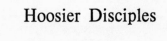

Hoosier Disciples

Hoosier Disciples

A COMPREHENSIVE HISTORY OF THE CHRISTIAN
CHURCHES (DISCIPLES OF CHRIST)
IN INDIANA

by Henry K. Shaw

WITH ILLUSTRATIONS

PUBLISHED BY THE BETHANY PRESS FOR
THE ASSOCIATION OF THE CHRISTIAN CHURCHES
IN INDIANA
1966

Copyright © 1966 by *Henry K. Shaw*

To
Edward, Samuel, and Kenneth
grandsons

In the fond hope that at least one may have the privilege
of serving in the ministry of Jesus Christ

Contents

CONTENTS

Foreword

This volume was prepared at the request of the History Commission of the Association of Christian Churches in Indiana. It was intended as a medium to extend the historical emphasis of the 125th State Convention of 1964, and as a contribution of the Christian Churches of Indiana to the observance of the sesquicentennial of the statehood of Indiana in 1966.

Information relating to the Christian Church (Disciples of Christ) movement was gained almost entirely from research of periodicals and other primary sources. It is hoped that this fresh approach to Indiana Disciples' history has provided also a fresh and new interpretation of the movement. Two categories of readers were kept in mind in the preparation of this book. They are laymen who may discover inspiration and develop appreciation for their Disciples' heritage and scholars who are seeking factual material. The text and the footnotes were, therefore, designed to tell the story as it happened and also to provide full documentation for future research.

One could not complete a work of this kind without being in debt to a great many people and institutions. The vast collection of Disciples' material, especially the periodicals, available in the library at Christian Theological Seminary was most helpful. Much encouragement was received from Dr. John W. Harms, general secretary of the Association of Christian Churches in Indiana. Dr. Beauford A. Norris, president of Christian Theological Seminary, by giving the writer permission to use great blocks of "school" time for research and writing, made it possible to meet the deadline set for the submission of the manuscript to the publishers. The writer is especially grateful to Dr. Ronald E. Osborn, dean of Christian Theological Seminary, for his wise counsel and careful reading of each chapter as it was prepared, The library staff of Christian Theological Seminary assisted in many ways— especially with the indexing of the book. Mrs. Sandra Mc-Mahan, a most capable secretary, spent many hours typing the manuscript and never wearied of doing sections over at the whim of the writer.

It is hoped that this book may fulfill the purpose intended by the History Commission and that each Disciple, after reading this volume, may feel that he is a partner in the history of the Christian Church movement in Indiana.

Henry K. Shaw

Indianapolis, Indiana
July 1, 1965

I

Wilderness Utopia

THE EARLIEST CHRISTIAN CHURCHES in Indiana were not planted in Hoosierland by some older religious body, nor were they the product of planned missionary expansion. They were an indigenous development—the outgrowth of the religious ferment common to frontier America at the beginning of the nineteenth century. These churches first learned about themselves, and then discovered the Stone and Campbell movements. Communication with these two movements some time between 1820 and 1830, by means of brash publications and itinerant preachers, resulted in a crystallizing of religious thought and in the development of common forms of faith and practice. When members of these churches learned of Alexander Campbell and Barton W. Stone they were impressed, at first because they were *against* the same things but later because they were in general agreement on principles. Reformation and change were in the religious atmosphere of the frontier, and evangelism became the catalytic agent of a melting pot of diverse religious cultures.

The Christian Church movement in Indiana, prior to the institutional stage, circa 1830, was a product of frontier religious thinking. The preachers in the movement, when it was in its embryonic stage, may have imbibed deeply from Reformation

11

wells, but they did not know it. They thought they had derived their views directly from the Bible. They firmly believed this, even though each of them had intellectual and spiritual roots in Reformation theology. In some cases Baptists remained Baptists, and Dunkards remained Dunkards a long time after they had actually embraced the new movement. Presbyterians, Methodists and Baptists were often in the Campbell-Stone axis even before they knew it themselves. Without outside aid or pressure, they were apparently caught up by the common religious ideas that were sweeping the American frontier.

The Hoosier Character

A thorough understanding of the Christian Churches (Disciples of Christ) in Indiana (and other Indiana institutions as well) is predicated upon an understanding of the Hoosier character. George Ade wrote of the Hoosier as, "a puzzling combination of shy provincial, unfettered democrat and Fourth of July orator." He added, "He is a student by choice, a poet by sneaking inclination, and story-teller by reason of his nativity."[1]

The people who came to Indiana in the early 1800's did not always know what they were seeking. Following the War of 1812 there was an economic depression in the East and a land boom in the West. This motivated great numbers of people to re-locate in the Northwest Territory, not a few of whom were mere land speculators; they were in the new country to make a fast dollar by buying land from the government agents and selling it at a profit to the settlers. In this period of American history there were hundreds of families on the move, never staying long in one place, always seeking the pot

---

[1]"George Ade, 1866-1944" (*The Magazine of Sigma Chi*, Memorial Issue, October-November, 1944), p. 68; cited by Arthur W. Shumaker, *A History of Indiana Literature* (Bloomington: Indiana Historical Society, 1962), p. 11.

of gold at the end of an imaginary rainbow. Great numbers of people came to Indiana because they had not been able to make good in either a financial or social way in their home environment, and the virgin soil of the new country provided a challenge for a fresh start and a new life.

French settlers and traders, mostly from Canada, were the first to come to Indiana, establishing a trading post at Vincennes in 1710. By 1775 there was quite a colony at this place. The Treaty of Paris in 1763, however, gave the English the territory east of the Mississippi River. This meant that in principle, at least, the English would be in possession of Fort Miamie (Fort Wayne), Fort Ouiatenon (below present Lafayette), and Fort Vincennes (Vincennes). Chief Pontiac and his Indian confederation took a different view of the matter and delayed occupation of the Indiana forts so that the British were not in control for long. Several skirmishes between the English and the Americans took place in Indiana during the Revolutionary War. Under the leadership of General George Rogers Clark the Americans took the offensive in the West, and this territory fell into their hands. This did not mean that the land was safe for settlers. Some 20,000 Indians with an estimated 5,000 warriors still populated the area directly after the Revolution. They were reluctant to give up their rights, but their power was broken by General Anthony Wayne at the Battle of Fallen Timbers in 1794. Indian resistance and raids on white settlements continued until the conclusion of the War of 1812.

Southeastern Indiana opened to settlers in 1794 when 150,000 acres of land north of the Ohio River opposite the present city of Louisville were awarded to soldiers who accompanied General Clark in his campaign of 1778-79. A series of land purchases from the Indians was made between 1803 and 1809 when William Henry Harrison was governor

13

of Indiana Territory. This opened all of southern Indiana for settlement. Subsequently, all the land in the territory was made available to immigrants. With the opening of the National Road east and west through the center of the state, and the Michigan Road north and south from the present Michigan City to Madison in the late 1820's and early 1830's, and availability of land at a basic figure of $1.25 per acre, central and northern Indiana became attractive to settlers. These people came from North Carolina, Virginia, New York and Pennsylvania; some came from the New England States, and a sprinkling from Europe. Many came by way of an interim of a few years in Kentucky, some leaving that state because of convictions against Negro slavery. Indiana thus became a melting pot for the opportunists, the dispossessed, the dissatisfied, and the underdogs of the older American culture. Not all would fall into this category, but for the most part they were not persons of social and economic stature in the older commonwealths.

When the settlers came to Indiana they brought with them an unconscious resentment toward eastern aristocracy and its ways, together with a fierce pride in their new status. Their coming bore some of the marks of a revolt against political, social, and ecclesiastical culture forms of the East. Cast from the same cultural mold, they shared a feeling of equality and respect for one another. They felt that they were "somebodies" in the Indiana country, and they liked it. It was worth the hardships they had to endure. As a result, they became intensely independent, quite self-reliant, and very articulate in their own way. Vachel Lindsay, Disciple poet, was describing more persons than his grandfather when he wrote:[2]

---

[2]Nicholas Vachel Lindsay, "The Proud Farmer" written in memory of his grandfather, E. S. Frazee, of Rush County. *General William Booth Enters Into Heaven and Other Poems* (New York: The Macmillan Co., 1917), pp. 111-112.

Into the acres of the newborn state
He poured his strength, and plowed his ancient name,
And, when the traders followed him, he stood
Towering above their furtive souls and tame.

That brow without a stain, that fearless eye
Oft left the passing stranger wondering
To find such knighthood in the sprawling land,
To see a democrat well-nigh a king.

By 1830 there began to develop in Indiana what could be called the typical "Hoosier" character, a rugged individualist with an easily recognizable mentality and outlook on life. Indiana, therefore, was fertile soil not only for the cultivation of farm crops but also for the development of indigenous social, religious, and political views. Though independent, Hoosiers with their log-cabin hospitality were noted for their concern over their neighbors and for travelers who came their way. They never felt any compulsion to hold back from expressing their views to all who would listen; their overpowering pride in the land, their joy in mastering their physical environment, and their love of freedom, marked them as being distinctively different.

Lack of the social amenities and education was never a handicap to the Hoosier. If the inferiority complex had been known in those days it would have taken an extensive bit of research to find a Hoosier who had one!

These Hoosiers could not write, but they wrote novels, short stories, essays, and even poetry that made a lasting impression on American culture. They were not men of letters, but they taught, established common schools and universities, and turned out great scholars. They could not preach, but their preachers converted thousands of people in great camp meetings and delivered sermons that changed lives and brought stability to the frontier. They were not theologians, but they

15

developed a homespun "back to the Bible" theological system that has since marked off American from European theology. They were not statesmen, but they produced many leaders of national and international stature in the Abraham Lincoln tradition. Those who knew these people before they came to Indiana probably would not have rated them as first-class farmers, but they made the forests resound with blows from the axe, the soil yield to their plowshares, and the acres produce an abundance.

This was the Hoosier character, not only of folklore but of fact. Among these people were those who laid the foundation for the Christian Church (Disciples of Christ) in Indiana.

Population Explosion

In the year 1800, when Indiana became a territory and General William Henry Harrison was governor, the Indians outnumbered the whites twenty to one. An estimated population of 6,500 white settlers was located in the southeastern corner of the territory, around the old town of Vincennes, and a scattering at the military and trading posts in central and northern Indiana. By 1810 the white population had increased to 24,520. Settlers who lived in the outposts were in constant danger of Indian attack. After the battle of Tippecanoe (near Lafayette) in 1811 and subsequent end of the War of 1812, the Indians realized they could no longer withstand the encroachment of the whites; reluctantly, and with a pitiful remuneration, they relinquished their claims and withdrew. Indiana became a state in 1816, and the first session of the legislature opened at Corydon in November of that year. A legislative census showed the population had increased to 63,-897. A United States treaty with the Indians in 1818 secured all the land in the state for settlement. The population accelerated rapidly after this, and the 1820 census claimed 147,178 settlers in the Hoosier State. By 1830, this number was increased to 341,582. Between 1820 and 1860 there was a tenfold increase in population; whereas in 1820 Indiana was the eighteenth state in population, by 1860 it was the fifth. As the years passed, settlers came in ever-increasing numbers. They came by way of the Indian trails, in flatboats and river barges down the Ohio, and by wagons and stagecoach through the mud and dust of bumpy roadways.

Religion—Hoosier Style

With the exception of the communitarian settlements in Indiana (Busro, Harmonie, New Harmony) and those of the homogenous sects (Quakers, Moravians), the various communities were a heterogeneous complex of religious interests and views. Catholicism, and most of the divisions of Protestantism, could usually be found in even the smaller settlements. There were Old School, New School, New Light and Cumberland Presbyterians; Separate, United, Primitive, Regular, Particular and Free-will Baptists; Dutch-Swiss-French-German Reformed adherents; as well as Lutherans, Episcopalians, and Methodists scattered throughout the territory.[3] Prior to 1830 there were few meetinghouses and even fewer trained ministers. It is no small wonder that in this religious milieu, fired often by emotional evangelism, there were

---

[3]Francis Trollope, *Domestic Manners of the Americans*, edited by Donald Smalley (New York: Alfred A. Knopf, 1949), p. 107 fn. 1. Mrs. Francis Trollope, a visitor from England, observed the frontier scene in 1828-29 during a temporary residence in Cincinnati. An excerpt from her notebook portrays a neat view of the vagaries of frontier religion as seen from the eyes of a sophisticated foreigner. She wrote, "The whole people appear to be divided into an almost endless variety of religious factions; I was told in Cincinnati that to be well received in society it was indispensably necessary to declare that you belonged to one of these factions—it did not much matter which—as far as I could make out, the Methodists were considered as the most pious, the Presbyterians as the most powerful, the Episcopalians and the Catholics as the most genteel, the Universalists as the most liberal, and the Swedenborgians as the most musical, the Unitarians as the most enlightened, the Quakers as the most amiable, the dancing Shakers as the most amusing, and the Jews as the most interesting. Besides these there are dozens more of fancy religions whose designations I cannot remember, but declaring yourself to belong to any one of them as far as I could learn was sufficient to constitute you a respectable member of society." Cincinnati had a population of about 20,000 people at this time.

frequent schisms, continual proselytism, and ready crossing of denominational lines; even new communions as the Reformers (former Baptists), and New Lights (Christian Connection) came into being.

Denominational Roots in Hoosierland

1. ROMAN CATHOLICS

The French, who were the first white people to occupy what is now known as Indiana, brought their Roman Catholic religion with them. Their activities centered around three trading posts on the Maumee-Wabash water route between Lake Erie and the Ohio River. One of these posts was at Vincennes, another was near the present city of Lafayette, and a third was located near the present site of Fort Wayne. These posts were garrisoned by the French government in order to provide protection for their political and economic interests. The existing edifice of St. Xavier's Roman Catholic church at Vincennes was started in 1826 and finished in 1850. Parish records go back to April 21, 1749. It was the first and only church in Indiana for half a century. There was no resident priest at Vincennes from 1763 to 1785, and this community and the other trading posts were served on a part-time basis by Catholic clergy from Detroit. The western see of the Catholic church was established at Bardstown, Kentucky, in 1808, with Father Benedict Flaget as bishop. When French interests in Indiana declined, Catholic church activity also declined. In 1821, Father John Leo Champomier of Vincennes was the only resident priest in the state. German and Irish immigrants who came to Indiana in the late 1820's and early 1830's more than augmented the French, however, and the Catholic movement was greatly strengthened. It is estimated that there were some 20,000 Catholics in Indiana by 1830.[4]

2. BAPTISTS

The Silver Creek Baptist Church, constituted November 22, 1798, is generally considered to have been the first Protestant congregation planted in Indiana. It was located near the present city of Charlestown. In 1802, the Baptists organized a second church in the "gore" (Clark's Grant), and a third church was established on the lower Wabash on the western side of the territory in 1806. Originally affiliated with a Kentucky association, after 1812 Indiana Baptists had their own Silver Creek association with nine churches. At first, Baptists were most numerous in southeastern Indiana and along the north bank of the Ohio River, but the denomination expanded with the population flow into central and northern Indiana, 1820-1850.

Though most of the early Baptist immigrants were from Kentucky, their former homes had been in Virginia and North Carolina. The Baptists, after being aroused by the revival of 1801, had much strength in Kentucky. At the close of the War of 1812 when the Indian danger had subsided, they overflowed into Indiana Territory. It has been estimated that by 1812 there were twenty-nine Baptist churches with 1,726 members in the territory, making it the largest Protestant denomination on the frontier. They brought all their inherited characteristic divisions to Indiana and soon added a few more. In their congregations, therefore, were United, Regular, Separate, Particular, Primitive, Free Will, and even German (Dun-

---

[4] R. Carlyle Buley, *The Old Northwest, Pioneer Period, 1815-1840* (Indianapolis: Indiana Historical Society, 1950), Vol. 2, pp. 469-471.

kard) Baptists. Theologically, most held to Calvinism in varying degrees, sometimes bespattered with a dash of Armin-
ianism; some believed in missions, and others were against missionary movements; some held to the Philadelphia Confession
of Faith while others opposed all creedal statements. Eventually, Baptists in the western part of the state, largely through
the influence of Isaac McCoy who was the first Baptist missionary to the Indians, embraced the Regular Baptist position.
Baptists in southeast Indiana, however, developed into a hot-
bed of dissenters. The principles upon which they all agreed
as Baptists—local autonomy, freedom to worship as they
pleased, right of private interpretation of Scripture—worked
against them as well as for them.

Frontier Baptists, lacking institutional character, had little
or no planned missionary strategy. The congregations usually
chose their preachers from among their own church members;
they were farmers or mechanics who lived and worked with
the people they served. Baptists seemed to prefer rural areas
or small towns, and their religious views were well suited to
their environment. Formal education as a standard for the
ministry was secondary to observable piety, ability to memo-
rize and quote Scripture, and speaking skill. Wherever the
settlers went there were sure to be Baptists among them;
wherever the Baptists went they usually took the initiative to
organize a church. Baptist expansion, therefore, was by chance
and providence more than by planning. Their numbers were
often increased by schisms within the congregations, opposing
factions withdrawing and forming new congregations. Even
associations were formed—and often divided—on this basis.
This resulted in a high church mortality rate. In spite of this,
Baptist growth more than kept pace with the increase in population. There were twenty associations formed in Indiana

by 1835.[5] Each association had the potentiality of becoming a little denomination in itself but staying within the framework of the Baptist movement. The various associations cooperated to the extent of sending official messengers to meetings of other associations and receiving messengers to their meetings in return.[6] Between 1820 and 1830 the Reformers, later called Disciples or Christians, gained a great many of these Baptist churches, especially in southeastern Indiana.

The German Baptists (Church of the Brethren), who differed from other Baptists by advocating trine immersion, love feasts, and the ritual of foot washing as an ordinance, were generally known on the frontier as Tunkers or Dunkards. They established the Four-Mile church in Wayne and Union counties in 1809, and the Nettle Creek church in Wayne and Henry counties in 1820. These two congregations are considered the mother churches of the Dunkard movement in Indiana. Members of the Four-Mile church organized the Raccoon (now Ladoga) church in Montgomery and Putman counties in 1826. When some members of the Nettle Creek church moved to South Bend in 1830 they formed a congregation at this place. The movement spread through Elkhart County, and a strong work was developed in this area.[7] In 1820, the Dunkard churches in Kentucky and Indiana formed a new association, separating from their brethren in Ohio and Pennsylvania. Some churches of the new association eventually broke from

---

[5]These associations were as follows: Wabash 1809, White Water 1809, Silver Creek 1812, Blue River 1816, Laughery 1818, White River 1821, Flat Rock 1822, Little Pigeon 1822, Salem 1822, Liberty 1824, Union 1824, Lost River 1825, Indianapolis 1826, Coffee Creek 1827, Danville 1827, Madison 1833, Tippecanoe 1833, Curry's Prairie 1834, Brownstown 1835, White Lick 1835.

[6]For information on early Baptist history in Indiana, *see* William T. Stott, *Indiana Baptist History, 1798-1908* (Franklin, Indiana: William T. Stott, 1908); John F. Cady, *The Origin and Development of the Missionary Baptist Church in Indiana* (Berne: The Berne Witness Co., 1942).

[7]Additional early churches in this movement were: Pyrmont 1829, Bachelor Run 1830, Elkhart 1830, and Portage 1831. *See* Otho Winger, *History and Doctrine of the Church of the Brethren* (Elgin, Illinois: Brethren Publishing House, 1919); Otho Winger, *History of the Church of the Brethren in Indiana* (Elgin, Illinois: Brethren Publishing House, 1917).

21

the Dunkard movement and joined with what were then called "Reformers." Among these churches was the Lost River (Old Liberty) church formed in 1819 in Orange County. Joseph Hostetler, ordained as a Dunkard minister, was a prime mover in spreading Reformer views among the Dunkards; he was responsible for organizing several congregations which eventually became known as Christian churches.[8] Many Dunkards joined the ranks of the Reformers (Christians) in the late 1820's, but there never was a mass hegira in this direction.

3. METHODISTS

Indiana Methodism had its beginning in 1820 when Samuel Parker and Edward Talbot came up from Kentucky and preached in the Springville settlement in what is now Clark County. The next year, as a result of the great revival at Cane Ridge, Kentucky, the Methodist movement on the frontier was stirred into intense activity. Concerning this phenomenon, James B. Finley wrote:

. . . we had a considerable decrease of members in the year 1795 and till 1801, when the great revival commenced and spread throughout all the western country; so that at the end of the conference year 1802, we had doubled our numbers from that of 1795. The revival also produced a great increase of local and traveling preachers.[9]

Indiana Territory had been formed a few months prior to the revival, and Bishop Francis Asbury placed it in the Western Conference. This conference included all Methodists on

[8]Madison Evans, *Biographical Sketches of the Pioneer Preachers of Indiana* (Philadelphia: J. Challen Sons, 1862), pp. 57-74.
[9]James B. Finley, *Sketches of Western Methodism: Biographical, Historical, and Miscellaneous*, edited by W. P. Strickland (Cincinnati: Methodist Book Concern, 1854), p. 74.

22

the western frontier and was under the supervision of Bishop William McKendree. It had twenty-six circuits and thirty-seven preachers by 1804. The Indiana District of the Western Conference was organized in 1808. The Whitewater Circuit which was formed in 1806, the Silver Creek Circuit which was set up in 1808, and the Vincennes Circuit which began in 1809 are generally considered the first regular Methodist circuits in the Hoosier state. By 1811, two more circuits were in operation. The Ohio and Tennessee conferences were formed from the Western Conference in 1812, Ohio receiving the circuits in southeastern Indiana, and Tennessee those in southwestern Indiana. By the time Indiana became a state in 1816 the Indiana circuits were divided between the newly formed Missouri Conference, the Tennessee Conference, and the Ohio Conference. The Indiana circuits were placed in the Missouri and Ohio conferences in 1818. Another change was made in 1824 when the states of Illinois and Indiana were made a part of a newly formed Illinois Conference.

Though the new jurisdiction was called the Illinois Conference it seems that Indiana was the primary center of activities. Five of the seven conference sessions held between 1825 and 1831 took place in Indiana towns. The first such session was held at Charlestown in 1825. The aura of the backwoods surrounded this meeting as forty-three circuit preachers arrived on horseback wearing their homespun and leather apparel. Among them were Joseph Tarkington, grandfather of Booth Tarkington, the Indiana author, and Peter Cartwright, the picturesque wilderness preacher. These were men who brought religion in the spirit of the Kentucky revival to the outposts of the American frontier, suffered great physical hardships for little financial reward, and preached the gospel as they knew it wherever they found people who would listen.

There were 755 Methodists in Indiana in 1810. This number was increased to 4,410 by 1820. It was not until 1826 that stations (settled pastorates) were established, and as these were increased the need for itinerants decreased. Some Methodists opposed the idea of settled pastorates and felt that they extinguished the spirit of the movement. Indiana Methodists established their own conference at a meeting in New Albany in 1832. Statistics, reported at this session, indicated that there were 19,853 white and 182 colored members within the conference. They were being served by sixty preachers.[10]

Methodist and Christian churches seemed to attract the same kind of constituency, and there was much crossing over of denominational lines in the early days. Some Methodists joined the Christian Church because they preferred a congregational polity, but for the most part the Christian Church made no great inroads on Methodism.

4. PRESBYTERIANS

The Presbyterians were better prepared for missionary expansion into Indiana Territory than any of the major Protestant denominations, yet they were relatively slow in gaining a foothold on this frontier. The Great Awakening in New England institutionalized the church, provided boards, missionary societies, and seminary-trained ministers for the task. But what should have been an asset to the Presbyterians turned out to be a handicap. The major population flow to Indiana in the early 1800's was from Kentucky. Kentucky Presbyterians were

---

[10]The following works contain much information on Indiana Methodism: William Warren Sweet, *Circuit-Rider Days in Indiana* (Indianapolis: W. K. Stewart Co., 1916); William C. Smith, *Indiana Miscellany: Consisting of People, and the Introduction of the Gospel and of Schools, Together with Biographical Notices of the Pioneer Methodist Preachers of the State* (Cincinnati: Poe and Hitchcock, 1867); F. C. Holliday, *Indiana Methodism: Being an Account of the Introduction, Progress and Present Position of Methodism in the State; and also a History of the Literary Institutions Under the Care of the Church, with Sketches of the Principal Methodist Educators in the State, Down to 1872* (Cincinnati: Hitchcock and Walden, 1873).

torn apart by constant theological strife, bitterness, and ecclesiastical trials; they lost great numbers to the New Lights
(Christian), Reformers, Dunkards, and Shakers. They were
also plagued with divisions within their own ranks such as the
Cumberland Presbyterian schism, and divisions into different
schools of theological thought. Presbyterian ministers who had
been inspired at the campfires of the Kentucky revival were
best prepared to cope with frontier problems and frontier people, but for the most part these men were *persona non grata*
with synod officials who preferred highly trained, orthodox,
"safe" young men from Princeton and Andover seminaries.
These young missionaries, through lack of experience and inclination, did not adjust well to the culture patterns of the
frontier or take too well to the backwoodsmen.

The General Assembly sent Thomas Williamson on a tour
through the lower part of the territory of 1805, and the West
Lexington Presbytery sent Samuel Holt on a similar tour the
following year. Samuel Rannels, James McGready, Thomas
Cleland and James Kemper made missionary incursions into
Indiana between 1804 and 1806 under the authority of the
Transylvania Presbytery. When Thomas Cleland traveled to
Vincennes over the old Wilderness Trace to preach in the Indian Council House he found that Governor William Henry
Harrison was in his congregation; it is claimed that on this
day he preached the first regular Presbyterian sermon ever
given in Indiana. Daniel Gray, Joseph Anderson, and James
Welch were sent to the territory in 1815 by the General Assembly. Because their service was so brief they were looked
upon as mere "horseback riders."

Samuel B. Robertson organized the first Presbyterian congregation in Indiana in 1806. It was called the "Church in
Indiana" and was located about two miles north of Vincennes.

25

When Samuel Thornton Scott became minister of this congregation the next year he was declared to be the first settled Presbyterian minister in Indiana Territory. Palmyra Church near Charlestown in Clark County was organized in 1807 by James Vance. It was the second Presbyterian church established in Indiana. Samuel Baldridge, who moved to Lawrenceburg in 1810, is considered to be the second settled Presbyterian minister in the state. John M. Dickey came to Indiana with his family and settled at the Forks of White River (near present Washington, Daviess County) in 1815, afterwards organizing several congregations. He is looked upon as the father of the Presbyterian churches in Indiana. In 1816, James McGready, under whose early preaching Barton W. Stone was greatly influenced, established congregations in Washington and Clark counties. By 1818, there were eleven churches in the state,

The Presbyterian General Assembly constituted the Synod of Kentucky in 1802. Most of the Presbyterian churches in Indiana were under this jurisdiction until 1826 when the Synod of Indiana was formed. The Synod of Indiana had four Presbyteries: Salem, Madison, Wabash, and Missouri; there were forty-three churches and ten ministers. By 1830 there were eighty-four churches in the state with a combined membership of 3,000 persons served by thirty-four ministers.

Since Presbyterian activity centered in the larger communities and the ministers had good academic preparation, interest in schools and education was emphasized, with the ministers often being the only teachers in the community. The Indiana State Seminary, established at Bloomington in 1825, became Indiana College in 1828. It was chartered as Indiana University ten years later. Presbyterian influence completely dominated this school in the beginning; its early presidents and many faculty members were Presbyterians.[11] Hanover Academy was founded by the Presbyterians in 1827 and was chartered as a college in 1834. Because of dislike for the theology being taught at Lane Seminary in Cincinnati a theological school was organized in connection with the Hanover project. This school moved later to New Albany, and finally to Chicago where it became McCormick Theological Seminary. Five Presbyterian ministers, desiring an institution in the state especially for training teachers, organized the Wabash Manual Labor College and Teachers' Seminary at Crawfordsville in 1833. This school became the present Wabash College.[12]

5. NEW LIGHT CHRISTIANS

James O'Kelly was the leader of a dissident minority which withdrew from the Methodist General Conference when it met at Baltimore in November, 1792. The schismatics objected to the right of bishops to appoint preachers to the circuits without giving them the right to appeal to the conference. In the debate on church polity (which was the fundamental issue at first) O'Kelly is reported to have protested, "Brethren, harken unto me. Put away other books and forms, and let this [holding up the New Testament] be the only criterion, and that will satisfy me." Efforts were made to reconcile O'Kelly and

[11]Baynard Rush Hall, who wrote under the pseudonym of Robert Carlton, Esquire, was one of the early teachers at this institution. His book is one of the early classics of Indiana literature. Although he disguised names, places, and events in fictitious terminology and his views are colored by his dislike of the administration, he, nevertheless, gives an insight into the early history of the institution that can be found in no other book. *See* Robert Carlton, Esq., *The New Purchase, or Seven and a Half Years in the Far West* (Princeton: Princeton University Press, 1916), Indiana Centennial Edition, edited by James Albert Woodburn.

[12]Information on Presbyterian history in Indiana may be found in, R. Carlyle Buley, *op. cit.*, Vol. 2, pp. 427-447; William Warren Sweet, *Religions on the American Frontier, 1783-1840, The Presbyterians* (Chicago: University of Chicago Press, 1936) Vol. II; Hanford A. Edson, *Contributions to the Early History of the Presbyterian Church in Indiana* (Cincinnati: Winona Publishing Co., 1908); William Henry Smith, *The History of the State of Indiana* (Indianapolis: Western Publishing Co., 1903) Vol. I, pp. 264-269. For sources of Presbyterian divisions on the American frontier *see* Robert Davidson, *History of the Presbyterian Church in the State of Kentucky* (New York: Robert Carter, 1847).

his followers to Bishop Asbury and the position taken by the General Conference. These failed, however, and the O'Kelly dissidents formed a new religious body at Manikin Town, Virginia, on December 25, 1793. Those who attended the Manikin Town Conference adopted the name "The Republican Methodist Church" to describe the new body. When the movement was one year old, Rice Haggard, one of the members, suggested that they call themselves "Christians."[13] By this time the new denomination claimed some 1,000 constitutents, the main strength being in Virginia and North Carolina. By 1809, the movement had 20,000 members. Some of these Christians (later known as "old" Christians to distinguish them from the followers of Barton W. Stone) moved to Kentucky and later on pushed into Indiana.

Abner Jones, a Baptist preacher in Vermont, came to the conviction that true piety alone and not the externals of it (sectarian names and human creeds) should be the test of Christian fellowship and communion. He organized a congregation on these principles in 1801 at Lyndon, Vermont. The next year he organized two more congregations, calling them "Christian" churches. Elias Smith, another Baptist, though with Universalist leanings (he eventually became a Universalist), joined with Jones and together they established a Christian church at Portsmouth, New Hampshire, in 1802. Since their religious views were similar, followers of the O'Kelly and Jones-Smith movements joined in 1811.

In the meantime, beginning in 1801 and continuing intermittently for several years, Kentucky was struck with the phenomenon of revivalism. The grounds around Barton W.

---

[13]For information on the O'Kelly schism *see* Charles Franklin Kilgore, *The James O'Kelly Schism in the Methodist Episcopal Church* (Mexico City: Casa Unida De Publicaciones, 1963). For information on the Christian Church denomination *see* Milo True Morrill, *A History of the Christian Denomination in America* (Dayton, Ohio: The Christian Publishing Association, 1912).

Stone's Cane Ridge Presbyterian meetinghouse became the site for a great camp meeting in which the main participants were Baptists, Presbyterians, and Methodists. Richard Mc-Nemar and John Thompson, Presbyterian ministers deeply involved in the revival, not only cooperated with the Methodists but preached like them. Because of this they were charged by the Washington Presbytery with holding "dangerous" Arminian doctrines. Since the Presbytery procrastinated in acting on the case the Synod of Kentucky censured it and took up the matter itself. As a result of this action the Presbytery withdrew from the Synod of Kentucky. A formal *Apology* was drafted in which the dissenters made a plea to the Synod "to adopt a more liberal plan, respecting human Creeds and Confessions."[14] This document, containing the views of the schismatics, carried the title, *An Apology for Renouncing the Jurisdiction of the Synod of Kentucky.*[15] It was signed by Robert Marshall, John Dunlavy, Richard McNemar, Barton W. Stone, and John Thompson.

After these five prominent revival preachers withdrew from the Synod they took immediate steps to organize an independent Springfield Presbytery. The Synod of Kentucky acted on this incident by suspending the preachers and declaring their pulpits vacant. Jobless, and without official ministerial standing with the Presbyterian Synod, they defended their stand by sending a circular letter to the congregations which they had been serving. A schism was thus promoted, but it is not known how many churches supported it. The preachers of the newly-formed Springfield Presbytery continued to preach as they had opportunity, and even organized some new churches. They soon came to the conclusion, however, that their Pres-

---

[14]Barton W. Stone, *The Biography of Eld. Barton Warren Stone, Written by Himself; with Additions and Reflections* by Elder John Rogers (Cincinnati: J. A. and U. P. James, 1847), p. 171.

[15]*Ibid.*, pp. 169-171. This is a complete text of the *Apology.*

bytery, even though it was independent of the Synod, was not consistent with their changing theological views. They decided to bring it to an end. This was accomplished through a facetious document, dated June 28, 1804, entitled, *The Last Will and Testament of the Springfield Presbytery.*[16] Their proposal was stated, "We *will,* that this body die, be dissolved, and sink into union with the Body of Christ at large; for there is but one body, and one Spirit, even as we are called in one hope of our calling." The *Last Will,* a protest against authoritarian church government and doctrines, and sectarian names, contained a plea for biblical Christianity in the spirit of mutual forbearance. By coincidence, Rice Haggard, who had given the name "Christian" to the O'Kelly movement, was present at the dissolution meeting. He suggested that this group also wear the name "Christian Church." The idea was gratefully accepted. Though this group was always known officially as the Christian Church, and its adherents as Christians, it was also called the New Light Church and members went by the name of "New Lights."[17]

John Dunlavy and Richard McNemar, signers of both the *Apology* and the *Last Will,* eventually defected to the Shakers. Because they were influential persons it is evident that they took many of the New Light Christians along with them. The fact that so many New Lights could be so easily led into Shakerism destroyed public confidence in the stability of the new movement. The storm this defection caused had hardly blown over when another one concerning the mode of baptism made its advent. It was finally agreed to allow freedom of conscience on this matter. The immersionist position

---

[16]*Ibid.,* pp. 51-53. This is a complete text of the *Last Will.*

[17]To avoid confusion with the general term "Christian Church," and to distinguish Stone's followers from the Reformers and the Disciples (all were at various times later called "Christians") the term "New Light" will be generally used in this connection.

had become popular with many by this time, and the liberal decision made some of the preachers quite uneasy. The group was also divided on the doctrines of the trinity and the atonement. Feeling the necessity for internal unity and a better public image the New Light preachers met in conference at Bethel, August 10, 1810, seeking a plan for more uniformity and appointing a committee to re-study their doctrinal position. When the committee reported at the next conference in 1811 it was apparent that there was disagreement on every issue. Robert Marshall and John Thompson had reverted to the orthodox trinitarian position; Stone and David Purviance opposed. Marshall and Thompson, as a result, returned to the Presbyterian fold, leaving only Stone of the original five leaders.[18] Doctrinal difficulties, the defection of leaders and members, and loss of prestige, combined with the non-institutional character of the movement, made planned missionary expansion nearly impossible for almost a decade after the new movement was launched. In the course of time the church recovered from its early misfortunes to gain a strong foothold in Kentucky and southern Ohio. It was not until then that New Light preachers could invade Indiana from the home base.

Christian Church movements in New England, Virginia, North Carolina and Kentucky eventually found common ground, and a loosely organized United States General Conference was instituted at Portsmouth, New Hampshire, in 1819. The conference was dissolved in 1832 and a General Convention was organized the next year. Stone's western Christian Church (New Light) movement was considered as a constituent body of the General Conference. Christians in the East were considered as being next door to the Unitarians in doctrine; according to Unitarian Charles H. Lyttle, ". . . Stone's

---

[18]*Christian Messenger,* October 25, 1827, pp. 263-269.

Christology and general doctrinal position were singularly like Channing's."[19] Lyttle also wrote that Unitarians considered themselves closely colligated with the Christians in the West for over thirty years. Unitarian strategy on the western frontier is well expressed in a letter from William Clarke to his brother James in Boston, published in the *Christian Register*, June 3, 1843:

> Their cause is identical with ours but they are able to do more to advance it among certain classes of society. They are breaking the rough land and gradually preparing it for the higher cultivation we may give it.[20]

Meadville Theological School, formed in the late 1840's, was a joint Unitarian-Christian Church project, and for some twenty years an equal number of ministerial students from each denomination usually attended.

Indiana's first congregation of the Christian Church was organized by Clement Nance in Floyd County, March, 1805. Nance was a Christian Church minister with a Republican Methodist background and is generally considered to be the pioneer Christian Church preacher in Indiana. By 1812 there were five Christian churches and four ministers of this denomination in the state. Daniel Roberts, who came from Maine to Dearborn County in 1817, formed a number of Christian churches in Indiana prior to 1830, especially in Switzerland and Jefferson counties. These early churches, organized by men under the influence of the eastern movement, were gen-

---

[19]Charles H. Lyttle, *Freedom Moves West, a History of the Western Unitarian Conferences, 1852-1952* (Boston: The Beacon Press, 1952), p. 15.

[20]*Ibid.*, p. 61. Alexander Campbell was suspicious of the Stone movement for many years because of this. He made frequent editorial attacks on the New England Christians through the columns of his periodicals because of the alleged Unitarian views of these Christians. When Stone collaborated with the Campbell movement (Lexington Unity Meeting of 1832 between Reformers and Christians) it meant ultimately that his followers (estimated at about fifty congregations) would be regarded as schismatics by the General Convention Christians. Stone's alliance with Campbell's Baptist Reformers had the effect of fragmenting the Unitarians, cutting off a number of what they considered to be their western churches, and possibly keeping them from becoming a major Protestant force in America.

erally referred to later as the "old" Christian churches. The Kentucky Christians (New Lights) did not expand into Indiana until recovery was made from the Shaker schism, and restoration was made from losses due to those who had returned to the Presbyterian fold. As for Barton W. Stone, compelled to earn a living for his family, he entered educational work for which he was well qualified. He operated an academy at Lexington for a while, then moved to Georgetown to pursue similar work. Short preaching tours around Kentucky and into Ohio where not neglected, but for the most part, so far as his religious activities were concerned at the time, he was on the defensive. The original Christian Church preachers in Indiana were of the O'Kelly or Smith-Jones persuasion, but some were followers of William Guirey of Virginia who had broken from the eastern group because of his belief in immersion as the proper mode of baptism. Since many of the early settlers in Indiana were from Virginia and North Carolina there were probably many of them who were already acquainted with the Christian Church position. Stone's status among these people increased gradually as the Kentucky New Lights moved into Indiana, and it became firmly established after he began publishing the *Christian Messenger* from Georgetown in 1826. Even after 1832 when Stone joined forces with the Reformers, his image was still bright with many of the "old" Christian churches.

The Christian Conference of southern Wabash County was organized in 1817. The *Christian Messenger,* once publication was started, reported several such conferences in existence in Indiana. At a conference in Harrison County in 1826 there were fourteen ordained and three unordained ministers present.[21] William Parker was ordained at the Indian Creek Con-

---

[21]*Christian Messenger,* December 25, 1826, p. 22.

ference in 1827 after it had considered whether or not it had the authority to take this action.[22] The Indian Creek Conference eventually organized the Flat Rock Christian Conference from the churches north of the Big and Little Flat Rock congregations. Correspondent Delana R. Eckels wrote to the editor of the *Christian Messenger* that a Christian conference and camp meeting was held at Blue Spring, near Bloomington, the first week in September, 1827, and that there were thirty to forty conversions. Christian Church conferences were voluntary associations; neither ministers nor churches were compelled to join them. Most of the time no records were kept of conference meetings, probably in fear that such records could become authoritative documents. A report from the Indiana Christian Conference of 1829 indicates why so few conference minutes exist today:

> The brethren, after conversing freely, unanimously agreed, to lay aside the Minute-Book for the present, for the following reason, viz: That some of our dear brethren were opposed to it.[23]

Early conferences were usually annual camp meetings (Kentucky style), followed by a special meeting of the preachers. The following letter from Dr. S. Roach, dateline Bloomington, December 22, 1830, illustrates this fact:

> At our Camp meeting the first Lord's day in Sept. [1830] ten professed faith in Christ. The brethren present with the Bishops, held a conference, named the spot Concord Camp-ground, and agreed to hold annual Camp-meetings there, on the first Lord's day of September. Preaching brethren were invited to attend with us. The spot is three miles south of Bloomington, Ia.[24]

---

[22]*Christian Messenger*, April 25, 1827, p. 139. They finally decided that "the eldership alone with the recommendation of the church, had the authority to ordain, when they concurred with the church in regard to qualifications of the person to be ordained."

[23]*Christian Messenger*, February, 1831, p. 40.

[24]*Christian Messenger*, December 22, 1830. Letter from Dr. S. Roach.

Joseph Badger visited many Christian churches in the west in 1826. The statistics he submitted to the *Gospel Luminary* ("old" Christian periodical) are probably a fair estimate of the strength of these churches in that period. He wrote that there were fourteen conferences in Kentucky, Ohio, Indiana, and Missouri; 225 preachers, and a total membership of 12,940. Membership in Indiana is listed as 1,200 persons.[25] According to Badger there were twenty-five ordained and four unordained ministers in this state.[26]

Early Christian churches in Indiana were made up of persons who were formerly, for the most part, Methodists, Baptists, and Presbyterians. They were frontier liberals, opposed to hierarchical control, the prevailing denominational doctrines (especially Calvinism), creeds, and what they considered to be sectarianism. Most members were anti-trinitarian (Arian) in their Christology. David Millard, editor of the *Gospel Luminary,* was quite forthright on this point when he wrote, "The people known by the name of *Christians,* are *anti-Trinitarians,* or if people please, they may call us *Unitarians."*[27] They were not immersionists at first, but through forbearance tolerated immersionist views. By 1830, many of the western Christians had accepted the immersionist position on the mode of baptism though they did not agree on its purpose. Their doctrine of salvation was quite simple, almost naive; they believed it was necessary only to search the Scripture in order to become Christians. The "old" Christians (New England)

---

[25]*Gospel Luminary,* April, 1826, pp. 91-92.

[26]*Gospel Luminary,* April, 1826, p. 91. Ordained preachers in the Indiana Conference were: Lewis Byram, Clement Nance, David Stewart, John Mavity, John Henderson, David McDaniel, Fletcher Mavity, Beverly Vawter, John Crafton, John Storm, ... Orbaurne, ... Oatmen, John Hubbard, James Dowdon, Thomas Johnson, John Herod, Jesse Hughes, ... Critzen, John Hibbs, ... Scott, ... Osborn, John Alkire, David Douglas, James Storm, Joseph Barry. The unordained ministers were: Jonathan Nichols, Eli Lee, Conrad Carns, and .... Hazzleton.

[27]*Gospel Luminary,* August, 1826, p. 192.

were not revivalists but fell into this pattern when they moved to the western frontier. Most of them seemed to regard their stand as primarily a "freedom" movement (Liberty and Freedom were popular local church names, and the *Herald of Gospel Liberty* was the name of their first periodical); they wished to be free from sectarian names, tenets, and control. Stone was not so much concerned with the freedom principle as he was with Christian unity. This was his main passion. Though they desired to be known as Christians, they were also referred to as the Christian Connection, "old" Christians, Christ-yans, New Lights, Marshallites, and Stoneites. This movement played a large part in the history of the Indiana Christian Church (Disciples of Christ).[28]

6. QUAKERS, RAPPITES, OWENITES, MORAVIANS, UNITED BRETHREN, SHAKERS

Baptists, Methodists, and Presbyterians were the major Protestant denominations to plant their faith in Indiana prior to 1830; but others also came to make contributions which were significant to Hoosier culture. Among these were the Quakers, the Rappites, the Owenites, the Moravians, the United Brethren, and the Shakers. Some came to stay; others were sojourners and strangers. But each made its own peculiar impact on Indiana religious, social, and economic life.

---

[28]There is much historical and biographical material in the book, Barton W. Stone, *The Biography of Eld. Barton Warren Stone, op. cit.* A series of articles by Stone in the *Christian Messenger* of 1827 contain valuable historical material on the Christian Church. These articles are entitled, "History of the Christian Church in the West." Charles Crossfield Ware is author of a valuable biography of Stone, *Barton Warren Stone, Pathfinder of Christian Union* (St. Louis: The Bethany Press, 1932). Davidson's volume, *History of the Presbyterian Church in the State of Kentucky, op. cit.*, also deals with Stone, especially in relation to the Kentucky revival. For a thorough study of Stone's theological views *see* William Garrett West, *Barton Warren Stone, Early American Advocate of Christian Unity* (Nashville: Disciples of Christ Historical Society, 1954).

The Quakers (Society of Friends) first came to Indiana in 1805, making their homes in the Whitewater Valley. Their first meetinghouse was built at the present site of Richmond in 1807. Soon, there was a steady flow of Quakers to this area; they were primarily from North Carolina, but some came from Virginia and Kentucky. Over 800 Friends were received in the Whitewater Monthly Meeting between 1809 and 1812. In 1817, the Ohio Yearly Meeting authorized the Indiana Friends to have their own Quarterly Meeting. The Indiana Yearly Meeting was established in 1821. There were forty families of the Society of Friends living in Richmond by 1822. One historian described Richmond, "A town on the Whitewater had replaced Philadelphia as the center of the Orthodox Friends in the United States." The Quakers came to Indiana primarily because of their antipathy toward human slavery; they could not bear to live in the South because of the slavery situation. The Underground Railroad is reported to have had its beginning in Fountain City where the periodical, *Genius of Universal Emancipation,* was published. In Indiana, as elsewhere, the Friends have witnessed as a social conscience toward the evils of society, and have become known for their devotion to simplicity, sobriety, industry, and interest in education. Though the Friends have had disagreements among themselves, as evidenced in the "Great Separation" into Gurneyite and Hicksite divisions, there have been no religious conflicts with other groups in the state.[29]

In 1815, after a temporary residence in Pennsylvania, some 800 Wurtenburg peasants established a religious colony in Posey County. They were German Pietists, followers of

---

[29]Bernhard Knollenberg, *Pioneer Sketches of the Upper Whitewater Valley, Quaker Stronghold of the West* (Indianapolis: Indiana Historical Society, 1945). Information on the faith, life, and polity of Indiana Friends may be found in, *Faith and Practice of the Indiana Yearly Meeting of the Religious Society of Friends* (Book of Discipline), Richmond: Yearly Meeting Session, 1850.

George Rapp. The Rappites considered themselves to be primitive Christians, had no written creed, and were organized as a celibate communitarian society. Because of their thrift and industry, the Rappites were able to build a successful and thriving industrial and agricultural community of factories, vineyards, orchards, mills, and granaries. They called their settlement Harmonie. For reasons now unknown—some believe it to be losses due to malaria—the Rappites sold their entire community to Robert Owen in 1824 for $150,000. When Rapp moved his colony back to Pennsylvania it is supposed to have had assets of over a million dollars. Owen, the new owner of the project, was one of the foremost social architects of his day; he was known throughout the civilized world. Owen planned to make the community site, re-named New Harmony, into a communitarian Utopia, and it was advertised far and wide as such. Intellectuals and socialistic-minded people were drawn to it as iron is drawn to a magnet. A coterie of the best minds of the East and of Europe came to the state to make their mark on Indiana culture. Though most of them were atheists they supported the New Harmony movement with an almost fanatical religious fervor. In spite of this the project failed in the same place where the simple-minded Rappite peasants had achieved phenomenal success. Many studies have been made of the New Harmony movement to determine why it did not succeed. Religious critics were quick to attribute the failure to Owen's atheistic views. Alexander Campbell, who debated Owen in Cincinnati in 1829, called the colony the forces of enlightened atheism. Nevertheless, the fact that the colony was over-supplied with intelligentsia and under-supplied with laborers seems to be the most reasonable explanation. An army made up of all generals and almost no privates was hardly prepared to win a battle against the wilderness.[30]

The Moravian story in Indiana is an unfortunate one. The Moravians (Unitas Fratum) were not interested in propagating denominational views; they were vitally concerned with Christianizing the Indians and teaching them a better way of life. Abraham Luckenbach with John Klage and his wife, consistent with Moravian missionary policy (Moravians were pioneers in the field of modern missions), established the White River Indian Mission in 1801. Mission outposts were set up near the present cities of Muncie and Anderson. They were doing quite well until it was learned that they were teaching Indians the means by which they could live on their own land in much the same way as the white settlers. This program was not acceptable to the whites. They did not want competition from the Indians, nor would they countenance any scheme of coexistence with them. The territorial administration seemed also to favor the view that the land was destined for occupation by the whites, and that nothing should be allowed which would encourage the Indians to stay permanently in the area. Because of this political position and the antagonistic attitude of the white settlers the mission project was doomed to failure. It was abandoned in 1806.[31]

The Church of the United Brethren in Christ had its Indiana origin in 1808 when John G. Pfrimmer established mission posts in Harrison and bordering counties. The first build-

---

[30]Among the eminent persons who participated in the New Harmony movement were: Charles Alexander Lessueur (botanist); Gerald Troost and John Chappelsmith (geologists); Leo Lesquereux and F. B. Meek (Paleontologists); Joseph Neff, E. T. Cox, Dr. Elderhorst, A. H. Worthen, Francis d'Arusmont, Sir John Lyell (Professors and lecturers); William Maclure and Thomas Say (scientists); and David Dale, Robert Dale, William and Richard Owen, sons of Robert Owen who distinguished themselves later in public service. For a full treatment of the Harmonie and New Harmony projects *see* George B. Lockwood, *The New Harmony Movement* (New York: D. Appleton and Co., 1905); Arthur Eugene Bestor, Jr., *Backwoods Utopias, the Sectarian and Owenite Phases of Communitarian Socialism in America: 1663-1829* (Philadelphia: University of Pennsylvania Press, 1950); R. Carlyle Buley, *op. cit.*, Vol. I, pp. 34-35; Vol. II, pp. 346, 597-616.

[31]Lawrence Henry Gipson, editor, *The Moravian Indian Mission on White River, Diaries and Letters, May 5, 1799 to November 12, 1806* (Indianapolis: Indiana Historical Bureau, 1938).

ing of this denomination was erected at Corydon in 1818. The United Brethren, Arminian in theology and Methodist in patterns and polity, were under the jurisdiction of the Miami Conference, organized in 1810 to include the area of Ohio, Indiana, and Kentucky. The first session of the Miami Conference to be held in Indiana took place in 1823 at Charlestown. John B. Pfrimmer was assigned to the Indiana District and John C. McNamar was appointed to the Whitewater Circuit which included Wayne, Fayette, Franklin, and Union counties. The Indiana Conference had its beginning in 1830. The United Brethren Church appealed to German-speaking immigrants; sermons were preached in the German language for many years.[32]

Shaker beliefs originated in England in the middle of the eighteenth century, and a society of "Believers in Christ's Second Appearing" was formed in Manchester in 1747. It was a millennial religion, the faithful holding that the end of the world was at hand and that all should be ready for the immediate coming of the Lord. It was a religion of prophecy and warnings, revelation and visions; emotional outlet was found in marching, dancing, singing, twisting, and shaking exercises. Several societies were formed in New England, and much opposition was encountered there. When the New England Shakers heard of the Kentucky revival of the early 1800's they looked upon it as a movement akin to their own and sent missionaries to the frontier to interpret its significance in terms of Shaker revelation. The missionaries—John Meacham, Benjamin S. Youngs, and Issachar Bates—after a pilgrimage of some 1,200 miles on foot, arrived at the Turtle Creek cabin of Malcham Worley in Warren County, Ohio, near Lebanon,

---

[32]Augustus Cleland Wilmore, *History of the White River Conference of the Church of the United Brethren in Christ* (Dayton, Ohio: United Brethren Publishing House, 1925).

in March, 1805. Worley not only opened his doors to these men but his heart as well, becoming the first convert to Shakerism in the West. His conversion was followed by that of Anna Middleton, a Negro slave. It is quite natural that Worley, a New Light Christian, should desire to share his new experience with Richard McNemar, his minister. McNemar, one of the original five founders of the Christian Church (New Light) movement, was so impressed that he, too, with his wife and children, joined the Shakers. Apparently a majority of McNemar's church members went along with him, and a community of some forty Shakers was soon established. In the meantime, the Shaker belief was taken to Cane Ridge, Kentucky, where the revival fires were still burning. Since this was the center of the Christian Church (New Light) movement, many converts were gained from among Barton W. Stone's followers. Among these was John Dunlavy, another of the five founders of the Christian Church movement.[33] This not only threw the New Light Christians into a state of confusion but embarrassed them before the eyes of other Protestants.

The Shakers invaded Indiana in 1809 when McNemar and three others journeyed to the Busro settlement in the southwestern part of the state (a community on the Busseron Creek a few miles above Vincennes) where they started a Shaker colony in 1810. Several contingents of Shakers joined them to set up a new kind of monasticism, a celibate community which apparently enjoyed success only temporarily. Sickness, danger from Indian uprisings, and violence at the hands of other settlers compelled them to make their exodus

---

[33]McNemar and Dunlavy were well educated and able men. Their defection was a terrific blow to Stone. Dunlavy became a Shaker theologian, writing a long treatise on Shaker doctrines, *see* John Dunlavy, *The Manifesto, or a Declaration of the Doctrine and Practice of the Church of Christ* (Pleasant Hill, Kentucky: P. Bertrand, Printer, 1818). McNemar's history of the Kentucky revival is considered one of the best early accounts of this phenomenon.

from Indiana in 1812. At this time, some 300 persons with their sheep and cattle left for Union Village, Ohio, a journey of eight weeks. Some returned in 1814, but by 1826 it was decided to abandon Busro forever.[34]

The Shakers, with their views on celibacy, millennialism, and communitarianism, together with a religion expressed in hard communal labor and shaking and dancing exercises, seem impractical and even fanatical today, yet they left a strange legacy of unique furniture design and labor-saving inventions that still charms and benefits American culture. If they were impractical in religion they were more than practical in industry, and there is no doubt that they almost succeeded in wrecking the Stoneite segment of the Christian Church movement.[35]

Seed-bed of Indiana Christian Churches

With the exception of those in certain minority groups such as the Rappites, Quakers, Shakers, and Moravians, who formed religious communities, the early Protestant settlers who came to Indiana came as individuals and in family groups. Thus, a small village of a few families could be made up of Baptists, Presbyterians, Methodists, a scattering from other denominations, and even a few atheists. Baptists and Presbyterians were, further, almost hopelessly separated into many divisions. It was impossible at this stage, therefore, for any one denominational group to institutionalize in a given community with any degree of success. A sermon by a roving preacher, given

---

[34]Peter Cartwright, a Methodist circuit rider, claimed that it was his preaching and debating in Busro that dispersed the Shakers. Peter Cartwright, *Autobiography of Peter Cartwright, the Backwoods Preacher*, W. P. Strickland, editor (New York: Methodist Book Concern, 1856), pp. 53-55.

[35]There are many interesting studies on the Shaker movement, as Anna White and Leila Taylor, *Shakerism, Its Meaning and Message* (Columbus, Ohio: Fred J. Heer Press, 1904); Edward Deming Andrews, *The People Called Shakers, a Search for a Perfect Society* (New York: Oxford University Press, 1853); Marguerite Fellows Melcher, *The Shaker Adventure* (Princeton: Princeton University Press, 1941).

in a shady grove or schoolhouse, was appreciated by all. When one denomination had strength in a given area a meetinghouse was built and a minister chosen, if not a professional, then one of their own members. In many instances the meetinghouses were used alternately by different religious parties. The settlers had many things in common (poverty, sickness, fear, insecurity), but organized religion was not one of these. If they worshipped together it was through expediency, not ecumenicity.

There was little extra-curricular activity to brighten the lives of the frontiersmen. A house-raising, a log-rolling, a corn husking, a singing school, a political rally, or a wedding occasionally broke the monotony of their humdrum existence. Travelers were usually welcome in Hoosierland. One such person wrote out of his personal experience:

A traveller enters without scruple any house near the road side, and breakfasts, or stays all night, even if the owner does not profess to keep a tavern: for every one is glad to have a stranger stop with him, as it gives him an opportunity of having some news, and also brings him a dollar or so, if he chooses to accept any thing for his hospitality.[36]

It is not strange, therefore, that the itinerent preacher was generally welcome, regardless of the peculiarity of his religious views, or that the camp meeting revival was the big social experience of the year. Everybody went to these revivals, some to pray and some to scoff; but nothing could keep the people away. Farm and home duties were usually put aside for the duration. The revival, more than anything else, became the social and religious catalyst of frontier culture.

---

[36]William Newnham, "An Excursion Through the United States and Canada, 1822-23, by an English Gentleman," cited by, Harlow Lindley, editor, *Indiana as Seen by Early Travellers* (Indianapolis: Indiana Historical Commission, 1916), p. 277. This volume contains many on-the-spot reports of early Indiana life as seen by outsiders.

Separated as they were from the East by hundreds of miles of wilderness trails, and with a genuine antipathy toward eastern culture and outside control, these pioneers developed their own forms and patterns of religion within the framework of traditional denominationalism. Though they were easy prey for charlatans and quacks, their common sense kept them from being too much victimized. The majority of the settlers knew little about fine-spun theological systems and cared less. A practical generation, the open Bible was its sole authority on matters religious. Some became quite proficient in quoting and explaining Scripture; they were chosen as resident ministers though they had to support themselves by means other than preaching. In their isolation from the theological world they gained some new insights in biblical study, insights that were to make Protestantism unique in America as compared with the Protestantism of Europe. These self-trained preachers of the backwoods spoke effectively to the backwoodsmen and became the forerunners of a great host of spiritual leaders who gave midwestern America a Christianity with a do-it-yourself flavor that it has never lost.

The wilderness Utopia of newborn Indiana, because of its isolated social and religious environment, contributed its share in bringing forth a new religious body in America, the Christian Churches (Disciples of Christ).

II

Ferment on the Frontier

IT WOULD BE PRESUMPTUOUS to point to any one congregation in Indiana and declare with assurance that it, or its successor, has a clear-cut claim to the distinction of being the first congregation of the Christian Churches (Disciples of Christ) in the Hoosier state. It is doubtful that any committee of historians among the Disciples could ever come to such an agreement. Many congregations now recognized as being among the earliest churches of the Disciples' movement in Indiana were first identified with other religious groups for many years. This makes it difficult to determine the precise date when each congregation went *all the way* into the new movement. Such decisions would have to be based on the timing and acceptance of any or all of the following criteria: (1) The renouncing of denominational names, (2) repudiation of authoritarian creeds, (3) dissolution of former association or conference structure, (4) abandonment of the mourners' bench test in conversion, (5) acceptance of immersion for the remission of sins as part of the conversion process, (6) observance of the Lord's Supper each Lord's Day, (7) efficacy of the ordinances when administered by non-professional persons, and (9) becoming a part of the structure of "cooperations" on various levels. Most congregations in the new movement eventually accepted most of these principles, but not at the same time nor in the same order.

Ryland T. Brown, a Disciple pioneer in the Hoosier State, wrote concerning this, "While Baptist churches adopting our plea have generally a well defined line of transition, it is often difficult to make any specific time when churches of this connection [New Lights] came fully to the adoption of the apostolic practice."[1] Before the middle 1830's the new body, which included several varieties of Baptists and New Lights as well as some defectors from other religious groups, was not yet born. No single pattern in any one congregation quite resembled that which characterized the Disciples of the late 1830's though the churches of the former Blue River Baptist Association seem to have come closer than others.

The "X" Factor on the Frontier

A secessionary spirit developed in the Baptist churches of southeastern Indiana in the 1820's; it eventually spread into almost every Hoosier settlement. There was a concurrent movement among the New Lights, not secessionary in nature but it pointed in the same direction. Neither Alexander Campbell nor Barton W. Stone can be held responsible for this development in Indiana prior to 1827. There were a number of "unions" between Baptist Reformers and New Lights after 1827; such unions were loosely structured. They were simply agreements to recognize each other as Christians engaged in a common mission. What happened could be illustrated by calling the New Lights "NL," the Baptist Reformers "BR," and the Disciples "D." In Indiana, at least, NL plus BR did not equal D. It was never this simple. Another

---

[1] *Christian Standard*, July 14, 1883. Article by Ryland T. Brown.

symbol stood for the active agent which worked on both NL and BR to produce D. The key to understanding what really happened is in the meaning of the Symbol X. It can be explained by calling it a special combination of nineteenth century rationalism and romanticism applied with a frontier twist to prevailing religious thought. In terms of equations it can be stated that NL plus X equaled D, and also BR plus X equaled D. If things equal to the same thing are equal to each other, then both Baptist Reformers and New Lights became Disciples when each was changed by the "X" ingredient.

The Hoosiers, a product of the older traditions of the East and South, found themselves isolated from these traditions, in a new and challenging environment. Old and long-suppressed resentment toward outside control, ecclesiasticism, and authoritarian theology came to the surface; in Indiana they could do something about it. They desired truth in matters of religion, and they were not afraid to explore the Bible in order to find it. For them, there was no other place where they could look. They did find some new light in Scripture, a light which found interpretation in a frontier context. The search led New Lights, Baptist Reformers, Dunkards, and some from other religious bodies to a common center; they were one people almost before they knew it themselves.

Baptists and New Lights, motivated by an inquisitive and sometimes rebellious spirit, added and subtracted from their original theological views many times before becoming an integral part of the third movement (Disciples of Christ), a movement which eventually became a common denominator of both. The New Lights that went into the new movement adapted quite easily, but the Baptist Reformers fought over every foot of theological ground before retreating or advancing from a position.

Free-Will Baptists

About the time that Alexander Campbell and his father were involved in the separated Brush Run congregation in Pennsylvania, John Wright and his father were promoting a similar program in southern Indiana. In 1810, the Wrights organized a Free-Will Baptist church in Washington County, about four miles south of Salem. This church was as different from the traditional Baptist churches as was the Brush Run Church from the Presbyterian denomination. Both were organized on the Protestant principle of the Bible as an all-sufficient guide in faith and practice. The Wrights held, even at this early period, that all creeds and confessions of faith were heretical and schismatical. John Wright,[2] assisted by Amos Wright, his father, and Peter Wright, his brother, organized several more congregations after the conclusion of the War of 1812 and before 1821. Some ten of these churches formed the Blue River Baptist Association in southeastern Indiana. In 1819, the original Blue River Baptist Church discarded what it called "party names" in favor of using the nomenclature of Scripture. It was known thereafter as the Church of Christ at Blue River (now Blue River Christian Church). As individuals, members preferred to be known as "Friends," "Disciples," or "Christians." They also agreed to lay aside what they called speculative opinions and contradictory theories that they might be better prepared to plead for Christian unity. Madison Evans wrote of them, "They then began in earnest the work of reformation, and with such success that by the year 1821 there was scarcely a *Baptist*

---

[2]John Wright (1785-1851) was born in North Carolina. His father Amos had first been a Quaker, then a Dunkard, and finally a Free-will Baptist. The family migrated from North Carolina to Virginia, then to Kentucky, and finally to Clark's Grant, Indiana Territory in 1807. John Wright became a Baptist in 1808. In 1810, with his wife, he moved to Blue River. In addition to operating his farm he preached for forty years in Washington and other southeastern Indiana counties. His father and his four brothers—Peter, Levi, Joshua, and Amos were also preachers, as was his son Jacob.

church in all that region."[3] The Blue River Baptist Association
was then converted into an Annual Meeting.[4]

The Blue River churches held this unique independent position for about seven years until they identified themselves,
along with fifteen Dunkard congregations which had joined
them, with the New Light Conference when it met at Edinburg in 1828. C. W. Cauble points out that the Blue River
church established a mission on the west branch of Mill Creek
in 1822 which did not become a separate organization until
1836. It finally developed into the Mill Creek Christian
Church around which the Mill Creek Conference of the Christian Churches was established with a permanent camp ground
about five miles southwest of Salem.[5] Chronologically, the
Blue River churches were first Free-will Baptist congregations,
then independent churches of Christ, then churches of Christ
combined with a Dunkard association which they had absorbed,
then New Light Conference (Christian) churches which absorbed them in 1828, and finally, Disciples of Christ.

German Baptists (Dunkards)

The German Baptists, better known as Dunkards, migrated
to Indiana after the War of 1812 and settled in Orange County
and in the surrounding area. By 1820 there were some fifteen
congregations in Indiana. Though a German-speaking people,
they, too, where influenced by the frontier spirit. Not being
quite like the Dunkards of Pennsylvania, they broke away
from their parent body and formed their own association

---

[3]Madison Evans, *op. cit.,* p. 32.

[4]The Mahoning Baptist Association in Ohio, with which Alexander Campbell was
identified, did not reach this position until 1830, some nine years later. The points
at which the Blue River Annual Meeting differed from the Disciples' position which
emerged in the mid 1830's was in the doctrines of conversion and baptism and the
weekly observance of the Lord's Supper.

[5]Commodore Wesley Cauble, *Disciples of Christ in Indiana, Achievements of a
Century* (Indianapolis: Meigs Publishing Company, 1930) pp. 31-32.

49

(Kentucky and Indiana) in 1820. Like other southern Indiana Baptists, they were motivated by a spirit of reform. During the first six years of the new association they debated matters of polity and doctrine, testing many traditional Dunkard views in the light of Scripture. They were called Universalist Dunkards by some of their opponents. Since they were questioning the propriety of authoritarian creeds, trine immersion, and even their denominational name, they were not far apart in their views from the neighboring Blue River "Christians" (former Free-will Baptists). As early as 1826, Alexander Campbell's *Christian Baptist* was being read by some of them. Joseph Hostetler[6] in particular was influenced by this periodical. He, with John Ribble and Peter Hon, even before being introduced to Campbell's writings, had conducted an unsuccessful attempt to prevent the new association from setting up regulations to govern the new body. Not willing to accept defeat in this matter, Hostetler engaged in an intensive study of the New Testament with special attention to Scriptural church polity. The *Christian Baptist,* once he started to read it, not only sharpened his antagonism towards creeds and sectarian names, but it provided him with a great deal of dialectical ammunition to use on his brethren. In 1826, he

---

[6]Joseph Hostetler (1797-1870) was born in Kentucky of a Dunkard family. Converted at the age of nineteen, he began preaching at once, accompanying his preacher uncle on several evangelistic tours. In 1817, he moved to a farm in Washington County, Indiana, where he engaged in farming, preaching on the side. He changed his residence to Orange County in 1819, and with the assistance of John Ribble organized what became known as the "Old Liberty" congregation. The founders claimed that this church was organized "on the foundation of the apostles and the prophets." Hostettler formed the White River Union Church, known as the "Old Union" church in Lawrence County, in 1821. He received ordination that same year at the Old Liberty church. Following this he made several preaching tours in Indiana, Kentucky, and Ohio. His next move was to Illinois in 1832, organizing a congregation on Okaw Creek which eventually became the Lovington Christian Church. The church at Decatur, Illinois, was organized by Hostettler in 1833, and he began to practice medicine at this place about the same time. He returned to Indiana in 1836, settling at Bedford. Between 1836 and 1849 he evangelized in Lawrence and surrounding counties, taught English grammar, engaged in a few public debates on religion, and published a pamphlet entitled, *Calumnies Refuted* as an answer to Methodist attacks on Campbell's views. He moved to Wisconsin in 1849 where he resumed the practice of medicine until 1855 when he returned to Indiana to preach in Washington County. In 1861, he returned to Lovington, Illinois, where he served as a county evangelist until his death.

opened a one-man campaign to reform the association by advertising that he would preach a sermon on primitive Christianity on a certain day in the community of Orleans. Some one thousand persons, including the majority of his preaching brethren, heard him discourse at this time on: (1) The Name, (2) The manner of becoming a Disciple, and (3) Creeds. This address stirred up a great deal of opposition. As a result he was notified that he would have to answer a heresy charge at the next association meeting. He defended himself so well at his trial the following year that he was not only acquitted but won over the majority of the members of the association to his position. Taking this as vindication of his reforming views he set out to promote the early dissolution of the association as an authoritarian body, a project in which he was successful but not quite in the way he had anticipated.[7]

Calvinistic Baptists

The majority of the Baptists who settled in southern Indiana in the first two decades of the nineteenth century were Separate Baptists from North Carolina and Virginia, who had lived a few years in Kentucky and had views modified by the Kentucky Revival. Originally they were back country, pietistic folk who revolted against esablished religion and the social aristocracy of the East and South. They had a firm dislike for liturgy, sacramental practice, episcopal polity and a professional clergy. Having suffered persecution from the established church they struggled for a complete separation from exterior political or ecclesiastical authority. They lacked in-

[7]Madison Evans, *op. cit.*, pp. 62-67. The dissolution of this German Baptist Association took place three years *before* that of the Mahoning Baptist Association in Northeastern Ohio with which Alexander Campbell was identified. The next chapter covers the union of the Blue River-Dunkard group with the New Lights at Edinburg in 1828.

stitutional character in Virginia and North Carolina, but desiring to be identified with the Baptist movement it was not long before they began to accept the standards of the Regular Baptists. In accepting this position they came under the creedal yoke of the Philadelphia Confession of Faith, a Calvinistic document, though they were never happy about it. The majority of Baptists who finally settled in Indiana were Regular Baptists nominally, but still retained views characteristic of the Separates. Therefore, conditioned by their tradition, they had a readiness to accept the views of Alexander Campbell as expressed in his *Christian Baptist*, views which appeared to them to be quite similar to those which they originally held.

Baptists who were members of the Silver Creek, Flat Rock and other Baptist associations in southern Indiana were, therefore, Calvinistic Baptists who had come to this position through the Separatist route, and they had warmed themselves by the camp fires of the Kentucky revival.

The change in theological views that led the Silver Creek Baptist Association out of the Baptist fold and into the Disciples' movement came very slowly. Minutes of the association do not indicate, except by inference, any serious conflicts within the association.[8] The association was constituted in the Silver Creek meetinghouse "the Friday before the fourth Lord's Day in July, 1812."[9] Jesse Vawter was elected moderator and James McCoy clerk. These men remained as officers in the association until 1827. At this time, John T. Littell became moderator and Absolem Littell clerk. The Littells kept this responsibility until the association was dissolved. The

---

[8]A copy of the minutes of this association is in the archives of Christian Theological Seminary at Indianapolis.

[9]*Minutes of the Silver Creek Baptist Association*, p. 1.

group originally consisted of nine churches[10] scattered through the present counties of Clark, Floyd, Washington, Scott, Jefferson and Jennings. As immigrants poured into the new country the Baptists among them organized new churches. By 1816, there were so many churches that the association divided east and west of the Knobs. At this time there were twenty-six churches with 582 members. The division left Silver Creek association with twelve churches and 365 members.

Prior to 1818 the association was in cooperation with the Baptist Board of Foreign Missions. That year, Isaac McCoy introduced a resolution to raise funds to assist the mission board in sending missionaries to the Indians. The association voted the resolution down, not believing it advisable to embark on such a venture. It also decided to settle all accounts with the Board and cease further correspondence. The next year when Jesse Vawter tried to read a letter from the Board, the association refused to hear it. It is apparent that a strong anti-missionary sentiment had developed within the group.

A second division of the Silver Creek association took place in 1827. This was a north-south division with border churches choosing which group they wished to join. The association was then reduced from twenty-eight churches with 1,015 members to thirteen churches with 430 members. The division was a friendly one, and for administrative reasons, but it left the association in the hands of the Littells and others who by this time had been reading Campbell's *Christian Baptist* and entertaining "reforming" views.

In the meantime, the Silver Creek church had its own refor-

---

[10]Churches making up the association in the beginning were: Silver Creek, Fourteen Mile, Knob Creek, Indian Creek, Upper Blue River, Lower Blue River, Camp Creek, and Salem. The association was an expansion of the Silver Creek Baptist Church, organized November 22, 1798, as "the church of Christ on Owen's Creek, in the county of Knox (now) Clark and territory northwest of the Ohio River, in the Illinois grant."

mation far in advance of the others. After discussing the issue, the church determined to be governed by the "word of God" rather than the traditional articles of faith. This caused a division of the congregation in 1829. A minority group withdrew, called itself the Silver Creek Baptist Church, and joined the Lost River Baptist Association. In an apology for this action the dissidents laid the blame on the writings of Alexander Campbell: "We wish to be plainly understood to refer to the views so widely and destructively diffused through the medium of a paper styled the *Christian Baptist*."[11] The Silver Creek Baptist Association tolerated the "reformed" church in spite of this, and it stayed in the association, yielding to many views with which it was no longer in agreement.

When the association met at the Silver Creek meetinghouse in August, 1836, the step that had seemed inevitable to the Littells[12] all along, was finally taken. The minutes of this meeting state, "Agreed by *unanimous* consent to amend our Constitution by erasing the Articles of Faith (finding them to be superfluous believing as we do that the Scriptures are of Divine Authority and the only infallible rule of faith and obedience)." This action did not indicate a flagging zeal; the group reported 160 baptisms for the year. One year later (1837) the association met at the Friendship meetinghouse in Washington County to take final action in separating from the Baptists. The minutes declare, "It is agreed to do away with the name of the association and to have an Annual Meet-

---

[11]W. T. Stott, *op. cit.*, p. 49.

[12]John Thompson Littell (1790-1848) and Absolem Littell (1788-1862), sons of Absolem Littell, a Presbyterian Elder, while still in their father's household settled on Silver Creek in Clark's Grant in 1799, one year after the Silver Creek Baptist Church was organized. They became members of this church after the ending of the War of 1812. John T. started preaching in 1816, and his brother started a year later. Absolem helped organize the New Albany church in 1820. John T. preached at Silver Creek and later at Muddy Fork. Beginning in 1827 and continuing the next ten years, John T. was moderator, and Absolem was clerk of the Silver Creek association. Both men evangelized in the area during their lifetime, and were probably responsible, more than others, for spreading the teachings of Alexander Campbell throughout the association.

ing in August on the same day of the year commencing on the Friday before the fourth Lord's Day in each and every year and to dispense with all form, and usuages belonging to authoritative bodies."

With the exception of the New Albany church which had declared its independence of the association the year before, the congregations which comprised the Silver Creek Baptist Association prior to the time it disbanded in 1837, were Baptist churches, even though they had embraced certain "reforming" principles in varying degrees in the years before that.[13]

Churches Withdrawing From Baptist Associations

There were many "reformed" Baptist churches in Indiana which did not carry their associations with them when they became a part of the new movement. In situations where they were the minority group, they simply withdrew and formed a new church. Sometimes this action was a friendly one; occasionally it was a matter of excommunication by the majority. When the Reformers had the upper hand the regular Baptists were forced out or withdrew voluntarily, losing their meetinghouse but continuing in the association. In a case where the entire congregation favored the "reformation," there was no special problem; either they sent word to the association that they were no longer a part of the group or the association took action to withdraw from the church. A few of the early Disciples' congregations were organized by Reformers who had been tried for heresy in Baptist congregations or who, in good conscience, could no longer be happy in the

---

[13]The last recorded list of the churches in the Silver Creek Baptist Association appears in the minutes of this association for 1834. The churches listed at that time were Silver Creek, North Washington, Muddy Creek, Charlestown, New Albany, Hopewell, Little Union, Mt. Edon, Friendship, Liberty, Jeffersonville, Mt. Pleasant, Camp River, and Mt. Lebanon.

Baptist fold. After the middle 1830's, churches in which there had been tension had resolved their difficulties by conciliation or separation, and internal conflict over "reforming" issues ceased. The new movement then began a process of structuring, and there was a modified planned expansion which resulted in the organization of new churches.

Because of the lack and/or loss of records and the fact that some of these churches became defunct after they reformed, many are no longer known. Such a church, for example, existed in the country about six miles from Indianapolis on the Bluff road, state route 37. Carey Smith refused to unite with the Baptist church in Indianapolis when he moved there in 1829, preferring this country Baptist church because it had adopted the New Testament as its creed, was independent in government, observed the Lord's Supper each week, and did not report to the Indianapolis Baptist Association. Some of the original members of Central Christian Church in Indianapolis (organized 1833) transferred from this little country church. The Indianapolis Baptist Association did not approve of the stand taken by this church, charged it with heresy in 1832, and withdrew from it.[14]

The Orange Church at Glenwood, Fayette County, was constituted by the Little Flat Rock Baptist Church in June, 1829. Known then as the Fayetteville Church, a mission of Little Flat Rock, it was refused admission into the Whitewater Baptist Association because it held the New Testament only as its Articles of Faith. The prime movers in the organization of the Fayetteville church were John P. Thompson, reforming minister of the Little Flat Rock Baptist Church, and two men from Scotland, William McPhearson and William

---

[14]Madison Evans, *op. cit.*, pp. 366-367.

Thompson. McPhearson had been influenced by the Haldanes (Scottish reformers) before coming to America. After being rejected by the Whitewater association the Fayetteville church continued existence as a church of Christ.[15]

The Hope Baptist Church in Bartholomew County near Columbus was organized in the early 1820's. The brethren of the congregation erected a log meetinghouse on the corner of Benjamin Irwin's farm. Joseph Fassett, the minister, became a reader of Alexander Campbell's *Christian Baptist* and was so greatly influenced by what he read that his new views were reflected in his sermons. The congregation apparently liked what they heard, but not so the Whitewater Baptist Association. A committee of the association was sent to investigate the soundness of the church. As a result, the association admitted that though it had no right to dictate articles of faith to the congregation, it could not accept the attitude of the Hope church in this regard. The position taken by the Hope church, that their "official" faith was based on the Bible (not the articles) was considered too general; it was not satisfactory to the association. When delegates from the Hope church attended the next meeting of the association they were warned to do better than this or the church would be dropped. The Hope church considered the ultimatum of the association and decided to separate rather than to conform to this ruling. On the first Sunday in October, 1829, the church, therefore, renounced its Baptist name and decided to call itself, "The Church of God in Christ in New Hope." In July, 1830, the congregation began the practice of observing the Lord's Supper weekly.[16]

---

[15]*Christian Standard*, July 14, 1883. Article by Ryland T. Brown.
[16]Hugh Th. Miller, *Tabernacle Church of Christ, Columbus, Indiana* (Columbus, Indiana: Privately printed, 1940), pp. 3-4.

John P. Thompson[17] started preaching for the Little Flat Rock Baptist Church in Rush County in 1822. In due time his religious views were changed by reading the *Christian Baptist,* conversations with reformers in Kentucky, and acquaintance with William McPhearson, the Scottish independent. Inspired by this "new" gospel, he not only presented it to his own congregation but preached it every night in schoolhouses and private homes in Rush and Fayette counties during 1828-29. His sermons called for immediate decision; he baptized the penitents at once after hearing their confessions of faith, accepting them into the church without requiring them to relate a "Christian experience" before the congregation, or allowing the church to pass on the soundness of their conversions. Many of his Baptist brethren looked upon Thompson's new position as heresy and accordingly filed charges against him in April, 1830. He was allowed a month in which to prepare his defense. When the case was tried and the vote taken, John P. Thompson, the defendant, was acquitted by a majority of three votes. The minority then proposed a peaceful separation. The majority group agreed to this, and the next day some forty of them entered into an agreement to constitute the Church of Christ at Little Flat Rock. Within the next three years the churches at Columbia, Connersville, Ben Davis Creek and Rushville were organized, all more or less connected with the mother church.[18]

Abner Davis and David Walford began reading the *Christian Baptist* about 1827. As a result, the creed question began

---

[17]John P. Thompson (1785-1871) was born in Washington, D. C., and came to Indiana by way of Kentucky. He started to read the *Christian Baptist* in 1826 but was not convinced of the position taken by Alexander Campbell until he [Thompson] revisited Kentucky and heard Raccoon John Smith preach. When he returned to the Little Flat Rock Baptist Church his preaching was tinged with "reform." The church divided over the issues, and Thompson continued as minister of the new group. He served the Little Flat Rock church for twenty-two years, and the Fayetteville church for nineteen years. Through his influence many churches of Christ came into existence in Rush and surrounding counties.

[18]*Christian Standard,* July 14, 1883. Article by Ryland T. Brown.

to trouble the old Maria Creek Baptist Church in Knox County where they were members. Joseph W. Wolfe and seventeen others requested letters of dismissal to organize a church at Shaker Prairie. Conditioned by the views of Walford and Davis, and by reading the *Christian Baptist,* they attempted to put together a scriptural statement of faith; the new church was organized on this basis. Eventually they began to ask themselves why they were adopting a few passages of Scripture and not the whole Bible. Finally they decided to use the preamble of their Statement of Faith, "We believe that the Scriptures are divinely inspired, and the only infallible rule of faith and practice—which we adopt as our creed and Book of Discipline." When delegates of the new church presented themselves at the next meeting of the Baptist association in September, 1830, a motion was made to eject them. B. W. Fields, pastor of the new Shaker Prairie church, explained their position but succeeded only in antagonizing the association. All connections with the Baptists were then broken, and the new church began observing the Lord's Supper each Sunday.[19]

John Bowman New[20] was a Baptist who apparently discovered the position taken by the reformers before he ever heard of Alexander Campbell. When he advocated this position among his brethren in the Vernon Baptist Church in Jennings County, to his surprise he was charged with preaching Campbellism. Because of the strife in the church, he and

---

[19]Madison Evans, *op. cit.,* pp. 389-390.

[20]John Bowman New (1793-1872) was born in North Carolina and came to Indiana by way of Kentucky. A cabinet maker by trade, he came to the same position as that of the reformers by self-study of the Bible. After a residence at Madison he moved to Vernon. In addition to organizing the church at Vernon he organized the church at Coffee Creek in 1832, and with Carey Smith, the church at Madison the same year. During the 1840's he moved about the state a great deal, organizing a number of churches. In 1849 he made Indianapolis his permanent residence. John Bowman New was the father of John C. New, publisher of the *Indianapolis News* and Consul General to Liverpool in 1889; grandfather of Harry S. New, senator and postmaster general of the United States.

several others obtained letters of dismissal to organize a separate congregation. Action was deferred for a year at the request of his Baptist brethren in the hope that an understanding could be reached. In the meantime, John B. New was baptizing "for the remission of sins." This was contrary to Baptist practice, and the church divided. New then organized the Church of Christ at Vernon. This was in November, 1831.[21]

In 1832, four years after a group left the Maria Creek Baptist Church to form the Shaker Prairie congregation, members of the Maria Creek church living around Bruceville asked for letters to organize a church there. The letters were granted, and the Bruceville Church of Christ came into existence. The old Baptist Church at Maria Creek, organized in 1809, was a mother church to many Christian churches, including those at Maria Creek and Vincennes.[22]

New Light Churches

For the most part, only those Christian churches (New Light) in Indiana that were touched by Campbell's "current reformation," became the congregations that were identified later with the Christian Churches (Disciples of Christ). Most of the New Light churches ("old" Christians) not affected by the Campbell movement either ceased to exist or survived as the Christian denomination which merged with the Congregationalists to form the Congregational Christian Church (now United Church of Christ).[23] As many Baptist churches in Indiana had reformed along Campbellian principles, a great

---

[21]Madison Evans, op. cit., pp. 87-88.

[22]C. W. Cauble, op. cit., pp. 64-65. The Maria Creek Baptist Church had a freed slave as one of its thirteen charter members, and Negroes were admitted to membership on an equal basis with the whites. Isaac McCoy, first pastor of the church, took a special interest in working with the Indians around the Vincennes trading post.

[23]Some of the New Light Christian churches did not identify with either the Campbell or the Stone movement. When the union took place between the Congregational Churches and the General Convention of the Christian Church in 1931 many of these churches participated; some of them did not enter the union and have remained as independent Christian churches.

number of New Light churches went through the same kind of reformation. Because the New Lights were loosely structured, placed what little ecclesiastical authority they assumed in the conference, and because they had a strong aversion toward minute books and official records on the basis that they might be construed as creedal statements, it is difficult to interpret their exact position in a given historical period, or to pin-point dates, places and events.[24]

Several families of New Lights from Kentucky moved into Clark and southern Jefferson counties in 1806.[25] These persons seem to have been connected with the "old" Christian movement though they knew of Barton W. Stone. They brought John McClung, their minister, with them. Churches, actually just neighborhood meeting places, were formed on Saluda Creek, on the White River in the Maxwell neighborhood (now Kent), at Clifty (three miles northwest of Madison), on the middle fork of the White River at William Ritchie's, on the Indian Kentucky near to the Thomas Jameson and John Eccles' settlements (now Liberty), and on the east fork of the Indian Kentucky in the neighborhood of George Myers and John McCullough. Monthly religious services were held in these communities, and usually two big evangelistic meetings were also held annually in each neighborhood. Since all of these communities were located in an area about twenty-five miles long and ten miles wide, any problem which concerned one group concerned them all. This area became a preaching center and home base for New Light preachers from Kentucky and Ohio who evangelized in southern Indiana. When land became available in central

---

[24]*Christian-Evangelist*, November 12, 1891. Love H. Jameson observed, "It will amuse you when I tell you that they were so much afraid of creeds and confessions of faith . . . that they would have neither church book nor register."

[25]*Christian-Evangelist*, November 12, 1891. The names of these families were Maxwell, Tilford, Henderson, McCullough, and others. Henry Brown, another New Light preacher, came to preach for them in 1814.

Indiana around 1820, many New Light settlers in this locality sold their farms and moved inland. People living around the White River settlement moved to Bloomington, called Barton W. Stone for an evangelistic meeting in 1826, and started a church at this place. The Clifty and Middle Fork settlers moved to Decatur County. Loss of members caused the failure of some of the original churches. The Indian Kentucky (Liberty) church, favored by the ministry of Beverly Vawter[26] and Daniel McMillan, became stronger.

A stranger appeared at the door of Thomas Jameson's home on the banks of the Indian Kentucky in April, 1818. He inquired the distance to the nearest tavern where he could find overnight accommodations. The Jameson family, with typical Hoosier hospitality, invited him to stay with them. The stranger turned out to be Joseph Bryant, brother-in-law of Alexander Campbell. Jameson and Bryant soon discovered they were both Scotsmen and that they both had departed from the traditions of the Seceder church. In the course of their conversation, Bryant informed Jameson of the Brush Run church experiment in Pennsylvania in which the Campbells were involved. Later, Bryant mailed Jameson a copy of Thomas Campbell's *Declaration and Address*. Love H. Jameson, son of Thomas Jameson, on recalling this incident, wrote, "I regard this as the first seed of the current reformation planted by Joseph Bryant in soil prepared by Barton W. Stone's coadjutors in the State of Indiana."[27] Jameson shared

---

[26]Beverly Vawter (1789-1872) was born in western Virginia but grew up among the Baptists in Kentucky. Unable to experience a "Baptist" conversion, he was attracted to John McClung, New Light preacher who baptized him in 1817. The New Lights ordained Vawter in 1819. He moved to Indiana that same year to operate a carding machine at Madison and preach in the vicinity. He brought the Baptist church at Hogan's Creek into the New Light movement in 1823. In 1824, he formed churches at Otter Creek and Vernon. He reorganized the church at Kent in 1832. He traveled with Love H. Jameson, his "Timothy" in religious work. Vawter left off preaching then for a number of years because of illness. In 1853, however, with his son, Philemon, he represented a six-county Disciple church cooperation.

[27]*Christian-Evangelist*, November 19, 1892. Article by Love H. Jameson.

the Campbell document with his neighbors; all were impressed by what they read.

Beverly Vawter, nephew of Jesse Vawter of the Silver Creek Baptist Association, became a popular preacher among the New Lights in this vicinity around 1820-25, organizing New Light churches and preaching in Jefferson, Switzerland, Ohio, Decatur, Scott and Clark counties. In his early ministry he was not acquainted with the teachings of Alexander Campbell, though he advocated many of Campbell's principles which he thought he had discovered for himself. He was often accused of being a "Campbellite" even though he was not introduced to the *Christian Baptist* by his friend, Thomas Jameson, until 1826. At that time Vawter represented the typical New Light preacher going through the transition period into the Campbell reformation. When he preached he would plead with the people to come to the anxious seat for pardon, and when they came he would say to them, "Why tarriest thou? arise and be baptized and wash away thy sins, calling on the name of the Lord" (Acts 22:16).

Just as the Baptists were disturbed about creeds and confessions, biblical terminology, the doctrine of election and ecclesiastical organization; so the New Lights had their problems. They began to question many of their own views and practices. Elijah Goodwin, a New Light preacher, claimed that though they had many converts in those days, nothing was ever said about baptism, and converts were accepted whether baptized or not. Michael and Job Combs, at the beginning of their ministries, converted many Quakers because baptism was not required. According to Goodwin, there were several preachers among the New Lights who were much concerned over the possibility that they were not following the gospel plan. After becoming readers of the *Christian Baptist* which apparently became well known to them about 1827, the New

Light preachers began to doubt the efficacy of camp meeting religion with its ranting, roaring and shouting; they came to prefer a simple confession of faith, and baptism for the remission of sins, to the "anxious seat" and the custom of "praying through" their converts to what they formerly thought was a salvation experience. When the Wabash conference met in the Old Union meetinghouse near Gosport in Owen County in 1827, James M. Mathes[28] found the anxious seat "in full blast." Mathes, though only nineteen at the time, had studied the Scriptures for himself with the view of learning how to become a Christian. He was so convinced of the truth of his discoveries that he undertook to teach "the way of the Lord more perfectly" to John Henderson,[29] one of the older ministers at the meeting. Henderson finally admitted the confession and baptism argument, as presented by Mathes, was in accord with God's plan even though contrary to his own experience. At the close of his first sermon after this discussion, Henderson invited any not disposed to come to the "mourning bench" but desiring baptism for the remission of sins as did the three thousand on the day of Pentecost, to come forward. Mathes and his sister Eliza responded at once, made the

---

[28]James Madison Mathes (1808-1892), born a Kentuckian and reared in the Baptist faith, became identified with the New Lights after self-study of the Bible, and the reading of Campbell's New Testament and *Christian Baptist* in 1827. Mathes reorganized the Old Union Church along reformation principles in 1831. He preached and taught school in the years 1830-38 and then entered Indiana University as a student. He left the university in 1841 and settled on a farm but continued preaching and occasionally engaging in public discussions on matters of religion. He began publication of a religious journal, the *Christian Record,* in 1843 to promote the interests of the Christian churches. Beginning in 1848, he also published the *Indiana Tribune* at Bloomington. That the *Record* could better serve the new North Western Christian University project (Butler University), Mathes moved his printing office to Indianapolis in 1851. There, in addition to editing the journal, he operated a book store and did occasional preaching for Central Christian Church. For a number of years Elijah Goodwin was associated with him on the *Record.* Mathes moved to Bedford in 1855. From 1859 to 1861 he was minister at New Albany. When he returned to Bedford he became president of the Bedford Male and Female College, Mathes authored and edited many books. Among these were: *Works of Elder B. W. Stone, Life of Elijah Goodwin, Letters to Thomas A. Morris, D.D., The Western Preacher, Mathes-Brooks Debate,* and *Voice of the Seven Thunders.* His unpublished autobiography in manuscript form is in the archives of Christian Theological Seminary.

[29]Other preachers at this meeting were: Joseph Berry, P. E. Harris (son-in-law of B. W. Stone), James Andrews, Cummins Brown, David McDonald and Jonathan Nichols.

"Good Confession" and were baptized in Lime Stone Creek. Mathes wrote concerning this in his autobiography, "I was the first person in Indiana so far as I know that was baptized for the remission of sins and my sister Eliza was the second."[30] As time went on, Michael Combs, Job Combs, Beverly Vawter, Elijah Goodwin, John O'Kane, and other prominent New Light preachers all came out against the "anxious seat" and in favor of what they called the gospel plan of salvation. Evangelism took the form of protracted meetings, and camp meeting religion gradually disappeared from among them.

About the time the New Lights in southeastern and lower central Indiana were undergoing a change in their theological views (called the current reformation), a similar change was taking place among their brethren in Montgomery, Putnam, and Hendricks counties, three counties located between Indianapolis and the western border of the state. Michael Combs[31] was the apparent leader of this group, but he was ably assisted by his brother, Job, James Hughes of Kentucky, John Secrist of Ohio, and Thomas Lockart. Combs settled on a farm in Montgomery County in 1826 and organized a congregation at this place. The church soon moved to Crawfordsville and became the Crawfordsville Christian Church. Using Crawfordsville as his base of operations, Combs preached throughout the White River valley in Montgomery and Putnam counties, organizing many New Light churches. He objected to the views of Alexander Campbell during the early part of his ministry, but by 1832, after having read Campbell's periodicals, he found him-

---

[30]James M. Mathes, *Life of Elder James Madison Mathes, Written by Himself for the Use of His Children When He Is No More* (Bedford: Unpublished Manuscript, *circa* 1870). Original and copies are now at Christian Theological Seminary.

[31]Michael Combs (1800-1872), born in Tennessee, was converted from the Baptist to the New Light faith by David Purviance while residing in Preble County, Ohio. Michael and his brother, Job Combs, started preaching in 1822. Combs organized a number of congregations in Montgomery, Putnam and Hendricks counties which he converted later to reformation views. Some years later he gave up the active ministry and went into the railroad construction business. He also tried politics for a time. In 1853 he moved to Illinois and from there he went on to Iowa.

self in agreement with the Bethany reformer. About 1833 he came out openly for the new movement. Elijah Goodwin, after hearing Combs speak at a New Light camp meeting at Bloomington, said that Coombs had gotten further into the reformation than any preacher that he knew.

The New Lights not only changed their views about conversion, but between 1825 and 1830 the whole structure of their movement was changed. Prior to this time, local congregations were essentially neighborhood religious fellowships. Elijah Goodwin,[32] evangelist for the Indiana and Wabash conferences in 1827, questioned the Scriptural validity of New Light church polity. He began to have his doubts on this matter in 1825 when he was admitted to the Indiana Conference by means of what he considered a very inadequate and superficial examination on the part of a special committee. It was the custom of New Light preachers, meeting in conference session (a business meeting which usually followed the big camp meeting) to license and ordain persons to the ministry, in complete disregard of, and with or without approbation of any local church. This produced, in effect, a self-perpetuating order of the clergy that operated independently of the lay

---

[32]Elijah Goodwin (1807-1874) was born in Ohio, moving with his parents first to Illinois and finally to Daviess County, Indiana; of Methodist background he joined the New Lights in 1821. He was licensed by the Indiana Conference at the age of nineteen. Two years later he was assigned a 600 mile circuit for the Indiana and Wabash conferences. Later, he organized several churches in Posey County. He began to have "reforming" views in 1828 and was instrumental in the disbanding of these conferences and bringing great numbers of his New Light brethren into the Campbell movement. He left Mt. Vernon in 1847 and moved to Bloomington where he became associated with J. M. Mathes on the *Christian Record*. In 1848 he became field agent to help promote the organization of North Western Christian University. He advanced his own personal project, the organization of the Indiana Christian Home Missionary Society, at the same time. In 1849 he accepted the pastorate of the Madison church, but in 1851 he returned to Bloomington to preach for the Bloomington and Clear Creek churches. After the death of his first wife he married Marcia Melissa Bassett, editor of the *Christian Monitor*, a woman's magazine. In 1856 he became pastor of Central Christian Church in Indianapolis. Three years later he purchased the *Christian Record* from J. M. Mathes and published this journal until 1861. He also assisted his wife in publishing the *Christian Monitor* for several years. In 1870 he was engaged as minister of Third Christian Church in Indianapolis, and in 1871 he served a church in Philadelphia. He died at Cleveland, Ohio, where he had gone to seek medical treatment. During his lifetime he engaged in ten public debates, mostly in the interest of temperance and religion. In addition to his editorial work he authored a book of sermons in 1856 which he titled, *The Family Companion*.

membership of the churches and ruled on matters of faith, order and polity. Though he said nothing about it at the time of his admission to the conference, Goodwin's doubts motivated him to further study of the Scriptures in order to find more suitable answers. This study led him to preach a "Sermon on the Law" at a camp meeting at Liberty in 1829. In this sermon he argued that "Christians need not go to the law of Moses to learn their duties, but to the system of grace and truth that came by Jesus Christ."[33] He may not have been familiar with Alexander Campbell's "Sermon on the Law," given before the Redstone Baptist Association in 1816, but there are startling similarities in the two sermons. Goodwin was given a public and abusive reprimand for his efforts, but he set the brethren to thinking.

At the meeting of the Wabash Conference in the fall of 1830, Goodwin, not a member of this conference, proposed another thought-provoking "reformation" idea. He introduced the proposition, "Is it scriptural for the meeting to be organized into a standing body, called a Conference, for the transaction of business, separate from and independent of the Churches?"[34] This resulted in a debate between William Kinkade[35] and Goodwin which focused attention to both sides of the issue. The matter must have been much discussed in the interval between the meetings of the Wabash and Indiana conferences because when the Indiana Conference met ten days later the issue was again considered, the discussion this time leading to the disbanding of the conference. Though responsible for the situation, Goodwin had not anticipated this sudden action. He explained later that he did not oppose

---

[33]James M. Mathes, *Life of Elijah Goodwin, the Pioneer Preacher* (St. Louis: John Burns, Publisher, 1880), p. 95.

[34]*Ibid.*, p. 118.

[35]William Kinkade was a popular and strong preacher among the New Lights but given to radical views. Once, in a camp meeting sermon, he attempted to prove that Jesus Christ was the Archangel Michael incarnate.

meetings for consultation but only meetings which operated as bodies separate and independent of the churches. He regretted that the conference, before it closed, had made no plans for future cooperation or annual meetings.[36]

Elijah Goodwin read Alexander Campbell's *Millennial Harbinger* in the years 1837-38 and compared Campbell's views with the Scriptures. As a result, he became convinced that faith in Christ and obedience to His commands constituted the Christian religion. Once, when he baptized a woman who had failed to get religion at the mourners' bench, he was accused of being a Campbellite.[37] By this time he was fully in the current reformation, as it was called, and started out to set the churches in the "gospel order" with elders and deacons, discarding the mourners' bench, and observing the Lord's Supper each week. From this time on, there were fewer camp meetings; protracted evangelistic meetings took their place, and the local church became an autonomous unit. The transition on the part of local congregations from the New Light position to that of the Disciples was a step by step progression —not sudden nor drastic—and any attempt to date it would be presumptuous speculation.

John Longley,[38] writing from Rush County to Barton W. Stone in 1832, stated that many churches formerly opposed to

---

[36]James M. Mathes, *Life of Elijah Goodwin, op. cit.,* p. 119. This action parallels almost exactly, even to time, to the actions of the Mahoning and Stillwater Baptist associations in Ohio.

[37]*Ibid.,* pp. 136-137.

[38]John Longley (1782-1867) was born in New York City. When he was eight years old his parents, who were Baptists, moved to Kentucky. While still a young man, Longley decided for the ministry. He was licensed as a Baptist preacher in 1805 although he was unhappy about Calvinistic theology. He met Barton W. Stone about this time, became interested in Stone's movement, and finally joined the New Lights. After preaching a few years in southern Ohio he moved to Rush County, Indiana, where, because of lack of meetinghouses, he preached from house to house. It was here that he met John T. Thompson, minister of the Little Flat Rock Church, just at the time when this church had separated from the Baptists. After a minor controversy with Thompson and the reformers, Longley embraced the new movement. He then moved to Yorktown in Delaware County where he organized a church and was instrumental in converting Benjamin and Daniel Franklin, young men who later became well known in the movement. He moved to Noblesville in 1840 and preached there for four years. His next move was to Lafayette where he preached for many years. Longley is reputed to have baptized over three thousand persons.

the "reformation" had ceased their opposition and had now fallen in with it. Not all New Lights, however, were in sympathy with the changes that had taken place. Longley wrote, "There are some of our brethren, that are making greater exertion in opposition, than the Methodists. Some of them have said, that they are able to put the reformation down, and they are determined to do it."[39] Since the New Light churches were loosely structured and conference membership was on a voluntary basis, many churches did not belong to any conference though they accepted conference preachers. The disbanding of some conferences did not necessarily mean that all the churches entered the reformation. There apparently was a division among the preachers and the churches, some going into the new movement and others eventually making complete affiliation with the original "old" Christian body which by this time had divorced itself from Stone and his followers.

Beginning about 1830 and continuing for about eight years, local New Light churches under the influence of such preachers as J. M. Mathes, Michael and Job Combs, Elijah Martindale, James Hughes of Kentucky, John Secrist of Ohio, Elijah Goodwin, Beverly Vawter, Love H. Jameson and John O'Kane went completely into the Disciples' movement (called the current reformation).

Whereas the Baptists in Indiana were structured in churches and their movement could be recognized as an association of churches, the New Lights did not really fit into such a category. Though they had churches, they were not churches in the theological sense in which the doctrine of the church is usually considered. At best, their churches were communities of persons—not always persons of the same mind—but of persons

---

[39]*Christian Messenger,* August, 1832, p. 246.

who were trying to follow Christ in complete freedom from the theological and ecclesiastical patterns of the nineteenth century. They believed in and advocated Christian union, provided such a union was completely unstructured. Their key words were "freedom," and "liberty." The New Lights seemed to feel a mission toward calling people out from under the authority of creeds, confessions, ecclesiasticism, denominationalism and even the "tyranny" of a structured local church. If Christians could be freed from these authorities, they thought, they would automatically be united as one Christian body; unity in Christ would be the inevitable outcome.

When people joined with them they were thought of as having "come out of something" rather than of having "gone into something." In this connection they frequently used the phase "coming out of Babylon" to refer to the action taken by those who left the traditional denominations. Elijah Goodwin proposed the following (now amusing) queries to Editor Barton W. Stone in 1828:

Brother Stone—As there is much said respecting coming out of Babylon: (1) Where is the road that leads out? (2) How must the church proceed, in order to get out? (3) How shall we know when we are out? (4) If Babylon is destroyed before the saints get out, what will become of them?[40]

Babylon, to the New Lights, was the armed citadel of erring and authoritarian sects which sought to dominate all religious life and stifle the spirit of God. They attacked their wilderness Babylon from within and from without, rejoicing at each person, each congregation, each ecclesiastical unit thus liberated. If they talked of union at this period it was not in the context of organic union—not even union through finding a common

---

[40]*Christian Messenger,* April, 1828, p. 156.

New Testament pattern—but unity in the sense of joining hands, hearts and minds in the project of gaining freedom for all Christians "enslaved" in structured ecclesiastical traditions. They did participate in "unions" with the Baptist reformers in the late 1820's, but these unions were looked upon by them as the uniting of forces to wage war on a common enemy rather than to bring forth a united church. If any of them thought of church unity in terms of one united Church of Christ, organized on a New Testament pattern, they put such thoughts aside for the duration of the action against Babylon.

The siege of Hoosier Babylon covered the period from about 1815 to 1835. Many outposts were captured, thousands were "liberated," but the Hoosier Babylon never really fell. Reinforcements from outside the state (new settlers) poured into Indiana from the camps of the Presbyterians, Methodists and Baptists. It is true that there were defections to the new frontier movement, but in spite of this, "Babylon" had a phenomenal growth. The denominational bodies were structured, had institutional characteristics, had a solid doctrine of the church, and soon became well established in the various Hoosier communities. The losses to the New Lights were great enough to allow the new body to grow to formidable strength, but replacements in the form of new settlers came to these denominations in such great numbers that their losses were scarcely noticed.

Baptist Reformers and New Lights Compared

Persons who became either Baptist Reformers or New Lights, who came to Indiana prior to 1830, had almost identical social and economic backgrounds. They followed the same migration pattern which funneled through Kentucky, and faced similar problems in the Hoosier state. Though originating from different theological traditions they sought the same goals in their religious pilgrimage. Many Baptist, New Light, and Dunkard congregations which had converted to these principles ceased to exist after a few years. This was due to population movement, shifting centers of community life, and lack of positive leadership rather than to divisive theological issues. Some thirty to fifty Indiana congregations surviving today originated on or before 1830.[41] Joseph Franklin explained it, "The people of these two reformative movements had come, but by different routes, to stand upon the same ground."[42]

Both Baptist Reformers and New Lights objected to creeds and articles of faith. The Reformers looked upon creeds as human inventions, divisive and heretical. The New Lights did not think of creeds as being the epitomy of evil but objected to them as binding and authoritative statements. Therefore, the New Lights found less difficulty in having fellowship with "creedal" bodies than did the Reformers.

Since both Baptist Reformers and New Lights had a deep distrust of authoritarian religious power, both sought freedom from it. The Reformers transferred authority from their associations and creedal statements to the local church by insisting on the "Bible alone" principle. The New Lights, on the other hand, attempted to free themselves from the authority of subjective inner experience, especially in conversion, by accepting this same "Bible alone" principle.

---

[41] It is not possible to list these congregations with any degree of accuracy. Many of these churches lapsed and were reorganized later, changed their names frequently, separated from the Disciples' movement and became independent or associated themselves later with the churches of Christ. Some of the earliest congregations did not become identified with the Disciples until the late 1830's. See *Our Rich Heritage, a Challenging Future*, the 125th Anniversary State Convention Program booklet (Indianapolis: Association of Christian Churches in Indiana, 1964), for a list of churches that responded to the appeal for statistical information on their origin. This list is neither accurate nor complete but represents the best information that could be compiled in consideration of the lack of local church records and non-interest taken on the part of some congregations.

[42] *Christian-Evangelist*, March 19, 1903. Article by Joseph Franklin.

Once this position was taken it was inevitable that applications be made in terms of ecclesiology, biblical theology, and biblical nomenclature. They each came to what they considered to be a biblical view of baptism and the Lord's Supper. Those who had formerly been Baptists had practiced immersion (baptism) as public confirmation of a conversion experience having already taken place. As Baptist Reformers, they took the position that baptism was an essential part of the conversion process, to be administered as a saving ordinance for the remission of sins, and that an unbaptized (unimmersed) person, however worthy otherwise, could not be considered by them as being a "saved" person. The New Lights originally were not concerned over baptism. They could take it or leave it, and the form did not matter. Baptism by immersion of the penitent believer for the remission of sins eventually became one of the tests by which it was known that a New Light congregation was leaning toward the Disciples' position.

The Baptist Reformers held the Lord's Supper in higher esteem than did the New Lights, but both bodies came to look upon this rite as being the center of corporate worship as well as an ordinance (law or command) that should be obeyed weekly. Anti-clerical views which they held in common made them deny that its administration (and the administration of baptism as well) was a priestly function, though they did consider their lay elders and deacons as having the proper ministerial authority to perform these rites; the idea that the administration of baptism and the Lord's Supper was a prerogative reserved for ordained clergymen did not enter the tradition until many years later and is not yet accepted by some of the churches. In general, the Lord's Supper came to have value in corporate worship only, and as a rite of fellowship which testified to unity in Christ as symbolized in the bread and wine.[43]

The New Lights, who had their inception in camp meeting religion, found that the camp meeting was the hardest thing to give up. In fact, even after they became Disciples they held occasional camp meetings. The Bethany Park Assembly and other Disciple "Chautauquas" so popular in the early 1900's were little more than an extension and a modification of the old camp meeting. The annual New Light camp meeting was often the one bright spot in the otherwise drab social life of the frontiersmen. It is clear that it filled a gregarious need in the lives of these people. Ryland T. Brown, who had experienced such meetings first-hand, wrote:[44]

If I were to give you a *fac similie* [sic] of the popular preaching and camp meeting worship of fifty years ago, you would accuse me of making a caricature of a grave subject. The religious teachings of these occasions, to put it mildly, was a mixture of theological speculations, traditional superstitions, and a wild fanaticism (I use this word in its literal sense—to see visions). The word of God, given us by the Holy Spirit, scarcely entered into the sermons of those times, further than to furnish a text.

As New Light preachers became more involved in the Disciples' movement they preached against "mourners' bench" or "anxious seat" conversions in favor of a simple public acknowledgment of faith in Christ as Savior, and a subsequent immediate immersion (baptism) for the remission of sins. Among the Baptists, the conversion test had been the relating of a "Christian experience" before a church group, and by the passing of representatives of this group on the validity of the experience. New Lights, after they became Disciples,

---

[43]Since every Disciple minister is his own theologian and interpreter of the movement, many will not agree with this analysis.

[44]*Christian Standard*, July 14, 1883. Article by Ryland T. Brown.

and Baptist Reformers eventually came to regard conversion as obedience to what they considered to be the Scriptural terms of admittance to the church.

Those who had been Baptists had originally held to a trinitarian position in their Christology. The New Lights were primarily unitarian in their belief, though many would not admit it. As they each moved toward the Disciples' position they came to accept Alexander Campbell's ambiguous Christological views by avoiding such "unscriptural" words as trinitarian and unitarian, an ambiguity that was as baffling then as now. Because of their strong emphasis on God's love and on the more positive aspects of religion, many New Lights were inclined to accept the popular view of universal salvation; the Baptist Reformers considered salvation as limited, not necessarily to the elect, but to those who obeyed what they considered to be the clear-cut demands of the gospel.

Both New Lights and Baptist Reformers claimed to center authority in the local church, though in actual practice this was not generally true. The New Lights organized in conferences and the Baptists in associations. Often the New Light conference was little more than a preachers' meeting held in connection with a big camp meeting. The conference proper, made up of preachers only, took the authority of licensing and ordaining ministers, though it also held that every man or woman who wanted to do so had the liberty to preach. Not many took advantage of this freedom because without the blessing of the conference there was little opportunity to preach. The Baptist Reformer system was one of using lay preachers (preaching elders) who supported their families by other means and preached as an avocation. This mutual type of ministry provided ministerial leadership for even the smallest of congregations, and some churches had two or more ministers who alternated Sundays in the pulpit. Whereas, the

New Light preachers were inclined to travel a great deal, sometimes in regular circuits like the Methodists, the Baptist Reformers were inclined to stay in one place where they farmed, pursued a trade, or followed a profession such as teaching, the law, or medicine. The central authority on the New Light system was in its ordained clergymen, though they exercised this authority very little except to perpetuate the clergy. The central authority for the Reformers had been in the association when they were still Baptists and in the Bible when they became Reformers. Authority in the Bible, as they held it, was tantamount to centering authority in the local congregation because interpretation of controversial biblical doctrines was in the hands of the voting majority of the local church. When the New Light conferences were dissolved, New Lights followed this same procedure.

Ferment on the Indiana frontier resulted in the dissolution of associations and conferences. This left the churches, for a time at least, in a state of near chaos. New Lights and Baptist Reformers, discovering they had arrived at about the same position though by different means, feeling a strong need for fellowship, began to work together in what they called co-operations (a unit made up of congregations in a limited geographical area). Churches in the cooperation shared traveling evangelists (the counterpart of modern clergymen), and even promoted a program of limited missionary expansion. From this "cooperation" structure they expanded into county and district organizations (larger cooperations), and finally to a State Meeting in 1839. By this time the Disciples movement (called Christian Churches in Indiana) had completely absorbed them both.

III

Cooperation with Compromise

1830-1846

RELIGIOUS FERMENT ON THE INDIANA FRON-
tier continued throughout the 1820's and into the beginning
of the next decade. By the middle 1820's the radical manifestation of religion (Rappites, Shakers, New Lights, and Owenites) had about run the course of fanaticism, and the newer
religious bodies were seeking a norm about which to structure
their faith. The place to seek this pattern, it was thought, was
in the Bible, particularly in the New Testament. For them,
the Bible became a "question and answer" book on all matters
of faith and order. Once an answer was found it was then
necessary only to obey or conform to the biblical precept.
Those dissatisfied with the doctrines of existing denominations
usually put them to the biblical test; they could then be accepted or rejected in accordance with how they thought they
measured up to the clear teachings of Scripture.

There was both strength and weakness in this approach. It
brought many people to a common ground, armed them with
spiritual truths, and provided a pattern for structuring a growing religious body. On the other hand, each thought that his
own views on biblical interpretation were the only correct
ones, that those who held different views must be in error, and
that a congregation which conformed "chapter and verse"

to what they considered to be New Testament church polity was a "true" Church of Christ.

Those who were like-minded in religious views were drawn to one another by mutual acquaintances, the efforts of itinerant preachers, and associations made at camp meetings. Evidence indicates that at least some were reading the *Christian Baptist* after 1825, the *Christian Messenger* after 1826, and after 1830, the *Millennial Harbinger*. These periodicals appealed to the frontier mind, carried on theological discussions in terms that could be understood, and occasionally printed news items of a local flavor. In some instances what was called the "new reformation" was carried into Hoosier communities by persons who had made direct contact outside Indiana with leaders such as Barton W. Stone, Alexander Campbell, Walter Scott and "Raccoon" John Smith.[1]

The new movement was an indigenous one, however, among the Free-will Baptist churches of the Blue River Baptist Association and in a German Baptist (Dunkard) association, both in southern Indiana. Under the influence of John Wright, his brothers and their father, the Blue River Baptist Church became the Church of Christ at Blue River as early as 1819, and the entire Blue River association converted into an Annual Meeting in 1821.[2] The Dunkard association, mentioned above, made up of fifteen churches in southern Indiana under the leadership of Joseph Hostetler, went through an almost identical experience in the years 1826-27.[3] When John Wright heard that these Dunkards were having a reformation similar to that experienced at Blue River he suggested that

---

[1] For example: Dr. Ryland T. Brown met "reformation" leaders in Cincinnati when he was a medical student in that city, Love H. Jameson and John O'Kane traveled with Walter Scott on evangelistic missions, John P. Thompson conferred with Barton W. Stone and John Smith while visiting in Kentucky, and John Longley was a friend of Barton W. Stone. Many other similar examples could be mentioned.

[2] *See* pages 48-49.

[3] *See* pages 49-51.

the two groups unite, face their problems together, and call themselves "Christians." This union was effected and became the first of such unions among the religious bodies which later became identified with the Disciples' movement in Indiana. This action was the inspiration for a more significant merger the next year between these two bodies and the New Lights.

The Edinburg Unity Meeting

John Wright and the newly-formed group of Free-will and German Baptist reformers, caught in the momentum of their own successful union, began looking for other groups with which similar "unions" could be consummated. They knew enough about the New Lights and their "Bible alone" principles to encourage them to look in this direction. Since the next New Light conference[4] was known to be meeting at Edinburg in Bartholomew County, beginning July 25, 1828, they determined to have representatives present with definite unity proposals. No transcript of the proceedings of this conference was kept (they were afraid that such documents could be construed as creedal statements), but enough evidence from various sources, when put together, gives a rather clear-cut picture of what transpired.

When Jesse Hughes, presiding elder, wrote a report of the meeting for the *Christian Messenger*,[5] he named the ordained and unordained ministers present and included John and Peter Wright in this list. Though these men were not New Lights—at least they did not come to Edinburg as such—

---

[4]It was officially announced as "The Second Conference of the United Churches of God in Christ of the State of Indiana and Kentucky, meeting at Brother F. Steinberger's in Bartholomew County the Thursday preceding the Fourth Lord's Day in July, 1828."

[5]*Christian Messenger*, Sept., 1828, p. 259. This list named the following ordained ministers as being present: Jesse Hughes, Jno. Wright, Peter Wright, Henry Logan, Jesse Frazier, Beverly Vawter, Jas. Doudle, James Daugherty, William Tracy, Wm. P. Ritchie, Thomas Johnson, Josiah Ashley, and Joseph Hatchitt. Those listed as unordained were Pliny Hatchitt, James McCoy and Henry Leonard.

the fact that they had come as representatives of another religious body was not mentioned. The Hughes' statement does not report a union of any kind as having taken place. Hughes did report that letters of correspondence from several conferences and churches were read, that Pliny Hatchitt was ordained and that James McCoy was licensed to preach. He also reported that John Wright, Peter Wright and Pliny Hatchitt were appointed to bear a letter of correspondence to the Christian conference on Buck Creek, Harrison County, and that John Wright was selected as one of the members of the Presbytery which was to ordain Pliny Hatchitt. The Hughes' correspondence shows that the Wrights were integrated into the conference but makes no comment concerning their former status, or of a union with the Baptist reformers.

Joseph Hatchitt, also a member of this conference, wrote a letter to the *Christian Messenger*[6] under the same dateline, a letter which inadvertently disclosed additional information concerning the presence of the Wrights. He stated:

> The Bros. Wrights, whose names you will see in the minutes, have been formerly denominated "Depending Baptists;" but lately have laid that name aside, and now call themselves "the church of Christ." I judge there are six or eight Elders among them, and many churches. When we met in conference together, we could find nothing to separate us asunder. In fine, we saw as nearly eye to eye as any company of Elders who have assembled in modern times —and then there was such a sweet spirit of love.

The primary purpose of Hatchitt's correspondence was to report his evangelistic activities to Barton W. Stone. Nevertheless, he was so impressed with the presence of the Baptist reformers that he was impelled to include a comment about them.

---

[6]*Christian Messenger,* September, 1828, pp. 260-261.

It is apparent that each of the groups read its own interpretation into the nature of the meeting. So far as the New Lights were concerned, a group of Baptists representing two former Baptist associations (though they did not mention Joseph Hostetler and the former German Baptist association) had dropped their Baptist names and creeds and joined with them. Hatchitt probably echoed this view when he wrote, "These people have freely and voluntarily come out of Babylon." The Baptist reformers were given full conference status and were accepted as brethren and co-workers. On the other hand, the Blue River-Dunkard group thought they had formed a union with New Lights at the Edinburg meeting, and often spoke of the event in these exact terms. According to Madison Evans, "a joint convention was assembled near Edinburg, where the union was readily formed."[7] Evidence seems to indicate that though the Baptist reformers thought they were uniting with the New Lights, the New Lights believed they had just "joined" their body. Perhaps they preferred to think of it in this way. The Baptist reformers, in describing this meeting later, claimed that Beverly Vawter was the principal speaker and that it was his arguments and conciliatory statements that brought the two groups together. The New Lights claimed that Joseph Berry was the great preacher at this meeting and emphasized the appeal he made for new converts. The Baptist reformers claimed later that the Littells of the Silver Creek Baptist Association were present also, but their names are not recorded in the Hughes' report to the *Christian Messenger*. It can be said with certainty, however, that there was a marriage of New Light Christians and Baptist reformers at Edinburg in 1828, although each group placed a different interpretation

------

[7]Madison Evans, *op. cit.*, p. 33. The New Lights held several annual conferences after the Edinburg meeting, even expanded and formed new conferences, and the former Baptist reformers were given assignments in the various conferences without regard to their prior affiliation.

on what happened. Assuming that the Baptist reformers symbolized the groom and the New Lights the bride, the marriage
could be said to be matriarchal in nature, *but the children
of the union took after the father!* If the New Lights thought
the Wrights and others had simply "joined" them to become
New Lights, they were mistaken; they "united" with them to
eventually escort them into the Disciples' fellowship.

Edinburg and Lexington Contrasted

The unity meeting at Edinburg occurred three and one-half
years before the celebrated New Light-Reformer union at Lexington, Kentucky. It was a union of three structured religious
bodies (two former Baptist associations and a New Light
conference) whereas the Lexington union was a meeting of
self-appointed delegates, none having conference or association backing and most of whom did not officially represent
even a local church.[8] The Lexington union of 1832, however,
did point the way toward many New Light-Reformer unions
in Kentucky communities in the years that followed. Evidence
seems to indicate also that union between these two bodies in
Indiana was always a step ahead of Kentucky; even the Indiana State Meeting was organized one year prior to the one
in Kentucky. Not only was a structured union a *fait accompli*
in Indiana before 1832, but many local-church unions between Baptist reformers and New Lights took place before
this time. John Longley of Rush County, Indiana, wrote to
Barton W. Stone under the dateline of December 24, 1831,

---

[8]Walter Scott wrote of the Lexington union, "It is one of so specific and local a
nature as to render it impossible for those who plead the cause generally to pronounce
upon either its propriety, or impropriety." *The Evangelist*, May, 1832, pp. 110-111. A.
W. Fortune, Kentucky historian, wrote of this union, "The action of the Lexington
meeting was not official, and did not consumate the union of the two bodies in the
state; it was merely an expression of the attitude of the leaders." Alonzo Willard
Fortune, *The Disciples in Kentucky* (Lexington: Convention of the Christian Churches
in Kentucky, 1932), p. 122. Alexander Campbell had another view of the Lexington
meeting. See *Millennial Harbinger*, March 5, 1832, pp. 138-139; May 2, 1822, pp.
193-195.

that "The Reforming Baptists and we New Lights are all one here, and we hope that the dispute between you and Brother Campbell about names and priority, will forever cease, and that you will go on united to reform the world."[9] The Lexington union involved several distinguished men and was followed by a joint editorship of the *Christian Messenger* by J. T. Johnson, the Baptist reformer, and Barton W. Stone, New Light leader; consequently, it gained wider attention than prior unions in Indiana which involved little known personalities and received no publicity at the time.

Beginning of Organized Missionary Expansion

When churches became a part of the "new reformation" they separated from prior associations or conferences to become self-governing or autonomous bodies. This seemed to be a desirable achievement but one with undesirable features. None were strong enough to give entire support to a minister, nor could the local congregations, by themselves, sustain an evangelist to carry the gospel to new Hoosier communities. They had, however, a strong compulsion for county-level missionary expansion and a desire for closer fellowship with their brethren in other communities. To accomplish this they began to organize what they called "cooperations." The cooperation had a dual function; to serve as a pastoral unity (two or more churches sharing the same pastoral ministry), and the financial support of an evangelist who had the missionary responsibility of organizing churches in communities where the need was determined. Sometimes the same man or the same team carried on both functions. The "cooperation" was regarded as a practical solution to the problem of maintaining the autonomy of the local church and at the same

---

[9]*Christian Messenger*, January, 1832, pp. 28-29.

time sharing the responsibility of missionary expansion with other churches. Though the brethren did not realize it then, the forming of cooperations was the first step in structuring the Indiana brotherhood. Cooperations were not regarded as ecclesiastical entities (though they were) but as expediencies for the propagation of the "new reformation" in the Hoosier state. As the influence of conferences and associations declined—presumably in favor of local church autonomy—the prestige of the cooperation increased. Few new congregations were formed after the early 1830's by either Baptist reformers or New Lights, but many were formed by the cooperations. New congregations organized under the cooperation system were not hybrid New Light-Reformer churches, but Disciples' churches (Campbell movement) known as Christian Churches in Indiana.

One of the first attempts of adjacent congregations to form a cooperation in Indiana was made at Crawfordsville in the fall of 1831. Madison Evans explained there were six ministers only in the group, "a number which clearly indicates that the Reformation in Indiana was then in its infancy."[10] From 1833 to 1839 James M. Mathes preached in Bloomington and other parts of Monroe County as the evangelist of a cooperation centering around Old Union Church in Owen County.[11]

The beginnings of Central Christian Church in Indianapolis is a good example of the significance of the cooperation plan. This church originated in a five-church cooperation in Rush County.[12] The first preaching in what is now downtown In-

---

[10]Madison Evans, *op cit.*, p. 286. Ministers who served in this cooperation were: Michael Combs, Andrew Prather, James R. Ross, A. Sears, John M. Harris, and William Wilson.

[11]James M. Mathes, autobiography, *op. cit.*, p. 47. He reported that he traveled, preached and organized churches during this period and that he received an average of thirty dollars per year for his services.

[12]These churches were: Little Flatrock, Fayetteville, Connersville, Columbia and Clarksburg.

84

dianapolis was done by John McClung, a New Light preacher who moved to the community from southern Indiana in 1821. He died that same year and is buried along Fall Creek two miles north of the city. When McClung preached at Indianapolis the Delaware Indians had just moved out of central Indiana and surveyors were laying out the town in preparation for moving the state capitol from Corydon to this site. In 1825, the legislature convened for the first time at this location. Between 1825 and 1835 the town was literally carved out of the woods. The Rush County cooperation apparently saw the importance of planting a church at Indianapolis, realizing its future as the state capital made it important to their cause. There was a small New Light congregation west of the city and a church of the Baptist reformers south of the city. John O'Kane, [13] who had held evangelistic meetings in Indianapolis early in 1833, was selected as the missionary evangelist of the Rush County cooperation and Indianapolis was chosen as his first field of missionary labor. As a result, "The Church of Christ in Indianapolis" was organized in the log dwelling of

---

[13]John O'Kane (1802-1881) was a colorful figure and influencial preacher. He was of Irish descent, born in Virginia and came from the Old Christian (O'Kelly) movement. Before locating in Wayne County where he preached and taught school in 1832, he had preached in Virginia and Ohio. He discovered some articles in the *Christian Messenger* by James E. Mathews of Alabama which appeared to savor of "Campbellism." Accordingly, he replied with an article which denounced these views. To O'Kane's surprise, Editor Barton W. Stone defended Mathews. Madison Evans wrote of this incident, "In a short time both he and Elder Stone were preaching the faith which both had sought to destroy." Apparently O'Kane had a conversion from the "old" Christian movement to the Disciples about this time. Because of this he was charged with being a Campbellite. That same year he joined with John P. Thompson, a Baptist reformer, in evangelizing in Rush, Fayette, and Decatur counties. With Dr. Ryland T. Brown he organized the Connersville church in 1833 and published a religious journal, *The Christian Casket*, from this city the same year. In June, 1833, as the evangelist of the Rush County Cooperation, he organized the Indianapolis church. O'Kane moved to Crawfordsville in 1837, preaching there and evangelizing in the surrounding area. He returned to Connersville in 1848 where he labored for one year. In 1849 he went into the bookstore business in Indianapolis and preached where needed. In 1851 he entered the North Western Christian University development project, taking the field as general agent. It was largely through his efforts that enough stock was sold in the enterprise to authorize construction of a university building. Some indiscreet remarks concerning Bethany College, made while in the field as agent for the university, antagonized Alexander Campbell and placed the whole educational project in jeopardy for a time. He moved to Independence, Missouri in 1859, and the Civil War cut him off from his Indiana brethren for a few years. Having organized several Disciples' congregations in Indiana and having successfully conducted a financial campaign for what eventually became Butler University, O'Kane has almost become a legendary figure among Disciples in the Hoosier state.

Benjamin Roberts on June 12, 1833.

The Indianapolis church is not only a good example of the result of missionary expansion through the "cooperation" unit, but of the successful integration of New Light and Baptist reformer traditions. The project was sponsored by Baptist reformers in Rush County, and the church was organized by John O'Kane of the "old" Christian movement. Among the charter members were Dr. John H. Sanders and his family, New Lights from Kentucky; Benjamin and Peter Roberts, New Lights; and Butler K. Smith and family, Baptist reformers.[14] There seems to be no evidence that members of this congregation at the time ever raised the question as to whether it was a New Light or Baptist reformer church or that they looked to either Alexander Campbell or Barton W. Stone as the sole founder and leader of the "new" Reformation.[15]

Regional Union of 1833

A union between Baptist reformers (former Calvinistic Baptists) and "reformed" New Lights took place on the Bluffs of the White River in Morgan County in August, 1833. It had its beginning in a business trip to Bartholomew County made by Michael Combs. Discussing religion with two elderly people at this place, one of them commented: "This stranger talks just like Jo Fassett." Combs then made a point of attending the New Hope church where Fassett preached. He

---

[14] Dr. John H. Sanders was a leader in the professional and social life of the new community. His daughter Zerelda became the wife of Governor David Wallace and a leader in women's suffrage, temperance, and missionary work. She was the stepmother of General Lew Wallace, author of *Ben Hur*. Peter H. Roberts was a lay-preacher of the New Lights and his brother Benjamin was a harness maker. Butler K. Smith and his brother Carey were blacksmiths. The Smiths had originally been Baptists and had changed their views after becoming readers of the *Christian Baptist*. Butler K. Smith was an overseer in the Indianapolis church, preaching occasionally before Love H. Jameson became pastor in 1842. At this time he was ordained as an evangelist-at-large, serving many cooperations in this capacity.

[15] The history of the founding of the Indianapolis congregation was taken from the 211-page typed manuscript, *The History of Central Christian Church*, by Francis M. Wiley, written in 1933.

86

discovered that this (now Disciple) church held to a theological position which was very similar to that which he had been preaching since he had changed some of his New Light views. Conversations between Combs and Fassett confirmed the similarity of their religious convictions and led to a program of uniting the Disciples in Montgomery and adjacent counties with the New Lights in Bartholomew and other counties to the north and west. They then called for a White River "unity" meeting. Some twenty of the "teaching" brethren (ministers) were present at this meeting, and the total attendance was about evenly divided between Disciples and New Lights. When each group had been heard from it was discovered all had renounced "human" creeds and that there was but little actual theological difference between them. The Morgan County unity meeting lasted three days and culminated in a union service where hundreds of persons, representing both original groups, participated in observing the Lord's Supper together.[16]

This regional union of 1833 is significant in that it originated from within the state, included hundreds of persons from several Hoosier counties, completed in the joint participation of the Lord's Supper, and was continued in three "cooperating" meetings the next year; one at Greensburg in February, one at Crawfordsville in March, and another in Indianapolis in April. Like the Edinburg meeting of 1828, the participants were largely unknown to their brethren outside the state, and the meeting received very little publicity.

Campbell, Stone and Christian Unity

The Baptist reformers learned of Barton W. Stone primarily through association with the New Lights. By the time of the Indiana "unions," Stone's prestige as a religious leader was

---

[16]Madison Evans, *op. cit.,* pp. 150-151. *Christian Messenger,* June, 1834, p. 63. The site indicated was probably what is now known as Blue Bluffs, near Bethany Park.

declining and Alexander Campbell's ascending. It is not strange that Stone's colleagues regarded him as a lovable, distinguished Christian; as early as the 1830's they no longer addressed him as *Brother* Stone but as *Father* Stone. By this time Barton W. Stone was a person to be honored, but Alexander Campbell was their guide and mentor. Stone was known among the New Lights of Kentucky, Ohio, and Indiana as a preacher and one of the founders of their movement. He was also recognized by this same group as their leading scholar and as editor of the *Christian Messenger.* On the other hand, Campbell was a person who had status beyond the western frontier as one who had won recognition from other religious groups than his own. There were many who did not agree with Campbell's views, but at least they knew him. His *Christian Baptist* magazine appeared three years before Stone's *Christian Messenger* and continued as the *Millennial Harbinger* many years after Stone's journal ceased publication. His New Testament translation, first printed in 1826, was published in several editions throughout the years. His hymnal was revised and enlarged many times after 1828. Campbell's *Christian System,* a volume containing his theological views, was published in 1835 and was popular for a half a century. He had many debates with such outstanding public figures as Robert Owen, Bishop John B. Purcell, and N. L. Rice. The debate with Owen at Cincinnati in 1829 was especially interesting to Hoosiers because of Owen's connection with the New Harmony (Indiana) experiment. Campbell had made numerous tours through the Midwest, South, and East, and he was known in Europe as well as in America. He was a man of wealth and influence who was at ease entertaining persons of national stature in his Bethany home; whereas Stone in his time was little more than a regional celebrity. In addition to this, when the Disciples' movement was advancing in Indiana,

Campbell was still vigorous and productive, whereas Stone had long since passed his prime. In 1835, for example, Campbell was forty-seven and Stone was sixty-three. There is little doubt that of the two leaders, Campbell carried more weight with more people in his time. Father Stone was loved, respected and appreciated by his followers, but eventually to these same people Alexander Campbell became "Mr. Big."

The idea of forming regional cooperations came from Alexander Campbell. He wrote a series of articles in the *Millennial Harbinger* in 1831 which set forth their necessity. Stone thought in larger terms at this time, the union of all Christian bodies into one fold in the shortest possible time. Campbell, the more practical of the two men, desired ultimate union on the basis of the restoration of what he called the "ancient order of things." He probably felt that the place to begin was in regional cooperations and on what he thought was the sound theological basis of a "restored" New Testament faith. Stone, on the other hand, was quite willing for all major religious bodies to unite on the principle of Christian love and forbearance, trusting that once so united, a common faith would develop. Stone's views on Christian unity were quite in keeping with his great spirit; but it must be also remembered that time was running out on him, and he knew it. On the other hand, Campbell had many more years ahead of him and could afford to wait for his idea of unity to develop from a grass roots theological basis. In any event, the idea of cooperations took firm hold in Ohio, Kentucky and Indiana, and they were the first steps in structuring a new brotherhood. A great number of county cooperations came into existence in Indiana during the 1830's. The brethren, even with their limited vision, could see "unchurched" communities in their own and nearby counties and were willing to consider these as a special concern, but their missionary spirit did not go beyond this.

First Indiana State Meeting

With so many small-scale cooperation meetings being held throughout the state it is not surprising that by 1839 the brethren thought in terms of a general "state-wide" cooperation meeting. The project had its origin in Indianapolis, indicating that although the Indianapolis area did not have the largest concentration of Disciples in the state, the brethren in this new community were exerting a quality of leadership and vision that could not be matched in the older communities. Butler K. Smith of the Indianapolis congregation, probably as the result of meeting held the early part of the year, submitted a notice to Disciples' periodicals concerning a statewide meeting, June 7-12, 1839, as follows:

It has been thought advisable by Brethren, in various parts of this state, to call a general co-operation meeting, to convene at this place, on *Friday, before the second Lord's day in June next*. The objects of said meeting will be, to promote the general prosperity of the good cause in Indiana—to endeavor, by the free interchange of views, to bring the united energies of the disciples to bear upon the accomplishment of some desirable objects.—Such as the procuring and sustaining of efficient and faithful Evangelists; the promotion of the cause of education in general, and of religious education in particular. In a word, to consult upon any matter that may be found conducive to the general advancement of the truth. It would be gratifying to the brethren here, to have said meeting numerously attended; not only by our brethren in Indiana, but also, those of the neighboring states; especially by such able champions of the faith as Campbell, Crihfield, Scott, Hall, Burnet, Johnson, and a host of worthies too numerous to name.[17]

---

[17]*Heretic Detector*, April, 1839, pp. 88-89. The announcement continued with a statement that the notice had been sent to the *Heretic Detector* and *Millennial Harbinger* for publication, in the hope also that it would be copied by the *Evangelist*, the *Preacher*, and the *Berean*. The use of the word "disciples" and the absence of the name of Barton W. Stone in the list of "able champions" which included only former Baptist reformers, may or may not be significant.

The meeting convened at the new Kentucky Avenue meetinghouse as announced, and John O'Kane presided over it with Persius K. Harris acting secretary. Francis W. Emmons[18] reported the proceedings to the *Millennial Harbinger*. There was no count of those present at this meeting other than the Emmons' statement that, "There were present about fifty public speakers,[19] among whom from abroad were Elders Barton W. Stone, Arthur Crihfield, and John Taffe." Probably not more than fifty male Disciples, therefore, plus the wives of some, attended in a quasi-official capacity, though the attendance at meetings other than the business sessions was probably much higher because of Indianapolis people who were interested in hearing the addresses and sermons.

One of the first projects of the meeting was to compile statistics of Indiana Disciples' churches to include names of churches, estimated membership, and names of leading persons in each congregation. These statistics, as published in the *Millennial Harbinger* and *Heretic Detector,* were no more than an educated guess, but they showed an estimated existence of 115 churches and 7,701 members. J. B. Hayward later reported a supplemental list,[20] which if added to the original report would raise the total membership to 8,219. Hayward estimated that membership in Indiana was really

---

[18]Francis Whitefield Emmons (1802-1881) was one of the few scholars among the Hoosier Disciples in the pioneer period. After graduating from Brown University in 1828 he was ordained to the Baptist ministry. He preached and operated an academy at Killingworth, Connecticut, about this time. By reading the *Christian Baptist* and the Campbell-McCalla *Debate* he became converted to Campbell's views. Emmons opened an academy at New Lisbon, Ohio, in 1831. At this time he contributed notes, emendations, and suggestions for the fourth edition of Campbell's New Testament. He moved to Noblesville in 1834 where he tried to unite a Baptist and New Light church. Emmons attended the Campbell-Purcell debate in Cincinnati in 1837 and took notes for its publication in book form. While in Noblesville in 1837 he wrote one major book, *The Voice of One Crying in the Wilderness, being an Essay to Extend the Reformation.* In addition to this he published several monographs and addresses. He returned to New England in 1842.

[19]*Millennial Harbinger,* August, 1839, pp. 353-357; in a report to the *Christian Preacher,* October, 1839, p. 203, J. B. Hayward stated there were sixty-five "preaching brethren" in attendance.

[20]*Heretic Detector,* November, 1839, p. 327.

about 15,000 persons and that there were about twenty-five evangelists, 150 capable of being evangelists and 150 capable of being "teaching Elders or Bishops." Since many churches at that time carried only the names of adult males on their membership roles and many churches also were not fully committed as yet to the Disciples' movement, it is impossible to ascertain with any degree of reasonable certainty what the Indiana membership was in 1839. Some of the churches named in the report remained autonomous and independent, and some stayed in the "old" Christian denomination; others eventually became identified with the Churches of Christ (anti-instrument) movement. Those churches which agreed in principle with Campbell's "new reformation" eventually were structured into the Disciples' brotherhood in Indiana. A more realistic estimate of the number of Disciples in Indiana at the time of the first State Meeting would be about 4,000.[21]

The Emmons' report also gave an account of several recommendations which, according to him, were adopted "very unanimously." These recommendations were directed to the churches of the state and covered the need of sending out evangelists (missionaries), the financial support of preaching brethren, encouragement to young men to become preachers, advice to the churches that these young men be assisted in getting an education, that education should be encouraged among the Disciples, that the Indiana State University at Bloomington be patronized, and that there should be a second State Meeting at Crawfordsville in 1840. There must have been some discussion concerning the need of a religious journal aimed specifically at meeting the needs of Hoosier

---

[21]C. W. Cauble's *Disciples of Christ in Indiana*, pp. 75-79, carries the Emmons' statistics, preceded by the explanation, "Then follows the list of the churches represented at this meeting with their location by counties." This is an unwarranted assumption as a study of the Emmons' report will show. It was a list of possible churches *but not specifically the churches represented at this meeting.*

Disciples because Barton W. Stone, who then lived at Jacksonville, Illinois, was requested to move to Indiana, to revive publication of the *Christian Messenger* in this state.

Barton W. Stone, who was not officially invited in the notice that gave special invitations to other prominent men, attended the Indianapolis meeting and was warmly received. He delivered five sermons with remarks especially directed to the young preachers. These sermons drew so many people that the Christian meetinghouse could not accommodate them and the Methodist church had to be used when he spoke. Concerning Stone it was reported, "Old brother B. W. Stone, of Illinois, attended, and spent some time preaching at Logansport, Bloomington, and other places with considerable success."[22]

Though statistical and factual information are important, more insight into the nature of this meeting is essential. Fortunately, Arthur Crihfield, editor of the *Heretic Detector,* was in attendance; he gave a rather full, though informal, report of his 400-mile round-trip from Middleburg, Ohio. It was published in a series of travel notes in his magazine. He complained of the roads in Randolph County and wrote of one especially, as "the roughest and most uncouthly bridged road we had ever seen . . . Thus we spent a half day going twelve miles, that is, from the State line to Winchester."[23] From Winchester he drove to "Munseetown" and finally to Yorktown where he lodged with John Longley. Leaving Yorktown he followed the White River through

---

[22]*Christian Preacher*, August, 1839, pp. 152-153. By this time Stone was becoming deaf, and his memory was dulled. He had a stroke of paralysis in the fall of 1841 from which he never fully recovered. He last visited Indiana when he attended the district meeting at Crawfordsville in September, 1843, accompanied by his son, B. W. Stone, Jr. Here he renewed acquaintanceship with John Thompson, one of the six signers of the *Last Will and Testament of the Springfield Presbytery* in 1804. Thompson had long since returned to the Presbyterian fold, and his sons had been instrumental in the founding of Wabash College at this place. Stone's daughter, Tabitha (Mrs. P. E. Harris) lived at Rockville, Indiana, and was the mother of two of his grandchildren.

[23]*Heretic Detector*, August, 1839, p. 199.

"Andersontown" and "Strawtown" to Noblesville where he stayed with F. W. Emmons. From Noblesville, it was a four-hour drive to Indianapolis at which place he enjoyed the hospitality of James Sulgrove.

In his comments on the Indianapolis State Meeting, Crihfield brought out the underlying issues connected with it. He stated that before leaving Ohio a brother in Indiana had written him, "Beware of the *horns* at Indianapolis."[24] He explained that many thought he had gone to some kind of a general assembly with the principal men among the brethren to form a creed and a book of discipline. Crihfield wrote that he found that this was a general concern among all who attended this meeting and warned that long experience had shown that there was a danger of a surrender of the peoples' power, when at such general meetings, an order is formed, committees appointed, resolutions adopted, and sundry recommendations made to the body at large. He compared meetings such as this to the origin of Baptist associations, Methodist conferences and Presbyterian general assemblies. According to Crihfield, such meetings oppressed the people by a power which the people gave them. He apparently was uneasy over the fact that the Indianapolis meeting adopted several *resolutions* "as though it had a power the churches had not."[25] He reminded his brethren that now that they had renounced "associations" they should beware lest they get the same thing under another name or no name at all.

Crihfield enjoyed the fellowship of the State Meeting. He wrote that he met men from nearly all parts of Indiana, many of whom he had never seen before. Named among those who preached were John O'Kane, James M. Mathes, G. T.

---

[24]*Heretic Detector,* October, 1839, p. 269.
[25]*Heretic Detector,* October, 1839, p. 270.

Harney, J. B. New, Watson Clarke, Newton Short, and
Barton W. Stone. He became quite fond of Elder Chauncey
Butler, Sr.,[26] and wrote that it pained him to have to separate
from him. Crihfield journeyed back to Ohio with Elijah
Martindale and John O'Kane accompanying him part of
the way. He also took pleasure in the hospitality of Samuel
K. Hoshour, head of the academy at Centerville, when he
passed through this community.

In spite of the limitations of the meeting it was a pioneer
project and had a great deal of significance. The fellowship
of Disciples was strengthened. Elijah Goodwin wrote that he
met Barton W. Stone here for the first and last time.
Others he mentioned in this connection were: James A.
Mathes, Michael Combs, John P. Thompson, Andrew
Prather, James R. Ross, Watson Clark, Love H. Jameson,
Butler K. Smith and John B. New.[27] In becoming acquainted
with one another the seeds of brotherhood life were sown.
The compiling of statistics, though inaccurate, proved to be
means by which they learned who they were and to some
extent where they were going. The passing of resolutions,
even though not binding on the churches, was the beginning
of ecclesiastical structure. Those who attended the meeting
must have done so with many reservations and not without
much fear of compromising their principles. The first meeting
was an experiment, and no one had any idea as to where it
would lead. The fact that it did become the state-wide first
Annual Meeting, and not the only such meeting, set a precedent that was never broken and one which was followed in
other states. It gave tacit approval to a principle that had

---

[26]Chauncey Butler, Sr. (1776-1840), the father of Ovid Butler, was the overseer
and evangelist of the Indianapolis church at this time. Formerly a Baptist, he had
recently accepted the views of the reformers. He had moved to Indianapolis only a
few months before this.

[27]J. M. Mathes, *Life of Elijah Goodwin, op. cit.,* pp. 150-151.

been rejected up to this time—the recognition of authority in church government beyond that of the local church. This was a difficult step to take, but once taken it opened the door for cooperation in missionary effort and sowed the seeds of institutional life (Butler University) within the framework of a state structure.

A District Plan that Failed

Before the Indianapolis meeting was adjourned it was decided to have a second meeting the next year at Crawfordsville. Very little is known about this meeting. About the only significant known fact concerning the third meeting at Indianapolis in 1841 is that Raccoon John Smith of Kentucky was the great attraction. Perhaps this paucity of news is the reason why John O'Kane and others kept insisting on the need of a state paper for the Indiana brotherhood. Lack of adequate communication among the brethren hampered the work. Dr. Ryland T. Brown[28] claimed that the matter of state-wide missionary expansion was discussed at Crawfords-

---

[28]Dr. Ryland T. Brown (1807-1890) was born in Kentucky and moved to southeast Rush County with his parents in 1821. Here at the age of fifteen he joined the Clifty Baptist Church. He read the Campbell-Walker debate in 1826 and subscribed to the *Christian Baptist* the same year. In the meantime the Flat Rock Baptist Association asked the Clifty church to adopt new articles of faith. Brown, by this time fully in accord with Campbell's views, suggested that the church first rescind the old articles. When this was done he made a motion that the church adopt the New Testament rather than the suggested new articles. Lest the church be accused of being against the New Testament his suggestion was followed, though most of the leaders were not in sympathy with the idea. Brown studied medicine at the Ohio Medical College in Cincinnati, 1826-29. When he returned to begin practice in Rush County he found John P. Thompson of the Little Flat Rock Baptist Church under fire for holding "reforming" views. Brown supported Thompson and consequently was labeled as a "Campbellite." The Clifty Baptist church passed a resolution, "That we will not fellowship the doctrines propagated by Alexander Campbell, of Bethany, Virginia." This resolution disfellowshipped Brown from the congregation, and the church refused to hear his defense. Always proud of this incident, he believed himself to be the first "martyr" to the cause in Indiana. In 1832 he moved to Connersville where he preached and practiced medicine. He was appointed as a state evangelist in 1842. In 1844 he located in Crawfordsville where he practiced medicine, preached, and used his leisure time to study in the Wabash College library. This college awarded him with an honorary A. M. degree in 1850. Governor Wright appointed him state geologist in 1854. In 1858 he accepted the Chair of Natural Sciences at North Western Christian University and in 1871 he received an appointment as chief chemist of the United States. Brown was an aggressive abolitionist and a temperance reformer. In addition to many articles for religious and scientific journals he authored the book, *Elements of Psychology and Hygiene.*

ville and at Indianapolis the next year, but nothing was done about it. A plan was finally adopted at the Connersville State Meeting in 1842 by which the state was divided into four quarters (called districts). An evangelist for each district was elected by ballot. John O'Kane was given the northwest quarter; Benjamin Franklin, the northeast; James M. Mathes, the southwest; and Ryland T. Brown, the southeast. These men were commissioned to visit the churches, obtain statistical information, and help set them in the gospel order.

Brown reported that he plunged into the work and visited every church in the district. Some churches, he wrote, refused to cooperate and others asked for time to consider the matter. Since the evangelists were to receive an annual salary of 500 dollars, and this was to come from the charity of the churches it posed a problem in stewardship; this was a subject that up to this time had not been considered very seriously. One-third of the churches in the southeast district promised a definite sum to be paid quarterly, but collections came in slowly and the State Meeting had no funds to support the work. The other three evangelists faced the same problem and were forced to abandon their districts before the close of the first quarter. Concerning this, Brown made the wry comment, "So ended the first state missionary enterprise."[29]

Marion County Pilot Co-operation Plan

Several proposals leading to better cooperation were made at the Noblesville State Meeting in June of 1843. One of them was that the elders, evangelists and brethren use their influence throughout the state to call the attention of the churches to a more liberal support of the ministry "that they

---

[29]*Christian Standard*, July 14, 1883. Article by Dr. Ryland T. Brown.

who preach the gospel, may live by it."[30] In spite of the failure of the first district plan the brethren were determined to find a way to make cooperation work. They decided to hold the next annual State Meeting at Indianapolis at the end of August rather than in June, 1844, so that Marion County Disciples would have time to set up a model project in county cooperation to serve as an example for the State Meeting to study the next year.

The Marion County brethren accepted this challenge. As a first step they instituted a program by which the brethren could become better acquainted with one another through a series of meetings in various parts of the county. These meetings were not well attended, however, because of failure of adequate communication. It was then decided to hold a mass meeting of Marion County Disciples at Indianapolis the first week in February, 1844. A great number of invitations were sent out at this time, and the attendance was very satisfactory. Ovid Butler[31] proposed a five-point program of cooperation at this meeting. He suggested: (1) that the meeting be regarded as the Marion County congregation of the Disciples of Christ, having no connection with any other congregation, and that meetings of this congregation would be held quarterly, (2) that this congregation select its own elders and deacons, (3) that the "credit system" be dispensed with and the liberality of the brethren be shown by their acts, rather than their promises, (4) that contributions made at

---

[30]*Christian Record*, October, 1844, pp. 91-93. *The Christian Record* began publication in July, 1843. Apparently the notes on the June, 1843 meeting were not available for this number. They were, therefore, published in 1844, following the information on the 1844 State Meeting.

[31]Ovid Butler (1801-1881) was the son of Chauncey Butler, Sr., early minister of the Indianapolis Christian congregation. The Butler family moved from New York to Jennings County, Indiana. Ovid Butler studied law and was admitted to the Bar at Shelbyville in 1825. He came to Indianapolis in 1836 and formed a law partnership with Calvin Fletcher. Butler became a wealthy and influential layman in the Indianapolis church. He was an abolitionist and took steps to form a "free soil" party in 1854. Butler was also instrumental in the organization of North Western Christian University, a school which later took his name (Butler University) because of his interest and benefactions.

the meetings be applied to aid the proclamation of the gospel within the county, and (5) that contributions of other specific articles as well as money be received. Two persons were then selected to preach the gospel within the county for the next three months.[32]

When the sixth annual State Meeting was held at Indianapolis six months later, Love H. Jameson submitted a formal report of the Marion County experiment. There seemed to be no objection to the manner by which the cooperation was structured although it was obviously a stratagem designed to circumvent fears of ecclesiasticism. It is doubtful if Ovid Butler and his friends at Indianapolis thought of the plan as a subterfuge to placate those who thought the cooperation was unscriptural and/or place the authority of the local church in jeopardy; rather they thought of it as a practical method of getting a job done and one that would not violate Scripture or the convictions of their brethren.

Before the sessions came to an end it was recommended that cooperation meetings should be held in each county to support the proclamation of the gospel and that such meetings be held as often as one each quarter.

Though the sixth State Meeting could be called a workshop on cooperation, several other items of concern were considered. John O'Kane and M. B. Hopkins had been doing missionary work at Logansport and the contributions taken at this meeting were given to them in support of this work. C. D. Hurlbutt, an agent for Bethany College, Alexander Campbell's new school at Bethany, Virginia, was present to tell the brethren about the school and to solicit patronage. The meeting adjourned with a resolution to meet at Bloomington in October the next year.[33]

---

[32]*Christian Record,* October, 1844, pp. 92-93.
[33]*Christian Record,* October, 1844, pp. 90-91.

A District Plan that Succeeded

The seventh State Meeting began as scheduled on October 3, 1845 at Bloomington. The subject of cooperation again received primary attention. As the idea of cooperation received implementation in various practical ways it is apparent that the brethren were reading new meanings into the word. They needed something like a denominational organization in order to be effective in propagating the new movement. Since they had protested against such organizations and "freed" themselves from ecclesiastical authority other than that of the local church—believing in good conscience they had acted in accordance with New Testament church polity—they faced problems of authority for concerted actions and the power to carry these actions out. The Bible, they thought, did not sanction any ecclesiastical authority other than that delegated to the local church; a cooperation of the churches did not violate this principle of authority. Because the cooperation, *per se,* did not need biblical authority it could take over the power responsibility and get certain jobs done that could not be done otherwise. Since they regarded the New Testament primarily in a legal sense as a book of rules and laws to be obeyed, working through a cooperation instead of an authoritative ecclesiastical body did not seem inconsistent to them. They had simply applied a legal twist to what they considered a legal document and felt secure in the interpretation.

Funds raised at this meeting amounted to $205.00. This was six times as much as was ever before contributed at such gatherings and represented a considerable amount in terms of salary usually paid to evangelists. John O'Kane suggested that the state be divided into districts north and south of the national pike and that the funds be distributed equally between these two districts. It was further decided to send two evangelists to each district, and this met with general agreement. The southern district selected the area west and southwest of Bedford to south of Vincennes as their field of service the next year, and the northern district chose Fort Wayne as its mission field. John O'Kane and Love H. Jameson were appointed as evangelists for the southern district, and M. B. Hopkins and James M. Mathes were assigned to evangelize in the north. The brethren in the southern district were so pleased with this arrangement that they pledged another $100.00 for work in their field.

The statistical report of Disciples' churches in Indiana was given at this meeting and published later in the *Christian Record*.[34] It indicated a membership of 3,917. A supplemental report from the Rush County cooperation claimed 1,200 additional members and another report from Hendricks County showed 800 members, This made a total of 5,917 members in Indiana in 1845. Since these statistics were actual reports and not estimates, the figures are more realistic and reliable than those worked out at the 1839 State Meeting.[35]

The eighth State Meeting opened at Columbus on October 3, 1846. J. B. New of Greensburg presided over the sessions; Benjamin Franklin[36] and James M. Mathes acted as secretaries. The problem of church polity again received attention.

---

[34]*Christian Record,* November, 1845, pp. 147-149.

[35]Minutes of the Bloomington meeting may be found in the *Christian Record,* November, 1845, pp. 143-146.

[36]Benjamin Franklin (1812-1878) moved from Ohio to Henry County, Indiana, with his parents in 1833. Franklin was of Methodist Protestant background though he professed no religion until converted by Samuel Rogers and Elijah Martindale. He began preaching at New Lisbon, Indiana, in 1842. Franklin started his *Reformer* in 1845 and soon changed its name to *Western Reformer,* publishing from Milton, where he moved in 1846 and printed the journal in his own shop. In 1850 he united the *Western Reformer* with Hall's *Gospel Proclamation* as the *Proclamation and Reformer.* Later, he became a partner of David S. Burnet in publishing the *Christian Age.* Finally, he established the *American Christian Review* which he published for many years. Franklin was helpful in the work of cooperations in Indiana, and gave his influence to the founding of Butler University and various national "societies." He changed his position in the 1850's and became a leader of the anti-societies movement. He was an abolitionist and a pacifist. He took part in over thirty religious debates, six of which were published. He also authored many books and tracts. The last years of his life were spent at Anderson, Indiana.

A committee appointed to prepare items for discussion suggested the following proposition as one suitable for investigation:

A Reformation of Christendom, in respect to *official* organization is imperiously demanded, and such reformation should by all means characterize the *current Reformation.*

There was a constant demand for church statistics on the part of leaders in the central part of the state. Congregations, cooperations, and districts were urged to report membership figures, the names of church officers and ministers, and progress in missionary expansion. Hoosier Disciples needed to prove their status to themselves and others, though they probably did not realize it. Motivated by practical reasons to form some kind of "official" ecclesiatical structure they had difficulty in doing so without violating some of the original principles of the movement. The Columbus State Meeting recommended that local churches set apart elders and deacons by fasting, prayer, and the imposition of hands, and that all evangelists (ministers) be ordained in the same manner. It was also advised that each church set apart one of its bishops to "the exclusive service of said church," and that the brethren support this bishop. They recommended that churches sending out evangelists (missionaries) should assume the support of these workers rather than to expect contributions from the missionary fields being served.[37] The meeting, therefore, was concerned with bringing order and responsibility to the churches, making Disciples aware of their missionary opportunities, and changing their status from that of a religious *movement* to that of a recognized religious body. The State Meeting at Columbus was a turning point

---

[37]Minutes of the Columbus meeting may be found in the *Christian Record,* November, 1846, pp. 150-153.

in the history of Hoosier Disciples.

Missionary Journey in Hoosierland

James M. Mathes had been commissioned at the Blooming-ton State Meeting in the fall of 1845. He set out the following May to do the work of an evangelist in the North. His experiences were reported in two travel letters published in the *Christian Record.*[38] Accounts of the day-by-day events in connection with this journey were written to indicate the progress of the gospel, but inadvertently they also served to describe the economic and social life of newly-opened northern Indiana. The fourth day after he left Bloomington he reached Lafayette "the terminus of the Wabash and Erie canal." He described the country as unsurpassed for agricultural purposes but known for "fever and ague, chills and fever, and bilious fever." There was a small congregation at Lafayette but no meetinghouse. He enjoyed the hospitality of Elder John Longley at this place. M. B. Hopkins joined him at Lafayette, and they held services at Longley's house. They expected to go to Delphi by water but since no boat was available they borrowed a horse and buggy to travel the highway. After preaching at Delphi they embarked on the "Lucy Neal" to Logansport. War excitement was high at this place. When Captain Tipton and his company of volunteers marched into the courthouse to the sound of martial music that night they heard Mathes preach on "Christian Warfare."

The next morning the two missionaries embarked on the "T. H. Benton" for Peru. Peru was described as a small town on the north bank of the Wabash, just north of the Miami Indian Reserve. Mathes wrote that some men in this region

---

[38]*Christian Record*, August, 1846, pp. 51-54; September, 1846, pp. 72-76.

had made a fortune "fleecing" the Indians. From Peru they went by buggy to Wabashtown where they found a congregation of some thirty Disciples. They met Benjamin Franklin, editor of the *Reformer* at this place, and he preached the evening sermon. The next morning they started on a forty-four mile trip to Fort Wayne by boat and were impressed with the great number of Indians that they saw on the way, "some drunk and some sober; and who, from their appearance, were as wild and uncultivated as they were in the days of Anthony Wayne." They reached Huntington by nightfall and learned that there was a small congregation at this place. The next morning at ten o'clock they arrived at the wharf at Fort Wayne.

It was Sunday, June 7, 1846, when John Johnson met the two itinerants at the Fort Wayne dock. Johnson gave them the hospitality of his home while they stayed in the city. The missionaries preached at the courthouse that evening. This was the opening sermon for a protracted meeting that was destined to have unusual competition. During the first ten days two companies of volunteers were raised for service in the Mexican War. Mathes lamented, "during that time our meetings were frequently forgotten, and broken up by war meetings; and even when we were permitted peaceably to meet in the court house . . . we were annoyed by the thunder of the cannon, roll of the drum, or the shouting and huzzaing of boys in the streets." In spite of these disturbing factors the meeting continued to June 22nd, a small congregation having been constituted on the fourteenth.

Mathes and Hopkins embarked June 22nd on a boat for Wabashtown, the journey taking a day and a night. P. P. Russell of Mishawaka, editor of the *Investigator* met them at this place. The next day they returned to Logansport where Hopkins addressed a small group at the courthouse that evening. Newton Herryman, a member of the Frankfort church, drove them to Frankfort in his buggy the next day. Milton B. Hopkins lived at Frankfort, and Mathes stayed over the week-end at the Hopkins' home, preaching at the church on Sunday.[39] Mathes then went on horseback to North Salem where he found a divided church. From there he visited his father's home near Stilesville, and the next day he returned to Bloomington.

The trip, which covered only a few counties in north-central Indiana, lasted thirty-six days. It was made on horseback, by boat and by buggy through an area in which Indians still lived and white men were coming in to settle. It was at the end of the "canal age" and the beginning of the steam railroad era. The missionary journey was one in which the itinerants faced the hazards of travel, epidemics, sectarian opposition, and competition from the Mexican War. In spite of this new congregations were formed, old ones were strengthened, the gospel was proclaimed, and converts were made to the cause.

Frontier Forensics

Debating was a popular form of communication (and entertainment) in Indiana in this period. Subjects under discussion varied from the inconsequential and irrelevant to serious theological controversy. A clergyman who could defend the faith [his convictions] with forensic skill was more likely to be popular in his community than one who was merely a good pastor. Some of these men were actually

---

[39]Milton B. Hopkins (1821-1874) was born in Kentucky and grew up near Rushville, Indiana. As a young man he preached and farmed; then practiced law in Noblesville. Entering the field of education he was in charge of Ladoga Academy for several years and the founder of Howard College at Kokomo. He was elected to the office of Superintendent of Public Instruction in the state of Indiana in 1870 and again in 1872. Robert M. Hopkins (1878-1955), president of the United Christian Missionary Society and leader in the World's Sunday School Association, was his grandson.

known for their ability to "capsize" Baptists, "sink" Methodists or "expose" Universalists and Mormons. If a non-Disciple community became threatened by the growing popularity of a Christian Church preacher it was not uncommon for "Campbellite killer" to be called in to defend the orthodox majority from being taken over by the new faith. These forays resulted mostly in crystallizing convictions already held, each side usually believing itself to be the winner. Most of these debates were minor and local; some were important enough to receive notice in frontier religious journals,[40] a few being published in book form. Some Indiana Disciples attended the large debates of the day[41] and were greatly influenced by them.

Authority of the Printed Word

Although the *Christian Baptist, Christian Messenger* and *Millennial Harbinger,* published outside the state, were probably more widely read by Hoosier Disciples than their own religious journals the Hoosier editors produced their share of periodical literature. These journals served often as the preachers, theologians and religious commentators of the community; the printed page was considered more authoritative than the spoken word. The episcopal system

---

[40]Some of the debates were as follows (Disciples listed first): 1829, Elijah Goodwin and _____ Richey (Methodist); 1832, Elijah Goodwin and Dr. H. Holland (Methodist) at Mt. Vernon; 1834, L. H. Jameson and John Pavy (Baptist); 1835, J. M. Mathes and John Bailes (Methodist) at Martinsburg; 1835, J. M. Mathes and Lorenzo D. Smith (Methodist) near Greencastle; 1836, Jacob Wright and _____ Emmet (Mormon) at Martinsburg; 1836, Jacob Wright and Dr. Suggs (on slavery) at Martinsburg; 1838, F. W. Emmons, and Lucien W. Berry (Methodist—pamphlet controversy); 1839, Jacob Wright and Philip May (Methodist) at Brownstown; 1841, J. M. Mathes and James Scott (Methodist) at Leesville; 1843, Elijah Goodwin and Joel Hume (Baptist); 1843, J. M. Mathes and Erasmus Manford (Universalist) at Greencastle; 1843, Jacob Wright and Erasmus Manford (Universalist) at Columbus; 1844, T. J. Edmundson and Erasmus Manford (Universalist) at Franklin; 1844, Joseph Hostetler and _____ Forbes (Methodist) at Fayetteville; 1844, J. M. Harris and B. F. Foster (Universalist) at Portland Mills; 1845, T. J. Edmundson and Philip May (Methodist); 1846, Jacob Wright and William Terrell (Methodist) at Clarksburg.

[41]Campbell-Owen debate, Cincinnati, 1829; Campbell-Jennings debate, Nashville, 1830; Campbell-Purcell debate, Cincinnati, 1837; Campbell-Rice debate, Lexington, 1843.

was denied, but the editors not only had the status of bishops within their own groups but wielded about as much influence. The *Christian Review* was published at Jeffersonville by Nathaniel Field[42] and Beverly James in the 1830's. During 1840-41, Field edited the *Journal of Christianity* at the same place. This was superseded by the *Israelite* in the early 1840's, with the same editor and published at the same place. John O'Kane was responsible for the *Christian Casket,* a short-lived paper published at Connersville in 1833. Daniel Cox started the *Primitive Christian* at Vincennes around 1845, and after publishing three numbers sold his subscription list to the *Christian Record.* Benjamin Franklin began publication of the *Reformer* at Centerville in 1845, changing the name of the journal to *Western Reformer* when he moved his headquarters to Milton the next year. The *Investigator* was published by P. P. Russell of Mishawaka around the years 1845-47. All of these Indiana periodicals were suspended after a few years because of lack of support.

The publication of the *Christian Record,* beginning July 4, 1843, by James M. Mathes, sometimes assisted by Elijah Goodwin, was a large factor in the solidification of the Indiana brotherhood. A monthly journal, it served in a quasi-official capacity as a means of exchanging views on religious matters and reporting the religious progress of the movement. When Nathaniel Field's *Israelite* suspended publication its patronage list was sent to the *Christian Record* so that unexpired subscriptions could be completed by this journal. This gave Editor Mathes a good subscription list for southern

---

[42]Dr. Nathaniel Field (1805-1888) was inclined toward radical eschatological views which were not accepted by the majority of the brethren though none rejected him for this. He held to "soul sleeping" and joined with William Miller in propagating the millennial expectations of 1843. Joseph Hostetler and Joseph Fassett also accepted Miller's theory. Dr. Field was a strong abolitionist all his life. He served in the state legislature, 1838-39. During the Civil War he was surgeon for the infantry forces. In 1868 he was elected president of the Indiana State Medical Society.

Indiana. An examination of the early issues of the *Record* indicates that in this period Indiana Disciples were strongly opposed to Universalism and Millerism, movements then sweeping the country with exaggerated zeal. Several articles and dialogues emphasized these themes. Other subjects that received attention concerned the nature of the church, Christian union, Christian ethics and various biblical doctrines. The *Christian Record* was published at Bloomington, 1943-51; Indianapolis, 1851-55; and from Bedford, after 1855. Elijah Goodwin published the paper in the years 1847-49 and again in 1859-66. The subscription list was sold to the *Christian Standard* when that publication began at Cleveland, Ohio, in 1866. The circulation of the *Record* varied from 5,000 to 8,000 subscribers but was down to 2,000 when it was finally sold. The *Record* never became more than a regional journal, but it was one of the best. It served for many years as a responsible and reliable medium of communication for the Indiana brotherhood.

Beginnings in Education

Hoosier Disciples, as a church body, had no incentive to establish educational institutions in Indiana prior to the period when a structural organization was being developed. Most of the ministers were self-educated; some had a little formal training but this was primarily of a classical and literary nature. Their interest was not in theological education as such but education for their children under the sheltered environment of Christian culture. An ambitious project that emphasizes this point was the attempt to establish a Christian college at New Albany, one which never advanced beyond the stage of receiving a charter from the legislature in 1833.[43]

---

[43]The incorporators were: John Cook Bennett, B. H. Mills, B. W. N. Fields, F. E. Becton, S. Woodruff, C. Bosworth, M. Cole, W. Scott and J. Bledsol.

Indiana had several academies which were organized and maintained on the initiative of persons who were members of the Christian Church. They were privately owned and operated, but because leadership centered around strong Christian Church personalities the brethren had a tendency to look upon them as their own. The Wayne County Seminary at Centerville was such a school. Samuel K. Hoshour, a prominent Disciple, became head of this institution in 1835. Many of his students, as Governor Oliver P. Morton and the generals Lew Wallace and Ambrose Burnside, had distinguished careers. A. C. Shortridge succeeded him in 1839 when Professor Hoshour assumed the leadership of Cambridge Seminary, ten miles west of Centerville, a position which he held until 1846. Milton B. Hopkins, prominent Disciple preacher, was in charge of Ladoga Academy for a number of years.

An interesting educational experiment was conducted in the Haw Creek church, located in Montgomery County between Ladoga and Roachdale. G. T. Harney, the minister, persuaded his congregation to erect a building which could serve as both an academy and as a house of worship. James Fanning and wife, schoolteachers of Kentucky, opened Haw Creek Academy in 1838 and the project was in operation one year.[44]

The Rush County Evangelizing Association started Farmington Academy in 1845 with George Campbell[45] in charge.

[44]The Haw Creek Church was largely responsible for the organizing of other near-by churches at Greencastle, Bowling Green, Russellville, Mechanicsburg, Thorntown, North Salem, Brownsburg, Parkersburg and New Maysville.

[45]George Campbell (1807-1872) was born and educated in Maine. He went to Ohio as a Congregational minister in 1833. On visiting his uncle in Fayette County, Indiana, he was influenced to Disciples' views by Dr. Ryland T. Brown and joined the Connersville church. Campbell, as evangelist for the Rush County Evangelizing Society in 1845, laid the groundwork for Farmington Academy and became its head that same year. He was a strong supporter of the North Western Christian University project. In 1848 he assisted Walter Scott with his *Protestant Unionist* in Cincinnati. He was one of the editors of the *Christian Age* which superseded the *Unionist* and along with James Challen promoted the calling of the first general missionary convention in Cincinnati in 1849. Later, he returned to Indiana and organized churches in Benton, Warren, Tippecanoe, La Porte and Montgomery counties.

In 1858 another school was started near Fairview in Rush County. It was called Fairview Academy and Allen R. Benton, a graduate of Bethany College, was called as first president.[46] The two schools merged as Fairview Academy, chartered in 1850. The Farmington and Fairview schools were not colleges but institutions on the academy or high school level. They served their communities effectively at a time when Indiana's system of secondary public schools was just getting under way.

The Dilemma of Progress

The passing of geographical frontiers in Indiana was accompanied by the passing of religious frontiers. Hoosier Disciples were saying much the same thing in 1846 as they were fifteen years before, but what they were saying was not reflected in what they were doing. This is seen especially in the development of ecclesiastical organization. They never ceased preaching about the autonomy of the church as described in the New Testament and the necessity for holding to this pattern. They also knew that there was a job to be done which could not be done without organization and structure. Torn between the static faith of legalistic theology and the dynamics of missionary expansion through organization, they sought ways to keep both. Cooperations, the State Meeting, district organizations, religious journals, and schools were eventually supported on the basis that they were not to be regarded as the church authorized by Scripture; just a common-sense means of getting an important job done which the churches could not do by themselves. This seemed to be a practical solution until authority began to shift away from

---

[46]He served for six years and was followed by Daniel Van Boskirk, William A. Thrasher, and Sterling McBride.

the churches to the organizations, and lasting tensions developed. Faced with the alternatives of holding to the autonomy, authority, and independence of the local church and consequent possible extinction of the movement, or of developing a program of extra-ecclesiastical activities and organizations to instill life and growth into the movement, they chose the latter.

IV

Inescapable Institutionalism,

1847-1855*

THE MOST AMBITIOUS PROJECT undertaken by Hoosier Disciples in the first century of their existence as a body of people was the founding of a university. Bacon College, established at Georgetown, Kentucky in 1836, and Alexander Campbell's Bethany College, chartered in 1840, antedate the Indiana project, but North Western Christian University (Butler University) has the distinction of being the first educational institution among the Disciples to originate through the concerted effort of the churches and as a specific project of the State Meeting. Benjamin Franklin, editor of the *Western Reformer,* pointed this out in 1849 when he wrote:

> The brotherhood as a whole or as a body, cannot, up to this day, say *we have a college.* Nor can they as a brotherhood, in any state, say, *we have a college.* As a body, they have never decided one question in relation to an institution of that kind. Nor have the brethren in any state ever acted upon, or decided any question respecting a college.[1]

The idea of a religious body establishing or maintaining an institution such as a university was contrary to the original

---

*Much of the information in this chapter was first published as an article by the author in *Indiana Magazine of History,* September, 1962, pp. 233-263.
[1]*Western Reformer,* March, 1849, p. 178.

theological views of the brethren. They held that there was no Scriptural precedent for the church functioning in this capacity. They could support a college as individuals, send their children to colleges for an education, but the establishing of colleges was not one of the prerogatives of the church; so they thought. Therefore, when the Disciples of Indiana added higher education to the responsibility of the churches they took a long step away from their original position and one in the direction of institutionalism. The desire to have a college of their own was so strong among the brethren that they acted first and later thought out their rationale. This position was not challenged until about forty years later when the anti-instrumental movement (Churches of Christ) began to crystallize; by this time the Disciples in several states were committed to a full program of institutionalism from which they neither could nor dared to retreat.

College Proposals Under Consideration

Some time in the summer of 1847, Elijah Goodwin and James M. Mathes, then co-editors of the *Christian Record,* held a protracted evangelistic meeting at Bedford, in Lawrence County. At the conclusion of their engagement they were approached by two men, Messrs. Malott and Short, of that community with a proposal concerning the establishing of a college under the auspices of the Christian churches. Prior to this time Lawrence County citizens had raised $10,000 in subscriptions to found a church college and preferred it to be under the patronage of the Christian Church. Goodwin and Mathes were impressed with the proposition, and after talking it over they promised to publicize the matter in forthcoming issues of the *Christian Record* and present it at the next State Meeting to be held at Greensburg in October, 1847.[2]

The college question was a major item of business considered at the Greensburg State Meeting. The Lawrence County proposal was repeated with the provision that the school be located at Bedford. Representatives from Rush County made a similar offer with the idea of locating the school at Farmington but had taken no steps to give this proposal financial backing.[3]

The State Meeting, after thorough discussion, finally adopted the resolution:

Resolved—That the Chairman of this meeting appoint a Committee of three, to report to this meeting the names of five brethren, to constitute a Committee, whose duty it shall be to meet in the city of Indianapolis, on the 2nd Monday in December next, for the purpose of receiving reports from the brethren and friends in Rush and Lawrence Counties, and as many other counties as may be disposed to bid for the location; and to determine the question of location; giving that point the preference which reports the largest amount of funds for that object, other things being equal; such as health, etc. The subscriptions in all cases, to be raised exclusively within the limits of the county, asking for the location.[4]

The committee[5] authorized by the State Meeting met at Indianapolis on December 13, 1847, as requested; all members were present except Thomas P. Connelly. Messrs. Short and Malott of Bedford renewed the Lawrence County offer, but no report was received from Rush County. The committee

---

[2]Goodwin and Mathes did not follow through on publicizing this offer in the *Christian Record*, but apparently they did present it at the Greensburg State Meeting. The story of the meeting of Goodwin and Mathes with the two Lawrence County men at Bedford appears in the book, James M. Mathes, *Life of Elijah Goodwin, op. cit.*, pp. 204-205.

[3]*Christian Record*, November, 1847, pp. 157-158. This was a verbal proposition made by George Campbell. Rush County Disciples were predisposed toward church responsibility in education as evidenced in the establishing of Farmington and Fairview academies.

[4]*Christian Record*, November, 1847, p. 158.

[5]The members were: Elijah Goodwin, Milton B. Hopkins, Thomas P. Connelly, Love H. Jameson, and Ovid Butler.

then decided that not enough information concerning the matter had been given to Disciples in Indiana, that it should be brought to the attention of all their brethren in the state and even to Disciples in Illinois and Ohio. The meeting was then adjourned with the agreement to come together again the following May.[6]

A letter from David Staats Burnet of Mt. Healthy, Ohio, to Editor Franklin of the *Western Reformer,* dated January 21, 1848, carried the information that there was a movement in Ohio to establish "Newton College with University privileges" in Hamilton County, Ohio.[7] In the meantime, Love H. Jameson wrote to Franklin, inviting him to attend the next committee meeting in Indianapolis on May 23. His letter showed an awareness of the Ohio project, and it was apparent that he objected to the Ohio plan of enlisting eastern Indiana brethren in support of an Ohio college.[8] In his comments in answer to this letter, Editor Franklin made it plain that he thought it would not be feasible for the brethren in either state to relinquish college plans and that colleges in both states would be desirable. He recommended that Indiana Disciples unite on their own project and that as many as possible be present at the next meeting in Indianapolis when the committee would further consider the matter.[9]

When the committee met, several sites were considered, though the Bedford offer was the only one sustained by subscriptions. Goodwin suggested that inasmuch as "no county

---

[6]*Christian Record,* December, 1847, pp. 187-188.

[7]*Western Reformer,* April, 1848, pp. 360-363. The letter as published in the *Western Reformer* listed seven reasons or "peculiar advantages" of this location. Burnet stated that he had written to Love H. Jameson, who in turn had conferred with Samuel K. Hoshour, Thomas P. Connelly, and Ovid Butler, with the result that these men recommended union of the two enterprises. Burnet added that the Ohio group had applied for a charter. The Ohio college proposal and the conflict between the Disciples of Lawrence and Rush counties points up the beginning of sectional rivalry for the location of the school, a rivalry which plagued the State Meeting for several months.

[8]*Western Reformer,* pp. 364-366.

[9]*Western Reformer,* pp. 366-368.

had made any effort worthy of comparison with the effort
made at Bedford" the committee should decide in favor of
this location. Others reasoned that Bedford was too far south
of the center of the state to be accessible to students from the
north, too close to the state university, and that the brethren
in the north and east were objecting to this location. It was
finally decided to refer the whole matter to the next State
Meeting at Little Flat Rock Church in Rush County.[10]

Controversy Over Location

Three of the nine items of business at the Little Flat Rock
State Meeting pertained to the college question and were
discussed with much feeling. They were:

3. That we hear the report of the committee appointed at the
last State Meeting to locate a college.

5. That we enquire: Is it expedient for the Christian brethren
of Indiana to proceed, at this time, to found a College or Literary
Institution in this State?

6. If so, where shall it be located? and what method shall we
adopt for raising the requisite funds?[11]

In response to item three, Love H. Jameson read the
reports of the college committee as published in the *Christian
Record*;[12] John O'Kane then offered a resolution that these
reports be received and the committee be honorably discharged. Stephen Younger, of the church at Leatherwood,
Lawrence County, immediately raised an objection. It appears

---

[10]*Christian Record*, June, 1848, pp. 376-378.

[11]*Western Reformer*, November, 1848, p. 742. The preachers registered at this
meeting were: John O'Kane, Crawfordsville; L. H. Jameson, Indianapolis; John Boggs,
Mt. Healthy, Ohio; G. Campbell, Fulton, Ohio; T. J. Mellish, Cincinnati, Ohio; John
B. New, Indianapolis; H. St. John Van Dake, Fort Wayne; P. M. Wiles, Fayette
County; Daniel Franklin, Middletown; T. J. Edmundson, Columbus; Benjamin Franklin,
Milton; M. B. Hopkins, Frankfort; A. H. Womack, Shelby County; J. P. Thompson,
Rush County; B. F. Reeve, Rush County; B. K. Smith, Marion County; H. R.
Pritchard, Fairview; Elijah Goodwin, Bloomington; Jacob Daubenspeck, Farmington;
A. R. Benton, Fairview.

[12]*Christian Record*, December, 1847, pp. 187-188; June, 1848, pp. 376-378.

116

that having read the committee reports in the *Christian Record* prior to the State Meeting, the Southern District was ready with a prepared statement which was subsequently read to the convention. It charged the committee with sectional favoritism and having acted in bad faith. A resolution was appended: " '*Resolved,* That it is the opinion of this meeting, that the committee should be severely censured for refusing to locate after undertaking to do so; and we do hereby, before God, and the world, wash our hands from all participation in, or approbation of their acts.' "[13] Fortunately, the report of the special committee was supported by George Campbell, John Bowman New, and others. They contended that the committee had not acted in bad faith and that its members "had a right to pursue that course which they thought best calculated to advance the interests of the Institution. . . ." The censuring resolution from the Southern District was tabled, and the original O'Kane resolution to receive the committee report was adopted.

When the fifth item of business was considered, four resolutions were proposed and accepted. The first of these, offered by George Campbell, stated: *"Resolved,* That it is the duty of the christian brotherhood in Indiana, to proceed to found and endow a college in this State."[14] The other three resolutions, as offered by John O'Kane, were designed to implement the Campbell resolution. They proposed that a circular be sent to all Indiana Christian churches to elicit views on the propriety of establishing a college in the state and the preference for its location, that competent brethren visit each church to lay the circular before the members and ask careful consideration of its contents, and that the State Meeting raise sufficient funds to compensate those employed

---

[13]*Western Reformer,* November, 1848, pp. 742-743.
[14]*Western Reformer,* November, 1848, pp. 743-744.

for this purpose.[15] H. St. John Van Dake was selected as general agent. In response to a call for volunteers to assist Van Dake in visiting the churches, ten men accepted the responsibility.[16]

Benjamin Franklin, editor of the *Western Reformer*, made a rough draft of the proposed circular and it was presented to the special committee for revisions and corrections. The circular, with a few slight additions, was then approved by the State Meeting.[17] The document explained the circumstances of the college proposal in detail, set forth the difficulties of the work of the special committee on location, and expressed a desire to learn the views of all the brethren in the state on the matter. The circular asked two specific questions: (1) Shall we build a college? (2) Where will we build it? It further stated that H. St. John Van Dake or other agents would visit within the year and hold a conference on the proposal and that each church was invited to be represented by a letter and a delegate at the next State Meeting in the Christian meetinghouse (now Central Christian Church) at Indianapolis, October 3-8, 1849.[18]

The Goodwin Survey

Van Dake declined the position as general agent, so Elijah Goodwin, his alternate, took the field at once in a

---

[15]The subscription to compensate the agents amounted to $98.30 and the cash was $22.00. Franklin wrote that the collection was made on Monday when the congregation was comparatively small.

[16]Volunteer assistants were: John Boggs (Jackson and Washington counties); George Campbell (Franklin and Union counties); B. F. Reeve (Rush County); John B. New (Shelby and Johnson counties); T. J. Edmundson (Bartholomew, Brown and Morgan counties); Benjamin Franklin (Fayette, Randolph, Henry and Wayne counties); Milton B. Hopkins (Boone and Clinton counties); Butler K. Smith (Marion and Hamilton counties); and Elijah Goodwin (Monroe County).

[17]*Western Reformer*, November, 1848, pp. 746, 747. The circular was signed by Benjamin F. Reeve, president; Benjamin Irwin, vice-president; Elijah Goodwin, secretary; and T. J. Melish, assistant secretary.

[18]Copies of the text of this circular may be found in the *Christian Record*, January, 1849, p. 218; *Western Reformer*, November, 1848, pp. 749-750. The complete minutes of the Little Flat Rock meeting were printed in the *Western Reformer*, November, 1848, pp. 741-750.

severe winter campaign. It was fortunate that Goodwin was willing to undertake the canvass. He was well known throughout the state; Goodwin had held pastorates, organized new churches and had taken part in several debates, even though he was then but forty-one years old. Regarding this campaign, Goodwin wrote, "I never stopped for rain, wind, snow, ice or storm." He usually sent circulars in advance of his visits and then preached a sermon before taking the vote of the members. He claimed later that he refrained from giving his personal opinion on the college matter until after the vote was taken. Goodwin summarized voting results in the following statement:

Nineteen churches, with an aggregate membership of 1,156, gave no vote; three, with an aggregate membership of 340 vote no college; thirty-six, with an aggregate membership of 2,272, Indianapolis; fifteen, with an aggregate membership of 859, Bedford; five, with an aggregate membership of 714, scattering.

This gave a majority for Indianapolis of 1,413, but the reports of local agents would swell that majority for Indianapolis to over 2,000. The largest portion of these churches were south of the old national road. Of course, none of the churches north of that road would have voted to locate the college at Bedford.[19]

In his report to the Indianapolis State Meeting on October 4, 1849, Goodwin stated that he had spent four and one-half months on the field, had visited forty counties, and had found a majority of the brethren in favor of building a college at Indianapolis. Six volunteer agents also gave reports which bore "about the same tenor as the statements made by Bro. Goodwin except as to its (the college's) location in relation to which there was some difference of opinion and wishes."[20]

---

[19]James M. Mathes, *Life of Elijah Goodwin, op. cit.,* p. 210.
[20]*Western Reformer,* December, 1849, p. 744; *Christian Record,* April, 1850, p. 260.

A committee was appointed by the State Meeting to study the reports of Goodwin and the other agents and recommend a plan of action.[21] This committee concluded that from the data before them the brethren in Indiana could not found and endow a university or college by themselves. They supported this report with two resolutions:

1st. *Resolved,* that this Annual meeting recommend to the Brethren the founding of a North Western University and that our churches North of the Ohio and Kentucky rivers and west of the Allegheny Mountains be requested to take the matter into consideration.

2nd. *Resolved,* that this Annual meeting appoint a committee to correspond with the Brethren and churches north of the Ohio and Kentucky rivers and West of the Allegheny Mountains on the subject of the foregoing resolutions.[22]

Ovid Butler objected to the "rivers and mountains" boundary clauses, preferring "North Western Territory," and other amendments were proposed at the session the next day. As no agreement could be reached, all resolutions and amendments were tabled until the following Saturday when John M. Bramwell moved the adoption of the following:

Resolved, That a North Western Christian University be founded at Indianapolis as soon as a sufficient amount of funds can be raised to commence it, and that a Committee of seven be appointed by this meeting to take the preliminary steps in reference to the founding and endowment of such an institution.[23]

John O'Kane offered a resolution to strike out the two original resolutions of the committee, which apparently had been considered as a preamble to the Bramwell resolution,

---

[21]Committee members were George Campbell, J. B. New, Benjamin Irwin, David Staats Burnet, and John O'Kane.

[22]*Western Reformer,* December, 1849, p. 745.

[23]*Western Reformer,* December, 1849, pp. 747-748; *Christian Record,* December, 1849, p. 186. The quotation is from the *Christian Record.*

and to adopt the Bramwell substitute. Ovid Butler, to fore-
stall future criticism, asked the Marion County brethren to
abstain from voting. They agreed; even without their support
the balloting resulted in the unanimous adoption of the
Bramwell resolution.[24] This action marked the first real
breakthrough on the college matter. It meant the end of
argument and delay over the selection of a location, the
choice of a name for the institution, a clear decision to go
ahead with the project, authority from the State Meeting for
implementing this decision, and the emergence of Ovid
Butler as one of the primary leaders of the project. A nominating committee was then appointed to select the college
committee contemplated in the Bramwell resolution. This
committee acted at once and their nominees were given
official approval.[25]

A Charter for the University

Ovid Butler, chairman of the new committee, was a prominent Indianapolis attorney and Disciple layman. A man of
acknowledged legal ability, financial means, and of influence
in the proper places, he was a desirable person to put the will
of the State Meeting into action. Because of failing health,
he had retired from the active practice of law at the age of
forty-six. According to M. C. Tiers,[26] when Butler escaped
death from a serious illness in 1847, he had the conviction
that God spared his life that it might be fulfilled in some
special service. It is possible that he considered North Western
Christian University to be his new mission in life. As chairman

---

[24]*Western Reformer,* December, 1849, p. 748.

[25]*Western Reformer,* December, 1849, p. 749. J. B. New, John O'Kane, and L. H.
Jameson made up the nominating committee. They chose Ovid Butler (chairman),
B. F. Reeve, J. B. New, Elijah Goodwin, A. E. Drapier, L. H. Jameson, and John
O'Kane for the college committee.

[26]M. C. Tiers, *The Christian Portrait Gallery* (Cincinnati: M. C. Tiers, Publisher,
1864), pp. 123-124.

121

of the college committee, Butler drafted what was considered to be a liberal charter. In a letter to J. M. Mathes a year later,[27] Butler indicated that he was thinking of an institution much more extensive than a mere church college or one which would be limited to the Disciples' constituency in Indiana. He envisioned a great university in the Northwest, one which eventually would compare favorably with the large universities in the East.

In describing the charter,[28] Ovid Butler declared that it proposed the founding and endowing of a university through the instrumentality of a joint-stock company with a capital of not less than $75,000 nor more than $500,000, divided in equal shares of $100 each. One-third of the capital stock, he wrote, would be expended on buildings, grounds and equipment; the remainder would be kept as a permanent fund for endowment. He explained that the subscriber could retain two-thirds of his subscription as a loan and be entitled to interest on the whole subscription in the form of tuition.

Subscribers were to have control of the institution through directors to be chosen by them triennially.[29]

Section three of the charter is a clear indication of what the committee had in mind for the new school:

Sec. 3. That the objects and purposes contemplated by this act of incorporation are hereby declared to be to establish, found, build up, maintain, sustain, and perpetuate, through the instrumentality of said company, at or in the vicinity of the city of Indianapolis, in the State of Indiana, an institution of learning of the highest class for the education of the youth of all parts of the United States, and especially of the States of the Northwest; to establish in said institution departments or colleges for the instruct-

---

[27]*Christian Record,* March, 1850, pp. 262-263.

[28]The charter was adopted by the State Legislature on January 15, 1850. Indiana, *Local Laws* (1849-1850), pp. 524-528. It is also printed in entirety in the *Christian Record,* September, 1850, pp. 73-76.

[29]*Christian Record,* March, 1850, p. 262.

ing of the students in every branch of liberal and professional education; to educate and prepare suitable teachers for the common schools of the country; to teach and inculcate the Christian faith and Christian morality as taught in the sacred Scriptures, discarding as uninspired and without authority all writings, formulas, creeds, and articles of faith subsequent thereto, and for the formation [promotion] of the sciences and arts.[30]

The charter named a board of commissioners[31] to be responsible for selling subscriptions for capital stock and managing the corporation until the election of a board of directors could be made under the charter. After 750 shares of stock had been subscribed, the commissioners were authorized to "appoint a time and place for holding the first election of directors." Twenty-one directors were to be elected by the stockholders every third year to serve three-year terms; the directors were authorized to choose a president of the board from among their own members, as well as a secretary, treasurer, and other officers from either their members or the stockholders.[32]

Board of Commissioners

The new board of commissioners held an organizational meeting in Indianapolis March 5, 1850. Ovid Butler was elected president; J. B. New, vice-president; and John M.

---

[30]Indiana, *Local Laws* (1849-1850), p. 525. (The word "promotion" appears in brackets in the *Local Laws*.) Emphasis on the Scriptures in the charter, coupled with a strong aversion towards creeds and confessions of faith was characteristic of the Disciples' movement. It was believed that these principles would guarantee that the institution would always be non-sectarian in nature.

[31]Commissioners named in the charter were: F. D. Wheeler, John K. Mentel, J. M. Mathes, Thomas Connelly, Benjamin Irwin, Elijah Goodwin, J. B. Craft, John O'Kane, B. F. Reeve, S. K. Hoshour, George Campbell, Jeremiah Smith, John Brownless, Ambrose D. Hamrick, Higgins Lane, James Ford, A. E. Drapier, Milton B. Hopkins, J. B. New, R. S. Browne, Michael Combs, O. Butler, L. H. Jameson, J. M. Bramwell, A. Houghton, Jacob Wright, T. J. Edmundson, E. F. Peabody, P. T. Russell, Paris C. Dunning, G. W. New, G. W. Smith, Corbly Martin, B. F. Flinn, M. Cole, D. C. Stewart, Stephen Younger, Thomas Lockart, John Longly, A. B. Cole, Alfred Davis, M. R. Trimbell, and Thomas M. Adams. Indiana, *Local Laws* (1849-1850), p. 524.

[32]*Ibid.*, pp. 525-526.

Bramwell, secretary. An executive committee, consisting of the president, vice-president, secretary, and two other commissioners, Elijah Goodwin and Albert B. Cole was appointed. The executive committee was given authority to select and employ agents to sell stock subscriptions. It chose Michael Combs to work in Iowa and Thomas P. Connelly to work in Ohio. The remaining commissioners were charged with the responsibility of procuring subscriptions for stock in Indiana communities. The hope was expressed that by the following May, when the commissioners were to meet again in Indianapolis, enough stock would have been purchased to authorize the election of a board of directors.[33]

The commissioners held their second meeting in Indianapolis on May 29, 1850. They were called upon, one by one, to report their success in selling stock. To the embarrassment of many who were present, Ovid Butler was the only commissioner who had actually sold any subscriptions. In spite of this, the group felt that the future for the university was encouraging.[34]

State Missionary Society Proposed

When Elijah Goodwin was surveying Indiana churches to ascertain views on the college question, many problems came to his attention. He discovered that a number of churches were in a weakened condition because they had no pastoral leadership. He also found that several of the brethren, capable of serving pastorates, could not afford to follow anything but secular pursuits. "In all southern Indiana," he wrote, "I do not remember of finding a single preacher who was giving his whole time to the work of the Gospel ministry." As a partial answer to this problem, he

---

[33]*Christian Record*, April, 1850, pp. 264-265.
[34]*Christian Record*, July, 1850, pp. 8-9.

worked out a plan for a state evangelizing society. This plan, together with a proposed constitution, was published in the *Christian Record*.[35]

The constitution called for an "Indiana Christian Evangelizing Society" to sustain the proclamation of the Gospel in all the destitute parts of Indiana. The society was to have officers and a board of directors; membership was based on annual dues of one dollar. Provision was made also for auxiliary societies.

Editor Mathes commented on the Goodwin plan, pointing out that there was no positive direct authority in the New Testament for such an organization and that the church itself was an evangelical society with every member obligated to engage in work according to his ability. He wrote that with a membership of some fifty thousand persons in Indiana, "and possessing, as our brethren do, a very fair proportion of the wealth," the Disciples should be fully able to sustain the Gospel in "every town, village, and neighborhood in the state." In spite of this, he wrote, "the churches sleep on!" It was his opinion, therefore, that under existing circumstances Goodwin's plan could do very well because it provided that every Disciple could go to work as an individual member of the body of Christ, uniting with others to "accomplish what they could not as individuals merely, or as churches, as now organized."[36]

The matter came up again when the State Meeting convened in Indianapolis in 1849. A committee was appointed to formulate a constitution for a State Evangelizing Society and report at the evening session on October 6th. The committee presented a constitution containing eight articles, in

---

[35]*Christian Record,* January, 1849, pp. 193-194. The letter and the proposed constitution also appears in, J. M. Mathes, *Life of Elijah Goodwin, op. cit.,* pp. 212-216.

[36]*Christian Record,* January, 1849, pp. 194-196.

principle much the same as the original Goodwin proposal. Instead of an evangelizing society, it was to be called a "Home Missionary" society to be supported by individuals rather than by churches. Some forty-five persons became members, presumedly by paying either one dollar annual dues, twenty-five dollars for a life membership, or fifty dollars to be a life elector. Annual meetings of the Society were scheduled for May so as not to conflict with the State Meeting which was usually held in October.[37]

Indiana Disciples at the First National Convention

The Indiana State Meeting of 1849 appointed seven official delegates to represent it at the first General Convention of the Christian Churches which convened at Cincinnati on October 23, 1849. Indiana was the only state represented with an official state-level delegation. In addition to the seven delegates, seventeen other Hoosier Disciples were present and were enrolled as delegates. The Indiana delegation was exceeded in numbers only by those from Ohio and Kentucky.[38]

John M. Bramwell of Indiana was appointed as temporary secretary of the general convention when it was being organized, and Elijah Goodwin was placed on a committee to define the order of business. John O'Kane was very prominent at the Cincinnati convention. It was O'Kane who read the

---

[37]*Western Reformer*, 1849, pp. 742-743, 746-747. The constitution and minutes of this meeting were not included in the annual report of the State Meeting. C. W. Cauble's book, *Disciples of Christ in Indiana, op. cit.*, pp. 101-103, states that the original record of this meeting, with the constitution as printed on page 102 of the Cauble book was discovered in an attic in Indianapolis.

[38]Appointed delegates as recorded in the *Western Reformer*, December, 1849, p. 750, were: John O'Kane, George Campbell, Elijah Goodwin, S. W. Leonard, Love H. Jameson, John B. New and James M. Mathes. Other delegates from Indiana, according to the *Report of the Proceedings of the General Convention of the Christian Churches of the United States of America* (Cincinnati: American Christian Depository, 1849), pp. 7-10, were: Milton B. Hopkins, Joseph M. Tilford, William C. Bramwell, Dr. D. G. Stewart, B. B. Stewart, Nathaniel Price, John M. Bramwell, William Begg, Samuel K. Hoshour, Peter M. Wiles, H. St. John Van Dake, Dr. Ephraim Clifford, Jacob Immel, Benjamin Franklin, G. W. Branham, V. Scott, and John Tait, Sr.

fraternal epistle from the Indiana State Meeting, the only
such communication submitted. The Indiana letter, dated
October 8, 1849, signed by Benjamin F. Reeve, presiding
officer, affirmed that the last State Meeting had been the most
interesting ever held in Indiana; explained the formation of
the Home Missionary Society, the organization of a State
Bible Society auxiliary, and indicated approval of the Cincinnati Christian Tract Society and the Sunday School
Library project.

Considering that Indiana had a State Meeting organized
since 1839, and had given public endorsement to the Bible
and Tract societies in Ohio, there is no question but that the
Indiana brethren had plunged more deeply into institutionalism than their Disciple brethren elsewhere. The institutional
momentum gained in Indiana is clearly reflected in an
Indiana State Meeting recommendation that the General
Convention consider the organization of its own missionary
society:

for the purpose of sending the gospel in the hands of a living ministry, to all the destitute, uncultivated portions of the Lord's great
field—which he declares "is the world." It is our hope—entertained
with the strongest desires of being realized—that this subject may
receive a due amount of attention, during the sessions of your
meeting; and that such a society will be formed, ere you adjourn.[39]

It is no surprise then that the delegates from Indiana took
an active part in writing the constitution of the American
Christian Missionary Society formed at the Cincinnati
General Convention, and in the article-by-article discussion
which preceded its adoption. When opportunity was given
for delegates to become life members of the new Society (at
a cost of $20 each), Indiana was represented by George

---

[39]*Report of the Proceedings of the General Convention, op. cit.,* p. 13; *Christian
Record,* December, 1849, p. 164.

Campbell of Fairview, Dr. D. C. Stewart and B. B. Stewart of New Albany, John O'Kane of Connersville, Elijah Goodwin of Madison, and John M. Bramwell of Indianapolis. S. W. Leonard of Jeffersonville, by a gift of $100, became a life director. The Indiana delegation pooled resources and raised $100 to make S. K. Hoshour of Cambridge City a life director; three friends of Love H. Jameson of Indianapolis did the same for him. When officers of the missionary society were elected, John O'Kane became one of the vice-presidents and Elijah Goodwin, one of the foreign managers.[40]

Alexander Campbell in Indiana

In the late fall of 1850, Alexander Campbell made his first extensive tour among the Christian Churches in Indiana.[41] This tour was a triumph for Campbell and the Disciples in many ways, but almost a disaster for North Western Christian University, as may be seen later. Arriving at Madison on November 6th via river boat, he gave an address at the Methodist Chapel in the evening, and left the next morning for Indianapolis on the railroad. There was a stopover at Columbus which included speeches that evening and the next morning. Before proceeding to the State Capital, the train was derailed at Columbus, due to the neglect of a switchman, but no one was hurt. The delay made Campbell late for his first speaking engagement at the City Hall that evening but the audience waited for him. This address must have made a good impression on Indianapolis citizens because attendance the next night, when he spoke at the same place, was greatly increased. On the following morning, which was Sunday, he spoke to a huge congregation made

---

[40]*Report of the Proceedings of the General Convention, op. cit.*, pp. 26-30.
[41]Campbell's tour of Indiana is reported in detail in the *Millennial Harbinger*, 1851, pp. 13-22, 76-82.

up not only of his Disciple brethren but of many delegates attending an Indiana Constitutional Convention (to rewrite the State Constitution), including even the Governor of the Hoosier State.

The next day Campbell received an invitation from the convention as follows:

Indianapolis, November 9, 1850

"Messrs. Badger and Wolfe: The following is a copy of a resolution adopted by the Constitutional Convention, on this day: 'Resolved, That Messrs. Badger and Wolfe be appointed a committee to wait upon Alexander Campbell, and request him to visit the Hall and open the Convention by prayer, on Monday morning next.'

Very respectfully,

WM. H. ENGLISH, Prin. Sec'y.
P. G. L. SITES, Assistant."

The invitation was accepted and Campbell opened the session by prayer as requested.[42] Robert Dale Owen, one of the delegates, son of Robert Owen with whom Campbell had debated in Cincinnati in 1829, greeted Campbell at the close of the business session. Campbell was delighted to meet him and inquired concerning the health of his father. The elder Owen was an antagonist whom he respected even though he was not in agreement with his philosophical, theological and political views.

Accompanied by Love H. Jameson, at whose home he had been staying, and John O'Kane, Campbell set out next day for Martinsville. There was a large audience awaiting him at the meetinghouse that night, including a number of mothers

---

[42]C. W. Cauble, *op cit.,* p. 129, records Campbell's prayer on pp. 132-133. Cauble also adds the comment that at the conclusion of the prayer one of the delegates arose, got the attention of the Chair and said, "Mr. Chairman and gentlemen of the Convention, I think it very appropriate to have a Badger and a Wolfe (Oliver P. Badger and Benjamin Wolfe) lead a Campbell (Alexander Campbell) into this hall to pray for 'Jackasses.' "

with babies. Campbell tried to preach but the crying and wailing of the infants in the congregation were too much for him, and he had to stop. John O'Kane, who had a strong voice, managed to lure the children into silence by his speaking. Campbell tried again, but with the same results as before. Not being able to meet this unexpected competition, and the exits being too crowded to allow mothers and babies to depart, Campbell was forced to dismiss the congregation and retire in defeat.

The next day the party journeyed to Bloomington where they were entertained at the home of James M. Mathes, editor of the *Christian Record*. On visiting the State University where O'Kane was scheduled to speak, Campbell renewed his acquaintance with his old friend President Andrew Wylie. Some thirty years before, when Wylie was president of Washington College, the two had engaged in a newspaper controversy over the compulsory observance of the Sabbath. The Presbyterians in western Pennsylvania had formed what they called "Moral Associations" to enforce by laws and fines the keeping of a strict Sabbath. Campbell took a liberal position and attacked the moral societies through satirical articles in the columns of the Washington (Pennsylvania) *Reporter,* writing under the pseudonym of Candidus. Dr. Wylie, writing under the pseudonym of Timothy, challenged Campbell's arguments and supported the "blue law" system. The *Reporter* essays attracted a great deal of attention and eventually public opinion was turned against the moral societies. Strengthened by Campbell's arguments, a citizen brought suit against the authorities for unlawful arrest on the Sabbath-breaking charge and won his case. This ended blue laws enforcement in the vicinity.[43]

---

[43]Robert Richardson, *Memoirs of Alexander Campbell* (Philadelphia: J. B. Lippincott & Co., 1868), Vol. I, pp. 526-530.

The next day the party moved on to Springvale where Campbell delivered a discourse and was entertained that night at the home of Milton Short. From Springvale they went to Bedford for a speaking engagement, and then returned to Bloomington where Campbell spoke at the university hall on both Saturday and Sunday. The following Monday, Campbell, with Jameson and O'Kane, drove back to Indianapolis.

Apparently Campbell, when in Indianapolis, enjoyed the hospitality of Governor Wright as well as that of his Disciple brethren. He was impressed with future possibilities of the city and by the moral tone of its citizens. He wrote especially of a pleasant evening spent at Ovid Butler's home on November 19th with a large number of his brethren. On November 20th he left by railroad for Rushville, via Edinburg, speaking that evening in Rushville. The next day he traveled to Fairview where he preached a sermon and visited Fairview Academy which was operated by George Campbell and A. R. Benton. He also first met Samuel K. Hoshour at this time. Next, he went to Connersville where he delivered a sermon in the meetinghouse. The following day he spoke at Fayetteville. During his visit there he was entertained at the home of Ephraim Frazee. Campbell returned to Rushville for the Sunday services which were held in the Methodist meetinghouse in the morning and in the courthouse in the evening. He spoke at a quarterly meeting of the Methodists in Metamora the next day. Campbell's last speaking engagement on his Indiana tour was at the Methodist Chapel in Brookville. He wrote of the Indiana tour as being exceedingly agreeable, saying:

> Our Indiana brethren have much in their power. They are second only to the Methodists in number, wealth, and influence. . . .

131

They are intelligent, liberal, hospitable, and remunerate their effective ministry with commendable zeal and liberality. They would not allow me to be at any expense, from the day that I put my foot upon the soil till the day I left it.[44]

John O'Kane, Field Agent Extraordinary

John O'Kane, who played such an important role at the General Convention in Cincinnati in the fall of 1849, was appointed by the commissioners of North Western Christian University the following May as their special agent to sell stock subscription for the proposed new school. He was forty-eight years of age, a six-foot-one-inch Irishman, straight and slender, with a reputation for wit, popular with the Indiana brethren as a person and as a preacher. He had tried his hand at many things, including the editing of a religious journal called the *Christian Casket* (Connersville, 1833), which survived for a year only. At the time of his appointment he was operating a bookstore in Indianapolis. He could not accept the new position, however, until he first sold his store. Ovid Butler and J. M. Mathes were so anxious for him to take the fieldwork position that they formed a partnership and bought him out for $1,500. He began his work on January 16, 1851. The commissioners looked forward to the sale of stock to the amount of $75,000, after which a board of directors could be organized, a site purchased, and suitable buildings erected.

The new agent made a whirlwind start, selling some $4,000 worth of stock subscriptions the first month. He wrote to Mathes, commenting: "My success thus far is beyond my most sanguine expectation." In this same letter he claimed also to have done something for the endowment of the chair

---

[44]*Millennial Harbinger,* 1851, pp. 81-82.

of ancient languages in Bethany College.[45] After being on the field six months, O'Kane accounted for the sale of stock to the amount of $25,000. Since he had visited but one-tenth of the Christian churches in Indiana and had already received one-third of the necessary $75,000 in subscriptions, the brethren began to feel confident that the remainder would be raised within a year.[46]

James M. Mathes, therefore, in an editorial in the *Christian Record*,[47] wrote in an optimistic vein concerning the future of North Western Christian University. He explained that O'Kane, with the aid of several brethren, had been able to get subscriptions amounting to $43,000 by December, 1851. The editorial also pressed strongly for support of the school project. Mathes argued that education in Indiana was fast assuming a denominational character. He mentioned Hanover College of the Old School Presbyterians, and Wabash College of the New School Presbyterians, as well as Franklin College, which was supported by the Baptist denomination, as examples. Other denominational schools cited in the same connection were Asbury College (Methodist) and St. Gabriel's and St. Mary's colleges (Roman Catholic). The article also explained the situation at the state university in Bloomington, declaring that this school had ample endowment and a superior faculty yet there were seldom over one hundred students in actual attendance at any one time. Mathes assumed from this data that the trend of higher education in Indiana was primarily denominational in

---

[45]*Christian Record*, March, 1851, p. 280. There apparently was some sort of an understanding between the commissioners and Alexander Campbell for O'Kane to raise funds to endow a chair of ancient languages simultaneously with the university project. The dual nature of O'Kane's commission later became a source of contention between Campbell and the commissioners.

[46]*Christian Record*, July, 1851, pp. 4-5.

[47]*Christian Record*, December, 1851, pp. 173-175.

character, and he seemed to be a little sorry for the plight of the state university, declaring that "the State University is left to take care of itself as best it can."

Writing from his Forest Home residence in Indianapolis on May 28, 1852, Ovid Butler announced that the establishment of North Western Christian University was no longer problematical, that the goal of $75,000 in stock subscriptions had nearly been reached, and that the commissioners were expected to meet in a few days to examine the stock subscriptions and order an election of directors.[48] Success apparently came sooner than was expected and it was necessary for Mathes to publish an extra edition of the *Christian Record* to carry the story. The proceedings of the commissioners, as reported in the extra, show that they met in the Christian Chapel at Indianapolis on June 22, 1852 under the chairmanship of Ovid Butler and the first order of business after establishing the validity of the meeting was to hear John O'Kane read his official report. O'Kane spoke of his eighteen months of labor on the field and of some three hundred discourses made to the churches. As evidence of his work he submitted papers to show $75,200 subscribed in stock.[49]

Board of Directors Elected

O'Kane's report was studied and then accepted. Jeremiah Smith made the motion to implement it with action:

Resolved, That the sum of seventy-five thousand dollars having been, to the satisfaction of a majority of the Commissioners of the North Western Christian University, subscribed as stock in said University, it is ordered by the Board that Wednesday, the 14th day of July next, at two P.M., be appointed as the time, and the

---

[48]*Christian Record*, June, 1852, p. 370.
[49]*Christian Record*, June, 1852 (extra), pp. 1-2.

Christian Chapel in Indianapolis, as the place for holding the first election of Directors, as required by the Charter, and that the President of this board preside at said election, and that he call to his assistance any two or four of the Commissioners or stockholders, to act as judges and clerks of the election, and that notice thereof be given in the Christian Record and such other ways as the President may deem proper and expedient.[50]

The above resolution, one concerning John O'Kane's salary, another dealing with the handing over of all papers pertaining to the project to the board of directors when organized, and a final one concerning the closing of the work of the commissioners, were passed.[51] The meeting marked another milestone passed for the university project.

The stockholders met, as directed in the resolution, on July 14, 1852, and twenty-one directors were elected for three-year terms.[52] The new Board of Directors had its first official meeting in the Christian Chapel in Indianapolis on July 27th. Ovid Butler was chosen president of the board; James Sulgrove, treasurer; and John M. Bramwell, secretary. This was a four-day meeting in which the directors worked on rules and by-laws, examined the financial potential of the proposed university, and appointed John O'Kane as collecting agent to try to persuade stockholders of the necessity of immediate one-third payment of their stock subscriptions.[53]

---

[50]*Christian Record*, June, 1852 (extra) p. 2.

[51]*Christian Record*, June, 1852 (extra) pp. 2-3.

[52]Minutes of the Board of Directors of the North Western Christian University, Book 1, July 27, 1852-September 30, 1863, pp. 2-3. (These minutes are hereafter cited as N.W.C.U. Minutes). The directors named were: George Campbell, Benjamin F. Reeve, Jeremiah Smith, Benjamin Irwin, Elijah Goodwin, Oliver P. Badger, Hiram St. John Van Dake, Daniel C. Stover, James Ford, Parmeter M. Parks, William H. Craig, Chauncy Butler, Perry M. Blankenship, James H. Marsteller, Ovid Butler, James M. Mathes, Love H. Jameson, Allen May, James Sulgrove, David G. Stewart, and Ephraim S. Frazee. These names were also reported in the *Christian Record*, July, 1852, p. 28.

[53]*Christian Record*, August, 1852, pp. 55-56; N.W.C.U. Minutes, Book 1, July 27-31, 1852, pp. 1-16.

Determined to Build

The directors met again on August 31, 1852, at the Christian Chapel in Indianapolis. They were concerned primarily with procedural problems, rules, and bylaws. In a couple of days they got around to considering building sites. After checking on several possible locations they voted to purchase a twenty-acre tract from Ovid Butler. It was a wooded area just north of the city limits of Indianapolis in the vicinity of the present Thirteenth and College streets. The brethren thought this location advantageous because the buildings, when erected, would be seen by passengers as they passed through the city on two different railway lines. Some board members thought the site was too far from the city, but the majority, being farmers, preferred a location in the open country. It was thought by a few of the directors that in view of the fact that Indianapolis was expanding, the university grounds might some day be within the corporation limits of Indianapolis.[54]

Ephraim S. Frazee offered a motion that the president authorize a premium of $50 for the best plans and specifications for a building, that the premium be offered on a competitive basis, and that it be open to all interested architects.[55] The motion was approved and Ovid Butler acted at once and placed advertisements in several midwestern newspapers, including the *Daily Journal* and *Daily State Sentinel* of Indianapolis.

Response to the advertisement launched William Tinsley on a long and successful career as a college architect, He had recently come to America from Ireland and was desperate

---

[54]*Christian Record*, November, 1852, pp. 151-152; N.W.C.U. Minutes, Book 1, August 31-September 2, 1852, pp. 20-35.

[55]N.W.C.U. Minutes, Book 1, August 31-September 2, 1852, p. 35. Butler raised the prize money to $100 in his advertisements. Frazee was the grandfather of the American poet, Vachel Lindsay, who wrote about Frazee in his poem, "The Proud Farmer."

for an opportunity to show what he could do. On reading Ovid Butler's advertisement in a Cincinnati newspaper he prepared alternate sets of plans immediately, one of which won the coveted $100 prize. He was then commissioned to proceed with the making of working drawings and supervision of construction.[56]

North Western Christian University's building was the first edifice designed by Tinsley in America, and it marked this architect's Collegiate Gothic style. Soon after designing the building, he was employed to make the drawings for Center Hall at Wabash College, and he supervised the construction of this building simultaneously with that of North Western Christian University.[57]

Preparatory School

The brethren could not wait for the erection of a building before actually starting the educational program. The first Monday in May, 1853, they opened a preparatory school in classrooms rented from St. Mary's Church (called St. Mary's Seminary by the Minutes of the Board of Directors of N.W.C.U.) near the center of the city of Indianapolis, north of the Circle. R. K. Krout, A.M., of Crawfordsville, was engaged as instructor.[58] Professor Krout resigned after a few weeks, and the school was temporarily suspended while the

---

[56]J. D. Forbes, *Victorian Architect: The Life and Work of William Tinsley* (Bloomington: Indiana University Press, 1953), pp. 65-66, 134.

[57]Forbes' volume, *Victorian Architect*, contains many photographic reproductions of buildings designed by William Tinsley. See also William N. Pickerill, "William Tinsley, Architect," *Butler Alumnal Quarterly*, Vol. 3 (October, 1914), pp. 116-120. Tinsley was also responsible for planning a building for Oskaloosa College (which later moved to Des Moines and became Drake University), the academic building at Indiana University, Bascom Hall at the University of Wisconsin, Ascension Hall at Kenyon College, and a building at Quincy College, Quincy, Illinois. His long career also included the designing of many public buildings, homes and churches. Christ Church (Episcopal) on Monument Circle, Indianapolis, still stands as a witness to this Victorian architect's ability.

[58]*Christian Record*, May, 1853, p. 348; N.W.C.U. Minutes, Book 1, May 24, 1853, pp. 65-66.

directors looked for a new teacher.[59] By November, 1853, Lyman P. Streator had been secured for the position, and forty boys were reported as being in attendance. James M. Mathes wrote concerning the school, "Students will have an opportunity of taking a thorough course, preparatory to entering the college proper when it opens, which we hope will be by next fall."[60] By the close of the second quarter some sixty-four students had been enrolled. Closing exercises held in Christian Chapel consisted of dialogues, declamations, and original compositions. The directors were pleased to report that three of these students "put on Christ in the institution of Christian baptism" and that they considered these three young men as the first fruits of North Western Christian University. They were also pleased that the experiment was a financial success; the school had sustained itself on tuitions. Then, just as the third quarter was beginning, Principal Streator's wife died, and he felt compelled to return to Pennsylvania with his children.[61] The Minutes of the Board of Directors of N.W.C.U. for May 25, 1854, show that the directors had confidence in him, for they had elected him to the permanent faculty of the new school. After Streator left, the directors decided to suspend the preparatory school until the university buildings were sufficiently advanced to receive the classes.

Altercation with Alexander Campbell

The resignation of Professor Streator and the closing of the preparatory school together with the difficulty of obtaining one-third payments from the stockholders to provide

---

[59]*Christian Record,* September, 1853, p. 94.
[60]*Christian Record,* December, 1853, p. 190.
[61]*Ibid.,* June, 1854, pp. 188-189. Streator, a Bethany College man, subsequently became president of Mayslick Academy, Mayslick, Kentucky, and later evangelist for the Pennsylvania Christian Missionary Society. The altercation between Campbell and N.W.C.U., hereafter described, may have been a strong contributing factor in his decision not to continue his post. For information on Streator, see the *Christian Standard* (Cincinnati), July 15, 1916, p. 1421.

cash for paying the various building contractors gave the directors much concern in the early months of 1854. These problems were of small import, however, compared with those raised by an antagonistic article in the January, 1854 issue of the *Millennial Harbinger*. Alexander Campbell, co-editor of the *Harbinger* and president of Bethany College at Bethany, Virginia (now West Virginia), was the acknowledged leader of the Disciples' movement. This was a time when the North Western Christian University project needed his tacit approval, if not his blessing, and antagonism from him might well prove disastrous.

The meeting of the directors on May 24th was the first session of the board since Campbell's article had appeared. Prior to this meeting, there had been correspondence between Ovid Butler and John O'Kane which Butler wished to share with his brethren. He first called attention to Campbell's article, "Notes of a Tour to Illinois," in which O'Kane was charged with using the slavery issue to bolster the cause of North Western Christian University and downgrade Bethany College.[62] Campbell had written:

I was, indeed, sorry to learn from several places in the State [Illinois] that he [O'Kane] made a new issue, one heretofore unknown amongst us as a Christian people. It was, in brief, that "Christians living on *free* soil, should not co-operate ["co-operate" had the connotation of "fellowship" with the Christian Church at that time] with Christians living on *slave* soil, in any seminary of learning." That in other words, political rather than *Christian* considerations, should rule and measure Christian co-operation in all seminaries of learning.[63]

Campbell also wrote that O'Kane was aware that the brethren in Illinois and Indiana had proposed to endow a chair of

---

[62]N.W.C.U. Minutes, Book 1, May 24, 1854, pp. 91-92.
[63]*Millennial Harbinger*, January, 1854, p. 42.

ancient languages at Bethany College and that his actions had hazarded his reputation and also that of the Indiana brethren for fair and honorable dealing.[64] In O'Kane's letter to Butler, read by Butler to the directors, O'Kane denied Campbell's charge that he had made a plea for patronage of North Western Christian University on grounds of political Free-Soilism. He admitted, however, that "he urged the fact, that its location was in a free State, and that students attending it would not be brought into contact with the habits and manners that exist in populations where slavery exists."[65]

The directors knew that they could not safely ignore Campbell's allegation, so they drafted a document with preamble and resolutions which was sent to the editors of the *Millennial Harbinger,* the *Christian Record* and the *Christian Age* with a request for publication "as an act of justice."[66] In this document they denied Campbell's "free soil-slave soil" charge on the basis that the university was pledged by its charter to the Bible and to no sectarian or political party; that it was not bound to receive or reject any doctrine or principle on a sectarian or political basis; that they had confidence in the activities of John O'Kane as agent of the school; that the university did not claim "exclusive patronage" on any ground whatever; and that the board never promised that John O'Kane, as its agent, would simultaneously urge the claims of Bethany College.[67]

The misunderstanding apparently had its origin in Ovid Butler's home at Indianapolis on the evening of November 19, 1850. Campbell, who had been on a tour through Indiana,[68] was entertained by Butler and some of his friends

---

[64]*Millennial Harbinger,* January, 1854, p. 42.
[65]*Christian Record,* July, 1854, pp. 210-211.
[66]The document was printed in full in the *Millennial Harbinger,* August, 1854, pp. 465-466.
[67]*Millennial Harbinger,* August, 1854, pp. 465-466.
[68]This was the tour described on pp. 128-132.

at a social gathering. During the course of the evening, Campbell must have pressed the claims and needs of Bethany College, an institution he had established ten years before at Bethany, Virginia, and a project very dear to his heart. If Campbell's recollections are correct,[69] many of the friends at the gathering that night were members of the former Board of Commissioners of North Western Christian University. After hearing Campbell's plea for Bethany College, this "board" retired to another room for some time to consider it. When the group returned, Ovid Butler told Campbell they had resolved to endow a chair at Bethany College and that John O'Kane would present the subject to the brethren at the same time that he presented the cause of North Western Christian University. As further evidence that such a decision was made, Campbell recalled that in many places in Indiana O'Kane actually did urge endowment of the chair.

A careful appraisal of the incident at Butler's home would seem to indicate that Campbell's memory, for the most part, was correct, but that some of his impressions were colored by his own enthusiasm for Bethany College. There seems to be little doubt that Campbell left the Butler home believing that when John O'Kane sold stock subscriptions for North Western Christian University he would also present the cause of Bethany College.[70] In O'Kane's frequent reports to the commissioners and in reports from district and state meetings of Indiana Disciples, as printed many times in the *Christian Record,* this seemed to be the case. The original commitment may

---

[69]*Millennial Harbinger,* August, 1854, p. 467. This explanation by Campbell was appended to the published document from the N.W.C.U. directors and was intended as a reply to the statement: "That *this* [italics mine] Board never promised that J. O'Kane 'as an agent for the N.W.C. University, would simultaneously urge the claims of Bethany College, that Indiana might endow one of its Chairs and El'd. Campbell is mistaken when he so affirms, the Board never had the subject before it."

[70]Campbell had made this understanding clear in the *Millennial Harbinger,* January, 1851, p. 52, and the Indiana brethren had never repudiated it before this incident took place two years later.

have been made unofficially by some of the commissioners who were present at the time, but under the terms of the charter the Board of Commissioners by this time had long since been discharged. The Board of Directors (which replaced the commissioners) was not the same board in 1854 even though some of the same men made up its membership. It would seem, however, that Campbell deserved to be treated with more candor than is indicated in the ambiguous statement that "this board never promised" to promote the Bethany College project along with its own.

According to the minutes of the Board of Directors, a single entry on May 24, 1854, with its preamble and resolutions denying Campbell's allegations, ended the matter. The document, as published in the *Christian Record, Christian Age,* and *Millennial Harbinger,* was the official "whitewash" of the affair. The unfortunate episode might have ended at this point had not H. St. John Van Dake added fuel to the fire in a letter sent to the *Christian Record.*[71] Campbell published this letter in his *Millennial Harbinger,* prefaced by a few caustic remarks of his own.[72] Van Dake's communication was couched in strong language but shed little light on the real issue. Ovid Butler, believing that his personal reputation was then at stake, wrote an explanation for the *Christian Record,* which was also published.[73] The *Millennial Harbinger*[74] carried correspondence from Jeremiah Smith in which he defended the position taken by the university and gave his version of the November 19, 1850 meeting at the Butler home. None of those who corresponded concerning the dispute ever really backed down on the positions they had taken. Campbell did admit, however, that he may have "miscalled the meeting"

---

[71]*Christian Record,* September, 1854, pp. 279-281.
[72]*Millennial Harbinger,* October, 1854, pp. 585-586.
[73]*Christian Record,* September, 1854, pp. 281-282.
[74]*Millennial Harbinger,* October, 1854, pp. 586-589.

at Butler's home, but he insisted "there was a called meeting there and then, held as before stated, and that *I was so informed at its close, I do most solemnly declare.*"[75]

Underlying Principles of the Dispute

To understand this unfortunate controversy it must be seen in its total context. It is not an isolated local conflict but one incidental to a larger maneuver of social and political forces within the total movement. The Bethany-Indianapolis episode was a vignette reflecting mounting tensions between the North and the South.

The Disciples' movement, of which Campbell was at this time the undisputed leader, had grown far beyond his dreams and expectations. But the slavery issue, which eventually divided nearly every major Protestant group, began to cast ominous shadows among Campbell's followers. Campbell preferred to see the question as primarily political rather than religious and wished to keep the controversy out of the churches. Finally, in 1845, under pressure to clarify his position, he wrote a series of articles on the subject.[76] A biblical scholar, he held to the master-servant relationship as he thought it was described in the New Testament and he believed that the slavery system should be upheld as long as it was the law of the land. Being a pacifist also, he objected to abolitionists and emancipators alike on the basis that they advocated force to gain their ends. Most of all, he was opposed to the sectional strife brought on by the slavery issue, which threatened to divide his country and his followers. After 1845, there was open alienation between Campbell and his followers

[75]*Millennial Harbinger*, October, 1854, p. 584.
[76]*Millennial Harbinger*, February, 1845, pp. 49-53; March, 1845, pp. 145-149; May, 1845, pp. 193-196; June, 1845, pp. 257-264; July, 1845, pp. 306-307; August, 1845, pp. 355-358.

in northern Ohio, and in other sections where strong abolitionist views were held.

By 1850, Campbell perceived that the cause of Christian unity and the restoration of primitive Christianity—principles to which he had dedicated his life—the Disciples' movement, his college, and even his leadership were in jeopardy because of what he considered a political situation. He knew his brethren on the Western Reserve in Ohio were getting out of hand but probably attributed it to the tradition of abolitionism in their New England heritage. He had made regular tours for many years through the South and Southwest and no doubt felt strongly entrenched in these parts. Because of his advancing age he no longer enjoyed extended tours among his constituents as before; yet a letter from Ovid Butler of Indianapolis jolted him into action again.[77] The letter informed Campbell of the incorporation of North Western Christian University and innocently implied that this school would have the patronage of some hundred thousand Christian Church members in Indiana, Illinois, Ohio, and Kentucky. Butler also implied that Bethany College need not be concerned because it had the support of the South and trained leadership for southern constituents. Butler, perhaps, had no intention of provoking Campbell, but the letter had two distinct results; it motivated an immediate caustic reply of disapproval[78] and compelled Campbell to make his first extended tour among the Indiana brethren. In his reply to Butler's invitation to visit Indiana which was one of several he had received through the years, Campbell gave as his excuse for never having visited the state, that Indiana was celebrated for fevers in the fall and its roads were impassable in the winter, the seasons during which he usually made his tours. If he really

---

[77]*Millennial Harbinger*, June, 1850, pp. 330-331.
[78]*Millennial Harbinger*, June, 1850, pp. 331-335.

believed this, his decision to make a tour of Indiana within five months after receiving Butler's letter concerning a proposed new university for the Disciples must have come because of strong inner compulsion.

When Ovid Butler and his friends, some of whom were N.W.C.U. commissioners, entertained Campbell at the Butler home on the evening of November 19, 1850, they were aware of the dim view Campbell took of their project. His reply to Butler's letter had made this plain enough. He probably made his position even clearer that evening by an impassioned plea for Bethany College. An off-the-record policy decision was inevitable. In the best interest of North Western Christian University it was deemed necessary for Indiana to support Campbell's project, the endowment of a chair of ancient languages at Bethany College. Any other decision would serve only to prove that Campbell's charges against them in reply to the Butler letter were justified. So Campbell was informed that O'Kane, as agent of the university, would add Bethany's project to his portfolio. It was a decision of appeasement, completely unofficial, and without approval of the State Meeting. There is no doubt that Campbell considered it otherwise and took the offer at face value.

The Fugitive Slave Act of 1850 crystallized antislavery sentiment among Disciples' churches in the North. Campbell wrote in support of the act:

Large and respectable meetings, ecclesiastic and political, have denounced it as unconstitutional and immoral, and have been advising, or at least countenancing, resistance and insubordination to its requirements. This, indeed, might have been more or less expected from those who are not well informed, either on the Constitution of the United States or on that of Christ's Kingdom. But that any one well-instructed in the Christian religion could recommend violence, or insubordination to a law, passed

145

by a Congress that merely represents and reflects the will of a sovereign people, is, to me, rather an unexpected development.[79]

With the passing of the Act and the publicity attending it, the brethren in Indiana and Illinois, following the lead of Ohio, became aroused. They were not sympathetic with slaveholders, did not agree with Campbell's views on slavery, and held that the "laws of God" were higher than the laws of Congress. Therefore, they could not support Bethany College, and John O'Kane was quick to find out that the chair of ancient languages at Bethany College had no chance of success in Indiana.

The Building Completed

The controversy with Alexander Campbell crowded out other news of North Western Christian University in 1854 so far as the *Christian Record* was concerned. Nevertheless, by the end of that year, J. M. Mathes reported that the building was nearly completed and that sessions of the preparatory school would commence at an early date.[80] The Indianapolis *Daily Journal* of April 2, 1855, carried a long account of the building enterprise. In this article the editor claimed: "It will be no slight gratification to a public spirited citizen to be able to say that Indianapolis has a college, which will compare favorably with any in the United States." The *Journal* described the new edifice as forming the western wing of a structure which would be about 250 feet long and 100 feet deep, standing immediately north of the old Bellefontaine Depot in the midst of a handsome grove of trees. The completed wing, the writer stated, was about 100 by 103 feet in dimension,

---

[79]*Millennial Harbinger,* January, 1851, p. 27. Much attention has been given to this issue because of what happened later between Bethany College and North Western Christian University.

[80]*Christian Record,* December, 1854, p. 378.

with towers, battlement walls, projecting windows, heavy stone sills, caps and ornaments. The interior was described as having black walnut staircases and massive balustrades. There were four recitation rooms and a room for chapel services or meetings of literary societies. The writer concluded: "It is worth the ride or walk of a mile and a half to look at it, and go through it."

Although the building was completed on record time, many disturbing financial problems remained. Through the columns of the *Christian Record,* N.W.C.U. stock subscribers were urged over and again to pay for their subscriptions. Ovid Butler wrote on March 1, 1855, that $6,000 was still due on contracts and that the directors had instructed the treasurer to bring suit against subscribers when he deemed it necessary.[81] In this same issue, Mathes declared that the building was finished but not out of debt. In a later issue he stated: "We could open next week if the stockholders could pay up their dues, so the directors would have something to pay the Faculty."[82] In the fall of 1854, Elijah Goodwin was appointed as agent for the university. He started his work early in 1855 and wrote of making a thorough canvass of Indiana "from Lake Michigan to the mouth of the Wabash river, and from Lawrenceburg to Terre Haute."[83] It was apparent to the directors by this time that continuous financial support from the Indiana constituency was a necessity.

Reconciliation with Campbell?

Alexander Campbell made a second trip to Indianapolis in late December of 1854. He made no point this time of ex-

---

[81]*Christian Record,* March, 1855, pp. 89-90.

[82]*Christian Record,* July, 1855, pp. 202-203.

[83]J. M. Mathes, *Life of Elijah Goodwin, op. cit.,* pp. 234-235; *Christian Record,* June, 1855, p. 192.

147

tending his visit in Indiana by having speaking appointments around the state. As a guest in Ovid Butler's home near the university building he had opportunity of inspecting the project. He was impressed and wrote of the university edifice as an admirable specimen of architectural taste and grandeur:

equal to any thing I have seen in the North-West, and speak[s] in unmistakable eloquence of the honorable pride and secular ambition of its enterprising projector and his worthy coadjutants. It is, and will long be, a proud monument of free soil jealousy, magnanimity, and generosity. It did not begin in the flesh, to be perfected in the spirit; but in the spirit to be perfected in the flesh.[84]

Following these stinging words, Campbell wrote of the conversation in the Butler home concerning the misunderstanding of what had been said there at the 1850 meeting. After mutual explanations, Campbell apparently exonerated his Indianapolis brethren, but with the reservation that he "could not fully reconcile their conduct to Christian candor and straightforwardness on their part."[85] Mathes reprinted the entire *Harbinger* article in the *Record* under the caption, "The Misunderstanding Settled," concluding with his own observations, "Bethany College and N.W.C. University, are not rival Institutions, but co-laborers in the great cause of Education, and Moral and Religious Reformation."[86]

Opened for Students

The preparatory school was reopened in the university building on April 9, 1855, with Allen Richardson Benton,

---

[84]*Millennial Harbinger,* April, 1855, p. 217-218. The Indianapolis visit was the last leg of an extended trip in Kentucky. Campbell's Indiana speaking engagements included only two addresses in New Albany and two in Indianapolis. He left Indianapolis on December 17th to go directly to Wheeling by railroad.

[85]*Millennial Harbinger,* April, 1855, pp. 218-219.

[86]*Christian Record,* May, 1855, pp. 147-149. Unfortunately this was not a lasting reconciliation as was proved by events of the next decade.

A.M.,[87] in charge. Benton, a graduate of Bethany College, had formerly been principal of Fairview Academy in Rush County. The school was advertised as being open to both sexes, "to give the female an equal chance to obtain a thorough education." Prior to this, Benton had been elected to the university faculty, and he served the preparatory school until a principal could be found to replace L. P. Streator. Silas E. Shepherd and Joseph Ray had also been elected to the faculty of the university, but they declined.[88] On August 8, 1855, the directors elected B. L. Long and Robert Milligan to the faculty, but they also declined.[89] The faculty roster was not complete until October 1, 1855. It was finally made up of John Young, A.M., professor of natural sciences; A. R. Benton, A.M., professor of ancient languages; James R. Challen, Jr., A.B., principal of the preparatory school; and L. H. Jameson, Challen's assistant. It was decided to leave the presidency vacant for the present.[90]

Twenty-one directors were elected for three-year terms on July 11, 1855, under the provision of the charter. Many of them had served a prior three-year term.[91]

Minutes of the meeting of the N.W.C.U. directors on October 1, 1855, show acceptance of the following resolution:

[87]Allen Richardson Benton (1822-1914) was born in New York State, united with the church in 1837, and graduated from Bethany College in 1847. He began preaching and teaching in Indiana in 1848. Benton was professor of ancient languages at N.W.C.U., 1855-1861; president of N.W.C.U., 1861-1868; president of Alliance College (Alliance, Ohio), 1868-1871; a founder of the University of Nebraska (Lincoln, Nebraska) in 1871 and later its chancellor; and president of Butler University, 1886-1891; professor to 1900. He died at Lincoln, Nebraska.

[88]N.W.C.U. Minutes, Book 1, May 25, 1854, p. 97.

[89]*Ibid.*, August 8, 1855, p. 127. Milligan, a professor at Indiana University, accepted a post at Bethany College instead of at N.W.C.U.

[90]N.W.C.U. Minutes, Book 1, August 8, 1855-October 1, 1855, pp. 126-130.

[91]According to N.W.C.U. Minutes, Book 1, July 11, 1855, p. 120, the directors elected were as follows: Ovid Butler, Love H. Jameson, Allen May, H. St. John Van Dake, John B. New, James M. Mathes, Elijah Goodwin, J. L. Martin, W. W. Thrasher, James Ford, B. F. Reeve, Jeremiah Smith, Higgins Lane, E. S. Frazee, D. C. Stover, William H. Craig, George Campbell, Chauncey Butler, R. B. Duncan, A. D. Hamrick, and Beverly Vawter. The *Charter and By-Laws of the North Western Christian University and an Ordinance for the Government of the Institution* (Indianapolis, 1847), lists the same men as members of the Board of Directors. Ovid Butler is president and treasurer in this list and Love H. Jameson is secretary.

"Resolved, that the Institution be opened on the first day of November next, the first session of which shall be nine months or to the first of August, 1856." Because of the shortness of time, and in lieu of a regular academic catalog, the directors issued a circular, dated November 1, 1855, in which an academic prospectus for 1855-1856 was given. According to the circular, the university was to be made up of six schools or general divisions: (1) the English and Normal Schools, (2) the Mathematical School, (3) the Classical School, (4) the School of Natural Science, (5) the School of Intellectual Science and Rhetoric, and (6) the Law School. The moral and religious training of the students was to be provided by daily lectures on such subjects as biblical criticism, natural theology, political economy, and analogy of revealed religion. Degrees for men included bachelor of arts and bachelor of science; women who completed the male collegiate courses were to receive either the degree of mistress of arts or mistress of science. The tuition was given as $30 per year for work on the college level and $20 per year for courses in the preparatory school.[92]

There was no formal dedication service for the new institution, but the school was officially opened with what the Indianapolis *Daily Journal* called commencement exercises.[93] On this occasion, James R. Challen, Jr. read from the Scriptures, H. St. John Van Dake led in prayer, and addresses were given by John O'Kane, Samuel K. Hoshour, A. R. Benton, and John Young.

Eight years had passed since the project was first proposed. There had been difficulties over the location of the school and even a major conflict with the acknowledged leader of the

---

[92]From a synopsis of the circular as printed in the *Christian Record*, March, 1856, pp. 86-88.

[93]*Indianapolis Daily Journal*, November 2, 1855.

Disciples' movement. Many of the problems which arose could have been handled better. The chief obstacle that faced the brethren, however, seems to have been the raising of sufficient funds. Ovid Butler's persistence and generosity, John O'Kane's perseverance in the field, and the publicity given the project by James M. Mathes and Elijah Goodwin in the *Christian Record* were major factors which brought the building project to successful culmination.

Vicissitudes of the Home Society

The Indiana Christian Home Missionary Society, constituted at the State Meeting of 1849, had its first annual meeting on May 29th the following year. Elijah Goodwin, making the major address at this meeting, claimed that Disciple churches were mostly confined to certain districts in central Indiana. He said that there were no churches "organized on the Christian Scriptures alone" south of the junction of the White rivers "until you reach Posey County." The need for a church at Evansville was pointed out, which "under the care of an efficient Pastor, would exert a powerful influence upon the surrounding country." Counties in which the Disciples had no churches were listed as: Pike, Vanderburgh, Allen, Noble, and LaGrange.[94]

The missionary society reported to the State Meeting, held at Indianapolis in October, 1850, that the *Christian Record* had been adopted as the organ of the Society and that after the following July this periodical would be published at Indianapolis. A proposal was adopted at the State Meeting that

---

[94]The full text of Goodwin's address appears in the *Christian Record*, August, 1850, pp. 33-43. The following men were elected as officers at this meeting: Ovid Butler, president; Elijah Goodwin and Butler K. Smith, vice-presidents; John M. Bramwell, recording secretary; and Berry R. Sulgrove, treasurer. Members of the Board of Managers were: Cyrus T. Boaz, James Sulgrove, William Wallace, Seth Bardwell, John B. New, Albert B. Cole, George Campbell, M. B. Hopkins, Benson Cornelius, P. H. Jameson, Joseph M. Tilford and James M. Mathes.

the state be divided into districts, bounded and numbered as were the existing judicial districts; that these districts each hold annual meetings composed of representatives appointed by the churches; and that the State Meeting be composed of representatives of these districts.[95]

Elijah Goodwin sent out a Circular Letter in support of the district plan adopted at the State Meeting. He claimed that though these meetings had been held annually since 1839, but a small portion of the brotherhood had been represented. Because of the voluntary nature of the meetings, he wrote, they were attended only by those who found it convenient to do so. He also stated that some of the brethren had expressed the fear that general meetings such as these would prove dangerous to the liberties of the churches. The district plan, Goodwin argued, would enable the strong churches to help the weak ones, be a means of obtaining better membership statistics, and through them the "voice of the whole brotherhood throughout the state" could be heard. He claimed that it was discovered at the State Meeting that some preferred to operate through the Home Missionary Society and others preferred to work through a committee appointed annually at the State Meeting; but because the Missionary Society was already in operation it was decided to stand by it and use it for this purpose.[96]

The second annual meeting of the Society was held at Indianapolis May 28, 29, 1851. According to a synopsis of the minutes[97] the entire attention of the meeting was given to procedural problems and the amending of the constitution. There is no indication of any actual missionary field work

---

[95]*Christian Record*, November, 1850, pp. 140-144. Minutes of the annual State Meeting.

[96]*Christian Record*, November, 1850, pp. 137-140.

[97]*Christian Record*, June, 1851, pp. 368-370. The constitution, as amended, appears on page 370.

having been accomplished. Nor does it appear that any missionary or evangelistic work of significance took place the next two years.

By 1853, opposition to the missionary society was so strong that it was decided to suspend it. It was thought that the State Meeting was the proper organization to carry on this work. The State Meeting was therefore reorganized with a new constitution (they perferred to call it a declaration of character) which provided for officers and a board of managers. The same judicial districts were used and many features of the missionary society were incorporated into the State Meeting. Life and annual memberships, however, were excluded in the new plan. When it was first set up the missionary society had its annual meeting in May so as not to conflict with the State Meeting in October. This was unsatisfactory, and by the time the missionary society was disbanded it was already holding its annual meetings in conjunction with the State Meeting.

It is easy to see that Indiana Disciples, completely unstructured at the beginning, in an effort to unify and strengthen their work, unwittingly set up competitive organizations. Because of this, they were never quite sure about administrative authority. By 1853, in addition to local churches holding power of independent action, they had cooperations, district organizations, a state missionary society and a State Meeting, all trying to do the same thing. In 1851, the State Meeting adopted a resolution to the effect that the State Meeting was a *mass* meeting, "composed of all accredited brethren of the church of Christ present." When the State Meeting was held at Indianapolis in 1854, "The President proceeded to call for delegates sent to the meeting; first, from the districts; second, from the county cooperations; and third, from the churches." There were delegates sent from districts 2, 3, and 10. Five county cooperations were represented by delegates

153

as well as were ten churches.[98] It is probably safe to assume that the State Meeting was composed of twenty-five or thirty persons only. This figure is probably typical of the attendance for many years. The work done by the Home Missionary Society had been sporadic and there was little improvement after the society was absorbed by the State Meeting. Regarding this, J. M. Mathes wrote, "At the State Meeting of 1853, a Missionary Board was created, to take charge of the Home Missionary field, and supply the destitute and help the weak, but up to this time nothing has been done by the Board for want of means."[99] From reports of the churches, made to the *Christian Record* in this period, missionary and evangelistic work was going on in the state, but primarily by local churches and county cooperations. It is doubtful whether even the brethren involved knew whether or not the State Meeting in this period was a mass meeting or a delegate convention. It is apparent that none was happy with the chaotic situation, that some were trying to bring order out of this chaos, and that no one seemed to know what to do about it.

---

[98]*Christian Record*, November, 1854, pp. 338-342.
[99]*Christian Record*, July, 1855, p. 203.

V

Slavery—War—Reconstruction

1856-1870

DISCIPLES OF CHRIST LIKE TO CLAIM that American slavery and the Civil War did not divide them. Actually, there was a *de facto* division among the Disciples over slavery and the war. It was not so obvious as divisions in the more highly structured religious bodies; it did not show as much. The division was apparent on a national level in the American Christian Missionary Society and on a state level in the various state associations. Slavery and the Civil War had a tremendous effect on the institutional life of the Disciples, especially in the field of higher education and missionary expansion. Since Disciples communicated their ideas primarily through religious journals, editorial views greatly influenced the thinking of the brethren. The Civil War broke this communication between churches of the North and the South, and it was never fully restored. If it had not been for the suspicion and hate engendered by the war and the victor-vanquished psychodrama which followed it, problems connected with the use of instrumental music in public worship and structured church cooperation to support missionary, benevolent, and educational work could possibly have been resolved. The war deprived the Disciples of the will to be a united brotherhood, and division finally came over issues that would have been considered as trifling before the war.

Hoosier Disciples had their first public confrontation with the slavery issue in 1854; it caused an altercation between the directors of North Western Christian University and Alexander Campbell.[1] The struggle for Kansas between those who wanted it to be a free state and those who wanted it to be a slave state, had serious repercussions in Indiana, especially among the Disciples. Pardee Butler, a Disciple abolitionist, moved to Kansas in 1855 and was successful in establishing several missionary congregations. Because of his strong antislavery views he was unable to get the support of the American Christian Missionary Society for his work. This antagonized antislavery (free-soil) groups among the Disciples, especially those who read John Boggs' *North-Western Christian Magazine* and the small circle of people around Ovid Butler[2] and his North Western Christian University clique.

A letter to the *Christian Record*[3] in 1857, and the reply by Editor Mathes indicate to some extent how Disciples felt about Negro slaves. Mathes was asked the following questions: (1) Is a colored brother's testimony to be taken in the congregation against a white brother? (2) Are colored members of churches entitled to an equal voice in the congregation in the transaction of business such as the election of officers, the reception and exclusion of members, with the white members? (3) Have the colored brethren equal privileges in the Lord's house with their white brethren? And should they be allowed to sit with the congregations in the house during

---

[1] This incident is discussed in the previous chapter, pp. 138-146.

[2] Butler was against the extension of slavery into the territories. He established the *Free Soil Banner* in Indianapolis in 1848. Though originally a Democrat, he served on the Free Soil electoral ticket and took the stump in the presidential campaigns of 1848 and 1852. Butler's financial contributions helped to establish the *Free Soil Democrat* in Indianapolis, a paper which merged with the *Indianapolis Journal* in 1854 with Butler in control. When the Republican party was organized that same year out of the antislavery men of all parties, the *Journal* served as their organ of communication. Butler also established a free soil newspaper in Cincinnati. See B. R. Sulgrove, *History of Indianapolis and Marion County, Indiana* (Philadelphia: L. H. Evarts and Co., 1884) pp. 175-178.

[3] *Christian Record*, July, 1857, pp. 240-242.

the religious exercises, such as preaching and the observance of the Lord's Supper? (4) Is it according to the law of the Lord for the white master to tie up and whip his colored servant, who is a member with him in the same congregation? (5) Is it the duty of Christian masters to teach their colored servants to read and understand, and obey the word of God?

Mathes replied to this communication by stating that one living in a free state could hardly appreciate the difficulties met with by a person living in a slave state, and that he had been inclined to leave such discussion to the political press. He regretted that his long silence on the matter could be construed as cowardice but asserted that this charge was not true. Mathes finally stated that the gospel made no distinction as to race and color and that "the blessings and privileges of the congregation belong equally to all." He admitted, however, that where their numbers justified it, he would prefer to have the colored brethren worship to themselves in a house of their own with their own colored preachers and church officers. On the other hand, he declared that no law of Christ regulated the matter and it would be wrong to make the colored people sit out of doors during worship *because* of their color. He concluded that the law of Christ gave no authority to any man to "tie up and whip" his Christian brother though he was a slave.

Rival Missionary Society Organized

The free-soil, antislavery movement among the Disciples reached its strongest position in a special convention held in Indianapolis in the fall of 1859. The purpose of the convention was to form a North Western Christian Missionary Society similar in structure to the American Christian Missionary Society, but with a constituency in the northern states and with representatives free to speak out on the evils of slavery.

157

Ovid Butler seems to have been the person responsible for is-
suing the call[4] for the convention, though it bore the signatures
of 600 persons.

Elijah Goodwin printed the "call" in the *Christian Record*[5]
but in his comments he claimed to differ with Butler on the
expediency of forming another missionary society. He held the
view, however, that a circular with 600 signatures could not be
ignored even though there was no evidence that the board of
the American Christian Missionary Society had ever imposed
the restrictions upon her agents that were implied in the "call."
Goodwin attended the various sessions of the convention so
that he could make a full report for his magazine. He wrote
that many persons in attendance were opposed to the movement but that it appeared that the convention was not called
"to investigate and determine the expediency of forming such
a Society, but to *form* it." Cyrus McNeeley of Ohio presided
over the sessions; G. H. Voss and T. Wiley of Indiana acted
as secretaries. According to Goodwin, the speakers claimed
that they were against division but spoke in terms of *we* and
they, i.e., "We don't intend to make division; if division is
produced, they must make it—we will not." Thus, believed
Goodwin, they showed that the line of separation was already drawn. Goodwin especially objected to a speech by
Jonas Hartzel on the grounds that it tended to promote divi-

---

[4]The "call" was a circular which announced that this convention would convene
on November 1, 1859 at the Christian Chapel in Indianapolis. The call stated in part,
"That as the American Christian Missionary Society of Cincinnati is avowedly an
effort to secure for missionary purposes a co-operation of the brethren from all parts
of the Union, and of every shade of opinion, upon the question of slavery, to ignore
that question is a necessity of that organism, and hence it consistently requires of its
officers, agents and missionaries, silence upon the subject of slavery. That those brethren
who regard slavery as no moral evil, may consistently co-operate together for missionary
purposes in the American Christian Missionary Society. That by a large majority of
the Northern brethren slavery is regarded as a moral evil, at variance with the principles of the Christian Code." The complete call was published in the *Christian
Record,* September, 1859 (2), pp. 282-283.
[5]*Christian Record,* December, 1859 (2), pp. 369-371, covers Goodwin's report of
the convention. For the contents of the circular, *see Christian Record,* September, 1859
(2), pp. 282-283.

sion between North and South and represented the Christian brotherhood in a false light.

When the Constitution Committee made its report, it was discovered that the subject of slavery was not mentioned. The delegates were astonished because they had anticipated that it would be an antislavery Constitution. Pardee Butler of Kansas, a rabid abolitionist, argued that because the new Society was to be a *Christian* Missionary Society, it was unnecessary to mention slavery. He contended that the name *Christian* automatically excluded slaveholders from membership. Others said they were doing the very thing they charged the American Christian Missionary Society was doing; "They were ignoring the subject of slavery, and that, unless an antislavery clause be inserted in the Constitution they would have nothing to do with it." Chairman McNeeley and Secretary Voss refused to become members. A Society of some fifty members was finally formed, fifty dollars in cash was raised, and pledges to the amount of $500 submitted. Goodwin was of the opinion that this was a small beginning considering that the Society was supposed to embrace the whole of the Northwestern states and territories as well as a part of Virginia. He advised his readers that the Indianapolis meeting was not a meeting of delegates from the churches nor could it be properly called a meeting of the Christian brotherhood in the Northwest; it was a meeting of a few brethren, living in various parts, who came together on their own individual responsibility to do what they did. Goodwin recommended that the new Society not be opposed lest the opposition be interpreted as persecution and create sympathy.

The states were embroiled in Civil War before the new Society had an opportunity to be tested. The political issues of the war soon corresponded with the moral issues raised by the sponsors of the new organization, obviating the necessity of its continuance.

Hoosier Disciples and the War Between the States

Hoosiers talked about the possibility of war in 1860 but had not considered it seriously. They were sure that armed conflict could be avoided, even after many of the Southern states had seceded. The fall of Fort Sumter on April 13, 1861, changed their views. They looked upon this incident as an invasion and as a national crisis; from this time on they felt that the rebellion should be put down. Events moved rapidly after the surrender of Fort Sumter; patriotic meetings were held throughout the state, General Lew Wallace[6] issued orders for companies to be formed and President Lincoln proclaimed a blockade of the South. Oliver P. Morton was Lieutenant Governor when Governor Henry S. Lane was elected to the United States Senate. This put Morton in an important position in a critical time. A Republican, he had difficulty in getting support for the war from a legislature made up mostly of Democrats. The legislators openly opposed Morton and President Lincoln, refusing to pass tax legislation to support the war effort. Governor Morton had to secure financial help from New York banking houses and from the Federal government, on his own responsibility, and without taxation. Since Christian Church members belonged to both parties, though the majority were probably Democrats at the time, tensions aroused by the war were present in every congregation. Republicans accused Democrats of being disloyal; many un-

---

[6]Lewis Wallace (1827-1905) was a lawyer, soldier, statesman and author. His stepmother was a charter member of Central Christian Church in Indianapolis. He attended Sunday school there though he never joined the congregation. Governor Oliver P. Morton named him adjutant general on April 15, 1861, and he was Indiana's top military leader for the duration of the war. Wallace served as major general in the Mexican army, 1865-1867; he was U. S. minister to Turkey, 1881-1885. His most popular book, *Ben Hur,* was published in 1880.

fortunate treason trials were held, and because of the direction the war finally took, the Democrats were temporarily discredited.

The war took a serious turn in Indiana when President Lincoln issued the Emancipation Proclamation, to take effect January 1, 1863. Hoosiers were willing to fight to preserve the Union (meaning the Union as it once was, slavery and all), but the emancipation of slaves had economic and social overtones to which they objected. At the time, even the Republicans became apathetic about the conduct of the war and military discipline was difficult to maintain.

Because those in leadership positions among the Disciples considered, for the most part, slavery and even the war itself as a political issue only, they thought that by ignoring slavery and war in their churches and journals they could escape tensions and conflicts and remain a united people. The war was on them almost before they knew it, and they were not prepared for it theologically. Elijah Goodwin explained this predicament in an article he wrote for his magazine[7] in which he declared that the war drums were beating in the towns and cities and the true Christian was asking himself, "What is my duty?" Goodwin advised that they should not give up the cause of Christ; that they should "pray more, preach more, and pray and preach more zealously, affectionately, and perseveringly" than they had ever done before. He wrote that they should not neglect a single Christian duty on account of the troublesome times; that they should "read their Bibles more, and, if possible, be more punctual than ever at the house of worship," Regarding their duties as citizens, he wrote, "We answer—sustain the government, peaceably if we can; forcibly if we must; and the sooner the question is settled the better for all concerned."

---

[7]*Christian Record*, June, 1861, pp. 173-175.

There was a number of genuine pacifists among the Disciples in this period, but their pacifism was generally interpreted as disloyalty. Benjamin Franklin, Hoosier-born editor of the *American Christian Review,* was one of these. Franklin wrote, "We doubt the whole business of Christians taking up arms and fighting, even *if drafted.* This is not *our country.* We are only pilgrims and sojourners here."[8] Goodwin considered these to be inflammatory statements that needed to be challenged. He proceeded to criticize Franklin in the columns of the *Christian Record*[9] by stating that when the *Star of the West* was fired upon, the *Review* had nothing to say on the subject; when Fort Sumter fell, the *Review* was still silent: "but when the government was driven to the necessity of calling on the loyal states for aid to suppress an armed rebellion, the *Review* says, 'We were not instrumental in bringing on the war, and therefore should not take part in it.'" Those who opposed the war generally followed a policy of silence concerning it, or took a position of pacifism; the northerners could not distinguish between the two and generally considered that those of their brethren who took either of these positions were either disloyal to the Union or sympathetic to slaveholders. The issue became crystallized at the Cincinnati meeting of the American Christian Missionary Society in 1861 during a heated debate over the propriety of passing a resolution in support of the Union.[10] This resolution, which was accepted with but one dissenting vote, was as follows: "Resolved: That we deeply sympathize with the loyal and patriotic in our country in their present efforts to sustain the government of the United States; and we feel it our duty, as Christians, to ask our brethren

---

[8]*American Christian Review,* July 9, 1861.

[9]*Christian Record,* November, 1861, pp. 347-348.

[10]*Christian Record,* December, 1861, pp. 375-376. It appears that though Dr. Robison of Cleveland introduced the resolution it would not have passed had it not been for the persuasion of his friend, Col. James A. Garfield (later President Garfield) of the 42nd O. V. I.

everywhere to do all in their power to sustain the proper and constitutional authorities of the Union." This resolution told the brethren who had formed a competitive missionary society at Indianapolis two years before, that their new Society no longer had excuse for its existence, that the missionary agency which represented the Disciples North and South had taken a position against the South, and that the only authoritative voice of the Disciples had sounded out in support of the war to suppress the rebellion. This was a *de facto* division of the brotherhood, one which continues to be ignored and un-acknowledged, and one from which the Disciples have never fully recovered. It contains the seed of the division recognized in 1906 between Disciples of Christ and Churches of Christ (anti-instrumental).

Some 208,000 Hoosiers were in military service before the war ended. Over 24,000 of these lost their lives in combat or were service-related casualties. The tragedy was felt in every church and in almost every home. Beginning in 1865, the word "reconstruction" was heard everywhere. The war freed the Negro from legal slavery, ended the secessionary movement among the Southern states, established the principle of the supremacy of the central government, and put the South under military rule for a few years. By 1870, the southern states, by act of Congress were re-admitted to the Union, carpetbaggers invaded the South, and reconstruction ended with a vengeance.

The Slavery Issue and Higher Education

The new university at Indianapolis seemed destined to tangle with Alexander Campbell and his Bethany College from the very beginning. Just when tension between the two schools had relaxed an incident took place at Bethany College which had repercussions at North Western Christian University. Because the Bethany College incident had jeopardized the school's image in the eyes of Northern patrons, Alexander Campbell gave a full explanation of it in the *Millennial Harbinger*.[11] He wrote that school policy was to maintain the strictly scientific, literary and moral character of the institution and to discourage student discussion of social and political issues. He believed, apparently, that this policy had been violated, especially by students of the Northern minority group. The Adelphian Society was made up of young men who planned to enter the ministry, and it was customary for these students to take turns preaching in the village church each Sunday evening. Campbell wrote that one of the students (apparently an abolitionist) violated the rules when he introduced the subject of slavery into a sermon on such an occasion. When a Northern student spoke on "The True Principles of Liberty," it was considered to be an antislavery address. On this occasion the Southern students hissed at the speaker and pounded the floor with their feet and canes; finally twenty or thirty of them walked out of the building and put on a noisy demonstration outside. Both speakers received anonymous communications which threatened punishment if they did not keep their antislavery sentiments to themselves. The Northern students then stayed away from classes and dictated conditions to the Faculty by which they would remain at the school. They insisted that the past be fully rectified; that those who were connected with the mob be arraigned before the Faculty and publicly reprimanded or expelled from college; and especially, they demanded the right to discuss, in public debate or in the pulpit, the issue of American slavery. According to Campbell, the Faculty resolved to put an end to the excitement and insubordination by dismissing the ringleaders

---

[11]*Millennial Harbinger*, January, 1856, pp. 54-60.

of the affair. These students were so informed; the Faculty further declared that order would be maintained on both sides, that disorder and violence would be punished immediately, no matter by whom perpetrated, so soon as the guilty could be identified. According to Campbell, five of the Northern students remained obstinate and were dismissed, and five other students left with them. Campbell took the view that the incident was primarily a matter of college discipline.

The event, as it was viewed by the students who left Bethany College, was described in an article in the *North-Western Christian Magazine*,[12] appearing almost simultaneously with the Campbell article in the *Harbinger*. The student explanation was similar to the one made by Campbell but took a different slant. It reported that there were some 130 students enrolled at the college; one hundred of these were from the South. As Southern students frequently discussed American slavery at public meetings, they (the Northern students) had no idea that the subject was against regulations. They cited certain speeches to which they had been compelled to listen, claiming these addresses were full of abuses against Northern men and principles and that they were received by the Southerners with deafening cheers. The statement that provoked the "hissing-stamping-walk out" demonstration was one made by a Northern student, "Satan's emissaries often misquote and misapply Scripture to sustain intemperance, spiritualism, and slavery." According to them, the speaker paused when the demonstration started; John Encell, a Northern student, called for him to "go on." For this, Encell was censured by the Faculty. The Faculty also frowned upon another student of known antislavery views, telling him to "keep his alien and seditious views locked within his own bosom." Following

---

[12]*North-Western Christian Magazine*, January, 1856, pp. 213-218.

the demonstration and the receiving of threatening notes, the Northern students claimed at a meeting in B. W. Johnson's room that they had resolved not to attend classes until matters were properly adjusted, the students who took part in the demonstration were arraigned for discipline by the Faculty, and that all students be guaranteed their religious rights as secured by the American Constitution. According to them, they were answered by W. K. Pendleton, representing the Faculty. He said in effect that in the future, slavery was not to be agitated at Bethany, a decision that brought boisterous and frequent applause from the Southern students; that certain Northern students were causing disturbances and trampling on College laws; that these students were young fanatics, "not capable of wearing respectable beards," and that they were poor specimens of Northern humanity. He also said that certain students had informed the Faculty on what conditions they *would* remain in college, and now he would tell them on what conditions they *might* remain, viz. "that they immediately return to their places in their classes." He is reported to have also informed them the Faculty would not grant their petitions or do anything further concerning the matter. Some Northern students submitted to this Faculty edict; five left Bethany that evening and five more the next day.[13]

The matter may have ended at this point if the public press had not played up the incident as a student riot at Bethany College and if North Western Christian University had not accepted some of the students who had left Bethany College because of it.[14] The acceptance of these students at the Indian-

---

[13]These students, some of whom later became prominent in the Disciples' brotherhood, were: Philip Burns, C. Mykranz, John Guffin, A. B. Way, H. W. Everest, J. Kimmons, John Encell, Leander McConnel, D. R. Van Buskirk, and C. C. Foot.

[14]The notoriety given the Bethany affair in leading newspapers around the country, the receiving of some of the students by N. W. C. U. and the church in Indianapolis, the publication of the students' story, which Campbell wrote was not true, and the refusal by most Disciples to view the case as a simple matter of discipline was a source of embarrassment to Alexander Campbell. He made another full explanation in the *Millennial Harbinger*, February, 1856, pp. 111-117.

apolis school led to an interchange of letters between the Faculties, communications which increased rather than diminished the tension. The Bethany Faculty declined to publish the N. W. C. U. letter (and a similar one from Hiram College) on the basis that it was not obligated to discuss its decisions just because they were not pleasing to everybody. They did, however, use the *Harbinger*[15] to publish a tirade against the students who had defected, North Western Christian University, and the church at Indianapolis. They claimed these young men were "under the wicked spirit of a politico-religious fanaticism," that they had "a puerile itching for even infamous notoriety," and that they had "falsely, recklessly, and slanderously represented the Faculty and students of Bethany College and the church and citizens of Bethany." They declared these students to be "beyond the pale of Christian fellowship," and "unfit for their own righteous companionship."

In a letter dated April 26, 1856, the Faculty at Indianapolis answered the Bethany charges. The letter admitted, among other things, that some men (not boys) had left Bethany and had been received by them. It explained that the N. W. C. U. Faculty believed these students had left Bethany voluntarily and that the students themselves had no idea they had been dismissed when they applied for admission at Indianapolis. The N. W. C. U. Faculty agreed that laws of comity among colleges were binding on them, but inferred that Bethany's laws were unusual. The letter then took a low blow at Alexander Campbell with the statement, "We can appreciate, to some degree, the labors of its [Bethany's] President, and we truly sympathize with him in the great purpose of these labors. We believe he has made an impression upon the world, which

---

[15]*Millennial Harbinger*, April, 1856, pp. 226-229.

the trembling hand of age will not have strength enough to deepen, although it may avail, to some extent, to dim and mar its beauty."[16]

Although the insinuations against Campbell in this letter were no worse than those Campbell had previously made against the founders of North Western Christian University, nevertheless, they were not in good taste and should not have been made.

The Minutes of the Board of Directors of North Western Christian University show the adoption of the following statement concerning this affair:[17]

Resolved: That we approve the course of the Faculty of this University in receiving and retaining some of the students who recently left Bethany College; that in so doing they are entitled to be regarded as doing what was just and proper in the case; and wrong to none: that the Institution has never sought war, but only peace with Bethany College; that the latter Instituion has no just cause of complaint against this University, its Board or Faculty; that having been assailed in the M. Harbinger, the Faculty of this University had a special right to the use of its columns in self-defense: that we regard the denial of that right by the Editors of the Harbinger: the mutilation of the reply of the Faculty of this University, and their repetition of the charges in the case on the pages of that work; as an act of injustice to this Institution; a repudiation on the part of the Editors of the Harbinger of its oft repeated profession of fairness in giving both sides, and a violation of gentlemanly and Christian courtesy.

North Western Christian University, 1855-1870

Although the school opened to receive students in the fall of 1855, it was impossible, because of lack of funds, to constitute a full faculty. By 1858 the situation was no better; the school had three professors, a principal of the English de-

---

[16]*North-Western Christian Magazine,* June, 1856, pp. 365-366.
[17]N. W. C. U. Minutes, Book 1, May 28, 1856, p. 145.

partment, and a tutor in the Primary department. The Directors did not name a president for three years, but Professor John Young[18] acted in this capacity as chairman of the Faculty. In 1858, Samuel K. Hoshour[19] became President and he held this office for three years. Allen R. Benton was President 1861-1868; he was followed in this office by Otis A. Burgess.

By 1859 the student body had increased to 265. The Faculty for the 1859-1860 academic year was announced as Samuel K. Hoshour, A.M., president and professor of ethics and intellectual science; Ryland T. Brown, A.M., M.D., professor of natural science; A. R. Benton, professor of ancient languages and literature; G. W. Hoss, A.M., professor of Mathematics and civil engineering; Madison Evans, A.M., professor of English and Normal School; and Mrs. N. E. Burns (Mrs. A. M. Atkinson) and Mrs. E. J. Price, teachers in the primary school. Of the 265 students enrolled, only 63 were in regular degree courses.

---

[18]John Young (1816-1885) received his education at Royal College, Belfast, Ireland and came to the United States as a missionary of the Baptist Irish Society. He learned of the Campbell religious movement about 1843 and accepted these views. He became minister of the Christian Church at Maysville, Kentucky, serving that congregation until 1853. During this pastorate he conducted private schools in the vicinity of Maysville. He was a friend of Walter Scott who was serving the Christian Church at May's Lick, Kentucky at this time. Young officiated at the wedding of Scott to Nancy Allen, a member of his congregation. Because of his academic background and experience as a schoolman, and because of views on education he had expressed in numerous articles written for the journals, he was called to the first Faculty of North Western Christian University in 1855. He served this school until 1858. At this time he left Indianapolis to practice law at Bloomington. Campbell met him in 1861 when he was visiting in that city. That same year Young became U. S. Consul to Ireland, serving throughout the Lincoln administration. He then returned to Indianapolis where he practiced law and lectured on medical jurisprudence at an Indianapolis medical college. He authored two books: *A Discussion of the Mode and Subject of Baptism* (with B. C. Grundy) in 1851; and *Pulpit and Platform*, 1854.

[19]Samuel Klinefelter Hoshour (1803-1883) was of German and French lineage, and as a young man was a Lutheran minister. Around 1834 he began to revise his religious views, especially those in regard to baptism. When this became apparent in his preaching it led to a break with the Lutheran Synod. He then moved to Centerville, Indiana. At this place he became actively identified with the Disciples. At Centerville, Hoshour was head of the Wayne County Seminary, holding this position for four years. He was elected a trustee of Indiana University at this time. In 1839 he became principal of the seminary in Cambridge City. He joined the Faculty of North Western Christian University in 1855 and was elected President in 1858. In 1862 he was made State Superintendent of Education. Hoshour read five languages and spoke three fluently. Among his pupils who became famous were General Lew Wallace and Governor Oliver P. Morton. Hoshour was author of a curious book entitled, *Altisont Letters* and edited an edition of Mosheim's *Church History* in 1847. His autobiography was published in 1884. In addition to his work in the classroom, Hoshour was often in demand as a preacher.

169

The school met with a normal degree of success until the outbreak of the Civil War. The conflict precipitated a huge loss of students and income. It became necessary in 1861 for the Board of Directors to cut back the program and dismiss several teachers. By commencement time, many students who were scheduled to graduate, had enlisted in the armed services and were not present to receive their diplomas.

It seems apparent that the school's loss of income and lack of support at this time was partly due to the strong antislavery, anti-southern rebellion position taken by Ovid Butler and a coterie of like-minded persons connected with the university project. The Minutes of the Board of Directors[20] quote a charge published in the *American Christian Review* that North Western Christian University "has been and is impeded in its prosperity and usefulness by its hobbyism and ultraism . . . and has departed from its legitimate work of education." Since the *Review* had taken a neutralist position toward the war and its editor was a pacifist there is no doubt about what he meant by hobbyism and ultraism. The Butler group had local support during the war, but this was not enough; very little encouragement came from southern Indiana where the movement had its greatest numerical strength. Judge Jeremiah Smith, president of the Board of Directors, felt that the position taken by Butler and his friends made it very difficult to hold the support of the constituency; in fact, he resigned his office when the following "loyalty" resolution was passed at the above-mentioned meeting:

Resolved: That while we deny that any action of this board, or of the faculty of the institution, has been either religiously or politically partisan in its character, we rejoice to be able to state

---

[20]N. W. C. U. Minutes, Book 1, July 2, 1862, pp. 362-363.

and for the first time we now state that the members of this Board and of the Faculty of the Institution are true and loyal to the Constitution and the Government of the United States, and warmly and deeply sympathize with the soldiers of the Union who are engaged in the suppression of the present wicked rebellion.

The catalog for the academic year 1863-1864, which listed the student body of the year before, indicated that by this time the enrollment consisted of one senior, five juniors, five sophomores, and twenty freshmen. An additional 143 students were enrolled as either irregular, special, or preparatory students. This issue of the catalog extolled the merits of the Mathesian, Pythonian, Sigournean, and Threskomathian literary societies; advertised board with good families at $2.50 to $3.00 per week; tuition at $10.00 per term in colleges classes and $8.00 in preparatory classes; and explained the advantages of the law school. The degrees of B.A. and B.S. were offered for work finished on the college level, and the M.A. degree, an honorary one, was "conferred on regular graduates of three years' standing, who shall have sustained, in the meantime, a good moral character, and have been engaged in professional, literary, or scientific pursuits."

The catalog for the academic year 1866-1867 named Elijah Goodwin as president of the Board of Directors and Mrs. M. M. B. Goodwin as secretary. The Faculty consisted of Allen R. Benton (President), Samuel K. Hoshour, Ryland T. Brown, W. M. Thrasher, and A. Fairhurst. There were 253 students enrolled, 57 in the regular courses. This indicated that with the war at an end the school had returned to normalcy, at least as far as enrollment was concerned. Including the class of 1866, the University by this time had sixty alumni which included nine teachers, nine preachers, five physicians, one editor, one Indian agent, one army lieutenant, four farmers, and one college professor.

By 1868 the school, still burdened with debt, faced a financial crisis. The seriousness of the situation was expressed by Editor Mathes,[21] "It would certainly be a burning shame for the Christian brotherhood in Indiana, now numbering nearly 80,000 to allow this great enterprise to fail." Because of pecuniary embarrassment it was necessary to reduce expenses in every possible way. President Allen R. Benton, probably because of a cut in salary, announced his resignation. Benton was an able administrator; the Board deeply regretted this action but did not have the means to prevent it. Otis A. Burgess[22] was chosen as his successor.

The catalog for the academic year 1869-1870 named twelve Faculty members[23] for the university. There were 209 students enrolled. The cost of board was advertised as from $4.00 to $5.00 per week; the tuition (in scrip) was $42.00 per season or $14.00 per term. There was a note to the effect that students who did not have the scrip to pay their tuition could purchase it at 50 cents on the dollar. Religion was not neglected; the catalog stated that "Students are required to attend public worship once, at least, every Sabbath, and the Sabbath lectures, at the University Hall."

[21]*Christian Record,* August, 1868, p. 233.

[22]Otis Asa Burgess (1828-1882) was born in Connecticut. He went to Illinois in 1847 where he taught school. In 1851 he enrolled at Bethany College, graduating in 1854. Burgess served as acting-president of Eureka College in 1855. At the outbreak of the war he became captain of a company of soldiers formed at Eureka College. Burgess served Central Christian Church in Indianapolis as pastor from 1862 to 1869. While still minister of the church in 1868 he was chosen as president of North Western Christian University, holding both positions. He accepted a call to First Christian Church in Chicago in 1870, and was there during the great Chicago fire. Called back to Butler University, he was again president of this school, 1874-1881. He resigned in 1881 to return to Chicago for another pastorate. Burgess was an outstanding brotherhood leader, wrote regularly for the Disciples' journals, and was in constant demand as a speaker.

[23]Faculty members were O. A. Burgess (president), Samuel K. Hoshour, Ryland T. Brown, W. M. Thrasher, Harvey W. Wiley, Catherine Merrill, W. F. Black, A. C. Alcott, Austin Council (tutor), J. W. Lowber (tutor), Mrs. Henry Griffin (music), and Mrs. E. J. Price (principal academic department).

Structure and Organization

By 1855, Hoosier Disciples had experimented with three types of state-level organizations: the simple State Meeting, the State Meeting plus a home missionary society, and a State Meeting with a special missionary board. Records of the work for this period show very little done in the missionary and evangelistic fields. Lack of financial support is usually given as a reason for this poor showing, but the cause probably goes deeper than this. In spite of the dissatisfaction with its structure and the weakness of organizational life the movement grew rapidly in Indiana; not through planned expansion, but on a do-it-yourself grass roots basis. Dr. Ryland T. Brown called attention to this in an address at the fiftieth anniversary of Central Christian Church in Indianapolis. He said, "The missionary history of our brotherhood in Indiana has been a paradox. While every plan which has been devised for carrying on the work by churches, or cooperation of churches, has been a failure, the work itself, thank God, has been an unparalleled, a glorious success."[24] The state organization, at each annual meeting, usually made plans for the year and employed agents to raise funds and hold evangelistic meetings, but plans were not followed and agents did not stay long on the job.

The Noblesville church provided an interesting test case on the authority of the State Meeting over the local congregation. The church had separated into two factions. Each faction claimed to be the church and sent delegates to the State Meeting in 1856. William C. Bramwell, who was presiding, did not want to accept either or both delegations. He reasoned that there was no choice that could be made which would not appear to influence the status of either or both factions before

---

[24]*Christian Standard*, July 14, 1883. Article by Dr. Ryland T. Brown.

proper investigation could be made.[25] Both sets of delegates, however, were seated when they agreed to permit a committee of disinterested persons to study their complaints and help them to resolve their differences.

A letter to the *Christian Record* from J. W. McAchran of Stilesville[26] pointed up a problem of authority posed by this decision. His letter questioned, "Has the State Meeting divine authority to determine questions of heresy or morality which may arise in the churches? and has it power to receive or reject delegates from congregations?" Editor Mathes responded that the State Meeting was a voluntary association and could perform no act that would be binding on any congregation; the most it could do would be to advise and assist congregations when called upon, in setting things in order. He claimed there was no divine law requiring a church to send delegates to a State Meeting and that a church could neglect to do so without violating any law of Christ. He added, "All deliberative bodies and associations of men have a right, by common consent and usage, to judge the qualifications of its members, and upon this ground may receive one and reject another." Mathes claimed the State Meeting had no jurisdiction over the churches and that its primary business was of a missionary character.

A committee of the State Meeting advised with both factions of the Noblesville church. As a result, it was thought that the issues which divided the brethren were finally resolved, but such was not the case. A new church organization, formed on the advice of the committee, soon divided. The faction in control of the church property wanted their old officers back and let it be known they wished to be called the Church of Jesus Christ in Noblesville, Indiana. The State

---

[25]*Christian Record,* November, 1856, pp. 321-333.
[26]*Christian Record,* March, 1857, pp. 88-90.

Meeting was asked to reassemble the arbitration committee so that it could decide which party violated the reconciliation agreement. President Goodwin held that the committee was chosen by both parties for a special purpose and that he had no authority to call it back. He ruled that if further investigation was necessary a new committee would have to appointed.[27]

The Circular Letter published by the 1857 State Meeting[28] was apologetic of the nature and policy of its own work. The letter admitted that the annual meetings had been poorly attended for several years and that contributions had been so meager that little could be done. The suggestion was made that if each of the 60,000 Disciples in Indiana would contribute five cents a week it would gross $156,000 annually, a sum sufficient to sustain an evangelist in every county, give $10,000 to the Bible Union, $10,000 to the Jerusalem Mission, $10,000 to North Western Christian University, and $26,000 to sustain evangelists in Kansas, Nebraska, and Minnesota. There is no indication that the State Meeting ever received even a fraction of five cents per member per week; by 1860 the offerings on the state level averaged a little over 1/100 of a cent per member per week, a substantial increase over the average in 1855.

The State Meeting for 1857 was held in the Christian meetinghouse at Lafayette.[29] There were no more than twenty persons in attendance. An address by H. St. John Van Dake,[30] can be seen as an answer to criticism from the brethren and as an apology for the continued existence of the organization. He stated that the State Meeting was just an

---

[27]*Christian Record*, April, 1857, pp. 113-114; May, pp. 152-153.
[28]*Christian Record*, November, 1857, pp. 333-334.
[29]*Christian Record*, November, 1857, pp. 329-333.
[30]*Christian Record*, December, 1857, pp. 368-373.

agency for good which Christians had the liberty to use. Van Dake declared that this organization learned of the needs of churches and communities in order to supply these needs, that it promoted Christian union among the Disciples, was an efficient missionary instrument, and that it presented an index before the world of the strength of the cause. He added that there was no reason to question its authority, the right of Disciples to have it, or the respect due to it. Van Dake also stated that North Western Christian University owed its existence to the State Meeting, but complained that the school was governed "not after the manner of the Christian Institution, but according to the laws of monetary corporations, and it renders homage to the capital which owns it." He further stated, "It was our movement, was built as ours, and should be held and managed as ours, *i.e.,* the brotherhood's." He pointed out that the financial aid given to the State Meeting for missionary work was very feeble, but that "though crippled in our operations, we should not be discouraged, for the work of faith, and patience of hope, and labor of love, cannot be in vain." There apparently had been some resentment toward permitting the evangelists and elders (professional clergymen) to serve as delegates to the State Meeting. Van Dake suggested that such men should not only be welcome to attend, but should be urged to take seats in the meeting. He admonished the brethren, "Should the refractory and discordant elements among us preponderate, we shall be weighed down and our energies crushed." He told them they should not heed the lament of the "croakers," and warned, "We must also resist the contagious malady of preacherphobia. Cripple your public men," he said, "and you cripple yourselves; dishonor your preachers, and you dishonor yourselves; slaughter your public servants, and you guillotine yourselves."

The fear of the authority of the State Meeting, the fear of the development of a clergy class within the movement, and an utterly inadequate sense of stewardship, prevented the State Meeting from becoming a constructive force for good for many years. The few who were loyal to the State Meeting felt that the answer to making it effective was in experimenting with different types of organization until the right one, acceptable to the brethren, could be found. They failed to see that no form of structure could succeed until there was a readiness to receive the principle of the State Meeting itself, and that structure-patterns *per se* were secondary to this.

There were only seven official delegates from three churches present at the 1858 Bedford State Meeting.[31] The few unofficial non-delegates who attended were given voting privileges. The next year when the group convened at Indianapolis,[32] four districts were represented by nine delegates and thirteen churches by eleven messengers. Elijah Goodwin was appointed corresponding secretary and general agent of the State Meeting on this occasion and was asked to give as much time to the work as he could spare from the editorship of the *Christian Record*. His salary was finally set at $500 annually, after several ineffectual attempts were made on the part of his friends to make it higher. Goodwin was commissioned to visit all the districts in the state, organize them, and set them in working order. He could not enter the field until January, 1860, but it appeared from the reports of the State Meeting at Greencastle[33] that he made a good start. Enough money was raised on the field to pay his salary! Goodwin recommended that the State Meeting employ

---

[31]*Christian Record*, November, 1858, pp. 326-330.
[32]*Christian Record*, October, 1859, (1) pp. 330-332.
[33]*Christian Record*, November, 1860, pp. 335-340.

a full-time secretary for the next year. As a result, H. Z. Leonard of Westville was named corresponding secretary and general agent for 1861. He immediately encountered problems raised by the war. In consequence, it was thought best to suspend his labors as agent.[34]

Even as late as the outbreak of the Civil War, Hoosier Disciples did not know who they were, what they were trying to do, or the meaning of their witness. The State Meeting was under a cloud of suspicion. Some of the brethren looked upon it as an ecclesiastical hierarchy and as a threat to their religious freedom. Therefore, the State Meeting found it necessary to issue statements from time to time to the effect that it would never devise or construct any creed or articles of faith to be imposed on the brethren; nor interfere with the rights, privileges, and scriptural independence of the churches. Elijah Goodwin wrote[35] that since some of the brethren wanted the state organization only as an annual meeting and others wanted it as a missionary society; both features were incorporated in the new constitution adopted in 1853. Under this arrangement congregations could send messengers to the annual meetings, county and district meetings could do the same, and any member in good standing in a Christian church could be an annual member by the payment of one dollar or a life member by the payment of ten dollars. The organization, under the new constitution, was called the Indiana Christian Missionary State Meeting. Recognizing this as a burdensome name it was changed to the Indiana Christian Missionary Society in 1862.

This was a period of decline for the State Meeting but not for preacher participation in public debates. Some eighteen

---

[34]*Christian Record,* December, 1861, pp. 366-369.
[35]*Christian Record,* January, 1861, pp. 27-28.

public discussions[36] are reported to have taken place between 1857 and 1862. Debating on religious issues ceased from 1862 until the close of the war. Most of these debates held prior to this time were with Universalists; some were with Methodists and Baptists.

Robert L. Howe[37] was named corresponding secretary at the State Meeting in 1863. He entered the field at once, and his work indicates that he was probably the first state secretary to envision the task as a full-time job requiring specialized service. When the annual meeting was held at Indianapolis in 1864 it was discovered that Howe had raised $1,539.72 during the year. This was far better than had ever been done before. In addition, he had been successful in organizing many of the districts and in the placing of ministers in churches. Beginning about 1865, the fortunes of the State Society seemed to change, the doldrums which had hung over the organization almost from its beginning, moved on; it was apparent that the State organization had turned another corner in its history. This could have been due to the restructuring of the organization, the employment of a

---

[36]These debates were as follows (Disciple contestant named first):
Henry R. Pritchard—B. F. Foster (Universalism), Fillmore, 1857.
Jasper J. Moss—_____ Chaplin (Universalism), Bluffton, 1857.
O. A. Burgess—W. W. Curry (Universalism), Indianapolis, 1858.
H. St. John Van Dake—B. F. Foster (Universalism), Shelbyville, 1858.
Jasper J. Moss—W. W. Curry (Universalism), New Albany, 1858.
E. Goodwin—R. Hargrave (Baptism and Justification), Oxford, 1858.
Thomas P. Connelly—E. E. Rose (differences with Methodists), Heltonville, 1858.
Benjamin Franklin—Joel Hume (differences with Baptists), Mt. Vernon, 1859.
William C. Beck—_____ Tucker (Baptism), Pierceville, 1859.
Jacob Wright—E. E. Rose (differences with Methodists), Worthington, 1860.
L. G. Pritchard—L. C. Wiley (Baptism), Johnson County, 1860.
Jacob Wright—Nathan Hornaday (materialism), North Salem, 1860.
Joseph Franklin—_____ Anderson (Baptism), Little Eagle Creek Church, 1861.
Elijah Goodwin—H. Wells (Baptism), Jalappa, 1861.
Jacob Wright—T. S. Brooks (differences with Methodists), 1861.
Elijah Goodwin—M. Mahan (Baptism), Henry County, 1862.
O. B. Wilson—Jacob Cozad (Baptism, creeds, etc.), Russellville, 1862.
John Chapman Miller—_____ Abbot (Universalism), Lick Springs, 1862.
[37]Robert Long Howe (1832-1892) was a native of Ohio. He was baptized by Jonas Hartzel and united with the church in 1851. After graduation from Antioch College he located with the church at Connersville in 1859. In the period 1863-1865 he served as corresponding secretary of the Indiana Christian Missionary Society, being the first full-time secretary in the modern conception of this office. He moved to Clark County in 1866 where he ministered to congregations for eighteen years. In 1884 he retired at Irvington.

capable corresponding secretary with vision, war-boom economics, or the final settlement of certain divisive issues by the outcome of the war. By the close of the year 1865, Howe was able to report that he had traveled 7,790 miles, given 280 discourses, sent out 1,705 letters, and had received $18,000 in cash and pledges. Under his inspiration and advice, seventy-three evangelists had given 3,042 days of service in Indiana churches during the year. This resulted in 2,868 additions to the church membership. Unfortunately, Howe's health failed under this strenuous pressure and by the end of 1865 he had to give up the work.

The attendance at the State Society meeting at Indianapolis in 1866[38] was considered large. By this time the brethren were using well-known Disciples from outside the state on their convention programs. Among the speakers at this meeting were W. K. Pendleton, M. E. Lard, L. Pinkerton, and D. Pat Henderson. It is possible that the brethren were now seeing the wisdom of giving less time at the convention to procedural matters and scriptural technicalities, and more time to fellowship and inspirational addresses. W. R. Jewell was appointed corresponding secretary at this meeting, but he served less than three months. J. H. Bauserman took his place and resigned after eight weeks.

The Sunday School Movement

The Sunday School movement was recognized as early as 1855 in Indiana when J. M. Mathes wrote[39] of the importance of organizing good Sunday schools in all the churches. The movement was also considered at the State Meeting of 1857, and a Sunday school convention was held in Indianapolis in

---

[38]*Millennial Harbinger,* November, 1866, pp. 523-525.
[39]*Christian Record,* October, 1855, pp. 301-302.

1858. The movement was not without opposition, especially from certain of the older people who believed that human effort for the conversion of men was a presumptuous attempt to aid God in a work that belonged to him alone. Elijah Goodwin complained in 1859 that these early impressions still lingered in the minds of Disciples, that many Sunday Schools were so poorly conducted that no good results could be witnessed, that it was hard to get suitable Sunday school literature for children, and that obtaining the right teachers and officers was a big problem.[40] A State Sunday School Association was formed at the state convention in Indianapolis in 1867, "to enlist the entire brotherhood of this state in an effort to promote the interest in the Sunday school."[41]

The Indiana Christian Missionary Society and the State Sunday School Association held a joint convention at Columbus in the summer of 1868. According to the reports made at this time it was a pleasant and profitable meeting. There were no special formal addresses, although a number of outstanding Disciples were present. It appears that this was a conference or "workshop" type of gathering which emphasized Sunday school work; as such, it was something new to the brethren.[42]

The State Society, probably because of the lack of progressive professional leadership, went into a temporary slump during the years 1867-1870. The president's report, given by Elijah Goodwin at the annual meeting in 1868, argued the means of cooperation, indicating that the brethren were still concerned about structure and organization. Membership in

---

[40]*Christian Record*, July, 1859 (2), pp. 214-215.

[41]J. H. Henry of Martinsville was elected president; W. W. Dowling of Indianapolis, corresponding secretary; J. H. Parsons of Noblesville, recording secretary; and A. C. Shortridge of Indianapolis, treasurer.

[42]*Christian Record*, July, 1868, p. 219. N. A. Walker, Corresponding secretary, named the participants as: Brethren Shackelford, Munnell, Filmore, Henry, Pritchard, Dowling, Gary, Goodwin, New, Brazelton, Robertson, and Bartholomew.

the Society was extended to all cooperating churches and to each member of these churches. It was decided to dispense with the office of corresponding secretary and with the thirteen-member Board of Managers; an Executive Board was empowered to administer affairs.[43] At the annual meeting the next year, 1869, the office of corresponding secretary was restored, and N. A. Walker was chosen for the position.[44]

The Indiana and American Christian Missionary Societies held annual meetings at the Christian Chapel in Indianapolis in October, 1870. The Indiana Society met on the 17th and 18th, and the American Society opened its sessions on the 19th. Both meetings were well attended by a large array of state and national celebrities.[45] An attendance of 800 to 1,000 persons was estimated. It was probably the largest "official" gathering of Disciples in Indiana to this time.

Between 1866 and 1870 Hoosier Disciples engaged in at least fourteen public debates.[46] Some of the ministers con-

---

[43]*Christian Record*, December, 1868, pp. 358-365. The Executive Board thus created was made up of the following persons: Elijah Goodwin, president; O. A. Burgess, Ryland T. Brown, and H. St. John Van Dake, vice presidents; John M. Bramwell, secretary; and Joseph M. Tilford, treasurer.

[44]*Christian Record*, December, 1869, p. 557.

[45]*Christian Record*, November, 1870, pp. 498-500. J. M. Mathes published the names of many important Disciples present. Among the older men he named: James Challen, Elijah Goodwin, H. T. Anderson, L. H. Jameson, George Campbell, S. K. Hoshour, J. B. New, B. K. Smith, J. P. Thompson, Thomas Lockhart, W. K. Pendleton, Thomas Munnell, Isaac Errett, Benjamin Franklin, Perry Blankenship, Ryland T. Brown and Jacob Wright. The younger men were named as: Jewell, the Frazees, Jones, Tyler, E. L. Frazier, Treat, R. L. Howe, W. J. Howe, Black, McCollough, Gary, Horner, J. L. Sweeney, Badger, Flower, Grigsby, the Walkers, Van Buskirk, J. C. Miller, W. H. Hopson, W. T. Moore, *et al*. Those just entering the ministry were listed as: George and Zack Sweeney, Lober, Council, Loos, Moore, and the two Flowers, etc.

[46]These debates were as follows (Disciple contestants named first):
Henry R. Pritchard—Thomas W. Brooks (differences with Methodists), Cloverdale, 1866.
O. A. Burgess—W. W. Curry (Universalism), Indianapolis, 1867.
C. P. Hollis—T. S. Brooks (Baptism), Jackson County, 1867.
William B. Chrisler—George W. Green (Materialism), Floyd County, 1867.
Jacob Wright—Robert Williams (Prayer etc.), 1868.
J. M. Mathes—T. S. Brooks (differences with Methodists), Bedford, 1868.
W. B. F. Treat—E. Hopkins (Creeds, baptism etc.), Pleasantville, 1869.
B. M. Blount—R. H. Miller (differences with Baptists), Howard County, 1869.
J. W. Stone—William Carter (Church identity), Belleville, 1869.
A. Ward—S. Bowers (differences with Methodists), Vincennes, 1869.
C. M. Robertson—Lewis Lovelace (Christian doctrines), Pike County, 1869.
J. S. Sweeney—J. W. Pike (Infidelity), Salem, 1870.
W. B. F. Treat—William McNutt (differences witth Baptists), Gosport, 1870.
J. Z. Taylor—Stephan Bowers (differences with Methodists), Bruceville, 1870.

sidered it a status symbol to be known as a debater. The comments of Professor John Young on one of these debates could be applied to most of them. He said, "Neither of the parties threw any new light on the subject." When reporting these encounters the Disciple contestant usually slanted his information to make it appear that he had won a signal victory. Writing of debates with Universalists, James Mathes declared, "We have debated with them all over the country, and 'though often vanquished, they can argue still."

Campbell's Last Tour of Indiana

Alexander Campbell had reached his "three score and ten" years when he made his last extensive tour of Indiana. By this time he had declined in health and his memory was faulty. Had it not been for the desperate need of Bethany College for financial assistance he probably would not have been motivated to attempt this arduous journey of seven weeks. The fact that he was accompanied by Mrs. Campbell and Isaac Errett indicates a concern for his health. Errett was an up-and-coming Disciples' leader and the corresponding secretary of the American Christian Missionary Society. He had just been offered a position as co-editor of the *Millennial Harbinger* and financial agent for Bethany College. While Campbell's image, as far as the issue of American slavery was concerned, was somewhat tarnished in Indiana in 1860, there was no question but that Errett was an antislavery man; as such, he would be an acceptable companion for Campbell and one whose presence would help to counteract what some Hoosiers erroneously thought to be Campbell's pro-slavery views. Elijah Goodwin and others arranged a schedule for the tour which included visitations in thirty-two places from Lafayette to New Albany and Vincennes to Richmond. The tour group met all its appointments and seventy-two discourses were given en route. The account of the tour, written by Isaac Errett and extended to two issues of the *Harbinger*,[47] provides a great deal of insight on Indiana Christian churches of the period.

The Campbells and Isaac Errett visited in Indianapolis as guests in the homes of Ovid Butler and J. M. Tilford over the Christmas holidays in 1860. In this city they met a great number of Disciple preachers, professors and students.[48]

The tour party started northwest from Indianapolis on December 27, and made a stop at Zionsville. At Lebanon, Campbell had a good audience in the courthouse. H. St. John Van Dake had just published a new pamphlet when the group visited his community, and he gave one to Errett for an appraisal. Errett's comments point up a typical Disciple view; it was too metaphysical. Errett believed that men were not to be brought to faith and repentance by metaphysical discussions, saying "it is best to load the gospel artillery with a full charge of Bible facts, evidences, promises and warnings, take steady aim at the heart, and fire away." They found the Thorntown church to be a good working congregation, but Lafayette was "feeble in religion" even though the brethren had a neat little house of worship and were under the ministry of Joseph Franklin.

From Lafayette they dropped south where they spent New Year's day in Crawfordsville. They met Governor Henry S. Lane at this place. Governor Lane was a Methodist although his mother and brother were Disciples. They went next to Ladoga where Campbell preached in the Methodist church. Errett wrote, "Our brethren have a flourishing academy here, under the care of Bro. Jno. A. Campbell, formerly of Bethany

---

[47]*Millennial Harbinger*, 1861, March, pp. 162-168; April, pp. 195-201.
[48]Among these persons were: Samuel K. Hoshour, Elijah Goodwin, Love H. Jameson, John B. New, Ryland T. Brown, Allen R. Benton, Butler K. Smith, John Bramwell, A. I. Hobbs, Madison Evans, and Perry Hall.

College. Several preachers reside here." The party next stopped at Bainbridge where they found a new meetinghouse. Higgins Lane, brother of Governor Henry S. Lane, was the minister at Bainbridge. From this place they went still further south to Greencastle, the home of Asbury University (De Pauw). Campbell was invited to preach in the Methodist church.

The next leg of their journey extended west to Terre Haute where the new city school auditorium, seating 1,200 persons, had been engaged for Campbell's appearance. From this city they dropped south again to Sullivan where they were entertained by Joseph W. Wolfe. Campbell spoke in the Methodist church at this place. They continued the journey southward until they reached Vincennes. Errett commented that this church was feeble but the spirit was good. An old Ohio acquaintance was minister at Vincennes. He was S. Burnet whose wife was the daughter of another old Ohio friend, Adamson Bentley.

From Vincennes, the party moved east to Washington where Campbell made a speech. The journey thus far had been by railroad; when it was necessary to speak at Bethany, five miles from Washington, it meant travel through five miles of mud. Errett wrote of this, "There is something quite unromantic and altogether unpoetical about mud—especially about Indiana mud." Returning to Vincennes, the group took the train to Bedford. Campbell spoke between train connections in a Presbyterian church at Mitchell. He then continued on to Bedford where he gave three discourses to "very attentive crowds." Leaving Bedford, the party traveled to Bloomington. University Hall, on the campus at the state university at Bloomington, was the setting for Campbell's next speaking engagement. The party turned south from this point, going to

185

New Albany but stopping at New Salem for a speech. Errett wrote of New Albany, "This is one of the few places in the state where we heard what we would call good singing." Campbell also heard some very disturbing news when visiting at New Albany. J. M. Mathes stated in his "autobiography" that when Campbell was staying at his home the news came to him that the Southern students at Bethany had raised the rebel flag over Bethany College. Mathes said the matter gave the old man great concern, and that he condemned this action by the Southern students and the faculty for permitting them to do it "in the most unqualified terms." Leaving New Albany, the group met an engagement at a Methodist church in Charlestown, making the journey in a comfortable carriage through deep mud. The trip up the river by steamboat to Madison was a much more pleasant one. Campbell had an audience of some 1,500 persons when he spoke at the court house on Sunday. Many Disciples came over from Kentucky to hear him.

Having reached the southern terminus of their journey the party turned North. Errett was impressed with the railroad incline outside of Madison and wrote that it was the steepest railway ascent he had ever known, an engineering feat that was a victory of mind over matter. On the way north a stop was made at Vernon. Campbell preached there, and the party was entertained in the home of Henry New. Arriving at Columbus, Campbell preached at the church. It was felt that there was great potential for good in the Columbus area. Errett considered H. R. Pritchard of that place to be an effective preacher but too much entangled in farming operations. He wrote of the church, "We have heard much of the backward condition of the cause in Columbus; but we must say, that at no point did we meet a heartier welcome, or a

186

more cheering response to our appeals. If the church is behindhand, it surely is not for lack of means to make it otherwise. The Washburns, the Cranes, the Irvins [sic], the Cobbs, and others whom we saw there, have the ability, and we cannot but believe, the *heart* to put the cause on a good footing. They have a good house—wealth—men of good judgment, and a superior worth."

At Edinburg, Campbell and Errett found a good meeting-house and a people of abundant means, but the church was not prosperous. They seemed to have more appreciation for Nineveh. Here, they found a flourishing church; John C. Miller, a Bethany graduate, was the minister. Errett wrote of this congregation, "They have here the best tact in bringing out and employing the members of the church, that we found in the State. In Bible reading, recitations, prayer and exhortations, the members are generally called into activity." Returning to Edinburg, the tour party took the train north to Franklin where Butler K. Smith was holding a protracted meeting. Campbell had to speak in the court house because the president of the college there was fearful of letting him preach in the church to which he belonged. Errett wrote, "We met only two or three such specimens of Calvinistic exclusivism on the route. They are amusing relics of a past age—regular fossils of the old Calvinistic orthodoxy, which deserve to be labeled and laid away in our museum of theological curiosities!" Going northward, the party stopped at Greenwood where Campbell spoke in the Baptist meetinghouse before going on to Indianapolis.

John B. New entertained the party in his home during the return engagement at the capital city. The Bethany College president also had an opportunity to speak to students at the North Western Christian University. He addressed the

Threshkomathean Society on the subject, "Literature, Science, Art, Politics, and Religion." Campbell met President Samuel K. Hoshour at this time and wrote that under his care the university was flourishing. On Sunday morning, Campbell preached at the Indianapolis church.

Following the Indianapolis visit, the party made a quick return trip to North Madison where Campbell preached in the Baptist church. From here they went north to Rushville where they reported a choice audience. The next engagement was at the Little Flat Rock church where Benjamin F. Reeve was the minister. George Campbell and Ephraim S. Frazee, two former Bethany College students, met Campbell at this place. The party then returned to Rushville to make train connections to Greenfield where Campbell spoke to a large assembly. They then moved on to Cambridge City. After a stopover at this place they continued on to Richmond, their last stopping place in Indiana. They found the Richmond church young and feeble, but Campbell preached to a large audience in Starr Hall, an auditorium seating 800 people.

On Monday morning, February 3, 1860, a tired tour party started back to Bethany. They had been gone from the home base over seven weeks; had traveled 2,000 miles by railroad, carriage, and steamboat; met every appointment on the schedule, and there were no accidents on the way. For a seventy-year old man in failing health it was a remarkable endurance test. Errett wrote, "Our success in pleading for Bethany College, was probably as great as, in these perilous and discouraging times, we could expect." The tour provided Hoosier Disciples with a last opportunity to see and hear Alexander Campbell and a first opportunity to get acquainted with Isaac Errett who was destined to play a large role in the history of the movement.

Literature of Hoosier Disciples, 1855-1870

Indiana Disciples produced a great deal of religious literature in this period. Professor John Young's book, *Pulpit and Platform*, was published in 1854 and became popular with the ministerial students at North Western Christian University. Elijah Goodwin prepared a volume of sermons in 1856 which he entitled, *The Family Companion*. The most significant book of the period was one published by Madison Evans in 1862. It was called, *Biographical Sketches of the Pioneer Preachers in Indiana*, and is a primary source of Indiana Disciple history. James M. Mathes was responsible for several books which were popular with Hoosier Disciples. He edited the *Works of Barton W. Stone* in 1859, and J. L. Martin's book, *Voice of the Seven Thunders*, in 1870. Mathes' *Letters to Thomas A. Morris*, D.D. was issued in book form in 1861. In 1865 he published a volume of sermons entitled, *The Western Preacher*. A few of the many debates held by Disciples in this period reached the stage of publication. They were: the *Burgess-Thompson Debate*, the *Franklin-Hume Debate*, and the *Mathes-Brooks Debate*.

The *Christian Psalmist*, a new hymnal by Silas Leonard and A. D. Fillmore, was used extensively by Hoosier Disciples at this time. It came out in three parts; the first part with round notes was issued in 1847; the second part was printed with "buckwheat" notes, and the third part with numerical notes.

In 1855, the *Christian Record* had the largest circulation of any Disciple journal except the *Millennial Harbinger*. J. M. Mathes was editor of this periodical until 1858 when he retired on his farm near Bedford and Elijah Goodwin assumed publication responsibilities. Weekly journalism became popular in the 1860's and a *Weekly Christian Record*

189

was issued along with the monthly, starting in 1862. When the *Christian Standard* began publication in Cleveland in 1866 Elijah Goodwin sold his subscription list to this magazine. This ended another phase of the *Record*. J. M. Mathes, however, revived the *Christian Record* in 1870.

Elijah Goodwin married Marcia Melissa Bassett in 1864. She was then editor of the *Ladies' Christian Monitor,* published in Cincinnati. This periodical was advertised as the only Christian magazine in the United States edited and published by a lady. It claimed to be devoted to Christianity, temperance, education, and a pure literature. When Mrs. Bassett became Mrs. Goodwin in 1864, the magazine was published at Indianapolis. Mrs. Goodwin added the *Mother's Monitor* to her publications; this was combined with the *Ladies' Christian Monitor* to form a new *Christian Monitor* in 1866. The *Christian Monitor* served as a news medium for missionary work among the Disciple women before the Christian Woman's Board of Missions was founded. Mrs. Goodwin also published the *Christian Monitor and Visitor* in 1866. It was advertised as a neat and attractive monthly conducted with taste and purity.

William W. Dowling's *The Little Sower,* a monthly for juveniles, began publication in Indianapolis in 1864. It was one of the first Sunday school papers among the Disciples. In 1866 this magazine became a semi-monthly. Dowling resigned his professorship at North Western Christian University to devote himself entirely to Sunday school work. By 1868, Dowling and Company of Indianapolis published *The Morning Watch,* a monthly for superintendents, teachers, and Bible classes; *The Little Sower,* a semi-monthly for children; and *The Little Sower and Little Chief,* a weekly for the Sunday school and family reading. The *Bible-Class Visitor* was a publication edited by William S. Winfield of Wabash,

1865-1867. Knowles Shaw edited his monthly Sunday school paper about this time from Rushville, though it was printed in Louisville. It was called *The Children's Friend*. In 1870 it was announced that the *Independent Monthly* had changed hands and would be published in Indianapolis by J. M. Tilford under the editorship of Professor Harvey W. Wiley of North Western Christian University.

End of an Era

The fifteen years, 1855-1870, which span the period before, during and after the Civil War, were perilous ones for the Disciples' movement in the Hoosier state. Indiana, though it had taken a position as a free state, had discordant political and social elements within its population which were reflected in the institutional life of the Disciples' brotherhood. The real problems rarely came to the surface in "official" meetings, except in the abortive attempt to form an antislavery missionary society at Indianapolis. They posed certain perplexing situations which hindered the growth and welfare of the movement. Neither the State Meeting nor the university project had much chance of success until the vital issues of the day were resolved by the outcome of the war.

This period of history ended the pioneer phase of the Disciples' movement in Indiana. It also marked the end of the careers of Barton W. Stone, Walter Scott, Alexander Campbell and of the original leaders of the movement in the Hoosier state. A new generation of Disciple leadership began to grapple with the problems left by the old order. The new leaders were aware of these problems and understood the sentimental attachments to the old watchwords, but they also felt a responsibility to the new era. There was a job that had to be done, and they sought expedient means of doing it within the framework of "first principles." The solutions they proposed rarely pleased the brethren. Nevertheless, persistent efforts on the part of the more progressive leaders preserved the movement in Indiana until 1870; but it was not really saved until after that time when the Sunday school movement came into its own, Disciple women began to take an active part in the life and order of the church, and some of the braver scholars dared to question the old shibboleths.

First State Meeting of Christian Churches, 1839

Kentucky Avenue Meetinghouse, Indianapolis, built in 1837 (now Central Christian Church). Hoosier Disciples held their first State Meeting here in 1839. Barton W. Stone (left) was a distinguished guest

Friday, June 7. — Pursuant to appointment many of the brethren from different parts of the State came together into the Christian Meetinghouse this day at 11 o'clock. Father Stone, of Jacksonville Ills. Bro. A. Crihfield of Middlebury Ohio, Bro. John Taffe, of Kentucky, and between 30 and 40 preaching brethren of the State of Indiana were present. Father Stone, bro. Crihfield, O'Kane & Taffe and others alternately proclaimed the Word through four successive days, and twelve persons were baptized during these days.

Lordsday, June 9, 1839. — Father Stone accepted an invitation to preach in the M. E. Chapel this day. — Audience large and attentive. Bro. Crihfield & Taffe preached in the Christian Meetinghouse. Not sufficient accommodations for the hearers. John Shortridge, Ellen Shortridge, and Esther McNabb, of the immersed this day, were added to the congregation. Supper at Candle-lighting.

Facsimile of church records concerning the event

Mrs. Zerelda Wallace Militant leader for temperance and women's rights

First Court House in Marion County, built in 1824-25. Housed State Legislature, State and Federal Courts, and County Offices

Governor's residence in Indianapolis. Governor and Mrs. David (Zerelda) Wallace lived here when Disciples had first State Meeting in 1839. Mrs. Wallace was a charter member of Central Christian Church. Location: northwest corner of Illinois and Markets Streets

Pioneer Christian Church Editors

Elijah Goodwin   *The Christian Record*   James M. Mathes

Benjamin Franklin
The Reformer

Mrs. M. M. B. Goodwin
The Christian Monitor

Nathaniel Field
The Israelite

Helen E. Moses
Missionary Tidings

Looking Back: Distinguished Indiana Ministers

John Chapman
Miller

Elijah Martindale

H. R. Pritchard

Daniel E. Lucas

Jabez Hall

J. V. Combs

Z. T. Sweeney

W. H. Book

Joseph C. Todd

Allan B. Philputt

T. W. Grafton

Frank E. Davison

Field workers of the Indiana Christian Sunday School Association. Photo taken at Bethany Park in 1908. Left to right: Garry L. Cook, T. J. Legg, C. M. Fillmore, and L. L. Carpenter

Fifth Annual Bethany Park Summer School of Methods, 1914

Administrative Districts of the State Meeting in 1842

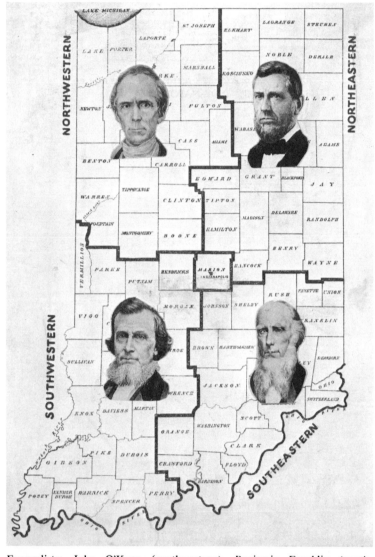

Evangelists: John O'Kane (northwestern), Benjamin Franklin (north-eastern), J. M. Mathes (southwestern), Ryland T. Brown (southeastern)

Administrative Districts of the State Society in 1914

Evangelists: A. L. Martin (northern), T. J. Legg (central-western), G. I. Hoover (central-eastern), Melnotte Miller (southwestern), Fred R. Davies (southwestern). Transportation was provided by "Model T" roadsters, the gift of Marshall T. Reeves

Butler University: Three locations

First building, Thirteenth Street and College Avenue, Indianapolis. Known as North Western Christian University, this building was occupied from 1855 to 1875

Photo of scale model of Butler University when it was located at Irvington, 1875-1927

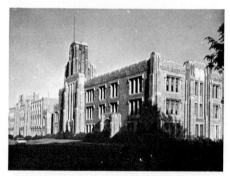

Arthur Jordan Memorial Hall, first building erected on the new Fairview campus in Indianapolis, 1928

Some New Buildings on the Butler Campus and Presidents in the New Construction Period

Irwin Library, dedicated 1965

M. O. Ross,
1942-1962

Alexander E.
Jones, 1963-

Clowes Hall, opened 1963

Educating the Ministry

Erected as the School of Religion building of Butler University in 1942, this building served as an educational center for training ministers until 1966 when Christian Theological Seminary moved to its new campus. Inserts: left, Frederick D. Kershner, dean 1924-1944; right, Orman L. Shelton, dean 1944-1958

College of Religion Faculty, 1927. Left to right, first row: Tobert L. Reavis, E. R. Moon, Bruce L. Kershner, Dean Frederick D. Kershner. Second row: Rabbi Morris M. Feuerlicht, Toyozo W. Nakarai, William F. Bacon, T. W. Grafton, Allena Grafton, William Shullenberger. Not shown: G. I. Hoover, H. Parr Armstrong

Christian Theological Seminary

Ceremony of laying the cornerstone of the School of Religion. Left to right: William G. Irwin, President D. S. Robinson, John W. Atherton, and Dean Frederick D. Kershner

Removing contents of cornerstone of School of Religion building on January 7, 1966. Left to right: Dr. Henry K. Shaw (Librarian), Dr. Robert F. Sullivan (Vice-President Butler University), Dr. David C. Pellett (C.T.S. Acting Dean), George L. Varnes (C.T.S. Trustee), and Dr. Beauford A. Norris (C.T.S. President)

Presidents of The United Christian Missionary Society

F. W. Burnham,
1919-1929

Virgil A. Sly,
1965-

H. B. McCormick,
1946-1951

A. Dale Fiers,
1951-1964

Stephen J. Corey, 1930-1938   Robert M. Hopkins, 1939-1946

Distinguished Christian Church Laymen

Ryland T. Brown

Ovid Butler

Joseph I. Irwin

Marshall T. Reeves

William G. Irwin

Hugh Th. Miller

J. Irwin Miller

Hilton U. Brown

Matthew E. Welch

Association Camp and Conference Grounds

One of five cabins at Barbee Christian Camp

Dining Hall and Lodge—Bedford Christian Camp

Retreat House—Indian Lake Christian Retreat

Camps and Conferences

Senior High young people attending conference at Indian Lake Retreat

Chi Rho campers at Bedford Christian Camp
in 1964

Discussion group at Christian Men's Fellowship Retreat at Indian Lake in
1963

Recent Significant Events

Celebrating the success of the United Capital Funds Appeal. Launched in 1962, the goal of $2,738,426 was exceeded by the deadline date in 1963. Insert shows Miss Elsie I. Sweeney, representing the Irwin-Sweeney-Miller Foundation, presenting a $200,000 check to Dr. John Harms and Doyle Zaring.

Group in lobby of Clowes Hall, Indianapolis, where the 125th annual State Convention of the Christian Churches was held in 1964

VI

New Horizons

1871-1882

THE OLD ORDER COLLAPSED for Hoosier Disciples in the early 1870's. The adoption of the Louisville Plan on a national level in 1869 was an attempt to get additional mileage from a worn-out ecclesiastical vehicle. The plan did not succeed in reaching its desired objectives, but it achieved limited success in some areas. Concurrent to the diminishing interest in the Indiana Christian Missionary Society in this period there developed an intense loyalty to the new Sunday school enterprise. The Sunday school provided an outlet for religious enthusiasm and became a center for experimentation in progressive faith. Because it was not thought to be the church, it did not come under the restrictions and limitations of the elder-deacon dominated local church body. It was free to function in the area of religion and morality in a manner consistent with the advancing thought of the times. The development of women's work, especially as it was expressed in the Christian Woman's Board of Missions, was another facet by which religious faith was made functional to a heretofore restricted group. The "sisters" came into their own in the middle 1870's and in due time assumed more than their share of ecclesiastical responsibilities. The Sunday school and the C. W. B. M. upset the old power structure of the local church and became a leavening influence which contributed to saving local congregations from self-imposed senility.

The Louisville Plan and the General Convention

The General Convention with its Louisville Plan was projected as an answer to the criticism leveled at the American Christian Missionary Society, that as an organization it had usurped the authority of the church. Many conservatives held that the Society was *not* the church, and that it had no right to act in the capacity of the church. They had missionary zeal for what they called the Disciples' *plea,* but they seriously lacked the stewardship to back up their convictions. Failing to understand this area of serious weakness they placed the responsibility for their missionary failures on structure and organization. The Louisville Plan, adopted in 1869, was received enthusiastically as a corrective measure which would return missionary control to the local church. Under the Louisville Plan[1] missionary work would no longer be supported by individuals—life members and life directors of the missionary society—but by the church itself, acting as the church. In principle, the plan had a great deal of merit; considered on the basis of practical results, the plan was a failure. Congregationally-governed churches in the seventies were not conditioned to act responsibly in the raising and disbursing of missionary funds.

The Louisville Plan was an attempt to structure the brotherhood in a quasi-hierarchical pattern; the churches sent official messengers to the district meetings, each district sent delegates to the State Meeting, and the State Meeting was entitled to be represented on the Board of the General Convention

---

[1]For a fuller discussion of the plan see, T. W. Grafton, "The Transition Period," J. H. Garrison (editor) *The Reformation of the Nineteenth Century* (St. Louis: Christian Publishing Company, 1901), pp. 296-305.

through its corresponding secretary, two delegates, and an additional delegate for each 5,000 members in the state.

The plan was accepted with enthusiasm in Indiana. J. H. McCollough, state evangelist, requested every church in the state to make a donation to missionary work.[2] He explained that the general plan which had been adopted by all the states anticipated that local ministers would request missionary offerings from the churches so that it would not be necessary to send agents to the congregations for this purpose; this was to keep overhead expenses at a minimum. Missionary money raised by this means would be sent to the district organization. The district would keep one-half of the amount to employ good evangelists to work within the district and send the other half to the State Society. McCollough advised that the churches pay the evangelist for his work if possible, and receipts over and above expenses should be designated as missionary funds and be sent to the state organization. It was thought that by this means the stronger churches could have the service of a minister and at the same time assist the weaker churches in the district to have preaching also.

To expedite this matter the state was divided into five missionary districts,[3] and attempts were made to organize each district into an effective working unit with its own board, corresponding secretary, evangelists, and quarterly meeting. The Indiana Christian Missionary Convention of 1871 was held at the city of Kokomo the following October. The large

---

[2]*Christian Record and Living Laborer,* January, 1871, pp. 16-18.

[3]The counties in these districts were as follows: (1) Hendricks, Boone, Hamilton, Hancock, Shelby, Johnson, Morgan, Marion; (2) Madison, Wayne, Henry, Howard, Randolph, Grant, Jay, Blackford, Miami, Wabash, Huntington, Adams, Wells, Kosciusko, Whitley, Allen, Noble, De Kalb, Tipton, Elkhart, Lagrange, Steuben, Delaware; (3) Putnam, Fountain, Warren, Montgomery, Tippecanoe, Clinton, Benton, Carroll, White, Newton, Cass, Fulton, Jasper, Vermillion, Starke, Pulaski, Marshall, Porter, Lake, La Porte, St. Joseph; (4) Owen, Monroe, Clay, Vigo, Green, Sullivan, Gibson, Martin, Lawrence, Davies, Knox, Orange, Crawford, Dubois, Pike, Perry, Spencer, Warrick, Vanderburg, Posey; (5) Fayette, Rush, Union, Franklin, Decatur, Bartholomew, Ripley, Dearborn, Jennings, Ohio, Switzerland, Jefferson, Jackson, Scott, Washington, Clark, Brown, Floyd, Harrison.

attendance expected at this convention was not realized. It was apparent that the districts had been strengthened under the new plan, but the state organization had been weakened. By the time the State Society received what little missionary money the districts thought they could release, there was little left over for division with the national organization. L. L. Carpenter was elected corresponding secretary at the Kokomo convention with a specific assignment of helping the districts to organize and become effective as soon as possible.

The plan produced good results at the district level in Indiana. It could hardly do otherwise with a man like L. L. Carpenter in the driver's seat. He went from church to church to hold protracted meetings, locate ministers and organize new congregations. He sent detailed reports of his activities to the *Christian Standard* and the *Christian Record*. Not even the "whistle stops" were too unimportant to be mentioned by Carpenter. The promotion of the Fort Wayne mission was the biggest project undertaken by the Board at this time. The general appeal made to the Hoosier brotherhood in the raising of building funds was so successful that N. J. Aylsworth, who preached at Fort Wayne, protested that solicitors from Tennessee, Kansas, Nebraska and Iowa, thinking Indiana to be a lush territory, had moved in to exploit Disciple resources for buildings in their own states.[4] Aylsworth commented, "Until a 'church extension fund' can be raised, each state and each county should do its own work." Twenty-two churches were organized in the state between the conventions of 1871 and 1872. Missionary work in the districts was one of the better features of the Louisville Plan.

The State Convention at Rushville in 1872 was one of the best of many years.[5] There were reports given from 261

[4]*Christian Standard*, April 19, 1872.
[5]*Christian Standard*, October 26, 1872.

churches. Of these, 47 had regular preaching each week, 87 had semi-monthly preaching, 99 had monthly preaching, and 42 reported no regular preaching. There were 213 organized Sunday schools with 1,917 teachers among the reporting churches. The statistics also show that $68,200 had been expended by the churches for regular preaching and $8,500 for transient preaching. The churches had raised $5,130 for missions. On the basis of the statistics of reporting churches the brethren estimated there were 625 churches in the state; these churches had approximately 65,625 members, 300 preachers, 510 Sunday schools, 53,550 persons in the Sunday school program, and 4,590 Sunday school teachers.

An article in the *Christian Record*[6] sounded a warning toward the direction being taken by leaders of the Disciples' cause in Indiana. It suggested that a mistake may have been made in using the words "missions" and "missionary work" to represent the systematic program of evangelizing the world and that an occasional visit from a traveling preacher, with the assistance of a "big meeting" once a year, would no longer suffice to build up and sustain churches. The author stated, "It takes a heap of money to keep up anything like missionary effort," and that "a man who waits for that perfect machinery in which grace only will grease the axles, and love alone furnish the driving power, while no bad men become preachers and no mistakes are ever made in our well-meant efforts to evangelize the world, will probably die with his hands in his pockets and his eyes set on empty space."

The brethren of the Rushville convention of 1872 determined to make a strong effort to raise $25,000 in the state the next year for missionary purposes. They estimated this would mean an average contribution of 75 or 80 cents per

---

[6]*Christian Record, December,* 1872.

member and one which could be easily realized. No mention is made in the journals of reaching the $25,000 goal by the time of the Wabash convention of 1873. The next year, however, it was reported at the Bedford convention[7] that over $25,000 had been raised in missionary money and that it had been judiciously expended in different parts of the state. Dr. Ryland T. Brown and John M. Bramwell, who had served as president and secretary of the convention for many years, declined re-election in 1874. They were succeeded in office by J. L. Parsons, president; W. W. Dowling, recording secretary; and W. R. Couch, corresponding secretary.

The Panic of 1873

The effects of the great panic of 1873 soon caught up with the brethren. For the nation, the panic meant the end of what has been since described as the "gilded age." Shortly after President Grant took office for his second term the national economic system collapsed. Currency inflation and easy credit had poured capital into business enterprises to the extent that production of consumers' goods soon exceeded consumption. Some 5,000 business concerns failed in 1873, and three million wage earners joined the ranks of the unemployed. This was also a period in which graft and corruption in politics were being exposed. It was five years before the nation returned to some degree of normalcy. Had it not been for the panic of 1873 it is possible that the Louisville Plan and the delegate convention system (with modifications) could have been saved. It was well-administered in Indiana by L. L. Carpenter. Though the Louisville Plan, *per se,* failed to provide adequate funds for missionary work abroad it was an excellent source of motivation for missionary expansion

---

[7]*Christian Standard,* November 14, 1874.

within the local districts in Indiana. Thomas Munnell, national administrator of the plan, wrote[8] that though the plan had been repeatedly pronounced dead and dying during its first five years, it had added 32,000 members to the churches, expended $309,000 in the task, encouraged thousands of weak churches and organized hundreds of new ones. He pointed out that among additions to the membership were some 5,000 Freedmen, and that a school to train Negro ministers had been established in Louisville.

When the convention of the Indiana Christian Missionary Society was held at Indianapolis in 1875 it was apparent that the economic depression had hurt the attendance. Many more persons were present, however, than were expected at the convention in 1876 when the brethren met at Fort Wayne. W. R. Couch, corresponding secretary, reported that he had not been able to give the Society much of his time during the year because of business problems. The convention elected L. L. Carpenter as corresponding secretary. He held this position through the conventions at Indianapolis in 1877, Noblesville in 1878, and Greensburg in 1879. Carpenter worked hard for the cause in Indiana. He wrote[9] that he knew of twenty-five places in the Hoosier State where churches could be opened with one protracted meeting costing $25 only. Twenty-five such meetings, according to Carpenter, would cost $625. He concluded that if each of the 625 churches in Indiana would contribute one dollar the amount could be raised.

The national economy had improved when the convention was held at Noblesville in October of 1878.[10] By this time the Indiana C. W. B. M. and the State Ministerial Association

[8]*Christian Monitor*, April, 1875.
[9]*Christian Standard*, April, 1875.
[10]*Christian Standard*, October 19, 1878.

were holding annual meetings in conjunction with that of the State Society. The Sunday School Association, however, had its annual meeting at another place on another date. According to J. A. Roberts, convention president in 1878, there were many inviting fields open to Indiana Disciples which could not be occupied at that time.

The attention of the convention was called to the unfortunate death of Knowles Shaw who had lost his life in a train wreck in Texas. Shaw, a Rush County man, had been ordained in the Milroy church and was known personally by most Disciples in this area. His evangelistic ministry had extended to the entire country. It was reported that some 20,000 persons had been converted in his meetings. Primarily a singing evangelist, he composed many gospel songs which found universal acceptance. Among these was his well-known "Bringing in the Sheaves." Shaw was so popular and well loved that 2,000 persons, representing many denominations, were present when funeral services were held for him in Courthouse Park, Rushville, June 13, 1878.

Announcements concerning the convention at Greensburg, October 7-9, 1879, stated that conventions had been small in recent years but now an "old time" convention was desired. Timothy Coop of England, Isaac Errett and other distinguished Disciples were featured as speakers. At the business sessions, J. A. Roberts was re-elected as president and L. Berry Smith became the new corresponding secretary.[11] The convention at Rushville in 1880 was a disappointment to the brethren because the attendance was small and the amount of money raised for state missions was insignificant. There was a major change of officers in the State Society made at this meeting. A. R. Benton was elected president; W. H.

---

[11]*Christian Standard,* September 13, 1879.

Drapier, corresponding secretary; Simeon Frazier, treasurer; and J. M. Bramwell, recording secretary.[12] The State C. W. B. M. and the Ministerial Association also held annual meetings at this time.

The report of Disciples' churches to the United States Census of 1880 was published in *The Evangelist*.[13] The information, gathered by a special committee of the General Missionary Convention, shows the comparative strength of the movement in five midwestern states.

	Churches	Preachers	Members
Illinois	775	650	85,000
Kentucky	595	485	79,525
Indiana	675	580	78,950
Missouri	565	395	60,950
Ohio	425	217	45,500

Many of the brethren took exception to these statistics and claimed they were not accurate. Nevertheless, they were probably as correct as could be obtained with existing facilities and resources. The population of Indiana was over two million people in 1880. Additional statistical material concerning religion and morality in the Hoosier State, prepared by the Bureau of Statistics which had been created by the Indiana Legislature in 1878,[14] provides an interesting study in Hoosierana. According to this report there were thirty-three different denominations or sects in Indiana; the Methodists led in sixty counties and the Disciples in six. The churches had a total membership of 820,833 persons, indicating that approximately 41 per cent of Indiana's residents were church members. The average annual salary for ministers was given as $454.45. There were 3,492 ministers and priests who served in 4,857 church buildings. The report also contained

---

[12]*Christian Standard*, October 23, 1880.
[13]*The Evangelist*, November 4, 1880.
[14]*The Evangelist*, September 29, 1881.

the interesting data than Indiana had 4,760 persons classed as "deadbeats" and 2,895 persons who claimed they were habitual drunkards. Taking this into consideration and the fact that the report also stated that Indiana had 3,060 lewd men and 2,777 lewd women at the time, it would seem that the church had a large work cut out for it.

Four Conventions in One

From 1878 to 1881 the State Society, State Ministerial Association and State Christian Woman's Board of Missions held annual meetings at the same convention. The convention of 1881,[15] held at Union City in August, included the State Sunday School Association also. Notices of this gathering stressed the idea of having four conventions in one. The striking feature of the Union City convention was the all-pervading Sunday school program. It was the chief interest of Hoosier Disciples in this period. The Sunday School Association used more convention time than all the other organizations combined. The Indiana Christian Missionary Society was in bad condtion; there was no enthusiasm for it, and nobody seemed to care. The total receipts for the year amounted to only $41.65. The disbursements were $6.98. This left a balance in the treasury of $34.67.

The General Missionary Convention of the Disciples was held at Indianapolis in October of 1881.[16] Some 500 persons attended the sessions of the General Society, Woman's Society, and the Foreign Christian Missionary Society. The convention accepted the recommendation of its Board of Managers that the Constitution of the General Society be amended to admit life members and life directors. This action was the death blow to the Louisville Plan.

---

[15]*Christian Standard,* August 13, 20, 1881.
[16]*The Evangelist,* October 27, 1881; *Christian Standard,* November 12, 1881.

The convention format, inaugurated at the Island Park[17] convention at Rome City in August, 1882, set a new pattern that characterized the Indiana conventions for many years. In fact, the meeting was not called a convention but an encampment. L. L. Carpenter and his colleagues were enamored with the "Chautauqua" idea and sought to make an application of it to the convention program. Island Park was a resort area with hotels, mineral springs, boating and other entertainment features; it was well suited to accommodate a program of this nature. The State Society was not only overshadowed by the Sunday School Association but by the encampment as a whole. This was not all; representatives from several states met here at the same time and as part of the encampment, to form the General Christian Sunday School Association with Constitution and By-laws.

There is no question but that Hoosier Disciples had reached a new period in their corporate life and were no longer satisfied with simple strategy and business meetings; they wanted to have a good time at their conventions. H. R. Pritchard, state evangelist, declared, "The Christian Church of Indiana, with nearly one hundred thousand men and women, is today a sleeping giant, and could, if properly aroused, revolutionize this western world, and all that is wanted is to quit nonsense and go to work."[18] It seems quite apparent that by this time the church no longer wanted to be the church; it wanted to be the Sunday school!

The Sunday School Movement Forges Ahead

A State Sunday School Association was organized in Indianapolis at the 1867 convention. Semi-annual meetings (conventions) were held with great success. By 1870, when

---

[17]*The Evangelist*, July 20, 1882.
[18]*Christian Standard*, September 2, 1882.

the convention was held at Wabash,[19] over one thousand persons were in attendance. The Sunday school movement created more interest, developed greater enthusiasm, and reached more people than any movement the Disciples had ever before embraced in Indiana. The Association was strong enough by 1870 to support a full-time worker in the field, and William W. Dowling was selected for this post. Dowling, a former faculty member at North Western Christian University, was the leading professional Sunday school worker among the Disciples, and he had been publishing Sunday school literature since 1864. The driving force behind the movement in Indiana, however, was Leewell L. Carpenter[20] who had moved to Wabash from Ohio in 1868. Carpenter served the Indiana Sunday School Association as president for five years and then became its state evangelist. The winter convention at Bedford in 1871 showed an attendance increase over the Wabash convention of a few months before. The Sunday school conventions were helpful and instructive; lectures and demonstration lessons were presented to the delegates. Attendance reports were featured at these meetings[21] and a spirit of friendly rivalry and competition among the schools was fostered with apparent good results. The summer convention of 1871 was held in the village hall at La Porte.[22]

---

[19]*Christian Standard,* September 17, 24, 1870.

[20]Leewell L. Carpenter (1832-1910) was born in Summit County, Ohio. After attending Mt. Union and Bethany colleges he located in Fulton County, Ohio (Wauseon) in 1857 where he preached, organized churches, and held evangelistic meetings. He moved to Wabash, Indiana in 1868, and this became his home for forty-two years. Carpenter was corresponding secretary and state evangelist at various times for both the Indiana Christian Missionary Society and the Indiana State Sunday School Association. An indefatigable worker, he held Sunday school institutes throughout the state, conducted evangelistic meetings, revived old congregations and organized new ones. Carpenter was the leading spirit in the Bethany Park Assembly project, serving as administrative officer for twenty-five years. He was said to have dedicated 752 church buildings (meaning he was an excellent money raiser) and he claimed to have baptized over 7,000 persons.

[21]*Christian Standard,* June 10, 1871. The average Sunday school attendance, as reported by the various schools, was as follows: Salem 50, Mitchell 50, Orleana 41, White River Union 45, Green Castle Junction 28, Green Castle 125, Seymour 35, Columbus 146, Campbellsburg 60, Bedford 200, Gosport 75, Vincennes 80, Stilesville 35, Bloomington 175, Greensburg 200, Kokomo 160, Logotee 90.

[22]*Christian Standard,* August 28, 1871.

Train excursions with special rates, stopping at principal cities
to pick up delegates, were arranged for this meeting. Sunday
schools were urged to have their delegates bring banners and
ensigns for display. The temper of the times was expressed in
an unusual speech by Isaac Errett, editor of the *Christian
Standard,* on this occasion. He told the convention that most
churches had too much preaching, calling it a "stuffing"
process whereby too much indigestible matter was given out
too frequently, resulting in a state of torpor. The Bible class,
he claimed, was the remedy.

The Sunday school picnic, delight of Hoosier Disciples for
many years, had its origin about this time. One such picnic
was reported at Mather's Grove near Clear Creek Station on
June 13, 1871.[23] W. B. F. Treat wrote that from 1,500 to
2,000 persons attended this event. They came from Mitchell,
Bedford, Clear Creek, Bloomington, Harrodsville, Smithville
and South Union. The Bloomington delegation alone filled
four coaches. Treat wrote that it was a glorious sight, the day
was fine, and the dinner abundant. He was impressed by
what he called a vast audience of happy people. In his opinion
it was evident that the "Reformation" was fast becoming a
power in the land.

The Sunday school convention at Greensburg in August,
1872,[24] was another "colossal" success. L. L. Carpenter presided over it, and Professor A. C. Hopkins[25] of Kokomo led
the delegates in the song services. The reports of this meeting
made the claim that Indiana Disciples now had 550 Sunday
schools with 6,000 teachers and 65,000 scholars. Editor W.

[23]*Christian Record and Living Laborer,* August, 1871.

[24]*Christian Standard,* September 7, 1872; *Christian Record,* September, 1872.

[25]Alexander Campbell and his brother John O'Kane Hopkins were sons of Milton
B. Hopkins. All three were professors at Howard College in Kokomo. Milton B.
Hopkins was also State Superintendent of Education. Robert M. Hopkins, president
of the United Christian Missionary Society and Disciple leader, was the son of
Alexander Campbell Hopkins.

B. F. Treat was so enthusiastic about Sunday schools that he compared them to catechetical schools of the early Christian era; he even claimed the modern Sunday school was better because "we have the Bible." His comments were constructive, however, in that he stated that in the future the Sunday schools should recognize the church and not be independent organizations. He believed that Christ should be taught in the Bible school and that the faithful performance of the Sunday school should be the responsibility of the church. The convention of 1873 was held at New Castle[26] with J. W. McGarvey as the featured speaker. Love H. Jameson was present; when this white-haired old patriarch sang his original hymns the convention was deeply moved.

The *Christian Record,* a journal that had always been somewhat on the conservative side, recognized the Sunday school movement in 1875 by changing its name to *Christian Record and Sunday School Worker.*[27] The magazine then began featuring a Sunday school department with articles and stories about Sunday schools in each issue. L. L. Carpenter became a regular contributor to the periodical after this. By this time Carpenter had been appointed as full-time agent for the Sunday school association and stated that he intended to visit every city in the state, hold institutes and conventions, and work with Sunday school superintendents. He wrote, "The time has come for a forward movement in the Sunday school work." By April, 1875, he had changed hats again; he informed Hoosier Disciples that he was taking the field as corresponding secretary of the Indiana Christian Missionary Society and planned to promote offerings for missionary work.[28] During his long career in general work in Indiana,

---

[26]*Christian Standard,* August 16, 1873.
[27]*Christian Record and Sunday School Worker,* January, 1875. This name was kept on the masthead but a few months.
[28]*Christian Record and Sunday School Worker,* April, 1875.

Carpenter served on and off with the missionary society and the Sunday school association and was president and corresponding secretary of both organizations at various times. There seems to have never been any criticism of his frequent changes of responsibility, and all the organizations were happy to get his services when possible.

The Sunday school convention for 1875 was scheduled for Greencastle but had to be cancelled because of heavy rains. Carpenter reported,[29] however, that Sunday schools had more than doubled in the last five years and that three-fifths of the church accessions came through the Sunday school program. No Hoosier Disciple ever excelled Carpenter in enthusiasm and optimism. He wrote of the Greencastle convention which was never held, "Could the convention have been held, we confidently believe that it would have been the largest, the most intelligent, the most enthusiastic, and, indeed, the *very best one* Indiana has ever held."

The temperature was in the nineties during the Columbus convention of 1876.[30] In spite of this the crowds were large, and delegates were attentive to the nine and one-half hours of program each day. The next June, in 1877, an interstate Sunday school convention was held at Union City. Carpenter presided here over a large delegation of Sunday school workers from Ohio and Indiana.[31] Two months later the Indiana Christian Sunday School Association had its own convention at Rushville.[32] In giving notice of the convention, Joseph W. Conner wrote, "The financial troubles through which the country has passed, have checked and sobered

---

[29]*Christian Standard,* August 28, 1875.
[30]*Christian Standard,* August 12, 1876.
[31]*Christian Standard,* June 9, 1877.
[32]*Christian Standard,* July 21, 1877.

many, so that they are now ready to hear the word." There were 125 schools reporting at the Wabash convention, August 6-9, 1878.[33] Carpenter was made state Sunday school evangelist at this meeting, and the state was districted into twenty-two sections, each presided over by a vice president. In the spring of 1879 the state Sunday school association held a convention at Columbus. Other state organizations were represented at this convention, but interest was centered in Sunday school work. The convention raised $1,200 to keep Carpenter in the field as Sunday school evangelist.[34] Within three months he had visited churches in eighteen counties and was holding Sunday school institutes in each community on his itinerary. By this time he was urging the use of the International Sunday school lessons and advocating the introduction of "temperance" instruction in the schools. The convention for 1880 was held at Danville. In addition to the local people some 400 persons were present from outside the community. This convention claimed to be one of Sunday school workers (not preachers).[35]

The church at Rushville, A. N. Gilbert, pastor, entertained the combined conventions in the fall of 1880.[36] The attendance was poorer than it had been for many years. The excuse was given that because the convention was held on the day after election the Republicans were feeling good, and

---

[33]*Christian Standard*, August 17, 24, 1878.

[34]*Christian Standard*, April 9, 1879.

[35]*The Evangelist*, August 19, 1880. Though it was reported that this was not a convention of preachers the following preachers were present: J. A. Beatty, B. A. Hinsdale, Isaac Errett, O. A. Burgess, G. P. Peale, J. M. Land, John Burns, T. M. Mason, L. H. Jameson, U. C. Brewer, S. J. Tomlinson, D. H. Gary, J. M. Mathes, R. T. Matthews, Aaron Walker, E. L. Frazier, William S. Winfield, A. H. Morris, J. S. Becknell, L. Berry Smith, J. L. Parsons, J. B. Maysfield, J. C. Barnhill, G. L. Harney, J. M. Monroe, C. T. Hendershot, H. B. Davis, J. P. Orr, A. N. Gilbert, T. M. Wiles, Amzi Atwater, Thomas Lockart, J. C. Tully, James W. Conner, Sr., R. M. Stevens, D. N. Goodykuntz, H. R. Pritchard, and H. H. Roberts.

[36]*The Evangelist*, December 9, 1880.

the Democrats bad, and "neither party was in first-class shape to attend a missionary meeting and attend to business as Christians should." The Indiana C. W. B. M. and the state ministerial association each held annual business meetings at this convention. The most significant action at the meeting was the selection of a Sunday school board and the placing of the Sunday school association and the state missionary society in the hands of one administration.

The political campaign which resulted in the inauguration of James A. Garfield as President of the United States on March 4, 1881, was the occasion for much publicity being given to the Disciples' movement. Garfield was a loyal Disciple and a former President of Hiram College; he was regarded as one of the "preaching" brethren because in his younger days he had preached in Disciple pulpits, held protracted meetings, conducted funerals and officiated at weddings. Garfield was the first Disciple and the only minister to have held the high office of the Presidency. He was wounded by an assassin's bullet a few weeks after his inauguration and never recovered. His death occurred on September 19, 1881. The anxiety following the shooting and the sorrow attending Garfield's death was felt by the whole nation. He was quite well known by Disciples in Indiana; North Western Christian University had conferred the honorary degree of Doctor of Laws on him in 1871 when he was then a congressman.

When the convention of the state organizations was held at Union City[37] in August of 1881 there was hope of Garfield's recovery, and many prayers were given on his behalf. The General Missionary Convention[38] was held in Indianapolis

---

[37]*Christian Standard*, August 13, 20, 1881.
[38]Francis M. Wiley, *The History of Central Christian Church, op. cit.*, p. 48.

in October of the same year. The attendance was estimated at about 600 persons among whom was the widow of Alexander Campbell. This was said to be the first convention in the history of the Disciples in which women took part on an equality with men. The national C. W. B. M. also observed an annual meeting at this convention. Mrs. Zerelda Wallace gave one of the addresses. Hoosier Disciples were proud of Mrs. Maria Jameson who presided over the C. W. B. M. sessions "with skill and grace."

The State Convention of 1882 at Island Park, near Rome City, held in August, set a new pattern for gatherings of Indiana Disciples, and one which was followed for many years.[39] The Sunday school movement, as usual, claimed the chief interest of the delegates.

Indiana Women Lead the Way

The status of women in American society began to change in the period following the Civil War. Certain leaders among them began to talk and write about women's rights and the equality of the sexes; the idea eventually took structural patterns which affected the whole social and political life of the nation. The National Woman's Suffrage Association and the Woman's Christian Temperance Union, formed in this period, are representative of organizations which challenged the long-established tradition of male leadership. The struggle for women's rights in America—even the methods used to obtain recognition for the movement—parallels the civil rights struggle of 1964-65. The women's rights movement had its repercussions in the churches. Women were no longer satisfied to play a minor and passive role in church life; they were not

---

[39]*The Evangelist,* April 27, July 20, 1882; *Christian Standard,* September 2, 1882.

too happy about the way men were running things, especially in regard to missionary work, and they were determined to do something about it.

According to a paper read by Mrs. Maria Jameson at Indianapolis and published in the *Christian Monitor*,[40] a small group of "Dorcas" women from Central Christian Church of Indianapolis were meeting in the home of Mrs. Zerelda Wallace in July of 1874, when a special letter from Mrs. C. N. Pearre of Iowa City, Iowa, was read to them. Mrs. Pearre was captivated with the missionary cause, and the letter proposed that Disciple women do as some women in other religious bodies had already done, *i.e.* form missionary societies in local churches. The Indianapolis women discussed the matter in subsequent meetings and finally decided to form themselves into a missionary society by the election of officers and the adoption of a set of rules. Mrs. Jameson stated that they desired at the time to encourage the missionary spirit, "The main idea being to enlist in our work every woman and child within reach; to pick up the crumbs, as it were, the pennies and nickles that are being wasted and thrown away for naught and scattered for the merest trifles, and devote themselves to this good cause." When the General Convention convened in Cincinnati that year many more members had been added to the local group, and the missionary society had expanded to include women from the other Christian churches of the city. This organization, therefore, was already tailor-made to furnish leadership for the Christian Woman's Board of Missions when it was constituted at the General Convention in 1874. Indianapolis immediately became the headquarters

---

[40]*Christian Monitor*, October, 1875; History Committee, *125 Significant Years, the Story of Central Christian Church, Indianapolis* (Indianapolis: McDaniel Press, 1958), p. 30.

for the national society, and Indianapolis women dominated the leadership of the organization for many years.[41]

Mrs. M. M. B. Goodwin[42] of Indianapolis, editor of the *Christian Monitor,* gave one of the principal addresses[43] at the Cincinnati General Convention of 1874. Speaking on behalf of the women in the Christian churches, she stressed the need of organized effort on their part to increase the sphere of their usefulness and inspire others to duty. Mrs. Goodwin claimed that about all that church women were allowed to do for the church was to distribute tracts, circulate subscription papers, teach Sunday school classes, prepare floral offerings and sing praises in corporate worship. She added that women were considered to be "one talent" church members, that talent for the most part being buried in the earth. The hope was expressed that the woman's missionary society, constituted at the convention, would afford scope for a portion of hitherto unemployed talent in the church. The pertinent observation was made, "The brother who contributes less to the missionary cause than he spends for tobacco, has not the true missionary spirit. The sister who thinks more of the lace on her handkerchief than the enlightenment of the soul of her washerwoman's child, has small conception of her religious duties." This was not a militant "women's rights" speech; Mrs. Goodwin declared she had no desire to discuss the rights of women, either in or out of church, but that she was appre-

---

[41]Mrs. P. H. (Maria) Jameson, daughter of Ovid Butler, was president 1874-1880, 1881-1890, and corresponding secretary 1880-1881. Mrs. William (Sarah) Wallace, daughter of Love H. Jameson, was recording secretary 1874-1876, 1887-1889, and corresponding secretary 1875-1880. Mrs. O. A. Burgess was treasurer 1874-1878, president 1880, 1881, vice president 1887-1890, and president again 1890-1902. Mrs. Sarah E. Shortridge was corresponding secretary 1881-1890, and editor of *Missionary Tidings* 1888-1890. Miss Marie Cole was recording secretary 1876-1878; Mrs. Naomi Tomlinson, 1878-1890; Mrs. Lizzie A. Moore, 1880-1887. Mrs. Ryland T. Brown was treasurer 1878-1880; Mrs. Mary C. Cole, 1880-1890. Mrs. M. M. B. Goodwin was first editor of *Missionary Tidings,* 1883. *See* Ida Withers Harrison, *Forty Years of Service, A History of the Christian Woman's Board of Missions, 1874-1914* (Indianapolis: C. W. B. M. n.d.) p. 113.

[42]Mrs. M. M. B. Goodwin was the wife of Elijah Goodwin.

[43]*Christian Monitor,* December, 1874.

hensive concerning the fearful brothers who saw heresy in women speaking from the pulpit and praying in public. Her speech was concluded with the stirring words, "Be faithful, then dear sisters, among a faithless generation, and go forward in this noble cause, and if you have a truth to utter, speak, and leave the rest to God."

The women at the Cincinnati convention drafted a simple Constitution for their organization. They planned for the Christian Woman's Board of Missions to engage in both home and foreign missions and made certain that their new Society would be under the complete control of the women. The Society gained convention recognition and support through a special resolution. The first officers were Mrs. Maria Jameson, president; Mrs. William Wallace, recording secretary; Mrs. O. A. Burgess, treasurer; and Mrs. C. N. Pearre, corresponding secretary. A vice president, a secretary, and one or more managers were elected from each state represented at the Cincinnati meeting. These, with the national officers, constituted the Executive Committee with headquarters at Indianapolis. It was apparent to all Disciples that the church women no longer intended to "keep silent in the churches."[44]

The first meeting of the Executive Committee was held in December, 1874, at Indianapolis. A sample Constitution was prepared for the use of local auxiliaries which the women hoped would be established all over the country. The Indiana women preferred the home mission field in which to start their work, but they were out-voted in favor of supporting missionary activity in Jamaica.[45]

The vice presidents of the national organization, one for each state, became the presidents of the state organizations.

---

[44]Ida Withers Harrison, *op. cit.*, pp. 22-25.

[45]F. M. Green, *Christian Missions and Historical Sketches of Missionary Societies among the Disciples of Christ* (St. Louis: John Burns Publishing Co., 1884) pp. 236-238; *Christian Monitor*, March, 1875.

Mrs. A. M. (Nancy) Atkinson[46] of Wabash became the first president of the Indiana C. W. B. M. and Mrs. J. T. Dye, the secretary.[47] The state officers of the C. W. B. M. served without remuneration for many years; they considered themselves fortunate if the local churches they serviced paid their traveling expenses.

Forming of Ministerial Associations

Disciple ministers in Indiana, in search of fellowship, formed a number of local and district associations which met at regularly scheduled times. In the spring of 1870, the Disciple preachers of Indianapolis and the ministerial students at North Western Christian University organized what was called the Indiana Christian Ministerial Association. O. A. Burgess was named as president of the organization, and N. A. Walker became secretary.[48] Plans were made for semi-annual meetings the first of which was held at Greensburg on June 15th.[49] The representation was better at the next meeting held at Dublin, Wayne County, in 1871. By this time subjects under discussion were such matters as family training, wo-

---

[46]Mr. and Mrs. A. M. Atkinson were indefatigable lay workers in the Disciple movement. He was connected with the pioneer period of Ministerial Relief; she worked in the C. W. B. M. She received a degree from North Western Christian University in 1856, the first woman to receive a degree from this school. Her first husband, Philip Burns, was one of the ten students expelled from Bethany College over the slavery issue and accepted at N. W. C. U. Mrs. Atkinson was vice president of the national organization 1892-1902 and was president the next four years. Under her leadership missionary work was opened in Mexico in 1895; in South America in 1905; the University of Michigan Bible Chair established in 1892. Other Bible Chairs established were University of Virginia, 1897; University of Kansas, 1901; and University of Texas, 1904. She took an active part in the commissioning of at least 150 missionaries.

[47]C. W. Cauble, *op. cit.,* pp. 231-234. Cauble lists officers for the first ten years as, presidents: Mrs. A. M. Atkinson, Mrs. Mary Armstrong, Mrs. C. W. Pearre, Mrs. Sarah Wallace, Mrs. Virginia A. Pollard, Mrs. Effie L. Cunningham, Mrs. Eva O. Taggart, Mrs. Frank Wells, Mrs. O. H. Greist and Mrs. J. D. Case. He lists the first ten state secretaries: Mrs. J. T. Dye, Mrs. Mattie A. Armstrong, Mrs. M. E. Shank, Mrs. J. C. Black, Mrs. S. A. R. Boor, Mrs. Effie L. Cunningham, Miss Ella Parkhurst, Mrs. Sallie K. Jones, Mrs. Lida B. Pierce (later Mrs. Ed. Jackson), and Mrs. O. H. Greist.

[48]*Christian Standard,* March 5, 1870.

[49]*Christian Standard,* May 21, July 9, 1870.

men's work in the church, evangelism, stewardship, and Christian unity. Critics were appointed for each discussion, and it seems that the preaching brethren, by means of mutual assistance, were trying to improve the quality of their ministries.[50]

Southern Indiana ministers apparently also desired an association. A representative group convened in the Christian Chapel at Seymour on July 1, 1873, and elected J. M. Mathes as president and M. T. Hough, secretary. According to the Constitution, written and adopted at this meeting, the group chose to call themselves the Christian Ministerial Conference of Southern Indiana. Membership in the conference included all elders, deacons, editors of church papers, and superintendents of Sunday schools. Resolutions passed at this meeting included one on adopting the *Christian Record* as their state paper; another looked with favor on the Bedford Male and Female College as an institution conducted on New Testament principles and worthy of patronage and confidence.[51]

A preachers' convention was held at Indianapolis on February 10, 1874. Thirty preachers from District number one were present. A Constitution was also prepared and accepted by this group. John C. Miller[52] was elected president; A. G. Thomas, vice president; and W. W. Dowling, secretary. The brethren wanted it known that they had agreed they had no

---

[50]*Christian Record and Living Laborer,* February, 1871.

[51]*Christian Record,* August, 1873.

[52]John Chapman Miller (1831-1901) was born on his father's farm near Nineveh, Indiana. He became a member of the Christian Church at Nineveh under the preaching of Richard Gosney. In 1855 he received the B.S. degree from Indiana University after which he studied law. About this time he decided to become a minister and went to Bethany College where he graduated in 1858. After travel in Minnesota and the Dakotas and serving a church at Madison he returned to Nineveh where he preached and conducted an academy. He served on the Faculty of North Western Christian University 1871-1873, and was a member of the Board of Directors 1873-1893. While living in Indianapolis he was pastor of Third Christian Church. In 1876 he returned to Nineveh, believing the rural environment better for the rearing of his children. Critical of the public schools, he educated his children at home. For many years he was minister of the Christian Church at Nineveh and a community leader.

right, desire, or power to bind the churches to anything ec-
clesiastically; they had a right to bind themselves to labor in
closer bond of fellowship than they had ever done before.[53]

The Southern Indiana Ministerial Conference had its second meeting at Bedford, June 2, 1874. On this occasion the
name of the organization was changed to the Consultation
Meeting of the Disciples of Christ in Southern Indiana. Among
topics considered by the older men was one entitled, "How
can young men best be encouraged to devote themselves to
the proclamation of the gospel?" The younger brethren inquired, "How can we solicit money from a congregation without making them think it is a *personal* matter?"[54]

A State Ministerial Association with A. R. Benton as president was organized at Rushville in 1877. Annual meetings
of this organization were held thereafter in connection with
the annual meetings of the Indiana Christian Missionary Society.[55] By 1878, there were local, district and state ministerial
associations among the preaching brethren. Evidence seems
to indicate that there was an element among the southern
Indiana preachers who rallied around J. M. Mathes and
W. B. F. Treat of the *Christian Record,* supported conservative
(though not reactionary) views, and favored the Bedford
Male and Female College over that of North Western Christian University.

The Beginning of Controversies

Thomas Munnell, in an article entitled, "The Six Questions," published in the *Christian Record,*[56] pointed out the
six leading questions which had been discussed in Disciple

---

[53]*Christian Standard,* March 7, 1874.
[54]*Christian Record,* July, 1874, pp. 315-317.
[55]*Christian Standard,* September 29, 1877.
[56]*Christian Record,* September, 1873, pp. 403-406.

journals in recent years. It was an attempt to show that while there were differences in the theological views held by the brethren there was really little ground for apprehension. The six questions over which Disciples had been concerned were listed as (1) Expediency, (2) Progress, (3) The Organ, (4) Independency, (5) Destiny of the Unimmersed, and (6) The Episcopacy. Munnell explained that under the general subject of *expediency* the brethren had shown anxiety over baptism, the Lord's supper, clerical garments, the Good Confession and the mourners' bench, but that these things had never really become a problem. Concerning *progress,* he stated that all affirm that unitarian, liberal Christianity progresses only in missionary work, education, the Sunday school, and a stronger ministry, but there is nothing to worry about because nobody is in favor of progressing beyond the Bible. The *organ,* he declared, was an unsettled question for a while. It need not cause apprehension because if the church abides on earth ten thousand years she will have unsettled questions. In regard to *independency,* he could see nothing in it so far that threatened the peace of the church. As to the *destiny of the unimmersed,* all would agree that God could save the mistaken soul. *Episcopacy,* he wrote, was ecclesiastical rule and "has no hold and never can have on the Disciples." He concluded that most of the discussions that had caused apprehension prior to 1873 were already closed and the problems and issues settled. Munnell reassured his readers that there was nothing very foreboding in the Disciples' ecclesiastical horizon except the tendency to be overly-alarmed and thus work up a panic that might do harm. If Munnell had written this article twenty years later it is doubtful that he would have been so optimistic or that he would have tried to "explain away" obvious facts.

A speech given at the Rushville State Convention of 1872 marks the beginning of theological controversy among the

Disciples in the Hoosier State. It was made by W. T. Moore,[57] pastor of the Central Christian Church at Cincinnati, then one of the largest and most influential congregations of the Disciples. Moore was one of the first Disciples to advocate a rethinking of the traditional Disciples' plea, and his orthodoxy was often challenged by his conservative brethren. The roots of "cooperative-independent" and "Conservative-liberal" schools of thought among Hoosier Disciples are to be found in Moore's address at the Rushville meeting.

The *Proceedings* of the Rushville convention, which included Moore's speech, were printed in a sixty-two page pamphlet and circulated throughout the state. The address was also reviewed in the *Christian Record*[58] and criticized by Editor Mathes. In the words of Mathes, Moore "is aiming to cut loose from the New Testament church as a model." Moore had stated that a complete reproduction of the apostolic church was clearly impossible and that it ought not to be reproduced even if it could. He held that much of what belonged to that church was incidental and appropriate only in that age, and that its principles and not its methods were all that were really important for the present age. Mathes took exception to this view and asked, "Were not her methods right?" He affirmed that the apostolic method of converting sinners was still right, the facts of Christianity still the same, and that its commands, promises, enjoyments and glorious hope had not changed. It made Mathes uneasy to hear Moore

---

[57]William Thomas Moore (1832-1926) was a Kentuckian who had graduated from Bethany College in 1858. When pastor at Cincinnati he lectured at Kentucky University and at the same time edited the *Christian Quarterly*, a scholarly religious journal. Moore had a long and useful career in England and in America. A great scholar and a liberal thinker, his views were often at odds with those of his brethren. He often said, "We have a right to differ but we have no right to divide." Moore lived to be ninety-four years old, having served the Disciples in many missionary, pastoral, academic and editorial positions. He was author of fourteen books, one of which was a comprehensive history of the Disciples of Christ. Moore was the recipient of an honorary L.L.D. degree from Butler University.

[58]*Christian Record*, February, 1873, pp. 83-88.

declare that the Jerusalem church was imperfect in its beginning; he inquired as to where else could one find a divine model.

W. B. F. Treat, co-editor of the *Christian Record,* supported Mathes in this view and wrote several articles on the Jerusalem church in an attempt to show his readers that it was a "perfect" congregation. These articles criticized Moore's Rushville address, paragraph by paragraph, and sounded the old Reformation cry of "The Bible alone, and Christianity as it was in the beginning." In a short time others got into the theological battle, either in defense of or in opposition to Moore's thesis. Isaac Errett of the *Christian Standard* and Thomas Munnell of the General Convention joined with ministers in Central Indiana in upholding Moore, especially in his right to express his views. Many Disciples, however, in southern Indiana did not agree and became alienated from their brethren.

The issue of the use of instrumental music in church worship also came to the forefront in this period. In 1875, anti-organ articles began to appear in the *Christian Record and Sunday School Worker.* The little reed organ, so popular in homes, was being taken into the churches. Sometimes this was accomplished to the satisfaction of the congregation, but more often it caused dissension. When an organ was introduced into the Third Christian Church at Indianapolis, twelve families left and organized another church. The congregation at Bloomington had a similar experience. The most serious schism occurred at Bedford. For a while the Disciples there had two congregations, one meeting in the court house and the other in the church. An arbitration board, appointed by the General Convention at Louisville, met at Bedford on November 27, 1882, heard both sides and rendered a verdict. The decision did not indicate the opinion of the board on the use of the organ in worship, but it did declare that both sides in the controversy were wrong.[59] Eventually the church was united.

The organ controversy had no serious consequences in Indiana. None of the larger urban churches were seriously affected, at least not for long; a few of the more isolated rural congregations looked upon it as a doctrinal issue and eventually found fellowship among themselves as a separated body. Many of the ministers who had qualms of conscience about the use of the organ in the church took a position similar to that of J. M. Mathes who wrote, "I do not refuse to fellowship with those who advocate its use, providing their lives are right."[60] Though he objected to the organ he would not allow it to drive him from his place in the Church of Christ nor from his duty as a disciple of Christ. An interesting observation on the "organ" question was made by W. B. F. Treat in the *Christian Record*.[61] He quoted "sister" Alexander Campbell as having said that a little organ such as the brethren have at Memphis, Tennessee, will not do much harm, but it would be bad indeed, to have a big one like that in New York which scared a foreign preacher until he imagined the house was falling down!

The Temperance Movement and Communion Controversy

The temperance movement fastened itself on the churches in America in the early 1870's. Francis Murphy's temperance clubs built up the temperance cause to an evangelistic pitch, and thousands of men, young men and boys took the pledge of total abstinence. Temperance was a live issue in the Sunday

---

[59]*Christian Record*, December, 1882, pp. 369-374.
[60]*The Evangelist*, March 31, 1881. Mathes defined his position in a six-point article.
[61]*Christian Record*, August, 1874, p. 366.

schools and almost became one of the tenets of the Christian faith.

The Woman's Christian Temperance Union was organized at Cleveland, Ohio in 1874. Indiana soon had its state organization, and Mrs. Zerelda Wallace[62] of Indianapolis became its first president and most militant leader. Prior to the growth of the temperance movement in the churches it was customary to use fermented wine in the communion service. Public notices for such wine appeared frequently in the church journals. Elder S. Burnet of Vincennes often advertised, *"Pure Grape Wine,* made from my own vineyard, expressly for communion purposes. Price $1.00 per bottle." Editor Mathes recommended the purchase of this product by the churches on the basis that most wines were made of burnt whiskey, bullock's blood, and some drugs; that these ought not be placed on the communion table of any church.[63] Mrs. Wallace was against the use of alcoholic wine any time, any kind, and at any place. She once wrote to Dr. Ryland T. Brown of her church, asking him to show her what analogy existed between the life-giving blood of the Saviour and an element seventeen per cent of which is poison.[64] This precipitated a theological argument carried on in several issues of the *Christian Standard* in which many prominent Hoosier Disciples participated. John Chapman Miller held that fermented or alcoholic wine was not essential to the integrity of the Lord's Supper and that Christians should choose non-alcoholic wine for this pur-

---

[62]Zerelda Wallace (1817-1904) was a daughter of Dr. John H. Sanders, pioneer Indianapolis physician. While still in her teens she married David Wallace, a widower with three children. Wallace soon became Governor of Indiana. One of her step-sons was Lew Wallace of *Ben Hur* fame. He is reported to have said later that Zerelda Wallace was his inspiration for the character of Ben Hur's mother. Mrs. Wallace was a charter member of Central Christian Church in Indianapolis. She began her career as a lecturer after she was fifty-seven years old. The liquor "evil" pushed her into this arena. She spoke often on temperance and woman's suffrage, even before the Indiana legislature. As a personal friend of Frances E. Willard, they often roomed together at temperance conventions.

[63]*Christian Record,* April, 1870, p. 185.

[64]*Christian Standard,* February 26, 1876.

pose. Dr. Brown agreed in principle but objected to the conclusion of Mrs. Wallace that alcoholic wine violated the integrity of the ordinance. His wife, an ardent temperance reformer, did not agree with him. The arguments continued until Mrs. Wallace made a test case of the issue on Sunday morning at Central Christian Church in Indianapolis. When communion was passed to her she stood up, got the attention of the congregation, and declared she would not commune that day or any day in the future when fermented wine was used.[65]

Needless to say, she won her point. The Disciples in Hoosierland soon began to use pure grape juice at the communion service, a practice which has continued to this day.

The temperance movement became very popular by the 1880's and articles on temperance and against the liquor traffic took more and more space in the religious journals. So far as Protestant churches were concerned, temperance was one of the first issues that took on an aura of ecumenicity among them. They might not agree on theological doctrines, but for the most part they presented a solid front on the liquor problem. The big "union" Sunday evening temperance service always drew a large and enthusiastic audience.

North Western Christian University Becomes Butler University

Otis A. Burgess, president and financial agent for North Western Christian University, 1868-1870, resigned this position at the end of the school year in 1870. He explained this action by saying that he considered himself to be a preacher rather than a teacher and preferred to enter again into the pastoral ministry. His resignation was accepted regretfully.[66]

---

[65]Francis M. Wiley, *History of Central Christian Church, op. cit.,* p. 59.
[66]N. W. C. U. *Minutes,* Book No. 2, June 6, 1870.

Burgess had been minister at Central Christian Church in Indianapolis when called to the presidency. His successor at Central church, William F. Black,[67] was asked to assume the presidency along with his pastorate. The fact that the school could afford only a part-time president is indicative of its financial situation.

In spite of its current financial problem the Board of Directors decided to establish a commerce college and a law school as part of the university.[68] The commercial department was instituted in the fall of 1870 with C. E. Hollenbeck as professor of bookkeeping and commercial law and W. W. Barker, professor of penmanship. A "female" professorship had been established the year before with Miss Catherine Merrill as professor of English literature and grammar. A substantial gift from Ovid Butler made it possible to develop this feature into what was called the Demia Butler Chair of English Literature a year later. The chair bore the name of Butler's daughter who was awarded a degree in 1862, the first woman to be graduated from the university in the regular four year program. By 1871 the law school was also a reality with H. C. Newcomb, B. K. Elliot, and C. P. Jacobs as professors of law.

The addition of new departments created a space problem, an indication that the school did not lack for students. An endowment fund of $140,000 was claimed by 1871, probably

---

[67]William F. Black (1840-1908) was a native of Putnam County, Indiana. He received his academic training at Asbury College (De Pauw) and was minister of the church at Greencastle when called to Indianapolis. His Indianapolis pastorate extended from 1869 to 1877. In the years 1870-1873 he was also president of N. W. C. U. After leaving Indianapolis he moved to Chicago where he was engaged in general evangelistic work.

[68]N. W. C. U. *Minutes,* Book No. 2, August 25, 1870. Faculty members in the period 1870-1872 were: W. F. Black, president and professor of Hebrew and Syriac; W. M. Thrasher, vice president and professor of mathematics; S. K. Hoshour, professor of Greek and Bible; A. Fairhurst, professor of natural science; Mrs. E. J. Price, principal of the academy; Scot Butler, professor of Latin; John Chapman Miller, professor of biblical literature; Gerald Maney, professor of French; Orren Reynolds, professor in the commercial department; H. J. Schoenecker, professor in the musical department; and Miss Ada Klum, principal of the academy.

because of Ovid Butler's gift to establish the Demia Butler Chair and his proposal to pay the tuition for all who wished to study for the ministry the coming year who desired such assistance. Butler resigned as president of the Board of Directors in 1871, and Joseph I. Irwin[69] was elected to take his place. Butler was then made chancellor of the institution, a position which was considered as an honorary one.[70] That same year the Faculty voted to confer honorary LL.D. degrees on Senator Oliver P. Morton, Congressman James A. Garfield, President A. R. Benton of Nebraska State University, W. M. Franklin, Governor Conrad Baker, Horatio C. Newcomb, and Ovid Butler. Professors S. K. Hoshour and H. W. Wiley resigned their positions. Hoshour, who wished to retire, had served the school for thirteen years.[71]

There were 330 students enrolled in the 1871-1872 academic year. Efforts were being made to raise a building fund of $100,000 to provide space for an expanded program. When William F. Black resigned as president, Otis A. Burgess returned from a ministry in Chicago to be inaugurated a second time in 1873. W. M. Thrasher and Scot Butler were granted leaves of absence at this time to study abroad. In its eighteen years of existence the school had two hundred graduates. Forty of these were lawyers, thirty-five were preachers, and thirteen were physicians.[72]

The corporation was appraised at $700,000 in 1873 and was declared to be the wealthiest institution west of the Al-

---

[69]Joseph Ireland Irwin (1824-1910) was born in Indiana near Columbus. He entered the mercantile business in that city in 1850. In 1871 he went into the banking business in Columbus and was president of Irwin's Bank until his death. Irwin was one of the organizers of the National Tin Plate Company in 1894, and he built the first interurban line out of Indianapolis in 1899. He became connected with the Union Starch and Refining Company in 1903. From 1868 to the time of his death he served on the Board of Directors of Butler University.

[70]N. W. C. U. *Minutes,* Book No. 2, February 7, 1871.

[71]N. W. C. U. *Minutes,* Book No. 2, May 23, 1871.

[72]*Christian Standard,* October 4, 1873. North Western Christian University catalogs, academic years 1871-1872, 1872-1873.

leghenies. It is difficult to explain the sudden prosperity of North Western Christian University in the light of the financial panic of 1873. It was probably due more to the expansion of the city of Indianapolis than to gifts from benefactors. When the College Avenue site was selected it was well outside the city environs. This is what the directors wanted. In the early 1870's the city limits moved north beyond the school, and its property became valuable as a business and residential area. Ovid Butler's property holdings near the school also increased in value, and he apparently shared this prosperity with the institution. The college needed to expand. Believing it to be more expedient to erect new buildings on another site than to add another wing to the existing building the directors were sympathetic to proposals made by a group of Irvington citizens to move the university to that place. Irvington was considered to be a beautiful residential suburb, and the people there desired to make it a cultural center. They offered several acres of land for a campus and a grant of $150,000 to be paid in five annual installments if the school would relocate in their community. The directors estimated that the sale of the old campus would increase their endowment fund to $275,000 and that the sale of additional land that the school possessed would bring between $150,000 and $200,000. Taking everything into consideration, it was the view of the Board of Directors that if the Irvington proposition were accepted it would not only solve their space problem but would increase the total assets of the school to $700,000.

By July of 1874 negotiations for the Irvington site were completed. It was planned that work on the new buildings should begin at once so that they would be ready for occupancy in the fall term of the 1875-1876 academic year. The

225

last graduating exercises on the old campus were held on June 16, 1875 with Isaac Errett, a member of the Board of Directors and editor of the *Christian Standard,* as the special speaker. By this time the law department had been suspended, causing a reduction in the number of students but creating no serious problem. The catalog for the 1874-1875 academic year shows that requirements for the degree of Master of Arts had been strengthened. It now required a year of graduate study and the presentation and acceptance of a satisfactory thesis to obtain this degree.

A new building on the Irvington campus was completed on schedule by the opening of the fall term in 1875. It was described as one of brick construction with stone foundation and trim which included a basement, two stories for classrooms and a third floor to serve as a chapel. It was erected at a cost of $50,000 and was planned to accommodate a student body of 500. The directors were proud to announce that the new building was heated by steam and that hot and cold running water was available. They were also happy about the two graded streets that ran to the building all the way from the city of Irvington.

Isaac Errett, commencement speaker in the old building three months before, was asked to give the dedication address for the new building on September 15, 1875. Speaking on the general subject of education[73] he said that education should be thorough, be extensive in range, thoroughly American, free to all without distinction of sex or race, and Christian. A gift of $20,000 from Jeremy H. Anderson[74] to establish a

---

[73]*Christian Standard,* September 11, 25, 1875; October 2, 1875. Errett is listed as a lecturer in homiletics in the 1875-1876 catalog.

[74]Jeremy Halleck Anderson (1813-1884) came to Franklin County from Kentucky to what came to be known as Andersonville. Anderson joined the Salt Creek Church of Christ in 1840. He thought of entering the ministry but went into business instead. Following an illness in 1877 he moved to Missouri. His gift of $20,000 to the school represented his interest in education. He was said to be, with the exception of Ovid Butler, the largest single contributor to the funds of the university.

Chair of Greek Language and Literature was announced at the dedication.

The first attempt to bring culture to the Irvington community was in the form of a lectureship by President B. A. Hinsdale of Hiram College. It was held in the chapel in the spring of 1876 under joint sponsorship of faculty, students, and Irvington citizens. Hinsdale lectured under the general subject of ecclesiastical tradition.[75] The first Commencement in the new building was held June 9, 1876. There were seven graduates. The school was beginning to feel the need for more students, and it was stated in the *Christian Standard*[76] that tuition was practically free, only $6.00 per year payable in N. W. C. U. scrip. When the Board of Directors had their June meeting in 1876 they reduced their number from twenty-one to eleven.[77] This action came under severe criticism later. It was also decided at the board meeting to accept Ovid Butler's generous offer of several lots in Indianapolis at College Corner (worth $50,000) in exchange for more shares in the corporation. This brought his holdings up to 750 shares and gave him legal control of fifty-one per cent of the stock.[78] A misunderstanding concerning the alleged proposed use of this control by other members of the Butler family also raised some serious questions later. Colonel W. F. Graham, brother-in-law of Joseph I. Irwin, purchased a large house on the campus and fitted it out to operate as a boarding house for female students. This was looked upon as a dormitory for

---

[75]The Hinsdale lectures were published later. *See* B. A. Hinsdale, *Ecclesiastical Tradition: Its Origin and Early Growth; Its Place in the Churches, and Its Value* (Cincinnati: Standard Publishing Co., 1879). This book is significant as the first published lectureship of the university.

[76]*Christian Standard*, June 17, 1876.

[77]The new directors elected were: Ovid Butler, P. H. Jameson, Joseph I. Irwin, W. F. Black, John C. Miller, A. C. Shortridge, B. M. Blount, John S. Duncan, Simeon Frazier, A. C. Thompson, and A. I. Hobbs.

[78]N. W. C. U. *Minutes*, Book No. 3, June 28, 1876.

women and was a welcomed addition.[79] Board at that time was four dollars per week.

On February 28, 1877, North Western Christian University at Irvington became Butler University. The directors explained it was a change in name only, an economical arrangement in regard to writing and speaking. They believed that the former name was tiresomely long, that "North Western" localized the school and no longer was significant, and a school of science, law, medicine, and polytechnics could hardly be called, with any show of propriety, a "Christian" school. In the process of selecting a new name they had observed that names of men, places, states and ideas were invariably chosen for colleges and universities. In consideration of these factors and in view of Ovid Butler's generous gifts of money and land which had increased in value through his oversight, the name was changed to Butler University in his honor.[80] The change of name seems to have been a happy one. There was no criticism or objection.

Butler University held its first summer program in 1877. It was called the Butler University Scientific Expedition and Summer School.[81] Professor David Starr Jordan, a pupil of the celebrated Agassiz and a scholar destined to be one of the brightest stars in the Butler Faculty galaxy, was the prime mover of the project. The expedition which took students from Indianapolis to Texas and return by way of Nashville and the Mammoth Cave was undertaken in the interest of geology and natural history. In addition to the students and Dr. Jordan the group was composed of Professors John A. Myers and Charles H. Gilbert of Butler University, Professor William R. Dudley of Cornell University and Professor Ernest

---

[79]*Christian Standard*, September 9, 1876.
[80]*Christian Standard*, March 10, 24, 1877.
[81]*Christian Standard*, March 24, 1877.

R. Copeland of Michigan University. A special study along the way was made of fish, birds, reptiles, insects, plants, and fossils.

By this time the school had seen many changes. It was in a new building on a new campus with a new name. Due to fortunate circumstances the financial outlook was encouraging. Many leaders on the Board of Directors and Faculty believed the time had come for the school to fulfill the roll envisioned by the founders—to become *the* great university of the midwest, equal if not superior to the great universities of the East and Europe. This was Ovid Butler's dream, and one shared by his son-in-law Dr. P. H. Jameson,[82] president of the Board of Directors. Such a university would be one with a strong liberal arts core, surrounded by colleges of law, medicine, science and theology. The anxiety to see this dream come true motivated Dr. Jameson and other members of the Butler family to hasty and expeditious action, precipitated the first real schism on the board, and placed the university in an unfavorable light with the public and its constituents. Dr. Jameson, because of his profession, was probably the one who made overtures to the two Indianapolis medical schools to become part of the university. The reduction of the personnel of the Board of Directors from twenty-one to eleven may have been the first step to restructure the institution. Before the negotiations commenced with the medical schools Ovid Butler had

---

[82]Patrick Henry Jameson (1824-1910) was the brother of Love H. Jameson and the son-in-law of Ovid Butler. After teaching school for four years he studied medicine with Dr. John H. Sanders of Indianapolis. Later he received his degree in medicine from the Jefferson Medical College of Philadelphia and returned to Indianapolis where he was associated again with Dr. Sanders and finally took over his practice. In 1861 he organized the post hospital at Camp Morton. He served two terms as commissioner to the Indiana Hospital for the Insane and in 1866 drafted and procured enactment of an ordinance for the establishing and maintaining of Indianapolis City Hospital. He was the agent for the sale of the large realty holdings of North Western Christian University in Indianapolis and the prime mover for the transfer of the university to the Irvington campus. He was a director of Butler University for thirty years and a respected and able man. John M. Judah, his son-in-law, was treasurer of Butler University in this transition period.

resigned as a director. It was generally understood that Dr. Jameson, in the future, would be his representative.

When it seemed possible to add a medical department to the university, Dr. Jameson appointed a committee to make the arrangements.[83] Discussions were carried on with the Indiana Medical College and the College of Physicians and Surgeons, rival Indianapolis institutions, with the view of absorbing them into the university complex. The agreement with the medical schools was an awkward and ill-advised arrangement. It provided that the medical department of the university would have its own trustees, name its own faculty, and manage itself. Directors of Butler University would have *ex officio* status with the trustees of the medical department. The university agreed to recognize the alumni of both former medical schools and pay the medical department $500 annually for the privilege of this association. Administrative control of the medical department was to remain in the hands of its own dean, and the university was to confer M.D. degrees on the graduates.[84] The faculty of the medical department was listed with the university Faculty,[85] and the combined board was to be known as the Board of Directors and Trustees of Butler University.

The addition of the medical department and the combining of boards (most of the trustees of the medical department were non-Disciples) made the Disciple constituency uneasy

---

[83]Butler University *Minutes,* Book No. 3, October 9, 1878.

[84]Butler University *Minutes,* Book No. 3, October 9, 1878.

[85]The new Faculty consisted of the following: O. A. Burgess, president; G. W. Mears, obstetrics; A. R. Benton, Greek; Theophilus Parvin, obstetrics; Graham M. Fitch, surgery; William M. Thrasher, mathematics and astronomy; John M. Comingore, surgery; Catherine Merrill, English; R. N. Todd, clinical medicine; Thomas M. Harvey, diseases of women; Isaac C. Walks, diseases of the nervous system; Scot Butler, Latin; David S. Jordan, natural history; William B. Fletcher, physiology; Henry Jameson, chemistry; Melville B. Anderson, modern languages; John Chambers, clinical medicine; C. E. Wright, materia medica; J. L. Thompson, eye and ear diseases; J. W. Marsee, anatomy; C. E. Hollenbeck, commerce; Charles H. Gilbert, natural history; Leland Sulgrove, assistant in chemical laboratory; Albert F. Armstrong, Greek; Demarchus C. Brown, Greek; James A. Young, history.

about the future administrative control of the university. In any event, when the Board of Directors (Disciples) met in 1879 a resolution was passed which declared "As soon as our obligations to those now in our employ will permit we recommend that all employees-elect in the Faculty or elsewhere be chosen from the aforesaid Christian Church." It was explained that this was a means of securing homogeneity in the general religious conceptions of the Faculty.[86] The resolution exploded like a bomb among non-Disciple friends of the university in Indianapolis and among the Disciple constituency in the state and whole brotherhood. A minority on the board tried unsuccessfully to pass a counter-resolution to the effect that a unity of sentiment in matters of religious faith was desirable for the Faculty, but removing competent teachers of a sound Christian faith and morality just because they were not Disciples was not good practice. The newspapers played up the story and interpreted the action of the directors as a move to oust David S. Jordan and Catherine Merrill from the faculty. Since these two persons were considered to be among the ablest members of the faculty the whole community was stirred, and charges of bigotry were heard.

The resolution had probably been formed in the background of fear for loss of control of the university but apparently was aimed directly at Professor David S. Jordan[87] who was supposed to have held liberal theological views. Inadvertently it included Miss Merrill who was unquestionably "sound" theologically and an ardent church worker. The

---

[86]Butler University Minutes, Book No. 3, April 24, 1879. Those voting in favor of the resolution were: Simeon Frazier, A. C. Thompson, A. C. Shortridge, John C. Miller, B. M. Blount, and A. I. Hobbs. Those against the resolution were: Dr. P. H. Jameson, O. D. Butler, and John S. Duncan.

[87]David Starr Jordan (1851-1931) was born in New York State and was a graduate of Cornell University in 1872. After teaching in Wisconsin he came to Indianapolis as a science teacher in the high school. From 1875 to 1879 he was professor of natural history at Butler University. In 1879 he became head of the Department of Natural Science at Indiana University and president in 1885. In 1891 he became president of Leland Stanford University. Jordan was a versatile and prolific scholar and became recognized as a national figure in American life.

231

resolution had been made general so that it would appear not to seem invidious. When the affair was reviewed in Christian Church journals the action was looked upon with favor. Dr. Jameson, who valued a good image for the school in the Indianapolis area, apologized for the board's action and stated that it would probably be changed at the next annual meeting.[88] A. I. Hobbs, a member of the board, presumed that Dr. Jameson was representing Ovid Butler's views, and that Butler intended to vote his majority-stockholder privilege at the next meeting and overrule the resolution. Hobbs believed that Butler had no moral right to do this.[89] Differences of opinion developed over the interpretation of the Charter of the university, especially in regard to the phrase, "To teach and inculcate the Christian faith and Christian morality as taught in the sacred Scriptures." John C. Miller and a majority of the directors interpreted the word "Christian" in a denominational sense. Miller reported to the *Christian Standard*[90] that he considered the Faculty part worldly and part Christian and that he looked upon the alliance with the medical college as the manifestation of a tendency to secularize the institution. He wrote that he had been trying to correct this for the past six years. Miller felt that it was now the responsibility of the Butler family and heirs to do something to restore confidence.

Ovid Butler apparently had taken no personal stand on the matter. He may not have known anything about the action at the time. He rarely attended board meetings and felt that other "family" members on the board could adequately represent his views. Word got around (whether true or not) that Butler was unwilling to yield to the majority, and if necessary he would cast all of his 750 votes to rescind the resolution.

---

[88]*Christian Standard*, May 3, 1879.
[89]*Christian Standard*, May 31, 1879.
[90]*Christian Standard*, June 14, 1879.

When Butler heard of this he was grieved that the brotherhood would think he would use his legal powers in violation
of a moral obligation. When his views were heard by proxy at
the annual meeting of the stockholders it was learned that he
wanted it known that the university belonged to and was to be
controlled by the people with whom it originated and in whose
interests it had been established, known in Indiana as the
Christian Church.[91] The unfortunate controversy was then
resolved by compromise based on the understanding that all
retiring directors should be re-elected and five new directors
added to the board.[92] The expansion of the board to include
more representatives from the Christian Church was a satisfactory solution. When this agreement was reached the directors
unanimously rescinded the controversial resolution. The secular press hailed this action as a victory for the liberal element,
and the Disciple journals looked upon it as a compromise
made in good faith.[93] Dr. Jordan was not discharged but soon
accepted a position on the Faculty of Indiana University.
Butler University lost prestige with the general public but
strengthened its position with the Disciples. An article in *The
Evangelist*[94] later praised the school and noted that there were
176 students in the literary department and 180 in the medical
department, making a total student body of 356. The statement was made that "Butler University is the wealthiest school
under the management of the Disciples, and none will surpass
it in thorough educational work." Otis A. Burgess, who had

---

[91]This analysis is based on articles in the *Christian Standard*, May 24, May 31;
June 7, 14, 28, 1879. *Old Path Guide*, July, 1879.

[92]Members of the new board were as follows (additional directors noted by *):
*Woodson W. Thrasher, *E. S. Frazee, *D. R. Van Buskirk, Joseph I. Irwin, A. C.
Thompson, John C. Miller, *John C. Hadley, B. M. Blount, A. C. Shortridge, John
S. Duncan, *Dr. S. A. Butterfield, Ovid D. Butler, Simeon Frazier, Dr. P. H. Jameson,
Alvin I. Hobbs.

[93]The motion to rescind the resolution may be found in the minutes of the Board
of Directors, Book No. 3, June 13, 1879. A full discussion of the matter is carried
in the *Christian Standard*, June 21, 1879.

[94]*The Evangelist*, July 15, 1880.

taken a neutral position throughout the controversy, resigned as president in 1881 to return to pastoral work in Chicago. Harvey W. Everest was elected to take his place.

Bedford Male and Female College

Though other schools in Indiana such as Howard College at Kokomo were owned and operated by persons who were members of the Christian Church the only serious contender to North Western Christian University, as a church related institution, was the Bedford Male and Female College at Bedford, Indiana. It was probably not the intention of the founders of this school to establish it as a Disciples' institution in 1871, but it is also apparent that J. M. Mathes and many Christian Church ministers in Lawrence and surrounding counties became disturbed by what they considered a departure from the Disciples' plea on the part of certain of their brethren in the central part of the state. They looked upon the support of W. T. Moore's address at the Rushville convention of 1872, the promotion of the Louisville Plan by the State Missionary Society, and the introduction of the organ into the worship of the church with a great deal of fear and apprehension. They even formed their own ministerial association in 1873, a body which passed resolutions to support the *Christian Record* and Bedford Male and Female College. The Bedford school advertised J. M. Mathes as president and head of the department of biblical literature. Others, actively associated with the school in a teaching capacity by 1874 were W. B. Crisler, Bruce Carr, W. H. Krutsinger and Theodore Hintz.

By this time plans were under way to build a suitable college building "that would be an honor to the brotherhood and the town of Bedford."[95] By 1877 J. A. Beattie was presi-

---

[95]*Christian Record*, July, 1874, pp. 330-331.

dent, and it was announced that this school was under the control of "our brethren."[96] Though a tract of land at the edge of the town had been purchased for a campus, financial difficulties were hard to overcome. When Southern Normal College was established at Mitchell, trustees of the Bedford school decided that this was a better location for the college and closed their institution. In the short period of its existence the Bedford school graduated some men who later distinguished themselves in the ministry of the Disciples. Among these were: Samuel B. Moore, Walter L. Kidd, W. H. Kern, Robert C. Bryant, J. W. Noe, William Ingraham, A. B. Philputt, Josephus Hostettler, and W. A. Spurgeon.[97]

Literature of the Period

A. Aron and Company had a bookstore in Indianapolis in 1871 which claimed to handle all the publications of the Christian Church.[98] Aron was active in Disciple Sunday school work in Indiana. W. D. Frazee and Son succeeded him in the book store business. Not many books were produced by and about Hoosier Disciples in this period, but among these were William Baxter's *Life of Knowles Shaw,* and Shaw's singing books, *Sparkling Jewells* and *Morning Star,* Joseph Franklin, son of Benjamin Franklin, collaborated with J. A. Headington to write the *Life and Times of Benjamin Franklin* and *A Book*

---

[96]*Christian Standard*, December 1, 1877.

[97]J. M. Mathes, *Autobiography, op. cit.,* pp. 110-111.

[98]*Christian Record and Living Laborer*, February, 1871. The advertising section of this paper listed available publications. The list is a good indication of what Hoosier Disciples were reading at this time. The books were as follows: Richardson's *Memoirs, The Living Oracles, The Christian System,* Campbell on *Baptism, Popular Lectures and Addresses, Campbell-Purcell Debate,* Franklin's *Gospel Preacher,* Moore's *Living Pulpit,* Milligan's *Reason and Revelation, Scheme of Redemption,* Goodwin's *Family Companion, Manford-Sweeney Debate, Brooks-Fitch Debate, Life of Elder John Smith, Universalism Against Itself, Sermons* by J. T. Walsh, *Braden-Hughey Debate,* McGarvey on *Acts,* P. T. Russell's *Materialism Against Itself,* Scott's *Messiahship, Works of B. W. Stone,* Lard's *Review of Campbellism Examined,* Anderson's *New Testament,* Hayden's *Hymn and Tune Book,* Martin's *Voice of the Seven Thunders,* McKnight on the *Epistles,* Campbell on the *Four Gospels, Campbell-Rice Debate,* Carpenter's *Bible vs. Spiritualism,* W. B. Hendryx' *Analytic and Synthetic Bible Lessons,* all of Knowles Shaw's and A. D. Fillmore's singing books, Christian Hymn Book, and Sunday school papers.

of Gems, Choice Selections from the Writings of Benjamin Franklin. Other books of the period include the *Burgess-Underwood Debate,* Ryland T. Brown's *Elements of Physiology and Hygiene,* Mathes' *Life of Elijah Goodwin,* and *Autumn Leaves,* a book of poetry by Mrs. M. M. B. Goodwin.

The great number of periodicals published in Indiana by Disciples show that Hoosiers placed great confidence in their magazines and their editors. W. R. Jewell of Lafayette issued *The Siege* in 1873, a paper which attacked immorality in all its forms. The Christian Record Printing and Publishing Company published a Sunday school paper called the *Sunday School Gem* in 1875. Professor H. W. Wiley and J. M. Tilford continued publication of the *Independent Monthly* at Indianapolis in 1870. The *Christian Foundation,* a journal of science and religion, was published by Aaron Walker of Kokomo, 1880-1884. W. W. Dowling of Indianapolis issued the *Little Sower, Morning Watch* and *Golden Lesson* at Indianapolis. These were Sunday school papers. Krutsinger and Crisler edited the *Common School Teacher* from Bedford in 1875. Mrs. M. M. B. Goodwin continued to edit the *Christian Monitor* throughout the period. In addition to this, she established the *Little Builder at Work* and the *American Housewife.*

When Elijah Goodwin sold the *Christian Record* subscription list to the *Christian Standard* in 1866 it ended this phase of the life of the *Record.* J. M. Mathes, however, revived the *Christian Record* in 1870. D. Oliphant of Canada, former editor of the *Banner of Faith,* had planned to publish a new monthly called the *Living Laborer.* Mathes persuaded him to combine his new paper with the new *Christian Record* and publish it as the *Christian Record and Living Laborer.* This merger lasted but two years. In 1872, *Living Laborer* was dropped from the masthead. When interest developed in the Sunday school movement, Mathes included a Sunday school

236

department in his paper and changed its title to *Christian Record and Sunday School Worker*. The new name did not last long; it was soon called the *Christian Record* again. In December, 1875, the *Record* combined with the *Evangelist* to become the *Record and Evangelist*. Although Mathes and W. B. F. Treat of the *Record* staff were contributors to this journal it soon bore the title of *The Evangelist*, with *Christian Record and Evangelist* as a subtitle. Later the subtitle was dropped. In 1882, Mathes again published a *Christian Record*, continuing until 1884. It was absorbed by the *Old Path Guide*. The *Christian Record* in its various forms, but primarily under the editorship of Mathes or Goodwin, spanned some forty-one years of Disciple history, being published in thirty of these years. In the period covered by its publication it is second only to Campbell's *Millennial Harbinger*. It also has the unique distinction of becoming a part of three facets of the Disciples' movement through mergers with the *Christian Standard,* the *Old Path Guide* and the *Evangelist.*

End of the Debating Era

Hoosiers in this period, 1870-1882, still liked to engage in public debates.[99] The frequency of these discussions, however, began to diminish after 1875. By the late 1880's Disciples no longer had to challenge outsiders in order to defend

---

[99]Debates in this period were (Disciple contestants named first):
W. B. F. Treat— . . . Land (Seventh Day Adventism) Lancaster, 1871.
W. B. F. Treat—G. W. Green (Soul Sleeping) Harrisonville, 1871.
W. B. F. Treat—Elders Land and Wagoner (Seventh Day Adventism) Gosport, 1871.
W. R. Jewell— . . . Hull (Spiritualism) Crawfordsville, 1872.
W. B. F. Treat—A. J. Nugent (differences with United Brethren) Lancaster, 1873.
Jacob Wright—L. Forbes (differences with Methodists) Clarksburg, 1874.
William Holt—L. B. Gandy (Universalism) Jefferson County, 1874.
A. C. Layman—George W. Marlow (differences with Baptists) Jasonville, 1874.
A. C. Layman—D. N. Horne (Baptism) Bethel, Owen County, 1875.
James Becknell— . . . Anderson (differences with Methodists) Charlottesville, 1875.
William Holt—T. E. Ballard (life after death) Ashby's Mills, 1875.
William J. Howe— . . . Curry (Universalism) Milton, 1878.
William Holt—Simeon P. Carleton (Universalism) Aurora, 1879.
Aaron Walker—L. Forbes (differences with Methodists) Shoals, 1880.
Aaron Walker—A. W. Bartlett (Sabbath) Kewanna, 1881.

237

their religious positions; there was sufficient difference of theological opinion among themselves to satisfy the urge for public discussion.

Advance Under Fire

By 1870 the Disciples' movement had progressed about as far as it could go in Indiana under its existing structural pattern. Had it not been challenged by the missionary emphasis inadvertently motivated locally by the Louisville Plan, the demand by Disciple women for a place in the work of the church, and the growth and enthusiasm of the Sunday school movement, the "plea" could have passed away with the pioneers. The Christian Woman's Board of Missions and the Indiana Christian Sunday School Association were powerful stimulants that not only kept the movement alive but provided motivation for advancing the cause. By 1882 the Disciples in Indiana were an on-going, forward-looking communion of people, notwithstanding the internal controversies through which they were passing. Their institution of higher learning also made progress in this period. The original building on College Avenue was outgrown in twenty years, and the move to the Irvington campus was a profitable one from the financial standpoint. The change in name from North Western Christian University to Butler University was a deserved tribute to Ovid Butler and a wise choice. The controversy over control of the university was unfortunate and could have been averted if better judgment had been used in the agreement made between the Medical College and the university. It served a good purpose, however, in clarifying some issues that had been troubling the brethren. There were still problems ahead for Butler University, lessons about ministerial education that had to be learned the hard way. Nevertheless, the school made remarkable progress in gaining financial stability and in academic achievement.

238

VII

Predilection to Maturity

1883-1896

A MANIA FOR CULTURE on the part of Hoosier Disciples marked the last two decades of the nineteenth century. The culture craze colored every phase of the movement but found the clearest local expression in the Bethany Park Assembly project. The Bethany Park program was a refined extension of the camp meeting and satisfied culture-hungry Hoosier Disciples for many years. In no other place could they find so much aesthetic enlightenment at so cheap a price.

The format for Bethany Park was set at the Island Park convention of 1882. After this occasion Hoosier Disciples were no longer satisfied with the old ways. They had to have a western Chautauqua of their own, one where religious, scientific, literary and moral assemblages could be held. L. L. Carpenter and the Indiana Christian Sunday School Association were prime movers in the project, but Hoosier Discipledom, as a whole, was more than willing to go along with the idea.

Plans for the Bethany Park project received final approval at the 1883 Island Park assembly. Since there was a great deal of sentiment toward a location near the center of the state a forty acre tract in Morgan County, eight miles north of Martinsville and thirty miles southwest of Indianapolis, was selected.

The project was financed by means of a joint stock company originally capitalized at $10,000 and increased to $25,000 in 1886. Shares sold for $20 each. The park and its program were under the administrative control of a superintendent appointed by a fifteen-member board of trustees chosen from among the stockholders.

The park was officially opened during the first sixteen days of August, 1884. A new tabernacle building was dedicated by L. L. Carpenter on the first Sunday. Excursion trains running out of principal Indiana cities brought hundreds of people to the site. Several acres of land were covered with tents. The project seemed to be a success from the start. Annual meetings of the General Christian Sunday School Association, the State Sunday School Association, the Indiana Christian Missionary Society, the Indiana Ministerial Association, the State Women's Christian Temperance Union, and the Indiana Christian Woman's Board of Missions were held on the campground.

In his book, *Churches of Christ,* John T. Brown described Bethany Park as it must have looked in 1904 when more fully developed.[1] He wrote:

On arriving at the park, you step out of the coach onto the platform, and you are at the gate of the park. At your right you see the magnificent Sanitarium building, one of the very best in the state, where you can bathe in its mineral waters, should you desire to do so. Near this is a fountain where at any time you can slake your thirst with the healing water of this artesian well.

In front of you you see the splendid summer hotel, with its broad inviting verandas, and surrounded with its acres of magnificently shaded lawn. We move on a few steps, coming to the quaint little boat house and its long dock lined with pleasure boats. To a lover of water what is more delightful than a row on Beth-

---

[1]John T. Brown, *Churches of Christ* (Louisville: John P. Morton and Company, 1904), p. 512.

any's lake, with its placid waters lined with rich foilage and forest trees.

From the lake we stroll through the grounds, the beautifully shaded lawns, surrounded by the buildings of the Standard Publishing Company, Cincinnati, Ohio; the New Castle cottage, the Annex, the Assembly cottages, a number of private cottages, the building of the Christian Publishing Company, St. Louis, etc. Then, "crossing over," the great tabernacle, with its splendid auditorium, capable of seating two thousand people, and one of the best in the country. This auditorium was built not only for conventions, lectures, musical entertainments, but in fact, for public gatherings of all kinds. Its acoustic properties are perfect. It is well lighted and ventilated, so that it makes a most desirable place for the purpose for which it was intended.

The last big summer assembly before going to Bethany Park took place at Island Park, near Rome City, in July, 1883. Four state boards and one national board held annual meetings at this time.[2] Mr. and Mrs. Timothy Coop of England were guests at the Island Park assembly. In addition to having a good time, holding meetings of the various boards, and listening to cultural programs, six missionaries were commissioned.[3] They were Mr. and Mrs. C. E. Garst and Mr. and Mrs. George T. Smith, who planned to go to Japan, and Mr. and Mrs. M. D. Adams who intended to work in India. Harvey W. Everest, president of Butler University, was the speaker at this service.

The commissioning of missionaries was an innovation to the Disciples and gave rise to certain questions among the brethren. The ceremony was looked upon as ordination, and John C. Miller protested the right of the assembly (considered primarily as a Sunday school association) to ordain,

---

[2]*Christian Standard*, June 16, July 28, 1883.
[3]*Christian Standard*, August 11, 1883.

and the scriptural authority of any group to ordain women.[4] Miller thus raised questions which have never been fully resolved to the satisfaction of the entire brotherhood.

Orthodoxy in the Civil Courts

One of the first court cases in which a Disciples' church became involved in the use of property and one in which the orthodoxy of the church was a matter of legal defense took place in the Noble County Circuit Court, June 19-21, 1883. Wide attention was given to this case.[5] It seems that when Salem Chapel, in the Haw Patch near Ligonier, was built in 1878-79, it was erected by means of funds obtained in a general community canvass. Though the chapel was controlled by the Methodist Protestant Church a provision had been made through a clause in the subscription paper to the effect, "and said house shall be free to all orthodox denominations when not in use by said Methodist Protestant Church." The system seemed to work to the satisfaction of all until J. H. Edwards, Christian Church pastor at Ligonier, who was holding afternoon services in the chapel, attracted a number of Methodists to his meetings. In addition to this, the Christian Church Assembly in near-by Island City focused attention on the Disciples. As the Christian Church movement appeared to become stronger in this community the Methodist Protestant officials became concerned. They took steps to prevent J. H. Edwards and his congregation from holding meetings in the chapel. Certain members of the Methodist Protestant church disapproved of this action and tried to get an order from the Circuit Court to maintain the integrity of the original agree-

---

[4] *Christian Standard,* October 6, 1883.
[5] *Christian Standard,* July 21, 28, 1883. The story of this court case was published in book form. *See* J. H. Edwards, editor, *Orthodoxy in the Civil Courts* (Cincinnati: Standard Publishing Company, 1884).

ment. Both plaintiffs and defendants in the case were members of the Methodist Church. Both sides employed legal counsel, and an impartial jury was chosen. J. H. Edwards and L. L. Carpenter were interrogated as witnesses for the orthodoxy of the Christian Church. Rev. B. Post and Rev. John W. Smith, Methodists, were questioned on the validity of their charge that the Christian Church, not being an orthodox denomination, was not eligible to use the building. The counsel for the plaintiff, in questioning witnesses, took the line that Disciples were orthodox because they held that "the Bible, the whole Bible, and nothing but the Bible" was the teaching of the Christian Church; faith, repentance, confession, and baptism as practiced by this church was in the main stream of Protestant thought, and that to maintain these beliefs was sufficient testimony of orthodoxy.[6]

The findings of the court in this case were "That the Christian Church denomination and the ministers thereof, are orthodox; and that J. H. Edwards, one of the ministers of said Christian Church, was, at said last mentioned date (January 1883), and still is, ready and willing to hold religious services in said building for his denomination." Therefore, for whatever it means, the orthodoxy of the Christian Church was conceded through jury trial in an Indiana circuit court. Edwards, and a great number of his brethren, seemed to look upon the favorable outcome of this case as a great victory. They never seemed to realize that the Christian Church had been defended as an orthodox *denomination,* and that defending the Disciples as a denomination they were arguing contrary to tradition. In any event, they saw fit to ignore a fundamental issue in the name of expediency. They wanted then, as now, to "have their cake and eat it, too."

---

[6]*Christian Standard,* July 21, 28, 1883.

Progress Report to 1890

The Sunday school movement, as the main attraction of Hoosier Disciples, was not hurt by the Bethany Park Assembly project. As the assembly program developed year by year, Bethany Park became the focal point of Indiana Discipledom, and the Sunday School as its main attraction commanded the chief loyalty of Hoosier Disciples. The holding of annual meetings of the various state organizations in the relaxed atmosphere at Bethany Park seemed to be a desirable thing at first, but after a few years the mood changed and the brethren began agitating for annual meetings at other places. The cultural aspects of the Bethany Park program usually took precedence over the business meetings. General Lew Wallace was a featured attraction in 1886.[7] He was advertised as an eloquent orator, erudite writer, and gallant soldier. Wallace lectured on Turkey and the Turks. As an added attraction, he read selected chapters from his novel, *Ben Hur*. Professor J. W. McGarvey of the College of the Bible in Lexington, who visited the Holy Land in 1879, was featured as a Bible lecturer. His use of stereopticon slides to illustrate these lectures was thought to be quite modern.

In the years 1884 and 1885 the State Society sought to perfect as many county organizations as were feasible, put evangelists to work in these counties, help pastorless churches find pastors, and organize as many missions in cities as possible.[8] T. M. Wiles of Connersville was employed as corresponding secretary beginning January, 1885. D. R. Van Buskirk was president of the Society at this time.[9] Apparently Wiles did not continue for long as corresponding secretary because

---

[7]*Christian Standard,* August 21, 1886.
[8]*Christian Standard,* January 12, 1884.
[9]*Christian Standard,* January 24, 1885.

by the middle of the year 1887 it appears that J. H. O. Smith was doing the work. Smith announced through the *Christian Standard*[10] that Indiana now had its own religious journal, *Indiana Central Christian,* a bi-monthly published by J. V. Coombs in Indianapolis with Z. T. Sweeney as editor-in-chief. The *Central Christian* was discontinued in the spring of 1889 in favor of an Indiana department in the *Christian Standard.* Smith sounded an optimistic note in 1887 concerning the Indiana work. He wrote, "Indiana is awake; she no longer lies like a sleeping monster, unconscious of her strength. Her 80,000 Disciples, awake at last to our perils and possibilities at home, are repairing the leaks in our ships, that we may sail secure in our own harbor, and be prepared to sail more boldly and fearlessly into *foreign* waters." Though the progress made in this period was by no means commensurate with Smith's oratory, ten of the twenty-eight districts of the state organized and employed evangelists.[11] It was announced the next year that fifteen evangelists were at work, including state evangelist J. P. Ewing and Sunday school evangelist L. L. Carpenter. All the State Society needed to make the Indiana work a great success, it was claimed, was "men and money."[12]

The ninth of the series of encampment meetings was held at Bethany Park, July 31 to August 18, 1890. In addition to the regular business sessions of the various state organizations, special days were featured. Among these special days were Children's Day, Christian Endeavor Day, State Ministerial

---

[10]*Christian Standard,* June 25, 1887.

[11]*Indiana Central Christian,* October 15, 1888. The districts thus organized and the evangelists employed were: I T. A. Hedges, III E. B. Cross, VII E. A. Pardee, XI M. McKinsey, XII L. C. Warren, XIII C. F. McHargue, XXI James and Matthew Small, XXIII George Barrows, XXVI A. L. Crim, XXVIII L. A. Coble. At the time, A. R. Benton was president of the Indiana Christian Missionary Society; L. L. Carpenter, vice president; Howard Cale, secretary and treasurer; and J. H. O. Smith, corresponding secretary. The Board of Directors consisted of A. F. Armstrong, P. S. Rhodes, Amos Clifford, A. C. Shortridge, William Wallace, E. J. Gantz, E. W. Darst, T. J. Clark, M. W. Harkins, W. S. Montgomery, John M. Bramwell, A. M. Atkinson, Joseph M. Tilford, A. R. Benton, and James W. Conner.

[12]*Christian Standard,* March 30, 1889.

Association Day, Indiana Missionary Society Day, Butler University Day, Christian Union Day, State Sunday School Association Day, and Christian Woman's Board of Missions Day; in order that no one would be missed, a Tourist's Day was also added.[13] The next year a large number of returned missionaries made personal appearances at the encampment.[14]

The State Society held a semi-annual meeting, February 25-27, 1890, at Kokomo.[15] When Love H. Jameson spoke to the group he caused "quite a commotion" by stating that although Alexander Campbell was opposed to praying for mourners, "it might be a good plan today to rig up a mourners' bench expressly for the use of church members." J. P. Ewing resigned as state evangelist shortly after this meeting, and J. L. Parsons of Indianapolis was appointed to take his place. There was no state evangelist in the field most of that year. In spite of this, a few new churches were founded. The State Ministerial Association, at its annual meeting in 1890, passed a resolution "to hail with delight" the existing tendency on the part of divided Protestantism to the "one Lord, one faith, and one baptism." They also endorsed the Young Peoples' Society of Christian Endeavor and acknowledged the excellence and superiority of the work of the sisters in the C. W. B. M. In addition, they made a strong pronouncement of being in favor of complete and legal prohibition of the liquor traffic.[16]

L. L. Carpenter had a busy twelve months in 1889-1890. As state Sunday school evangelist he reported 326 days spent in the field. During this time he conducted 21 normals (teacher training courses), held 13 Sunday school institutes and

---

[13]*Christian Standard,* July 19, 1890.
[14]*Christian Standard,* August 1, 1891.
[15]*Christian Standard,* March 29, 1890.
[16]*Christian Standard,* August 23, 1890.

seven Sunday school conventions; he gave 190 sermons and 238 Sunday school lectures, baptized 137 new converts, dedicated 16 meeting houses, traveled 17,250 miles (no automobile), and sent out 2,000 letters and cards (not mimeographed).[17]

Young People's Society of Christian Endeavor

The Christian Endeavor movement, destined to play an important part in Hoosier Disciple history, came to the front in Indiana in the last years of the nineteenth century. Within a short time societies were organized in a majority of the Christian churches; the movement became a department in the State Society with its own full-time superintendent, a Christian Endeavor cottage was erected at Bethany Park, and a column on Christian Endeavor was featured in the religious journals.

Christian Endeavor had its beginning in a local society organized by Francis E. Clark, a young Congregational minister at Williston, Maine, in 1881. It found general acceptance in less than five years. The Christian Endeavor movement was ecumenical in scope, being embraced by the major Protestant communions. Regular conventions were held on county, state, and national levels; it was *the* youth movement of the early twentieth century. When it became a structured organization it had its own literature, its own *modus operandi,* and its own administrative hierarchy. It provided a youth program on the local church level that was not dominated by adults, and one in which the young people had opportunity of expressing themselves in a practical way. Though the C. W. B. M. had youth organizations and the Sunday school reached the young people with a program of Bible instruction, it was Christian Endeavor that really met the social and spiritual needs of

---

[17]*Christian Standard,* September 6, 1890.

church young people. The roots of the present youth movement in Disciple churches are to be found in Christian Endeavor.

Five Years of General Work, 1891-1896

The Bethany Park encampment continued to be popular
with Hoosier Disciples for many years. L. L. Carpenter managed to import new and attractive features for the program
each season. This drew large crowds. There was much emphasis on music and musicians; opportunity was given for
special study in vocal and instrumental music. Carpenter even
gave special prominence to a phonograph, a new and wonder-
ful invention on which he claimed great instrumental music
and the speeches of distinguished Americans could be heard.[18]
Two things, however, that dampened Bethany Park enthusiasm
eventually made their appearance. It was acknowledged that
the Bethany Assembly had a worthy program, but people complained that it was so crowded with good things of a cultural
nature that the business of convention delegates was relegated
to second place on the schedule. Some of the brethren advanced the view that the annual meetings of the state organizations should be held in the large cities so that more attention
could be given to the state work and that local communities
could feel the impact of the Disciples' movement.[19] The second
deterrent to Bethany Park's progress was the development of
active competition in the form of rival encampments in Indiana. The Fountain Park Assembly had its beginning in a
park near Remington, Indiana, in 1896. It was advertised as
not being a rival to Bethany Park, but supplemental to it so
that those who lived too far away from Bethany Park could
be served at Fountain Park. Robert Parker, Christian Church

---

[18]*Indiana Christian,* July 18, 1896.
[19]*Indiana Christian,* April 1, 1893.

248

member at Remington and president of the bank in that community, was a leading spirit in the inauguration of this assembly. Fountain Park claimed to emphasize evangelism more than Bethany Park, but a study of the annual programs of both groups indicate that it was a "me too" project.[20]

Seeking a better means by which the Indiana Christian Missionary Society could do its work, what was called the "Ohio Plan" was adopted in 1891. This plan centered administration in the district rather than in the State Board.[21] Each of the fourteen newly-formed districts had responsibility for raising and disbursing its own missionary money. One-half of the money raised was to be kept in the district for district work, and the other half was to be divided between the state organization and the General Convention. The State Society asked the Sunday school board for the release of L. L. Carpenter because it was believed that he was a man who could do the job that was required. Carpenter found it hard to get rid of the old organizations but had moderate success. He was most effective in what was called "grouping" the congregations (pastoral unities) so that several churches could have the service of one man.[22] J. V. Coombs pointed up this situation when he wrote that it was lamentable that so many congregations in Indiana were without preaching. He stated that in the Wabash Valley south of Lafayette in particular, there were scores of congregations that were once prosperous but had become thoroughly disorganized. He mentioned that there were six or eight congregations within six miles of Rock-

---

[20]*Christian Standard*, July 11, August 1, 1896. Fountain Park was the first of the rival organizations in this field. In a few years the Disciples had several such "Chautauquas" operating in the Hoosier state.

[21]*Christian Standard*, November 21, December 3, 1891. The "Ohio Plan" looked good at this time. However, there were weaknesses which showed up later. District boards could not see any farther than their own districts when it came to planting new churches. Churches were desperately needed in the cities because of the population flow, and there was no money to finance them.

[22]*Christian Standard*, March 5, 1892.

ville that were either too poor or too indifferent to have regular preachers; other churches wanted a "big" preacher or none at all.[23]

E. B. Scofield became state evangelist (sometimes called state manager) in September, 1893, replacing L. L. Carpenter. His job was to go into the districts and raise money for district and state work. Whenever possible, he was to place evangelists in the field to hold meetings under state society management. A drive was made at this time to encourage rural churches to supply parsonages for their ministers.[24]

The year 1893 was significant for the opening of the World's Fair in Chicago and the ushering in of a major economic depression. The Fair was enjoyed, but the depression brought hard times to Hoosierland and made it very difficult to raise funds for religious work.[25] Professional evangelists began to play a larger role in religious life in this period. Indiana Disciples were proud of their preachers who entered this field. Status-wise, a professional evangelist in those days was one step up the ladder above the local pastor. Among these evangelists were J. V. Updike, J. H. O. Smith, J. V. Coombs, and James Small. By the middle of the year 1893, Updike had held over 160 meetings; it was claimed over 2,000 persons a year were being added to the churches through his efforts. J. H. O. Smith, special evangelist for the State Society, established nine mission churches in a twelve-month period. His congregation at Valparaiso had the distinction of having the largest Christian Endeavor Society in the world. J. V. Coombs set a record of speaking for 190 consecutive nights—six months and ten days—without missing an appointment. He held meetings on the free-will offering basis

---

[23]*Christian Standard*, September 26, 1891.
[24]*Christian Standard*, September 16, 1893.
[25]A more complete description of this panic may be found pp. 263-264.

throughout the country. James Small was another Indiana evangelist in great demand. He had 387 additions in one meeting at Martinsville.[26]

Hoosier preachers were not only evangelists, but they were lecturers as well. A. M. and S. M. Conner established a lecture bureau to supply lecturers on themes amusing and instructive at reasonable rates. The names of the lecturers were D. R. Lucas, F. D. Power, Z. T. Sweeney, B. J. Radford, A. L. Crim, and other notables. The following lecture titles were advertised: "Are Preachers Fools?" "Thoughts and Tears," "Blockheads," and "James A. Garfield." The lectureship bureau, whistling and singing preachers, and the various "Chautauqua-like" encampments could be considered as evidence of an inner drive for culture that dominated middle-class Hoosier society at the time.[27]

In response to the demand for a state convention of the Indiana Christian Missionary Society, to be held apart from the Bethany Assembly, one was held at Columbus on April 10-12, 1894. Sermons and addresses were given by John S. Sweeney, Z. T. Sweeney, E. T. Lane, E. B. Scofield, D. R. Lucas, T. H. Kuhn, and A. B. Widger. H. S. Riggs, minister of a church supported by the State Society, was reported to have made his own salary the past year "by his unique entertainment of recitation, lecture, song, and whistling." The brethren were happy to learn that he would employ the same techniques in the coming year.[28]

When L. L. Carpenter transferred to the State Society from the Sunday School Association in 1892, C. M. Fillmore succeeded him as Sunday school evangelist. Fillmore's first job was to tour the state to find out the needs. Before the year was

---

[26]*Indiana Christian*, July 1, 1893.
[27]*Christian Standard*, October 5, 1895.
[28]*Indiana Christian*, May 1, 1894.

over he gave up this work, and T. J. Legg[29] took it over. The next year L. L. Carpenter was appointed as missionary evangelist of the Sunday School Association with the understanding that his work would not conflict with that of Mr. Legg.

The business depression was still being felt in 1894 and 1895. It was reported at the annual convention of the State Society in 1895 that although there had been severe financial problems several new buildings had been erected and others remodeled. By 1896 the financial situation began to look better. A total of $26,324 was raised by the Indiana organizations that year, The State Society reported $9,100, the largest amount; the C. W. B. M. and Foreign Society each had contributions of over $5,500. E. B. Scofield served as corresponding secretary and state evangelist in 1896 and was asked to continue in this position. H. R. Pritchard was his associate in the work.[30]

Indiana Christian Woman's Board of Missions

Christian Church women in Indiana continued their interest in the C. W. B. M. and sought to strengthen the organization in this period. Mrs. Mary Shank of Irvington served as secretary until 1890 when the work was taken over by Mrs. J. C. Black. Mrs. Black was succeeded by Mrs. S. A. R. Boor of New Castle who did an outstanding work for several years. Attempts were made to organize as many local church auxiliaries as possible. It was reported that Indiana had fifty-five

---

[29]T. J. Legg (1849-1919) a native of Rush County, became a member of the Christian Church in 1869. He started teaching school that same year. Following his teaching experience he traveled for eight years in Indiana as an inspector and underwriter for fire insurance. As superintendent of the Sunday school at Logansport he showed much ability in this field. He became Sunday school evangelist in 1892 and spent the next twenty years with the Sunday School Association and the State Society. He is credited with organizing 116 churches as well as doing his regular job of holding Sunday school institutes, organizing Sunday schools and Christian Endeavor societies and conducting Sunday school rallies.

[30]*Indiana Christian*, August, 1895; *Christian Standard*, August 29, 1896.

auxiliaries and seven hundred members in 1885. The next year the number was raised to sixty-five auxiliaries and 1,375 members. By 1887 the number of auxiliaries was raised to seventy-five. The women were never satisfied with the progress being made because their goal was to have auxiliaries in every congregation.[31] A great number of life memberships were held by Indiana women.[32]

The thirteenth annual convention of the C. W. B. M. was held at Central Christian Church in Indianapolis in 1887 in connection with other national meetings of Disciples' boards. A review of the work on a national basis indicates the women were supporting missionary activities in Jamaica, India, the mountain mission at Hazel Green, Kentucky, and home mission work in Montana Territory. The Montana mission points were at Helena, Deer Lodge, Anaconda, Fish Creek, Chestnut, Highwood, Corvallis, Butte, Stevensville and Missoula.[33]

National headquarters for the C. W. B. M. at 160 N. Delaware Street, Indianapolis, was usually a bee-hive of activity. Much volunteer and sacrificial labor was given to the cause, especially by Indianapolis women. In 1896, *Missionary Tidings,* a thirty-two page periodical, was in its fourteenth volume, and the *Little Builders at Work,* a sixteen-page magazine for children, was in its seventh year. The former magazine had a circulation of about 11,000 copies, and the latter, 7,000. Indiana, and especially Indianapolis, was the hub of the C. W. B. M. wheel in matters of administration and promotion, but for some strange reason (or perhaps no reason at all)

---

[31]*Missionary Tidings,* November, 1885; December, 1886; June, 1887.

[32]*Missionary Tidings,* December, 1886. Life Memberships in Indiana were held by the following persons: Mrs. Zerelda G. Wallace, Mrs. Harriet Judah, Mrs. Sue Robinson, Mrs. H. N. Radibaugh, Mrs. A. S. Hale, Mrs. E. E. Shortridge, Mrs. F. E. Frazier, Mrs. E. E. Graham, Mrs. M. A. Stanley, Mrs. Margaret Wilcox, Mrs. Lydia Anderson, Miss Jennie Laughlin, Mrs. Isabelle C. Ross, Mrs. Mary Coe Smith, Mrs. Alice Sidener, Mrs. Lavina Smith, Mrs. Josie Walk, Mrs. Ira J. Chase, Fannie Frazee, Mrs. Caroline Neville Pearre, Mrs. R. T. Blount.

[33]*Missionary Tidings,* July, December, 1887.

Indiana produced few missionaries for the field in this period when compared with the number of recruits from other states.

Indiana and the Ministerial Relief Fund

There probably would have been a relief fund and pension plan for Christian Church ministers eventually, but the death of Ira J. Chase, preacher and former governor of Indiana, pointed up its immediate necessity. Chase died while holding an evangelistic meeting in Maine in 1895, leaving a nearly blind and destitute widow, and children at Wabash, Indiana. Chase was well liked by Hoosier Disciples and had served as pastor of the churches at Wabash and Danville. A Union Army veteran, he had also served the G. A. R. in Indiana as both chaplain and commander. In 1888 he was elected lieutenant governor of Indiana while still serving the church at Danville. When Governor Alvin P. Hovey died in 1891, Chase completed his term. While governor of Indiana, Chase often preached on Sundays. He was a very popular speaker at the Bethany Assembly and at other church gatherings. Some sixty-six ministers attended his funeral when it was held at Indianapolis.[34]

Alonzo M. Atkinson of Wabash, an intimate friend of Ira J. Chase, was very much disturbed at what happened to the Chase family after his friend died. He instituted a "Chase Fund" through the brotherhood papers, in an effort to raise $2,000 to buy Mrs. Chase a home. Atkinson started the fund by making a personal subscription of one thousand dollars. Constant notices in the church journals brought good results, and contributions were received from people in many states, and even from England. The Chase Fund served to point up the shabby manner by which the brotherhood treated its faith-

---

[34]*Indiana Christian*, May, 1895.

ful ministers,[35] and motivated A. M. Atkinson to dedicate his life to the cause of ministerial relief. J. V. Coombs wrote in the *Indiana Christian.*[36]

We seldom go to conventions without hearing appeals for some worthy brother. Brother A. M. Atkinson of Wabash has proposed a Ministerial Relief Fund. He starts the fund with $1,000. No greater enterprise has been started since the organization of our Church Extension Society. As the plan is started by an Indiana brother this state must not go limping behind. With Brother Atkinson as manager the enterprise is sure of success.

The General Missionary Convention at Dallas in 1895 voted to organize a Board of Ministerial Relief with authority to raise funds for the relief of destitute ministers. Headquarters were established at Indianapolis with Howard Cale of that city as president, A. M. Atkinson as corresponding secretary, and Amos Clifford as treasurer. Atkinson, Cale, and Clifford made a great triumvirate of Christian businessmen; as laymen, they could not be accused of having personal pecuniary interests.[37] The Board formed a legal corporation in Indiana in 1897, a corporation approved by the General Christian Missionary Convention the next year.[38]

Among the first applicants for ministerial relief was a preacher in Kansas, forty-two years old, disabled, with seven

[35]In 1887 the Indiana C. W. B. M. raised money to pay rent for the home of J. M. Mathes; John Longley received an offering for medical help in 1859; Mrs. Knowles Shaw was left destitute when her husband was accidentally killed in Texas. These cases could be multiplied many times over.

[36]*Indiana Christian,* November 1, 1895.

[37]A biographical sketch of Mrs. Atkinson appears on page 214. Howard Cale was a deacon and Sunday school superintendent at Central Christian Church in Indianapolis. He was graduated from North Western Christian University, 1866, and was a law associate of Benjamin Harrison before and after Harrison's term in the White House. Cale also was a trustee of Butler University. Amos Clifford was a flour and grain dealer in Indianapolis and helped to organize three Christian churches in that city.

[38]Among the Indiana "incorporators" were: D. R. Lucas, John E. Pounds, George H. Clarke, L. L. Carpenter, W. M. Cunningham, Burris Jenkins, A. L. Orcutt, William D. Owen, E. B. Scofield, W. F. Sellers, Samuel Ashby, Mrs. M. E. Shank, Mrs. M. E. Showers, John M. Canfield, Dr. W. H. Boor, R. W. Clymer, G. H. Clarke, M. E. Henderson, and John Davidson.

children to support. The next applicant who received help was the sixty-eight year old widow of Knowles Shaw. She had no home and was in deep poverty.[39]

The cornerstone for a permanent loan fund was laid by 1896. The plan contemplated the investment of 75% of money received; 25% was for immediate use. All trustees and officers served without remuneration. It was decided to adopt a special day on which the churches were to make an appeal for ministerial relief.[40] The first annual report was published on September 30, 1896. It showed $1,144.70 expended for relief the first year; fifty-six persons, including widows and children of ministers and missionaries had been aided.[41]

More Public Debates

It is probable that Hoosier Disciples engaged in occasional public debates after 1883, but none was reported in the journals until 1890. Even those reported after this date were fewer than in other periods, indicating that interest had declined in such controversies. The Disciple "hero" was no longer the fair-haired debater on a public rostrum who challenged his "enemy" to forensic combat.[42]

The Literature of the Period

Ira J. Chase authored a book entitled, *The Jewish Tabernacle, Two Lectures,* which was published in 1893. *Under*

---

[39]*Indiana Christian,* December 15, 1895.

[40]*Indiana Christian,* February 15, 1896.

[41]For a comprehensive account of Ministerial Relief and its successor, the Pension Fund, *see* William Martin Smith, *For the Support of the Ministry* (Indianapolis: Pension Fund of the Disciples of Christ, 1956).

[42]Debates recorded in this period (Disciple contentant named first) were:
H. R. Pritchard—Lemuel Potter (conditional salvation) Fairview, 1890.
Ira Scott—Joseph Chartrand (differences with Roman Catholics) Huffman, 1892.
S. H. Creighton—Jersee Beals (Baptism) Cuyuga, 1893.
W. B. F. Treat—John Hughes (Universalism) Lexington, 1894.
J. A. Frank— . . . Harvey (Quakerism) Plainfield, 1896.

Ten Flags, a volume written by Z. T. Sweeney, was published in 1889. Sweeney was the traveling companion of Isaac Errett when they both visited the Holy Land in 1887. The book describes the places visited. *Talks to Young People,* a book by J. Z. Tyler, pastor of the Euclid Avenue church in Cleveland, Ohio, was published in 1896. It is significant to Hoosiers because it contains the addresses he made to the young people at Bethany Park Assembly the year before. E. V. Zollars was another Ohioan, but his book, *The Great Salvation,* published in 1895 , was written as an answer to the teaching of Hugh C. Garvin, Bible professor at Butler University. Harvey W. Everest of Butler University was author of *The Divine Demonstration,* written while he was president of Butler University in 1884. J. H. Edwards published the proceedings of the Noble County Circuit Court in the famous "orthodoxy" case of 1883 in a book entitled, *Orthodoxy in the Civil Courts.* A new song book entitled *The Gospel Call* was issued in 1890 by J. V. Coombs, J. T. Reese, and S. S. Jones. The publishers claimed that this book was free from sectarian and unscriptural phrases.

Though Hoosier Disciples produced but few books in this period they did publish a great number of periodicals. The first issue of *Missionary Tidings,* publication of the Christian Woman's Board of Missions, appeared as a four-page monthly in May, 1883. Mrs. M. M. B. Goodwin was editor. She became ill later that same year, and the journal was edited by a committee. When Mrs. S. E. Shortridge became editor in 1884, some 4,000 copies were being issued. By 1890, the circulation had increased to 40,000. *Little Builders at Work* was a monthly magazine for children published by the C. W. B. M. The first number was issued in 1890. The *Northern Indiana Christian Evangelist,* published at Valparaiso by B.

F. Perrine, was a six-page periodical issued in 1890. It probably had a very short life. A. M. Laird of Butler, Indiana, published the *Gospel Magnet* in 1896 which was said to be "fresh and newsy." The *Octographic Review,* edited and published by Daniel Sommer, was moved to Indianapolis in 1894, and published from that city for many years. The *Review* represented the views of the brethren who had taken a position opposed to instrumental music, missionary societies, church colleges, and numerous other alleged "innovations."

In response to the need for a news medium for Indiana Disciples it was decided to issue the *Central Christian* in 1887. This was a bi-monthly paper published by J. V. Coombs at Indianapolis. Z. T. Sweeney was editor-in-chief; W. S. Brown, W. H. Kerr, J. H. Edwards, Charles Fillmore, J. H. O. Smith, and L. L. Carpenter were on the editorial staff. Mary Coe Smith looked after the women's department. By the spring of 1889 the function of the Central Christian was transferred to the *Christian Standard.* The *Central Christian* then became the Indiana department of the *Standard.* The *Christian Standard* for January 17, 1891, carried the announcement that the *Indiana Standard* was then being issued with L. L. Carpenter as editor-in-chief. It was described as a monthly paper devoted to the interest of the Christian churches and as a cheap medium of communication in state affairs. This was probably an Indiana supplement to the weekly *Christian Standard.* A subscription drive was projected in an effort to get 50,000 readers of the new journal. The *Indiana Christian* first made its appearance under the publishing date of December 1, 1892. W. T. Sellers was listed as business manager for the periodical. This monthly magazine for Hoosier Disciples was destined to survive for some time. J. V. Coombs became editor-in-chief in October, 1895.

Butler University

The catalog of Butler University for the academic year 1882-1883 named Harvey W. Everest[43] as president. The university still included the large medical faculty which was controlled by a special board of trustees, and an enlarged board of directors to which the non-medical personnel had responsibility. A Bible course, given on the graduate level, was offered by the department of biblical literature and moral philosophy. Scrip, a form of interest given to stockholders for their investment in the university corporation, sold at 12½ % of normal value ($6.00 worth of scrip could be purchased for 75¢) and could be obtained by students and applied to their tuition. This same scrip was furnished free to ministerial students.

There was no medical department listed in the catalog for 1884-1885, indicating that this feature of the university organization had been abandoned. Seven students were graduated at the commencement exercises of 1886. The enrollment at the time was 181 students; twenty of these had definite plans to enter the ministry. The school apparently had financial problems during these years. Because of an operating deficit it was finally decided to lower salaries and reduce expenses in other ways. The cut-back in operating costs may have been the reason for the resignation of Harvey W. Everest as president. Beginning in the fall of 1886, Allen R. Benton[44] became president of the university. The Board of Directors, at the

---

[43]Harvey William Everest (1831-1900) came from New York State. He received his education at Western Reserve Eclectic Institute (Hiram), Bethany, and Oberlin colleges. He was president of the "Eclectic" at Hiram for a short time after graduating from Oberlin. He became president of Eureka College in 1864 and held this position for eight years. Following a short period in the pastorate he became a professor at Kentucky University. In 1877 he became president of Eureka College for the second time. He served as president of Butler University from 1881 to 1886. Everest then went to Wichita, Kansas, to help organize Garfield University as its chancellor. Later he became president of Southern Illinois State Normal University until he was called to Drake University as dean in 1897. He was elected president of Drake University in 1889.

[44]For a biographical sketch of Allen R. Benton, *see* p. 149.

annual meeting of 1887, made the announcement that the university property was now worth $360,000 and that two chairs had been endowed. These were the Demia Butler chair of English literature and the Jeremy H. Anderson chair of Greek language and literature. The endowment figure for the chairs was $20,000 each. Since the assets had been given at nearly $700,000 ten years before, values must have been depressed considerably.

Plans were made in 1889 for the erection of a new building on the campus for the use of the Preparatory Department (High School) and to provide quarters for the library. By the fall of 1889, the foundation for this new three-story $30,000 building (later called Burgess Hall) was laid. An observatory was also being built on the campus at the time. It was needed to house a new $3,000 telescope, apparently a gift from Joseph I. Irwin. The telescope had a six-inch object glass with an eight-foot focal length. The new observatory was completed and the telescope mounted by the spring of 1890. Faculty and students were delighted when construction began on the new street railway between Irvington and Indianapolis. Of course, it was rather slow going when completed, the car being pulled as it was by a team of docile mules. There was partial compensation, however, in the fact that the fare was only five cents.[45]

Z. T. Sweeney[46] was elected chancellor of the university in

---

[45]*Christian Standard,* February 16, October 5, November 9, 1889; March 8, 1890.

[46]Zachary Taylor Sweeney (1849-1926) was the son and grandson of a minister and had three brothers who were ministers. Guyrn Emerson Sweeney, his father, moved the family from Kentucky to Illinois because of his abolitionist views. Z. T. Sweeney graduated from Scottsville Seminary in Illinois and later attended Eureka and Asbury (De Pauw) colleges. After preaching two years at Paris, Illinois, Sweeney was called to the Tabernacle Christian Church at Columbus, Indiana, where he served from 1872 to 1898. It was here that he married Linnie Irwin, daughter of Joseph I. Irwin. During this pastorate he conducted twenty-two evangelistic meetings in the church, each lasting about six weeks. The congregation grew in membership from 180 to 1,500 persons during his ministry. In these years he also had interim pastorates at New York City, Richmond, Virginia, and Atlanta, Georgia. In 1887 he toured the Mediterranean and the Holy Land with his friend, Isaac Errett. Butler University conferred an honorary LL.D. degree on him in 1888 and elected him chancellor the

the spring of 1889. His special responsibility was to be in the field of selling stock in the corporation and in recruiting students. He resigned this position before he started, because of bronchial trouble. The board, hoping he would recover, would not accept the resignation.[47]

The school seemed to enter, at least temporarily, upon a more prosperous era beginning in 1889. The Board of Directors established a Bible department that year. Hugh C. Garvin, who had been teaching languages, was placed in charge of it. W. M. Mullendore of Noblesville was employed as financial agent for the school, and an effort was made to increase the endowment to $1,000,000. A gift of $20,000 from Mr. and Mrs. Addison F. Armstrong of Kokomo made it possible to endow a chair of Germanic languages in 1890. T. C. Howe, who was to take over this professorship, went to Germany for a year of preparation before assuming the responsibility.[48]

Irvington was fast becoming a religious center for Disciples at this time. Including student ministers who preached frequently in surrounding areas there were some fifty ministers living in Irvington. A protracted meeting was held in the college chapel each winter. A. R. Benton and Hugh C. Garvin, who alternated their preaching on Sundays, had frequent accessions to the church. There was usually a large and enthusiastic audience at the prayer meetings. The college Sunday

next year. Sweeney served as U. S. Consul-General to Turkey, 1889-1893, receiving his appointment from President Harrison. After this, he lectured on the Redpath Lyceum Bureau. He was much in demand as a church dedicator because of his ability to raise money. He is reported to have dedicated 166 churches. He was commissioner of fisheries and game in Indiana, 1899-1911. In 1904 he was president of the American Christian Missionary Society. Sweeney had the confidence of the brotherhood and played a large part in the construction of the International Convention. He authored many pamphlets and wrote articles for the church journals. Among his published books are: *Under Ten Flags* (1899), *Pulpit Diagrams* (1897), and *The Spirit and the Word* (1919). He was editor of three volumes of collected material which appeared under the general title of *New Testament Christianity*, Vol. I (1923), Vol. II (1926), and Vol. III (1930).

[47]*Christian Standard*, March 9, April 27, 1889.
[48]*Christian Standard*, August 10, October 5, 1889; March 18, April 26, 1890.

school class was in a flourishing condition with attendance ranging between 150 to 200 young people. One hundred young men were enrolled in Professor Iden's Sunday school class. Sunday evening meetings conducted by the Y. M. C. A. and Y. W. C. A. were well supported.[49]

Burgess Hall, so named in memory of Otis A. Burgess, former president, was dedicated September 9, 1890. Mrs. O. A. Burgess was present as a special guest. Lieutenant Governor Ira J. Chase delivered the invocation, B. J. Radford gave the dedicatory address, and John C. Miller conducted the formal dedication on behalf of the board. Visitors were invited to inspect Burgess Hall, and it was announced that it would serve the preparatory and music departments and house the library.[50]

The curriculum in 1889-1890 added a new course of study for the school. The project anticipated Bible study on a more advanced level and was under the supervision of Professors Hugh C. Garvin and A. R. Benton. These advanced classes for ministerial students (which would be understood sixty years later as seminary level courses) were in New Testament and Patristic Greek, Hebrew, church history and archeology. They required preliminary training in German, Greek, and Hebrew languages.[51] The catalog for the academic year 1891-1892 indicated that a Bible college had been formed (it was called a Bible school) within the framework of the university. It was not a department of the liberal arts college but a separate school, apparently on a graduate level. A four year ministerial program is described which included Bible study, church history, doctrine, Hebrew, Latin, Greek, and German. Students were to be trained in exegesis and original investigation and were required to have a knowledge of the "best theo-

---

[49]*Christian Standard,* March 29, 1890; June 3, 1891.
[50]*Christian Standard,* August 30, September 20, 1890.
[51]*Christian Standard,* March 22, 1890.

logical works." The curriculum was divided into *Quarta, Tertia, Secunda,* and *Prima* divisions. Courses in the *Secunda* and *Prima* divisions were regarded as graduate courses, and the M. A. degree was conferred on those who completed the work. The university at this time also included a preparatory department which apparently was regarded as the High School for the city of Irvington, and, in addition, there was a school of music.[52] Construction of a gymnasium began in 1891. It was completed the next year.

When the Board of Directors met on June 10, 1891, they elected Scot Butler[53] to succeed A. R. Benton as president. Benton continued at the school in a teaching position. Scot Butler was the son of Ovid Butler and the first president who was not a minister. Because he was experienced as a teacher and educated in Europe and America, the board believed Butler was a man of great promise. The next year the board authorized the establishing of a chair of history and Hugh Th. Miller[54] was elected to fill it. To prepare himself better for this position, Miller was granted a one-year leave of absence to study in Paris and Berlin.

The university seemed to enjoy financial prosperity and general popularity until about 1893 when the nation was

---

[52]Butler University Catalog, 1891-1892.

[53]Scot Butler (1849-1931), son of Ovid Butler, was born in Indiana and had his early schooling in Indianapolis. He was a student at North Western Christian University at the outbreak of the Civil War. Rather than purchase a commission he enlisted in the 33rd regiment of the Indiana Voluntary Infantry in 1862 and saw service in Kentucky, Tennessee and Georgia. After the war he returned to N. W. C. U. where he was graduated in 1868. He was an assistant instructor at Indiana University, 1869-1871, then joined the N. W. C. U. faculty to teach Latin. He was a student at Halle and Berlin, 1873-1875, returning to the Indianapolis school to become professor of Latin. He became president of Butler University in 1891.

[54]Hugh Th. Miller (1867-1947) was born near Nineveh, Indiana. When his father, John Chapman Miller, became pastor of Third Christian Church in Indianapolis and a member of the faculty at North Western Christian University in 1871, he brought his family to the city. Miller was graduated from Butler University in 1888, and became instructor in French and History at the school the next year. One of his students was Nettie Sweeney, daughter of Z. T. Sweeney, who later became his wife. He moved to Columbus in 1899 where he became cashier in Irwin's Bank. Miller was elected to the Indiana legislature in 1902, and in 1904 was elected lieutenant governor of the state. At the time of his death he was president of the Irwin Union Trust Company of Columbus, president of the Union Starch and Refining Company, and a Director of the School of Religion at Butler University.

struck with a major financial depression. The panic of 1893 was fully as severe as the one in 1873. Paralysis and fear gripped the business world. Over 8,000 business firms failed, many banks had to close their doors, and 156 railways went into receivership. Unemployment was acute everywhere. In the winter of 1893-1894 masses of unemployed persons formed themselves into "armies" to demonstrate against conditions. "General" Coxey, in a spectacular move, marched one of these detachments to Washington. Butler University, heretofore in a fairly secure financial position, accumulated a substantial indebtedness by 1894. Failure of a local bank in which the university funds and the accounts of many university stockholders were held greatly aggravated the situation.[55]

The university was desperately in need of money at this time, and so were the stockholders; since the financial institutions were not in a position to lend money, the school turned to Indiana Disciples for help. Knowing that the Disciple constituency was uneasy about the power structure of the university, Scot Butler based his appeal to the Indiana Christian Missionary Society to purchase $100,000 in stock from the stockholders on the premise that such a purchase would give the Society a controlling interest in the university. Under the charter, and with full control, the Society could then elect its own Board of Directors. It was made clear that such a move would give the State Society control of over a half million dollars' worth of assets in buildings and endowments. It was estimated that $25,000 could be raised for this purpose from the alumni, $25,000 from patrons, leaving but $50,000 for the Society to raise.[56]

Negotiations apparently went on for two years. The State Society appointed Daniel R. Lucas, pastor of Central Chris-

---

[55]Butler University *Minutes,* Book No. 5, July 11, 1894.
[56]*Christian Standard,* April 29, 1893.

tian Church in Indianapolis, as its agent; the university directors approved the choice. The matter was presented at the annual meeting of the State Society, to the State Ministerial Association, and explained in the Disciple journals. It seems that it was just as difficult for the Society to raise money at this time as it was for the university; after agonizing over it for several months the matter was finally dropped.

By means of cutting back on operating costs and by personal sacrifice of those involved, the school continued to operate. When the depression finally lifted, the school's immediate financial problems also passed away. Founders Day was observed for the first time on February 7, 1894. This seemed to be such a good idea that the Board of Directors decided to make the event a tradition. It was hereafter observed on this date, the anniversary of the birth of Ovid Butler, each year.[57] There were sixteen graduates at the Commencement of 1894; six were preachers. When the Board of Directors had their annual meeting at this time they increased their number to twenty-one.[58]

Controversy over Hugh C. Garvin

The financial problem at Butler University, occasioned by the panic of 1893, was infinitesimal compared with the uproar over the alleged heretical teachings of Hugh C. Garvin. There was a need for a Bible chair in the university, and Garvin was elected to it in 1889 as professor of Biblical literature and modern languages. He was very competent in linguistic studies and had become acquainted with Biblical criticism and theology in Germany. In establishing a Bible chair the university

---

[57]*Christian Standard,* March 3, 1894.

[58]Names of the directors at this time were: A. M. Atkinson, Joseph I. Irwin, M. T. Reeves, Howard Cale, U. C. Brewer, A. F. Armstrong, P. H. Jameson, Chauncey Butler, H. U. Brown, C. E. Thornton, William Mullendore, Carey E. Morgan, T. H. Kuhn, S. D. Noel, A. W. Brayton, A. M. Chamberlain, C. E. Hollenbeck, John S. Duncan, Albert Johnson, R. F. Kantz, and Dr. Strong.

had a desire to bring the newest and best in theological scholarship to the school. Professor A. M. Hall described the program by writing that clear-eyed criticism was sweeping away the traditional and theological cobwebs by examining every nook and corner of the *sanctum theologicum,* and that Butler University was trying to do its share. This was about the time that wide publicity was being given in the East to the "heresy" trials of Professor Charles A. Briggs and others. Though the Disciples knew very little about higher criticism, they were sure they were against it. They talked much about freedom and the right of individual interpretation of the Bible, but they were much concerned when they thought the new criticism had infiltrated into the university. Garvin apparently was trying to develop the Bible chair into a program of what now would be called academic excellence, but in so doing he encountered the enmity and suspicion of his preaching brethren. If he had been as knowledgeable in public relations as he was in academic pursuits the crisis might have been averted. Instead of giving direct answers to charges of heretical teaching he countercharged by telling his accusers (preachers, editors, and college presidents alike) that since they could not read the Bible in the original languages, did not know German, and were even weak on English grammar, their charges were unworthy of his attention. This was a poor way to win friends and influence people, as he later learned.

When the graduate program in theology got under way, ten students enrolled to pursue the courses. Professor Garvin was assisted by Professor Benton and President Butler. The quality of the program was popular with the serious students and the few who knew what was being attempted. It emphasized mastery of the Biblical languages and German. It envisioned the reading of the whole Old Testament in the unpointed Hebrew text, and the reading of the New Testament in the Greek text. Textual criticism, evidences, and exegesis were included in the curriculum. Theology, church history which included the patristic period, and hermeneutics were not neglected. Garvin's program was, without a doubt, the most original, ambitious, and advanced program of ministerial education ever undertaken by any Disciple school to this time.

The new Bible department was anything but popular with the Disciples' ministers in Indiana. The Indiana churches needed *preachers,* and Butler University was answering this need with scholars. This attitude is summed up editorially in the following excerpts from the *Indiana Christian:*[59]

> The educated physician is he who can save his patient. What is demanded today in the pulpit is great preachers, not great scholars. . . . The great scholar will never save the world.
>
> For eight years we have heard about this scholarship. How many souls have these two professors and ten or twelve preachers who accept their scholarly teaching rallied around the banner of Christ? . . . How many congregations have they organized and builded up?
>
> This scholarship has divided congregations and sown discord. It has rejected the commandments of Christ and turned away from primitive Christianity. This scholarship has made Congregational and New Light preachers out of our young men. From such scholarship, God deliver us.

The same editorial claimed: "J. W. McGarvey is the best Bible critic on the continent," and that "true scholarship everywhere quotes him as high authority." The use of McGarvey as an authority and as an ideal indicates that the primary difficulty was not with Professor Garvin's teaching (he made mistakes but was not a heretic), but with a certain spirit of anti-intellectualism that had permeated the thinking of the brethren by this time, coupled with a genuine fear that the new scholarship might jeopardize the validity of the Disciples' plea.

---

[59]*Indiana Christian,* June 15, 1896.

By the spring of 1894 the Indiana brethren were ready to take direct action against Professor Garvin. When the third district convention was held at Crawfordsville a resolution aimed at Professor Garvin was adopted.[60]

Resolved, That it is the judgment of this Convention that the churches of Christ in this District should reject all teachers who teach any or all of the following named doctrines:
(1) Repentance before faith in the salvation of sinners.
(2) Baptism of the Holy Spirit and of fire as taking place now.
(3) Judaism as being the religion of humanity, and Christianity as only a new Spirit put into it.
(4) That the death of Christ had no more to do with the salvation of the world than that of any other good man.
(5) That the Gospel of Christ is only a power among other powers in the salvation of men.

The editor of the *Christian Standard,* on reading this, expressed the view that this was condemnation without trial and asked that once begun, where would it lead? The editor of the *Christian-Evangelist,* in an article entitled, "A Dangerous Precedent," stated that the missionary convention was not the place to deal in theology. He further stated that the only heresy he had heard against Professor Garvin was that he taught that repentance precedes faith, a matter in which a majority of evangelical theologians would concur.

A letter, dated April 20, 1894, was sent to Professor Garvin. It was signed by fourteen ministers of the third district. The letter[61] stated:

Knowing you are not in harmony with the Disciples on some points of their teaching, and to the end that the churches be not alienated by your teaching from Butler University, we kindly ask you to resign the position you hold in the university.

---

[60]*Christian Standard,* May 12, 1894; *Christian-Evangelist,* April 26, 1894.
[61]*Christian Standard,* May 5, 1894.

A similar letter was prepared, signed by twenty-six ministers attending the State Society convention at Columbus in 1894, and sent to Professor Garvin.[62] Concerning this matter, Z. T. Sweeney wrote that these ministers had no intention of trying Professor Garvin for heresy, nor of preferring charges against him. He claimed they had no disposition to abridge Garvin's Christian liberty of thought or speech; they did ask him to transfer to another department of the university.

Butler University and the Irvington community in general remained loyal to Professor Garvin. The Board of Directors, at their annual meeting in 1894, took cognizance of the matter. Their decision was recorded in the *minutes:* "Resolved, that this Committee find nothing in the present situation requiring action of the Board."[63] President Butler made it plain to all that Professor Garvin would not be asked to resign. In an effort to find a way out of the impasse it was arranged for Garvin to lecture at the Bethany Park Assembly in the summer of 1894. His three lectures given at this time to the Ministerial Association were supposed to have had the purpose of clearing up misunderstandings concerning his theological views. The speeches, however, turned out to be so evasive and ambiguous that they did no more than to lead to further confusion. The carping and the criticism continued for another two years. Under pressure for further clarification Garvin wrote three articles for publication in the *Christian-Evangelist*.[64] J. H. Garrison, editor of the *Christian-Evangelist,* took the view that Garvin not only perverted and distorted the views of Alexander Campbell but that the articles were deliberately ambiguous and meandering in details. Garrison concluded his comment by writing, "It is now manifest as light

[62]*Christian Standard,* May 19, 1894; *Christian-Evangelist,* April 26, 1894.
[63]Butler University *Minutes,* Book No. 5, June 13, 1894.
[64]*Christian-Evangelist,* January 23, February 13, March 26, 1896.

itself that Professor Garvin is teaching a view of the gospel that is antagonistic to and subversive to the principles of the Reformation for which we have contended from the beginning. Either he is wrong or we have made our pleas in vain."[65]

The university tried to maintain its Bible School (seminary) in spite of the criticism leveled at it from all directions, The Board of Directors recorded in their *minutes* in 1895 that, "There is $40,000 in the Bible School endowment, and the board by the terms of Ovid Butler's gift is obligated to maintain a Bible department with two instructors."[66] The next spring the special course in Bible study for ministerial students was temporarily suspended because of "lack of funds." Professor Garvin was requested by the Board to transfer from the chair of Biblical philology to the chair of Germanic languages during Professor Howe's leave of absence. The Board of Directors also decided on the reorganization of the Bible School, to have a separate board of control "chosen by those contributing to the fund for the maintenance of said school."[67] The last official note concerning Professor Garvin stated, "The college loses the service of Hugh Carson Garvin this year [1897]. He has retired from the teaching profession and gone to West Virginia to pursue his studies to complete writings for publications already well advanced. He left an impact of scholarship on hundreds of students. The Board thanks him for his labors."[68]

The University of Indianapolis

The catalog of Butler College [the name had been changed by this time] for the academic year 1895-1896 indicated that the university had been merged into a collection of institutions

---

[65]*Christian-Evangelist*, January 23, February 13, March 26, 1896 (editorials).
[66]Butler College *Minutes*, Book No. 5, October 14, 1895.
[67]Butler College *Minutes*, Book No. 5, April 8, 1896.
[68]Butler College *Minutes*, Book No. 5, June 22, 1897.

in Indianapolis under the general name of the University of Indianapolis. Under this arrangement, Butler University became Butler College, a school of liberal arts. Other institutions included in the merger were the Medical College of Indiana, the Indiana Law School, and the Indiana Dental College. The merger contemplated further expansion into other professional fields. Under the terms of the merger agreement the new relationship did not affect the autonomy of Butler College, and control of all matters affecting internal management remained as heretofore with its own board of directors. The University of Indianapolis had a fifteen-member Board of Trustees; the president of the University and the mayor of Indianapolis were *ex officio* members of this board.[69] Academic matters were under the supervision of a Senate composed of one representative from each school, except Butler College which had two representatives. Scot Butler soon became president of the Academic Senate.

Open Membership Becomes an Issue

Open membership was introduced into the South Side Christian Church in Indianapolis in January, 1896. The case was reported in the *Christian Standard*[70] in an article which stated that the officers and pastor of this church had determined to admit persons to membership without immersion. The congregation met in the I. O. O. F. Hall on Virginia Avenue. The decision, made by minister George E. Hicks and his board, was not approved by all the members of the congregation; some twenty members transferred to other churches.

---

[69]The trustees named at this time were: P. H. Jameson, Thomas Taggart, Sterling R. Holt, Scot Butler, Eli Lilly, Benjamin Harrison, M. J. Osgood, Hilton U. Brown, A. C. Harris, Edward S. Dean, J. W. Marsee, and W. P. Fishback.

[70]*Christian Standard,* January 18, 1896. This is the second recorded case in the brotherhood. The first was the Cedar Avenue church in Cleveland. *See* Henry K. Shaw, *Buckeye Disciples, A History of the Disciples of Christ in Ohio* (St. Louis: Christian Board of Publication, 1952) pp. 288-290.

Open membership at South Side church was not very successful in its application. Hicks, with the remainder of his congregation, eventually became identified with another religious
body. Critics of Butler College were quick to hurl the charge
of "Garvinism" on minister and congregation. There was also
a tendency to thus stigmatize all of Professor Garvin's former
students, and suspicion of open membership was cast on some
of the churches where these students had been preaching.
Hoosier Disciple heresy hunters had a "field day" out of the
incident, but, fortunately, it was limited to a short period of
time.[71]

Extremism and the Sand Creek Platform

The most serious schism in the Christian Churches occurred
in southern Indiana, beginning in late 1895. It seemed to center in Lawrence and Owen counties. The congregations in this
area, for the most part, were extremely conservative, independent, and uncooperative. Their leaders objected to Sunday
schools, missionary societies, the Christian Endeavor movement, salaried (professional) pastors, and most of all to the
use of instrumental music in church worship. The "ruling
elders" in these congregations had faith only in the Bible, the
Firm Foundation, the *Christian Leader,* the *Octographic Review,* and in their own ability to determine truth in religion.
They held to the view that those who became members of a
missionary or aid society, a Sunday school, or an Endeavor
society were heretics and should be rejected by the church.
One congregation excluded twenty-six members for belonging to Christian Endeavor, and a like number of "sisters" were
excluded from another church for belonging to an aid society.[72]

---

[71]*Christian Standard,* February 1, March 14, 1896; *Indiana Christian,* April 15, 1896.
[72]*Christian Standard,* June 6, September 12, December 5, 1896.

272

Communication between these brethren and those in churches cooperating with Disciple institutions and agencies began to cease in the middle 1880's and almost came to an end by 1890. When a congregation took this extremist position it was usually indicated by stating that it had accepted the "Sand Creek" platform. In Indiana, the Sand Creek platform, Daniel Sommer, and the *Octographic Review* were almost synonymous terms. They meant schism.

The Sand Creek platform was the position taken in the *Sand Creek Address and Declaration.* The authors, obviously impressed with Thomas Campbell's *Declaration and Address,* probably thought they had produced a document of the same order and importance. Before P. D. Warren read the "Address and Declaration" at the Shelby County, Illinois yearly meeting, held at the Sand Creek church in 1889, Daniel Sommer delivered a lengthy address.[73] Sommer, editor of the *Octographic Review,* made a vigorous attack on the "innovations" such as the organ, missionary societies, etc., that had infiltrated the heretofore "pure" church of Christ. The Sand Creek *Address and Declaration,* which bore the signatures of officers of several congregations (this in itself was not consistent with the position taken), stated that there were now among them persons who taught and practiced things not taught and found in Scripture, *i.e.,* church festivals, instrumental music, choirs, societies, and the one-man pastorate; such persons were advised to turn away speedily from these things. The crux of the document is in the concluding phrase, "If they will not turn away from such abominations, then we can not and will not regard them as brethren." In this manner, therefore, the Sand Creek brethren built a creedal wall around themselves; others had to agree to the principles of the *Sand*

---

[73]*Octographic Review,* September 5, 1889.

Creek Address and Declaration, or fellowship was denied to them. The declaration was amended in 1892 with a clause which was recommended for use in the property deeds of churches. It declared, "No instrumental music or other innovations should ever be used on the premises."

The Sand Creek platform gave the ultra-conservatives a tangible statement which could be used as a test of fellowship. The congregations accepting it became a part of a separated group, and by its terms no longer in the Christian Church (Disciples of Christ) movement. Like-minded extremists and churches sympathetic to the Sand Creek point of view soon found one another. It was not long before the Sand Creek platform and program invaded southern Indiana. Daniel Sommer moved his *Octographic Review* to Indianapolis in 1894, and became the spokesman and recognized leader of the movement in this state. E. B. Scofield of the Indiana Christian Missionary Society was very much concerned over the future of southern Indiana for the Disciples. He wrote that there was "a campaign to stampede as many churches as possible and close them to constructive enterprises."[74] By 1896 a separation had already taken place. The religious census of 1906 recognized two distinct church bodies, one known as Disciples of Christ, and the other known as Churches of Christ.

Emergence of a New Disciple Image

The period 1883-1896 was one in which Hoosier Disciples began to lose their smug complacency about the inviolability and sanctity of their distinctive plea, and the idea that the whole religious world would eventually have to turn to them and accept their ideas. This was the period also when Disciples awoke to the fact that they could not live in isolated

[74]*Christian Standard,* June 6, 1896.

security and maintain their spiritual integrity. To their credit they developed a wholesome desire for self-improvement and expressed this through their "Chautauqua-type" summer assemblies, emphasis on the work of the Sunday school, promoting the new youth movement, and even in the establishing of lecture bureaus. They began to show evidence of maturity in the sharing of church leadership with the women of the congregation, supporting the various missionary societies, and in taking a vital interest in the work of missionaries at home and abroad. The establishing of a board of ministerial relief indicates an awakening of a social conscience. By this time they began to see what really needed to be done to fulfill their mission, and they were willing to take the steps necessary to organize for action. In the Butler University "Garvin case," the fact that mistakes were made on both sides does not alter the argument that by this time Hoosier Disciples were vitally interested in an educated ministry and felt responsibility toward it. A court battle to prove they were not a "queer" sectarian group, but in the main stream of Christianity, indicates a desire for public approval and acceptance. The fact that extremist elements (right and left) in their midst separated from them during this period is a clear gauge of the direction the main body was taking. Hoosier Disciples were beginning to "grow up." The image of the mid-twentieth century Disciple made its first shadowy appearance over the Hoosier horizon at the end of the nineteenth century.

VIII

Struggle for Status and Numbers
1897-1913

AT THE TURN OF THE CENTURY the Disciples were still disassociating their religious views from the world about them. Existing social movements (with the exception of Prohibition), political events, economic development, and population change were subjects rarely mentioned in their journals and never seriously considered. Even the Spanish-American War, popular with most Americans, was scarcely considered worthy of attention. Members of the Christian Churches lived in this world, were a part of it and enjoyed it; they even let some of the world get into the church, but they were careful not to let the church get into the world.

With them, evangelism took the form of salvation from the "wickedness" of denominationalism by offering full security in the "Scriptural" church. The brotherhood of the Disciples was concerned with white, middle-class, American-born, "solid" citizens in order to win them to their "plea" and add them to their numbers. It would not be correct to state that they were not interested in the spiritual welfare of these people because they were vitally concerned at this point; but neither can it be denied that in the period 1897-1913 their primary motivation was to advance their status and increase their numbers. There was a tremendous emphasis on professional evangelism during the latter part of this period, but if it had not been for this emphasis the Christian Churches (Disciples of Christ) may not have become a major American religious body.

The Great Evangelistic Campaigns

Indiana felt the impact of professional evangelism much as, if not more than, other states in this period; some of the strongest professional teams originated in the Hoosier state. Evangelism, for the Disciples of the early twentieth century, was the proclamation of their "plea." The chief result of evangelism, they believed, was the winning of the Christian world to the Disciples' position. Those who were in the mainstream of Disciples' thought were of the opinion that the "plea" as they understood it, was the *sine qua non* of the Christian faith. It was their firm conviction that it was indispensable and necessary for the unity and ultimate victory of Christ's church. Though their evangelists adopted the methods of interdenominational evangelists of the day, their message was not the same. Their sermons, especially those preached in specific campaigns, were variations on themes related to the "plea."[1] There is no question but that they were happy when souls were saved, but news reports indicate they especially rejoiced when they won people away from the traditional denominations.

The evangelism of the early twentieth century was almost completely identified with special intensive membership drives sometimes called evangelistic campaigns or revival meetings.

---

[1]This can be illustrated by sermon titles characteristic of Disciple evangelistic meetings. A typical sampling of subjects could contain the following: The Church of the New Testament, The One Baptism, The Gospel Plan of Salvation, What Church Did Jesus Establish? The Sect Everywhere Spoken Against, Are The Churches of Christ a Denomination? The Church Lost and Found, The Good Confession, How to Become a Christian, Why I am a Christian Only, The Lord's Supper, Christian Union, Baptism in a Nutshell, Bible Repentance, Defense of the Faith, The Significance of Names, The Infallibly Safe Course, Terms of Discipleship, etc.

Before professional evangelism became popular "meetings" were either conducted by a local pastor for his own congregation, by a neighboring pastor who was borrowed for the occasion, or by district and county evangelists. Some of the men apparently had more success in this work than others and found themselves giving more and more time to it. As evangelistic campaigns became popular the demand for evangelists increased. The full-time professional evangelist soon came to be recognized as one who belonged to a "special" order of the Disciples' clergy. In due time the professional evangelist expanded his program far beyond that of a one-man preaching mission. The evangelistic meeting then became a campaign, promoted and conducted by a company of several persons, each skilled in a particular area. Such companies consisted of an evangelist who always had top billing; the song leader who, though important, rated second place; other musicians who were responsible for huge volunteer choirs and entertainment features such as the playing of unusual "musical" instruments, *i.e.,* hand saws, wine glasses or cow bells; children's workers, laborers, and a business manager. Sometimes the capital outlay in tent or tabernacle quarters, rentals, furniture, song books, printed tracts, posters, prizes, advertising and salaries ran into fabulous figures. The campaigns were big business, usually so well organized, advertised, and administered, that success in terms of new converts (usually called additions) could almost be predicted, if not guaranteed.

Evangelistic preaching was natural for the pioneer preacher. He was not a settled pastor anyway, but an itinerant evangelist who looked after several congregations. When settled pastorates became popular they were hardly ever of long duration, usually for a few months only; at that time a settled pastorate was little more than an extended evangelistic meeting. By the

278

end of the century, however, the evangelistic meeting became an important phase of the annual work cycle of the church. Hundreds of meetings were held in Hoosier churches on this basis.[2]

In the early 1900's the State Society began the practice of employing persons whose sole responsibility was in the evangelistic field. The state evangelist gave full time to the holding of evangelistic meetings and to the directing of a large number of part-time evangelists who continued in their pastoral charges while serving two or three months of the year on the field. The state evangelist held twenty-seven meetings in 1903, resulting in 507 accessions; thirty-four additional meetings were held by part-time evangelists under the direction of the State Board, resulting in 624 accessions. Salvation was not free, but it was not too expensive. The cost of the 1,131 accessions for the year was reported as $1.07 per new member.[3]

Profile of an Evangelistic Campaign

A typical large-scale evangelistic campaign was held at Marion in July, 1905.[4] The Tabernacle and Central churches united their efforts to promote a city-wide campaign. Plans

---

[2]For instance, among the churches reporting evangelistic meetings in 1899 were the following: Anderson, Aurora, Central (Indianapolis), Corrunna, East Columbus, Edwardsport, Elkhart, Elwood, Englewood (Indianapolis), Evansville, Flora, Gilead, Hammond, Hartford City, Huntington, Ingalls, Kendallville, Knox, Kokomo, Lebanon, Lynn, Martinsville, Mill Creek, Montpelier, Nashville, Noblesville, Osgood, Pennville, Remington, Shoals, Smithfield, Sullivan, Union (Morgan County), Wabash, Walesboro, Winamac, and Winchester. Preachers engaged in holding these meetings were reported as being J. C. Anderson, J. C. Ashley, D. W. Campbell, J. M. Canfield, L. L. Carpenter, J. D. Carson, C. C. Cline, A. P. Cobb, J. V. Coombs, . . . Crim, C. H. De Voe, A. J. Frank, E. L. Frazier, . . . Hackleman, J. E. Hawes, . . . Harkins, T. H. Kuhn, A. Martin, Eugene Martin, . . . McGowan, H. C. Patterson, A. B. Philputt, M. F. Rickoff, J. O. Rose, C. R. Scoville, J. L. Sharitt, . . . Starr, S. A. Strawn, W. B. F. Treat, P. O. Updike, J. H. Vincent, Earl Wilfley, and M. W. Yocum. The prefix "brother" in some reports, rather than first names or initials, makes it impossible to identify some of the men precisely.

[3]*Indiana Christian*, October 15, 1903. This is a report of Allan B. Philputt, president of the State Board. State evangelistic efforts were primarily directed to establishing new congregations in unoccupied county seat towns. Philputt claimed that churches were needed at Albion, La Grange, Columbia City, Crown Point, Bluffton, Newport, Booneville, Cannelltown, Petersburg, Jasper, Versailles, Goodland, Paoli, and Vernon.

[4]*Christian Standard*, July 15, August 12, 19, 1905.

were made three months in advance of the meeting. W. S. Buchanan was minister at the Tabernacle church, and Merritt Owen served the Central congregation. They both believed the Disciples were completely overshadowed by the "denominations" in Marion, and the campaign was to be a program of doing something about it. They stated that their main objective was the reaching of Marion citizens with the Disciples' plea. The project had its beginning with a community census which indicated there were 150 Disciples in the city, not identified with the Christian churches. Evangelists employed for the work were R. F. Fife of Kansas City, T. J. Legg of Indianapolis, and J. M. Elam of Rensselaer. H. H. Saunders of Noblesville, Edward McKinney of Dorsey, Illinois, and P. A. Parsons of Plainfield, New Jersey, were engaged as singers and helpers. Tents were set up in the central, western and southern parts of the city so that three programs could be conducted simultaneously. The stores, railroad stations, factories and telephone poles were plastered with 1,000 large posters. Regular articles on the Disciples, who they were and what they were doing, were splashed across the front pages of local newspapers. Thousands of tracts were distributed, and 6,000 "extra" newssheets (containing campaign propaganda) were thrown on front porches. The projected meeting soon became the talk of the town. When the campaign proper got under way, prayer meetings were held each morning and afternoon. Also, special services were held on the public square. It was reported that 20,000 people attended the Sunday and weeknight services in the three tents during the month, resulting in 130 additions to the churches. A union communion service was held in the central tent at the close of the campaign. T. J. Legg organized a church in South Marion as a by-product of the evangelistic emphasis. The entire expense of the program, covered by voluntary offerings, was under $1,000.

The Scoville Meetings

Hoosier-born Charles Reign Scoville[5] was one of the most successful of the professional evangelists of this period. As early as 1901 it was reported in the *Indiana Christian* that Scoville had the qualities of all the greatest evangelists, and that "he had taken more scriptural confessions in one year than any other preacher on the continent. Chapman, Mills and Moody are far behind." Many of his campaigns were held in Indiana. Among these were meetings at Butler, Noblesville, South Bend, Muncie, Indianapolis, Lafayette, Connersville and Anderson. The revival at Anderson, where T. W. Grafton was minister, was considered highly successful. There were 1,561 additions in the first Anderson meeting of 1906. A second meeting was held at the same place in 1909. Scoville was a forceful speaker and an excellent organizer and administrator. He was one of the first of the few Disciple evangelists to enter the interdenominational field. Because of this, one Disciple editor accused him of losing his faith! He made an evangelistic tour around the world in 1912, concentrating on many huge campaigns in Australia. The party on this trip consisted of Scoville, his wife, Arlene Dux Scoville, soloist; C. R. L. Vawter, assistant evangelist and cornetist; Mrs. Caroll E. Marty, personal worker; and H. F. Phillippi, assistant evangelist. The Scoville campaigns were always thoroughly organized with as many as fifteen local committees to look after

---

[5]Charles Reign Scoville (1869-1938) was born in De Kalb County, Indiana. He received the B.S. degree from Tri-State Normal College in 1892, the A.B. from Hiram College in 1897 and the A.M. from the same school in 1898. Drake University honored him with the LL.D. degree in 1901. Scoville held numerous revivals while still a student at Hiram College. After a pastorate at the Metropolitan Church, Chicago, 1901-1905, he conducted numerous local church campaigns in the brotherhood. In 1917-18 he entered the service of the Y.M.C.A. to do field work in military camps. Following World War I, he became primarily a "union meeting" evangelist. Scoville helped to organize the National Evangelistic Association of the Disciples of Christ and was president of this organization, 1920-1925. For further biographical information *see* H. H. Peters, *Charles Reign Scoville, the Man and His Message* (St. Louis: Bethany Press, 1925). He authored the book, *Evangelistic Sermons* (Des Moines: Christian Union Publishing Company, 1902) and several song books in collaboration with E. O. Excell, W. E. M. Hackleman *et al.*

such matters as building erection and maintenance, advertising, devotions, ushers, music, finance, young people, transportation, entertainment, personal workers, instruction, and conservation of converts.

In the work of Charles Reign Scoville the "big team" professional type of evangelistic campaign for the Disciples reached its zenith of popularity. There were other highly successful professional companies that followed this pattern, but for the most part, interest in such campaigns began to decline in the late 1920's; evangelism began to be equated with the normal function of the pastorate as a year-round program rather than as a series of sporadic efforts.

The State Society, Restructure in 1897

Apparently E. B. Scofield declined to serve as corresponding secretary after 1896. T. J. Legg had this office beginning in 1897, and J. V. Coombs served with him as state evangelist. The State Board needed a wider base of support for its program, and it was thought that this could be accomplished through restructure. To the fifteen members of the State Board were added the fourteen district secretaries who served in an *ex officio* capacity. Each county was urged to organize itself with a president, vice president, secretary and treasurer. Officers of the county boards were then to become *ex officio* members of the district boards. It was also recommended that each church appoint a missionary secretary to be responsible for missionary collections the first week of each calendar quarter. The funds were to be raised on a five-year subscription plan based on a uniform stewardship canvass in each county, and were to be expended only in preaching the gospel in the weaker churches.[6] The State Convention held at

---

[6]*Indiana Christian*, October 15, 1897.

South Bend, June 14-16, 1898, was a delegate convention. Each church contributing $5.00 was entitled to one delegate, and one additional delegate for each additional $5.00 contributed. Individuals who paid an annual fee of $1.00 were also considered members of the voting body. The convention enrolled 117 delegates that year.[7] The Irvington church entertained the convention the next year. The Constitution of the organization was revised at this time and its name changed to *The Missionary Society of the Churches of Christ in Indiana.* No one liked this name; the name *Indiana Christian Missionary Society* was preferred, but the brethren thought they had to use the name under which they were incorporated and hoped that the charter could be changed in the near future. Under the revised Constitution, adopted at Irvington, the organization in the future was to be made up of members and delegates of churches.[8]

An alphabetical list of Indiana Disciple preachers in 1897, together with information on where they preached, appeared in the November 15th issue of the *Indiana Christian.* There were 356 names. Many of these Hoosier preachers became well known later as brotherhood leaders.[9] The State Ministerial Association held its 34th annual convention at Muncie, May 10-12, 1898. Burris A. Jenkins and John L. Brandt lectured to the men. The preachers enjoyed Muncie, at this time a city of 25,000 people, and they especially liked the conducted street car excursion to the glass factories and foundries in the vicinity.[10]

---

[7]*Indiana Christian,* March 15, July 15, 1898. New officers elected at this time were E. B. Scofield, president; H. C. Kendrick, vice president; W. E. M. Hackleman, secretary; and Amos Clifford, treasurer.

[8]*Indiana Christian,* June, 1899.

[9]Among them were Edward Scribner Ames, A. R. Benton, B. M. Blount, W. C. Bower, John L. Brandt, J. V. Coombs, Jabez Hall, B. A. Jenkins, T. J. Legg, John E. Pounds, H. R. Pritchard, Perry J. Rice, C. R. Scoville, Z. T. Sweeney, J. V. Updike, and E. P. Wise. The *Year Book* of the American Home Missionary Society for 1897 also contains a list of Indiana preachers.

[10]*Indiana Christian,* April 15, June 15, 1898; *Christian-Evangelist,* May 19, 1898.

Christian Endeavor

Youth work in this period was expressed primarily through Christian Endeavor. B. L. Allen was state superintendent of Christian Endeavor for the Disciples in 1897. He stated there were 500 Endeavor societies in the Christian churches of Indiana and that this was one hundred more than any other communion in the state could claim. The South Bend society, with its 102 members, was the largest; Angola, with 99 members, was next in size. Christian Endeavor was in such a flourishing condition that by 1899 the *Indiana Christian* began to carry a column on Christian Endeavor prayer meeting topics. This was in addition to another full column on the activities of the various societies. Disciple Endeavorers in Indiana cooperated with the interdenominational State Union but felt that they did not get their share of recognition and that they were deliberately kept out of the power structure of the organization.[11]

Prohibition Becomes an Issue

The cause of Prohibition was the one socio-political issue that the Disciples took seriously. Temperance, preached in the churches prior to the last decade of the nineteenth century, came to mean the prohibition by law of the manufacture and sale of intoxicating beverages. Scarcely a sermon was preached in the beginning years of the twentieth century in which the saloon was not the target of the preachers' oratory. Charles M. Fillmore, rabid prohibitionist, in a strong article entitled, "Face the Facts,"[12] wrote to the effect that the saloons did the devil's work; they ruined man physically, mentally, mor-

---

[11]*Indiana Christian*, September 15, 1897; April 15, December 15, 1898; June, 1899.
[12]*Indiana Christian*, August 15, 1898.

ally, financially, politically, socially, and spiritually; they were the enemies of the home, the church, and the state; they were anarchists, ballot corrupters, the resorts of criminals, and common nuisances. C. M. and J. H. Fillmore edited a special hymnal in 1900 entitled, *Fillmores' Prohibition Songs.* The hymns bore interesting titles such as: "The Saloon Must Go," "We'll Vote for Prohibition," "Bibles and Beer," "Stand Up for Prohibition," and "The Saloonatic." The words in the refrain of one of the songs express the intense feeling held against the saloon:

We stand for Prohibition	Complete extermination,
The utter demolition	Entire annihilation,
Of all this curse of misery and woe;	The saloon must go.

Most of the churches of that period (and lodges as well) refused fellowship to drinkers and venders. All those connected in any way with the liquor business had little if any status in the Christian community. The Anti-Saloon League of America, the Prohibition Party, and the Woman's Christian Temperance Union were strong forces in Hoosier Disciple churches. The cause of Prohibition developed into a national crusade in this period and eventually gained tremendous political influence and power.

Brotherhood Convention in Indianapolis

Burris A. Jenkins headed the local committee in Indianapolis which was responsible for entertaining the national convention of the Disciples, October 14-22, 1897. Indianapolis, with its population of 200,000 people, had twelve Christian churches with a total membership of 4,000. Rooms and breakfasts were provided free to delegates, and some

285

1,700 persons took advantage of the generous hospitality. Distinguished Disciples,[13] many of them representing Christian Church agencies, gave addresses at Tomlinson's Hall. For many Hoosiers, not only was this a first introduction to some famous Disciples but to other religious leaders such as Booker T. Washington. Washington, well-known Negro leader, was welcomed to the rostrum of the convention in a storm of applause. The convention format in 1897 was much the same as is now in use, even in the communion service. Some 5,000 persons were present at this service, and the hall was decorated with flags from many countries. Large portraits of Alexander Campbell, Isaac Errett and John O'Kane were displayed at the front of the hall; portraits of James A. Garfield, Raccoon John Smith, Otis A. Burgess, S. K. Hoshour, Love Jameson, and Benjamin Franklin, together with mottos and slogans, appeared on the side walls. The Governor of the state was a special guest, and D. R. Lucas was described as the "generalissimo" of the occasion.[14]

The State Society, 1900-1905

The state convention for 1900 met at Valparaiso on May 15 in conjuction with the ministers' institute. Publicity emphasis was placed on the fact that this city of 9,000 people was the home of Northern Indiana Normal College, the "largest normal college in the world." The school was described as having 3,000 students and a faculty of 60 to 70 professors. H. C. Brown, founder and president, was a member of the Chris-

---

[13]Among these were the following: Charles L. Loos, A. McLean, F. M. Rains, Clinton L. Lockhart, C. B. Newman, W. C. Payne, W. R. Lloyd, C. S. Medbury, H. W. Everest, B. C. Deweese, J. P. Pinkerton, W. P. Aylesworth, M. M. Davis, Benjamin L. Smith, B. B. Tyler, John Henry Barrows, B. C. Hagerman, A. M. Atkinson, G. W. Mulkey, C. C. Smith, G. A. Hoffman, R. H. Waggener, J. Z. Tyler, F. D. Power, Herbert L. Willett, J. A. Lord, J. H. Garrison, George Darsie, Granville Jones, P. Y. Pendleton, Alexander Proctor, Carey E. Morgan, Mark Collis, and D. R. Dungan.

[14]*Indiana Christian*, October 15, 1897; *Christian-Evangelist*, October 28, 1897.

tian Church.[15] Statistics,[16] published in 1900, showed that the Disciples had 500 preachers in Indiana, and that 425 were cooperative. There were 891 congregations with a total membership of 119,000 persons. The convention met at Anderson in 1901, and at Terre Haute in 1902.

The *Indiana Christian* proved to be a good medium of communication for the State Society, especially in the early part of this period. B. L. Allen retired as managing editor at the end of 1898. Under his able leadership the journal had increased in circulation from 1,500 to 5,500 copies. He was followed by E. B. Scofield who continued Allen's editorial policies, though the paper was reduced in size and published by the firm of Scofield and Hackleman. W. E. M. Hackleman took entire charge of the paper beginning in 1901. There was a noticeable change in the editorial policy at this time. There was less news and articles were slanted against persons suspected of holding liberal theological views. For example, it was stated in one issue, "Professor Willett has written a book. The professor should not have done it." Delicate subjects were not always handled with tact. The Ministerial Relief number, for example, compared the retired minister to an old horse who "is not as spry and useful as he was twenty or thirty years ago, but he is well loved and cared for by the family." The paper must have ceased publication in 1903; there are no numbers extant for the period 1903-1914. An announcement was made at the Bedford convention in 1905 that the State Society planned to start a monthly paper, and the *Indiana Christian* is supposed to have been resurrected in 1906. It is possible that a few numbers were printed at this time, but there is no evidence of consistent, continuous pub-

---

[15]*Christian-Evangelist*, May 24, 1900; *Indiana Christian*, June 1, 1900.

[16]*Indiana Christian*, November 1, 1900. The *Year Book* of the American Home Missionary Society for 1900 lists 844 churches, 107,000 members, 756 Sunday schools, and 507 ministers.

lication until volume one, number one, appeared as the *Indiana Worker* in January, 1914.

The State Society was giving assistance to a number of mission points by 1903.[17] This was an era of good feeling, and optimism prevailed among Hoosier Disciples.[18] Cephas Shelburne wrote, "Indiana is taking the plea of the Disciples as her religion; the Disciples are taking Indiana as their representative state." He claimed that Indiana had more Disciples to the square mile than any other state in the union, and that it was the geographical center of the brotherhood.[19] This burst of optimism and confidence seems to have stemmed from the reading of the statistics published in the *Year Book* for 1903. Professor Amzi Atwater of Bloomington, in an analysis of the *Year Book* figures, wrote that Indiana had 924 churches with 123,000 members. He claimed that 324 of these churches were strong and active, 300 were doing passably well, and 300 were weak and dying out. He explained this situation by writing that some churches had been planted unadvisedly, some had experienced bad leaders, and that many, after a promising start, had not followed up their program by Christian nurture.[20] The *Indiana Christian* used the *Year Book* for a comparison study. According to this source Indiana ranked second among the states in Christian Church members, excelled only by Missouri; in Bible schools she ranked first, having a total enrollment of 120,000. Other comparisons claimed first place for Christian Endeavor (660 societies), fourth place in the value of church property, and eighth place in the amount of money raised for state missions.[21]

---

[17]These mission points were named as Plymouth, Stroh, Akron, Attica, Cambridge City, Fountain City, Peru, Seymour, Spearsville (Brown County), Mt. Vernon, Bourbon, Walton, Cave Mills, Middle Fork, and "other minor points."

[18]*Indiana Christian*, January 15, 1903.

[19]*Christian-Evangelist*, March 19, 1903.

[20]*Christian-Evangelist*, March 19, 1903.

[21]*Indiana Christian*, February 14, 1903.

Allan B. Philputt[22] was president of the Sixty-fourth annual State Convention at Greenfield, May 13-15, 1903. As a new feature of the convention, the Christian Woman's Board of Missions, Young People's Society of Christian Endeavor, and the State Sunday School Association met in cooperative sessions.[23] The convention was held at Lebanon[24] in 1904. A report issued later that year showed that 42 churches had been organized between September, 1903, and March, 1904; the report also showed that thirteen evangelists and missionaries had been supported by the State Society during the year. There were sixteen projects called "standing missions" in the state at this time. J. O. Rose was called to be corresponding secretary that fall.[25] The Bedford church entertained the convention held May 16-18, 1905. J. H. Garrison, editor of the *Christian-Evangelist,* visited this convention as a guest of his son Winfred E. Garrison, president of Butler College. He reported later that A. B. Philputt was a model presiding officer, that he was impressed by the semi-centennial announcements concerning Butler College, that Indiana had a larger element of anti-organ people than any other state, that the convention authorized the publication of a monthly paper, and that "Indiana has its face turned toward the future."[26]

---

[22]Allan B. Philputt (1856-1925) was born in Tennessee and his parents brought him to southern Indiana at the close of the Civil War. He was graduated from Indiana University in 1880. Later, he studied at Harvard University and the Episcopal Divinity School at Philadelphia. He held pastorates at Bloomington, Indiana; Philadelphia, Pennsylvania; and Indianapolis. The Indianapolis pastorate was at Central Christian Church and extended from 1898 to 1919. He served as president of the American Christian Missionary Society, on the board of directors of both Butler College and the Christian Board of Publication, and on the Board of Managers of the United Christian Missionary Society.

[23]*Indiana Christian,* May 15, 1903.

[24]*Christian-Evangelist,* May 5, 1904. The officers and workers that year were A. B. Philputt, president; E. B. Scofield, Sunday school evangelist; T. J. Legg, state evangelist; W. E. M. Hackleman, secretary; and W. S. Moffett, treasurer.

[25]*Christian-Evangelist,* May 25, 1905.

[26]*Christian-Evangelist,* May 25, 1905.

School of the Evangelists

A school for preachers had its inception at the Bethany Park Assembly in 1904. It was sponsored by the State Ministerial Association. Many Disciple preachers in Indiana had never received formal academic training in the ministry and desired to take some "professional" courses. There were others who felt the need for "refresher" studies. The school of preachers, eventually known as the School of the Evangelists, was projected by the Assembly as part of its responsibility; sessions followed the annual meeting of the State Ministerial Association, and an impressive faculty was brought together for the experiment.[27]

An Experiment with a Hospital

The Disciples in Indiana launched their first experiment in hospital care for the sick in 1905. With the aid of the National Benevolent Association and the Christian church at Valparaiso, the Loring Hospital in that city was purchased and set in operation as the Valparaiso Christian Hospital. The building was remodeled ten years later. Many favorable comments were received on the hospital, but it never had much more than local character and local support. In 1937, the National Benevolent Association, the organization holding title to the institution, sold the hospital to the Christian Hospital and Training School for Nurses. N. B. A. officials stated at the time of the sale that the organization had never definitely intended to enter the field of hospital care and that the disposal of the property would free them to give entire attention to benevolent work for the aged and orphans.[28]

---

[27]*Christian Standard*, July 23, 1904. Faculty members: E. B. Wakefield of Hiram College, B. C. Deweese of Kentucky University, J. B. Briney of Louisville, Jabez Hall of Butler Bible College; C. B. Newman and A. B. Philputt, Indianapolis ministers.

[28]F. M. Rogers, editor, *Fifty Years' March of Mercy* (St. Louis: National Benevolent Association, 1937) p. 27; *Christian-Evangelist*, August 22, 1912; *N. B. A. Family Talk*, March, 1937, p. 6.

The State Society Restructured Again, 1906-1909

The state convention met at Lafayette in 1906. J. O. Rose[29] who was corresponding secretary by this time, claimed a forty-one per cent gain in cash receipts and a sixteen per cent gain in the number of churches contributing to the work of the State Society. During the year there had been sixty-one evangelistic meetings held, resulting in 1,404 accessions. Rose also reported that twelve new churches had been organized, thirty-nine new buildings had been erected and sixteen more remodeled.[30]

At the suggestion of W. E. M. Hackleman,[31] secretary of the Bethany Park Assembly, it was decided to have the annual meetings of all the state organizations meet at Bethany Park the next year in one convention of eight days with interwoven programs. These organizations (Indiana Christian Missionary Society, State Sunday School Association, State Christian Endeavor, Indiana C. W. B. M., State Ministerial Association and Butler College) heretofore each had their own week of activities, and it spread the total program out over too long a period of time. It was thought that the telescoping of all these meetings into eight days would also solve the problem offered by the competition of recreational facilities which formerly had detracted people from the formal business sessions. The new plan envisioned a week of annual business

---

[29]J. O. Rose (1864-1941) was born in Steuben County, Indiana. He attended Tri-State Normal College at Angola and The College of the Bible at Lexington. Rose held pastorates at Kendallville, Lebanon, and Warsaw, and was corresponding secretary of the Indiana Christian Missionary Society, 1903-1909. He went to Angola in 1913 to assume a Bible Chair professorship at Tri-State College, one established by the Indiana C.W.B.M. After continuing in this work for seventeen years he turned his attention to the building up of the Lake James Assembly project.

[30]*Christian Standard*, May 12, 1906; *Christian-Evangelist*, November 1, 1906.

[31]W. E. M. Hackleman (1868-1927) was founder and president of the Hackleman Book-Music Supply Company of Indianapolis. He began as an evangelistic singer in 1885 and subsequently worked in 300 evangelistic campaigns. He is supposed to have directed the music in over 500 conventions, many of them assemblies of other religious groups. Hackleman led the singing of 35,000 people at the Communion Service of the Pittsburgh Centennial Convention in 1909. He served at different times as both secretary and president of the Bethany Park Assembly and was on the board of the Indiana Christian Missionary Society for many years.

meetings, a week for the program of the School of the Evangelists, and a third week reserved for "Rest, recreation, innocent amusements, religious instruction, sweet fellowship, and very many things that will advance the interest of the Redeemer's kingdom, and to make all who attend better and stronger to do brave work for the Master." Those who promoted the new plan firmly believed that it would attract at least 3,000 people to Bethany Park.[32]

Bringing the annual meetings of all the state organizations back to Bethany Park in 1907 led to another change in the structure of the State Convention. J. O. Rose, corresponding secretary of the state missionary society, explained that whereas there had been but seventy-one preachers and a few other persons in attendance at the 1906 convention at Lafayette, over one thousand people attended the 1907 convention at Bethany Park. The success of the union project at Bethany Park led to the consolidation of the Sunday School Association and State Christian Endeavor organization as departments of the Indiana Christian Missionary Society. Rose further explained that in the future there would be one state treasurer, W. S. Moffett, but separate bookkeeping accounts would be maintained. Increased convention attendance in 1907 was not reflected in the treasurer's report. The total amount received by the Society from all sources was $4,503.89. The requirements of the delegate system were apparently overlooked at the Bethany Park meeting, though a reporting system to the *Indiana Christian* was developed whereby the counties were linked to the districts and the districts to the state. According to Secretary Rose, 645 of the 800 Christian churches in Indiana did not support the state missionary work. Rose also reported that there were seven evangelists under the direct

---

[32]*Christian Standard,* January 26, June 1, 1907.

pay of the State Board; these men had held 43 meetings in the past year, obtained 751 additions, organized six new churches and reorganized fourteen more.[33]

The annual conventions of the state organizations continued to meet at Bethany Park in 1908 and 1909. Austin Hunter served as president of the convention during both of these years. Although the great crowd of people that had been anticipated by the return to Bethany Park was not realized, the financial situation of the State Society began to improve about this time. In 1909 the permanent funds increased from $11,-000 to $28,000; the regular offerings increased to $7,119.67. The salaried workers that year were J. O. Rose, corresponding secretary; T. J. Legg, state evangelist; William Chapple, special evangelist (Marshall T. Reeves of Columbus paid half his salary); and Melnotte Miller, special evangelist. There were 786 Christian churches in the state; 155 had full-time preaching and 224 no regular preaching at all. The State Society sponsored a great number of evangelistic meetings during the year, and seven new congregations were organized.[34]

The City Union Movement

Population growth in urban centers was a stimulus to Disciples to organize new congregations in these places. When a city had several Christian churches it became important to have them structured in what was called a "City Union." One of the first of such City Unions in the Hoosier state was organized at Indianapolis in 1896. The organization was composed of Christian churches in the city and suburbs and was

---

[33]*Christian-Evangelist,* October 17, 1907.
[34]*Christian Standard,* August 21, 1909. Evangelistic meetings were conducted at Epsom, West Point, Marysville, Mooresville, South Scott, Milford, Bloomingdale, Marshall, Liberty, Williamsport, Brownstown, Fredericksburg, Rochester, Gary, Center Square, New Carlisle, Windfall, Delphi, Painesville, Orland, Burnet's Creek, Hazelwood, Whiting, Indiana Harbor, Michigan City, Westville, and Sauktown.

chartered under Indiana law. In general, its purpose was to bind the churches together in a closer fellowship, strengthen the weak ones, and establish new congregations where needed. By 1906 the Indianapolis Christian Church Union claimed fourteen congregations in the city.[35]

On the Sunday School Front

The Indiana Christian Sunday School Association continued to have regular annual conventions for many years. The primary emphasis was on numbers, big Sunday schools and big classes. The state Sunday school evangelist conducted institutes and sponsored county rallies which were effective and well received. Beginning about 1907 the emphasis shifted to teacher-training courses in the local churches. This project was sponsored by the *Christian Standard,* and much publicity was given to the movement. Unfortunately, attention was focused on numbers, and recognition was given to schools with the largest number of teacher-training classes and classes with the largest enrollment. The quality of training became, probably inadvertently, a secondary consideration. When L. L. Faris became associate pastor at Third Christian Church in Indianapolis he concentrated his efforts on the teacher-training classes of the city. The claim was made at the time that Indianapolis was ahead of all the cities in the world in the number of students involved in training courses; there were 764 persons enrolled in these courses in the fourteen Christian churches of greater Indianapolis.[36] Bethany Park Assembly got on the teacher-training bandwagon and included a National Congress and Teacher Training Institute on its summer

---

[35]*Indiana Christian,* January 15, 1897; *Christian Standard,* February 10, 1906.
[36]*Christian Standard,* November 9, 1907.

schedule for many years. The big aim for religious education in 1909 was for every Bible school teacher and officer to hold the teacher-training diploma, a status symbol for Sunday school workers.[37]

Garry L. Cook[38] was called to Indiana in 1909 to serve as state Sunday school superintendent. His ministry marked a new era for religious education in the Hoosier state with attention drawn more to quality of education rather than quantity of numbers. Under Cook's leadership several experimental programs were undertaken which were adopted later on a national level. The American Christian Missionary Society and the Indiana Christian Missionary Society entered a joint partnership arrangement in 1911 whereby they could function as one unit in the religious education field. Cook was the representative of both organizations in Indiana. Largely through the influence of Garry L. Cook, the Sunday school perspectives of the Bethany Park Assembly began to turn toward more modern concepts of religious education. The Bethany Park School of Methods for Sunday school and missionary workers was established in 1911. Hazel Lewis, Robert M. Hopkins, E. W. Thornton, Charles T. Paul, F. M. Rains and Peter Ainslie were among the instructors. There were 175 Bible school workers enrolled the first year. This feature at Bethany Park soon attracted hundreds of workers from Indiana and other states.[39]

---

[37]*Christian Standard,* April 4, 1908.

[38]Garry L. Cook (1873-1951) was born in Trumbull County, Ohio, graduated from Hiram College and attended the University of Chicago. He was called from a pastorate in Ohio in 1909 to become state Sunday school superintendent for the Indiana Christian Sunday School Association. In 1918 he became district director (Indiana, Illinois, Wisconsin) for the Bible school department of the American Christian Missionary Society. Cook went to Texas in 1922 to become professor of religious education at Texas Christian University. Later, he became pastor of the W. Morris Street Christian Church in Indianapolis, serving there until his retirement in 1939.

[39]Roy W. Ross and John W. Harms, editors, *Disciples of Christ Silver Anniversary of Religious Education,* Indiana edition (St. Louis: Department of Religious Education, U.C.M.S., 1935); *Christian Standard,* August 19, September 2, 1911.

The Congress Movement

Ministers, interested in projecting a more scholarly image for the Christian Church movement, scheduled a Disciple "Congress" at St. Louis in 1899. In contrast to the traditional conventions that had been held for the purpose of popular preaching, fellowship, and agency reports, promoters of the Congress movement desired assemblies which would emphasize research, scholarly presentations, and dialogue. They wanted to bring the impact of higher learning on brotherhood concepts of faith and order. Since those who made addresses usually emphasized biblical criticism and touched on social problems the conservative brethren soon looked upon the Congresses with suspicion and as an attempt by atheistic scholars to capture the brotherhood.

The second congress of the Disciples was held at Central Christian Church in Indianapolis. It had eight sessions which covered the fields of Holy Scripture, biblical criticism, education, Christian liberty, unification of agencies, sociological studies, civic responsibilities and social obligations. The topics were discussed pro and con with two speakers being responsible for introducing each session.[40]

The congress returned to Indianapolis in 1906. J. H. Garrison was head of the general committee, and A. B. Philputt was chairman of the local committee. Several non-Disciple speakers were on the program which was held at Central Christian Church and Butler College.[41]

The State Society, Restructure Continued, 1910-1913

Ennis M. Barney succeeded J. O. Rose as corresponding secretary on January 1, 1910. The Anderson church enter-

---

[40]*Indiana Christian,* March 1, 1900. Principal speakers at this congress were Hiram Van Kirk, George A. Peckham, F. D. Power, C. C. Smith, Mrs. Helen E. Moses, D. R. Dungan, Herbert L. Willett, J. B. Briney, Robert Moffett, C. B. Newman, Mrs. H. M. Meir, Alva W. Taylor and Graham Taylor.
[41]*Christian Standard,* March 24, 1906.

tained the state convention May 16-19, 1910. This convention was significant because a new constitution was adopted for the state organization, one which incorporated the Indiana Christian Sunday School Association and the Indiana Christian Endeavor Society into its organization which was called the *Indiana Christian Missionary Association.* The new constitution provided for a state board of twenty-one men, ten of whom were to be Christian businessmen. Articles of Incorporation were filed with the State so that the association would be in a favorable position to receive and administer trusts under its new name.[42]

L. E. Murray became corresponding secretary of the state association on January 1, 1911. About this time the brethren became concerned over the plight of the country churches. There had been a great exodus of Disciples from these churches as they were caught up in the rural to urban population movement. Many local church leaders and their families were among those who moved to the cities; in many cases this left the country church destitute of leadership and finances.[43]

The Tabernacle Christian Church of Columbus played host to the state convention, May 15-17, 1911. Those who attended expressed appreciation for the hospitality of W. H. Book, pastor of the church, and of his colleague, Harley Jackson of the Central church. One of Indiana's first brotherhood banquets was held on this occasion. The speaker was Professor Charles T. Paul, principal of the new missionary training school at Irvington. This was the seventy-third annual State

---

[42]*Christian-Evangelist,* June 23, 1910. The businessmen on the board were T. C. Howe, W. A. Kelsey, F. R. Lindell, George C. Wyatt, M. O. Reeves, W. E. M. Hackleman, C. M. Shattuck, W. S. Moffett, and H. G. Murphy. Officers of the association were E. L. Day, president; T. C. Howe, vice president; W. S. Moffett, treasurer; W. E. M. Hackleman, secretary; Ennis M. Barney, corresponding secretary; Garry L. Cook, state Sunday school superintendent; T. J. Legg and William Chapple, evangelists; and E. H. Clifford, Christian Endeavor superintendent.

[43]*Christian Standard,* February 18, 1911.

Meeting, and it was considered to be the best attended of any such meeting in many years.[44]

The brethren complained about the great number of days specified for special offerings in the churches. To remedy this situation the State Association and the American Society entered into an arrangement whereby appeals for both organizations would be made on the same Sunday. Members were asked to give at one time what they would normally give to both organizations in two offerings. Secretary Murray pointed out later that the new system did not help the causes but actually diminished the total offerings.[45] The convention met at Hammond in 1912, and at Indianapolis in 1913. L. E. Murray continued as corresponding secretary. As a result of a survey made in 1912 it was decided that some 200 churches in the rural areas and small towns in Indiana needed revival meetings. Ministers were advised to volunteer their services for these meetings by getting in touch with T. J. Legg, state evangelist.[46]

Butler College and Butler Bible College, 1897-1913

The annual catalog for 1897-1898 described Butler College as the Department of Arts of the University of Indianapolis. President Scot Butler headed a distinguished faculty,[47] many of whom held doctoral degrees from eastern universities and had studied in Europe. The solid core of the University of Indianapolis was really Butler College.

After Professor Garvin retired from the department of religion in 1896 no work was offered at the college in the

---

[44]*Christian-Evangelist,* April 20, May 25, 1911; *Christian Standard,* June 17, 1911.

[45]*Christian Standard,* December 23, 1911.

[46]*Christian-Evangelist,* July 25, 1912.

[47]Faculty members: A. R. Benton, W. M. Thrasher, Demarchus C. Brown, Hugh Thomas Miller, Thomas C. Howe, H. L. Bruner, Flora Bridges, J. D. Forrest, Edward Scribner Ames, W. J. Karslake, Marietta Kies, Jabez Hall, Burris A. Jenkins, W. E. Garrison, Bertha Thormyer, Omar Wilson, J. L. Zink, Evelyn M. Butler.

field of ministerial training. The educational board of the American Christian Missionary Society appointed a special committee (Burris A. Jenkins, John E. Pounds, E. P. Wise, Z. T. Sweeney, and J. H. McNeill) to confer with the college administration to remedy this situation. As a result of the discussions which followed it was decided to set up an entirely new program of ministerial education. Jabez Hall,[48] was called to head up the new project, and Butler Bible College had its inception in 1898. The Bible College had its own board of trustees[49] and controlled its own finances. A graduate school for the training of ministers, it was an innovation in Disciples' educational circles, the first three-year graduate seminary in the brotherhood.[50] The Indiana Christian Missionary Society endorsed the project wholeheartedly. The Butler Bible College catalog for the academic year 1898-1899 had a listing of its first faculty members.[51] Through a working agreement with Butler College the Bible College could use Butler College facilities, and undergraduate students at Butler College could take a major in religion at Butler Bible College to apply on

[48]Jabez Hall (1837-1924) came from England to America by sailboat when he was fifteen years old. The journey took forty-four days. After clerking in stores in northern Ohio he took a job at Georgetown, Kentucky. Hall was a Baptist who disliked Calvinistic doctrines. When he heard "Raccoon" John Smith, pastor of the Georgetown Christian Church, he was impressed with the religious views of the Disciples. Smith gave him some preliminary training in Bible study and sent him to Bethany College with a letter of introduction to Alexander Campbell. Hall stayed at the Campbell home and waited on Alexander Campbell in his last illness. The last food and medicine given to Campbell was administered by Jabez Hall. Hall's ordination papers were the last that Campbell signed. After graduation at Bethany he served the church at Wheeling. From here he had an eighteen-year pastorate at the Euclid Avenue Church in Cleveland. Hall was minister at Richmond, Virginia when he was called to Indianapolis for the Bible college project.

[49]Trustees: E. P. Wise, Burris A. Jenkins, George W. Snider, Z. T. Sweeney, J. H. McNeill, E. S. Ames, William V. Morgan, A. J. Frank, A. B. Philputt, S. M. Cooper, A. McLean, John E. Pounds. William G. Irwin and Jabez Hall were added the next year.

[50]*Christian-Evangelist*, August 12, 1897, January 13, 1898; August 17, 1899; Butler College *Minutes*, Book No. 5, January 12, 1898 contains the agreement between Butler College and Butler Bible College. The minutes for April 13, 1898, show also that Butler College agreed to furnish the equivalent of a full-time professor in the Bible College and to cooperate in meeting the salaries of some of the faculty members of Butler Bible College.

[51]Faculty: Jabez Hall, A.M., dean; A. R. Benton, A.M., LL.D., biblical theology; Burris A. Jenkins, A.M., B.D., New Testament Literaure and exegesis; W. E. Garrison, B.D., Ph.D., church history; Edward Scribner Ames, A.M., Ph.D., philosophy and pedagogy; Jacob Dorsey Forrest, A.M., sociology and economics.

their B.A. program. The B.D. (Bachelor of Divinity) degree was offered by the Bible College to all graduates of respectable colleges who completed the course requirements of the three-year graduate program. The Bible College was opened officially on October 3, 1898. Among its students were graduates of Drake University; Hiram, Bethany, Franklin, and Abingdon colleges. Some already had considerable experience in the pastoral ministry.[52] According to the catalog the first person to receive the B.D. degree under this program was Willis Judson Burner who was graduated in 1901. Before coming to Butler Bible College he had received the degrees of A.B. and A.M. from Hedding College.[53]

Once the Bible College was established it became necessary to make plans for a permanent endowment. With a goal of $100,000 in view for the Bible College, Joseph I. Irwin pledged $25,000 toward it on condition that an additional $75,000 would be raised.[54] Some fifty Indiana ministers attended a retreat at Central Christian Church in Indianapolis in December, 1900, where the needs of a school of ministerial training were freely discussed. The group recommended that the Indiana brotherhood raise $100,000 at once to endow Butler Bible College and that this project be considered as the Twentieth Century Movement.[55] Apparently their enthusiasm was not matched by their dollars; nothing more was heard from the campaign. The faculty was of the highest quality, but they were not persons likely to restore the confidence of the Indiana brotherhood in professional ministerial training, especially after the Garvin fiasco. Garrison soon re-

---

[52]*Indiana Christian,* October 15, 1898. Other Bible colleges of the Disciples in existence at this time were undergraduate professional schools, though in some cases an M.A. was given for an additional year of work.

[53]Burner served as a missionary in South America 1905-1912, and later taught sociology at Columbia University. It is probable that he was the first person to receive a three-year graduate B.D. degree from a Disciples' school.

[54]*Indiana Christian,* March 1, 1899.

[55]*Indiana Christian,* December 1, 1900.

turned to St. Louis to work on the *Christian-Evangelist,* Ames was absorbed by the University of Chicago, and Jenkins became president of Kentucky University where his views eventually became a "thorn in the flesh" to arch-conservative Professor McGarvey of the College of the Bible. The Butler College catalog for 1906-1907 had the announcement that it was not possible to continue with the full Divinity School program and that the B.D. degree would not be granted until further notice; but it was the purpose of the college to establish a Graduate Divinity School again in the future. The A.M. degree, however, with a major in religion, was continued. The Butler College Catalog for 1912-1913 announced the restoration of the three-year graduate B.D. program under the department of ministerial education instituted in 1910.

Affiliation with the University of Chicago

President Scot Butler of Butler College and President William R. Harper of the University of Chicago worked out an arrangement in 1898 whereby the Indianapolis school gained much needed strength and recognition. Under the Articles of Affiliation Butler College standardized its work with that of the University of Chicago, and the University of Chicago agreed to give Butler College graduates the same credit as if they had matriculated at Chicago. The Butler College graduate with the highest grade point average at the time of Commencement was automatically awarded a corresponding degree from the Chicago school. Other Butler College graduates were eligible for a University of Chicago degree by doing one quarter's resident study at the Chicago institution. Three one-year free tuition fellowships were granted annually by the University of Chicago to Butler graduates, and Butler faculty members were to receive free tuition for graduate courses pursued at Chicago. The affiliation agreement also specified

301

that the administration of Butler College should consult with the administration of the University of Chicago upon all cases of appointment or removal of instructors before such recommendations should go to the trustees, and that the president of Butler College would become a member of the University Council of the Chicago school.[56] President Harper of the University of Chicago was the Founders Day speaker at Butler College the next year. John E. Pounds, Butler College field secretary, in reporting the event, commented on the school's affiliation with the University of Chicago by writing, "It is practically saying that the college course at Butler is on a par—equal in all respects—with that of Chicago University."[57]

Burris A. Jenkins, minister of Third Christian Church in Indianapolis and professor at Butler Bible College, was elected in 1899 as the first President of the University of Indianapolis. He was officially installed in office at an impressive convocation at Tomlinson's Hall. One thousand persons were in the parade which followed the academic procession. Hoosier Disciples were proud of the selection of Jenkins for this office, but within a year he had accepted a call to a pastorate at Buffalo, New York, and the year 1901 found him installed as President of Kentucky University.[58]

Libraries and the Disciple Book Collection

The Butler College library had its beginning in 1852 with a gift of a $10.00 Bible. The book next donated to the school was a copy of the debate between Alexander Campbell and Robert Owen. Other books were acquired in due time for the library, but it was not until Butler Bible College was established that attention was turned to the special literature of the Disciples of Christ. Dean Jabez Hall announced in 1900:

---

[56]*Indiana Christian*, August 15, 1898; *Christian-Evangelist*, October 13, 1898.
[57]*Indiana Christian*, February 1, 1899.
[58]*Indiana Christian*, March 1, 1899.

"Butler College has begun the work of collecting a library of literature of the Disciples of Christ, and parties having books of this character would do a good part in presenting the college with such books as they may now possess."[59] This was the beginning of the valuable collection of Disciples' literature now held at the library of Christian Theological Seminary. Because of early attention to this matter the collection developed into the largest of its kind in any college or seminary; the periodicals' section is the most extensive to be found anywhere. Butler Bible College began in 1901 to acquire general theological books for a theological library separate and apart from the Butler College collection. Student ministers appealed to their churches to donate books and money to the project. This was the nucleus of the general collection of 70,000 religious books now cataloged at the Christian Theological Seminary library.

The new Bona Thompson Memorial Library building on the Butler campus at Irvington was dedicated on December 20, 1903. It cost $43,000 and was made possible through a gift from Mr. and Mrs. E. C. Thompson. The Mayor of Indianapolis spoke at the dedication. Arrangements were made so that this library could also be used as an Irvington branch of the Indianapolis City Library.[60]

The $250,000 Endowment Campaign

Winfred E. Garrison[61] taught church history at Butler Bible College for two years, then resigned to do editorial work in

---

[59]*Christian-Evangelist*, April 12, 1900; *Indiana Christian*, June 1, 1900.

[60]*Christian Standard*, January 16, 1904.

[61]Winfred Ernest Garrison (1874-   ) was born in St. Louis, the son of J. H. Garrison, long-time editor of the *Christian-Evangelist*. He received A.B. degrees from Eureka and Yale colleges, the B.D. and Ph.D. degrees from the University of Chicago. In addition to these, he holds several honorary degrees, including a D.D. degree from Butler University, awarded in 1955. Garrison was Dean of the Disciples Divinity House of the University of Chicago, 1897-98; taught church history and Hebrew at Butler Bible College, 1898-1900; was assistant editor of the *Christian-Evangelist*, 1900-1904; president of Butler College, 1904-1906. Following this he had a long academic and editorial career and authored a great number of significant books.

St. Louis for the *Christian-Evangelist*. He was soon called back to Indianapolis to become President of Butler University, beginning April 1, 1904. Garrison was thirty years old at the time, perhaps the youngest college president in the United States. College authorities, in the meantime, had determined to embark on a campaign to raise $250,000 for the permanent endowment fund. It was anticipated that Garrison would head up this program. In his first annual report to the board after he had been president but three months (incidentally, the first president to make use of a typewriter for this purpose), Garrison stated that he was getting adjusted to administrative duties but as yet had not found time to do any fund-raising. The report showed, however, that he already had a comprehensive grasp of the educational problems at the college, and the ability to handle them.[62]

The semi-centennial or fiftieth anniversary year of Butler College was selected as a time for the raising of $250,000 to add to the permanent endowment of the institution. The promise of a gift of $100,000 from Joseph I. Irwin of Columbus, provided the additional $150,000 would be raised, was a strong incentive to wage a vigorous campaign. Soon, other large gifts ($25,000 from Andrew Carnegie, $12,500 from Charles T. Whitsett) were received.[63]

Representatives from Butler College and the State Ministerial Association met at Bethany Park in the summer of 1905 to organize the Indiana Christian Educational Society. William J. Russell, minister at Frankfort, was made president; T. W. Grafton, minister at Anderson, was elected vice president. The purpose of the new organization was announced as an effort to unify educational sentiment in favor of Butler

---

[62]*Christian-Evangelist*, August 7, 1904; Butler College *Minutes*, Book Number 6, July 13, 1904.

[63]*Christian-Evangelist*, November 9, 1905; July 5, 1906; April 4, 1907.

College. It was probably part of a plan to interest Hoosier
Disciples in supporting the $250,000 financial drive.[64] When
the campaign was well under way, President Garrison's health
failed, and he was compelled to seek a milder and dryer cli-
mate. Demarchus C. Brown was then appointed as acting
president. He served a few months in this capacity and then
resigned on October 10, 1906, to become Librarian of the
State of Indiana. Professor Thomas Carr Howe was then
chosen to complete the campaign. He was ably assisted by
Hilton U. Brown, president of the Board of Directors. The
campaign slowed down after the first year had passed, and
the big gifts had been received. Y.M.C.A. and Y.W.C.A.
financial campaigns the following year divided the interests
of the community. College officers decided to concentrate
their efforts on a whirlwind finish; with the support of the
newspapers, the Commercial Club of Indianapolis, and Christian churches, the program picked up momentum. Students'
pledges of over $6,000 and a gift of $25,000 from Marshall
T. Reeves of Columbus put the campaign over the top to the
amount of $251,637.90. The drive was declared closed on
March 25, 1907.[65]

The $250,000 campaign was significant for Butler College
because it succeeded under severe handicaps. The $100,000
gift from Joseph I. Irwin was reputed to be the largest single
gift ever received by a Disciples' educational institution up to
that time, and first approaches were made to non-Disciple
donors such as Andrew Carnegie. Even William Jennings
Bryan is supposed to have made a pledge of $500.00. Though
only minor amounts must have been received from Indianapolis businessmen it meant a great deal to the school to be en-

---

[64]*Christian Standard*, September 16, 1905.
[65]Butler College Minutes, Book No. 6, January 31, 1906. *Christian-Evangelist*,
April 4, July 4, 1907.

dorsed by such organizations as the Commercial Club; it opened the door for future contributions.

Scot Butler became interim president, 1906-1907. He resigned in June, 1907, in order to become eligible for an annuity pension from the Carnegie Foundation.[66] Thomas Carr Howe,[67] who had been dean and acting president following the resignation of Butler, was elected president of the college in 1908. Howe, an alumnus of the college who had studied abroad, had received the Ph.D. degree from Harvard University in 1899.[68] His academic qualifications, administrative experience gained in the $250,000 campaign, and his popularity with non-Disciple as well as Disciple constituents made him a wise choice for this position. He served as president for many years.

Changes in Academic and Administrative Policies

There were many changes made in the academic and fiscal policies of the college during the period of the $250,000 endowment campaign. Connection with the University of Indianapolis was broken in 1905. It had never been a firm alliance; campuses of the affiliated schools were many miles apart, and none of the participating institutions were really strengthened by the association. Actually, it hampered the securing of endowment funds and raised embarrassing administrative problems. The Butler College Faculty, in 1906,

---

[66]Butler College *Minutes,* Book 6, June 19, 1907.

[67]Thomas Carr Howe (1867-1934) was born in Charlestown, Indiana, the son of Robert L. Howe, first full-time secretary of the State Missionary Society. Butler College granted him the Ph.B. degree in 1899 and the A.M. degree in 1893. He studied at Harvard University, gaining the degrees of M.A. and Ph.D. He occupied the Armstrong Chair of Germanic Languages at Butler College, 1890-1910; dean 1907-1908; president 1908-1920. Howe was an active Christian Church layman, being an elder at different times of both the Downey Avenue and Central Christian churches. He was a trustee in the Board of Ministerial Relief and later president of the Pension Fund of the Disciples. He was an active member of the Commission on Budgets and Promotional Relationships. Howe served also as president of the Church Federation of Indianapolis and once was a candidate for mayor of Indianapolis.

[68]*Christian-Evangelist,* April 30, 1908.

asked the Board of Directors to strike out all references to the University of Indianapolis in its next catalog. It was listed in the catalogs, however, for 1906-1907 and 1910-1911. The last named issue and the one following named the dental and law colleges as affiliates, but they made no mention of the University of Indianapolis. After the death of President Harper of the University of Chicago, and beginning in 1910, the Chicago school adopted a policy of severing its affiliations with small colleges.[69] Therefore, by 1910, Butler College, free from the University of Indianapolis and the University of Chicago, was again pursuing its own administrative and academic program.

Control of the college by a joint stock company got to be a very unwieldy administrative structure by 1908. This type of organization had served a good purpose in the past but now stood in the way of receiving large grants from foundations, and the task of accounting for outstanding stock grew more difficult each year. It was also apparent that something needed to be done to remove a fear on the part of the Disciples' brethren that some group might organize, buy up the stock, and gain control of the college. To meet this problem the directors took advantage of an act passed at the Sixty-sixth Regular Session of the General Assembly of the State of Indiana in 1909.[70] It authorized universities, colleges, and other institutions of learning to have self-perpetuating boards. Since two-thirds of the stockholders of the college corporation voted to accept this provision, steps were taken to make

---

[69]*Christian-Evangelist,* July 4, 1907.

[70]Indiana *Statutes,* Acts 1909, ch. 52, section 1, p. 128. "An act entitled an act authorizing universities, colleges or institutions of learning heretofore organized under general laws of the state of Indiana, or created by special charters, or hereafter organized under the laws of the state of Indiana, to provide for the election of directors or trustees by the board of directors or trustees from time to time instead of by stockholders or subscribers to its funds, and to provide for the transfer of its capital stock to the board of directors or trustees with authority to hold and vote the same for its benefit and to cancel such stock, and providing methods for effecting such ends and declaring an emergency." In force March 3, 1909.

it effective as soon as possible.[71] It was then necessary to call in all outstanding stock, and notices were published to this effect. Some of the stock was never found, though stockholders owning $261,900 in the corporation gave approval of the change at a meeting held June 10, 1915. Following this the board declared all outstanding stock to be null and void. The stock company was then disbanded, a new financial system was instituted, and the Board continued as a self-perpetuating body.[72]

Plans were projected in 1911 to add another $500,000 to the permanent endowment fund in the next five-year period. By 1913 it was possible to announce that the school possessed $400,000 in unencumbered endowment, and that the total income for the academic year 1912-1913 h a d b e e n $43,745.96.[73]

One of the large gifts which was made in the $250,000 campaign in 1907 was a $25,000 subscription from Marshall T. Reeves[74] of Columbus. Reeves added $5,000 to this later to make up for a possible shrinkage in contributions. The Reeves gift was designated to endow a chair of biblical literature. William Charles Morro, dean of the College of the Bible at Lexington, was called to the Reeves chair and to head the department of ministerial training, beginning with the academic year 1910-1911. A comprehensive plan for ministerial

---

[71]Butler College *Minutes,* Book No. 6, June 17, 1909.

[72]Butler College *Minutes,* Book No. 6, June 10, 1915.

[73]*Christian-Evangelist,* July 31, 1913.

[74]Marshall T. Reeves (1852-1925) was born on a Rush County farm. He conceived of several labor-saving improvements for farm implements and eventually went into the farm implement manufacturing business at Columbus. He was very successful, and at the time of his death was president of the Reeves Pulley Company of Columbus. Reeves was an elder in the Tabernacle Church of Christ at Columbus and served on the Board of Trustees of Butler College. In his lifetime he made a great number of large contributions to Christian work. In addition to providing funds for the Bible chair mentioned above he was a liberal supporter of the Indiana Christian Missionary Association, the Cunningham mission in Japan, Cincinnati Bible Seminary, Milligan College, and Johnson Bible College. Reeves was a moving spirit in the founding and program of the Christian Foundation. He was reported to have contributed over three-fourths of a million dollars to Christian causes.

education was projected in 1913. It included a thirty-hour graduate program for the M.A. degree and a ninety-hour graduate program leading to the B.D. degree.[75] By this time the College of Missions had been established on the Butler campus at Irvington. Though they were controlled by separate boards the two schools interchanged academic work and together could command a respectable faculty in the field of ministerial and missionary education.[76]

College of Missions

When goals were projected in 1906 for the Centennial Convention of the Disciples of Christ in 1909, the Christian Woman's Board of Missions in Indiana assumed the responsibility of raising money for a building to serve as a missionary training school and as its national headquarters. A large gift from Mrs. Maude D. Ferris, given in memory of her mother, Mrs. Sarah Davis Detarding, enabled the project to get underway. Cornerstone ceremonies for the new building took place on August 10, 1908; the finished building was dedicated at a missionary conference in Indianapolis, August 18, 1910. It was of colonial brick and Bedford stone, four stories in height, with classrooms, dormitories, and space for a library and museum as well as for offices of the national board.[77]

The new institution, originally called the Sarah Davis Detarding Missionary Training School, published a prospectus with announcements for the academic year 1911-1912. Charles T. Paul, who had achieved phenomenal success at

[75]*Christian Standard,* July 1, 1911; *Christian-Evangelist,* July 31, 1913; *Butler College Bulletin,* Religious Education Number, September, 1913.

[76]The combined faculty in the religious field was made up of the following: Thomas Carr Howe, Ph.D., president; William Charles Morro, B.D., Ph.D., professor of New Testament and head of department; C. B. Coleman, A.B., B.D.; C. E. Underwood, Ph.D., professor of Old Testament; Charles T. Paul, A.M., president of the College of Missions; Harry Clark Hurd, A.M., M.D.; and Fred Elmore Lumley, B.D., Ph.D.

[77]W. R. Warren, general editor, *Survey of Service* (St. Louis: Christian Board of Publication, 1928), pp. 521-523; *Christian Standard,* September 5, 1908; September 3, 1910.

Hiram College in training young people for the mission field, became principal. He prepared the first curriculum, one made in conformity with a report of the Edinburgh Ecumenical Conference of 1910. A working agreement for the exchange of credits and teaching service was made with Butler College, and a competent faculty was enlisted.[78]

The catalog for 1911-1912 indicated that the name of the school had been changed to College of Missions, the Sarah Davis Detarding Memorial; Charles T. Paul was listed as president. There was an increase in faculty and student enrollment the next year. The College of Missions proved to be a source of strength to the entire brotherhood for many years. Its location on the Butler College campus enabled students to receive part of their training at Butler College. Many College of Missions students received Butler College degrees while in training to be missionaries. The College of Missions faculty also gave strength to the program of ministerial education at Butler College.

Bloomington Bible Chair

Disciple students at Indiana University formed a Disciples Club at this place in 1897. A majority of the half hundred students in the club were young men; some of these wanted to supplement their income by preaching for small southern Indiana churches. These churches needed pastors, but they were not particularly responsive to those identified with the university. Southern Indiana, by this time, had the largest

[78]First faculty: Charles T. Paul, M.A., principal, teacher in the fields of comparative religion, missionary history and linguistics; Harry Clark Hurd, B.A., M.D., teacher in the fields of science of missions, anthropology, and tropical medicine; Miss Mary Graybiel, teacher of Hindi language and history of India; W. C. Morro, M.A., B.D., Ph.D., Butler College dean of department of ministerial education (New Testament literature, history of interpretation); Jabez Hall, A.M., Butler College professor (Biblical theology). Archibald McLean, president of the Foreign Christian Missionary Society, and A. B. Philputt, minister of Central Christian Church in Indianapolis, were listed as lecturers.

group of extremist anti-organ, anti-missionary society people in the state. The Indiana Christian Missionary Society had come to look upon this area as a mission field, long neglected and deserted.[79]

It was generally thought that if only a Bible Chair could be established at Indiana University it would prove to be an effective witness in that part of the state for the mainstream of Disciples' thought and polity. Disciple students at the university petitioned the Christian Churches of Indiana in 1910 to place a religious worker in the state university, one who was competent to give instruction in biblical and religious subjects. They claimed to represent some 175 to 300 Christian Church students from 150 churches in the state. The brethren in Indiana were interested, and initial steps to establish a Bible Chair were taken at once. An association was formed and incorporated with eleven directors to be responsible for establishing and maintaining the work. Dr. W. L. Bryan, president of the university, and his trustees were cordial to the proposals. The immediate need, however, was for financial backing of the project. Joseph C. Todd, minister of the Christian Church at Bloomington, became financial secretary of the organization and was very active in bringing this need to the attention of the Indiana brotherhood.[80]

The Christian Church at Bloomington responded immediately by donating a piece of property to the Bible Chair movement. It was not long before $10,000 was raised and it was possible to call a man to the field. Walter S. Rounds of the Flatbush church in Brooklyn was chosen to be campus

---

[79]*Indiana Christian,* May 15, 1897.

[80]*Christian-Evangelist,* July 7, November 17, 1910; *Christian Standard,* November 26, 1910. The first directors of the association were Edgar F. Daugherty, president; J. E. Martin, E. L. Day, Dr. Rodney D. Smith, Joseph C. Todd, R. W. Abberly, Ira C. Batman, E. R. Edwards, E. M. C. Hobbs, L. C. Howe, and J. M. Rudy.

311

minister for the Disciples. While Joseph C. Todd[81] was in the field trying to raise an endowment fund of $60,000, Rounds took his place in the Bloomington pulpit. Joseph C. Todd became university pastor at Indiana University under the Bible Chair program in the fall of 1912.[82]

Profile of Sixteen Years

The period of 1897 to 1913 has been designated as a time of struggle for status and numbers on the part of Hoosier Disciples. The *Year Book* figures for 1897 show 100,000 members in Indiana. Sixteen years later (1913) the same source indicated a state membership of 84,000. Samplings of statistics taken between these years show that the total membership reported in the state was at times as high as 120,000 persons. Either the membership was fluctuating with tremendous gains and correspondingly high losses or the statistics of the period are not reliable. The latter seems to be the case. The means of gathering statistics at the beginning of the century were not adequate. Figures on church growth, for the most part, were optimistic guesses. By 1914, the churches had become more stabilized, and the reporting of numbers was more realistic. There were gains and losses in this period. While this cannot be overlooked it is also true that gains and losses were not as extreme as the statistics indicate.

Indiana Disciples were not prepared to cope with the rural to urban population trend. Essentially a rural people, the

---

[81]Joseph Clinton Todd (1879-1953) was born in Boone County, Missouri. He was graduated from Missouri Valley College in 1901. He served the Booneville Christian Church as pastor, 1902-1903, and the Monroe City, Missouri, Christian Church in the same capacity in 1904-1905. Columbia University granted him the A.M. degree in 1908. He became pastor of the Kirkwood Avenue Christian Church in Bloomington in 1908 and served until 1912 when he became identified with the Bible Chair movement. When the Bible Chair developed into the Indiana School of Religion, Todd became dean. He was president of the national convention of the Disciples in 1911; was awarded an LL.D. degree by Culver-Stockton College in 1922, and was fraternal delegate to the World Council of Churches meeting at Amsterdam in 1948.

[82]*Christian-Evangelist*, December 1, 1910; September 5, 1912; *Christian Standard*, February 4, 1911.

main strength of the Christian churches prior to 1900 was in the open country and small towns. When thousands of people were pouring into Indiana's industrialized urban centers the Disciples were still concentrating their efforts on building up rural and small town churches. Many Disciples who moved to cities were absorbed by older communions that had been in the cities for years with programs geared to city life. Though the Disciples still counted the anti-organ, anti-missionary society Churches of Christ in south-central Indiana in the early 1900's, a *de facto* separation had already taken place. The religious census of 1906[83] recognized the division; after this the Disciples no longer included the Churches of Christ in their statistics. According to this census report the Churches of Christ in Indiana had 106 congregations and 10,259 members at that time.

Criticism is sometimes leveled at the concept and character of the program of evangelism during this period. It should be remembered that this was the only way the Disciples knew how to reach urban Indiana, and that if there had not been a strong program of professional evangelism in this period it is possible that the church would have been tremendously weakened.

During this period the State Society changed its name several times and restructured itself over and over again. This indicates strength rather than weakness. The leaders knew there was a big job to be done, that it was not being done effectively, and they were not afraid to experiment to find means of best promoting the cause. If their emphasis was on numbers and in striving for status among the other religious

---

[83]Special Reports, Religious Bodies: 1906. Bureau of the Census, Part I (Washington: Government Printing Office, 1910). This same census showed that Indiana had 228 "old" Christian churches (then called Christian Connection) with 21,397 members.

bodies it was because they believed this was the most expedient way to witness for the Disciples' plea.

Hoosier Disciples in this period followed the same pattern in regard to Butler College. In entering and breaking affiliation with the University of Indianapolis scheme, in experimenting with ministerial education on a graduate level, in affiliation with the University of Chicago to get recognition for the quality of work being done in Indianapolis, and in the abandoning of the old stock company structure, they were seeking excellence in the field of education. They made mistakes, but they also broke new ground for the brotherhood at large.

The advance made by the Indiana auxiliary of the Christian Woman's Board of Missions in its publication program and in establishment of the College of Missions paved the way for making Indiana, especially Indianapolis, the center of brotherhood life for the Christian Churches (Disciples of Christ).

Bertha Lockenour had a strong feeling for Hoosier Disciples and composed a song for them. It was published in the *Indiana Christian* on February 15, 1898. Sung to the tune of "America," it reflects the spirit of Hoosier Disciples in the early years of the twentieth century:

> Our Hoosier State for Christ,
> Our grand old Hoosier State,
> This song we sing.
> Still let this be our cry,
> And we shall win or die,
> Yes win it by and by,
> Our State for Christ.

IX

New Center of Brotherhood Life
1914-1930

WHEN THE FIRST NUMBER of the new *Indiana Worker* was issued in January, 1914, neither its editors nor its readers in the Hoosier state knew that before the end of the year Europe would be embroiled in a terrible war which would make a terrific and lasting impact on American culture and church life. Church people in general were not too much concerned with the events on the other side of the Atlantic; President Wilson had assured them of American neutrality and appealed to them to be impartial in their views.

Long before the United States declared war on Germany in April, 1917, the Christian Woman's Board of Missions was aware of what was going on and of possible consequences. At least the C.W.B.M. column in the *Indiana Worker* indicated this. An article by Mrs. J. McDaniel Stearns[1] showed a deep concern over the perilous world situation. She wrote of civilization being broken down and of Edinburgh, Oxford, and the great German universities being deserted; the flower of young manhood was dying in the trenches. She wondered if the church had also collapsed! The article pointed out that half of the world's missionary work had been carried on by European mission boards whose resources were now cut off,

---

[1] *Indiana Worker,* July, 1915.

315

and that the Christian churches in America were now being weighed in the balance against the world's appalling need.

Men and Millions Movement to the Rescue

Disciples answered this challenge in part, at least, through the instrument of the Men and Millions movement, a project already under way when the war started. The movement had a modest beginning in 1912 when the China mission asked for $200,000. A. E. Cory, one of the missionaries to China, then led a drive to raise a million dollars for the Foreign Christian Missionary Society. The American Christian Missionary Society and the Christian Woman's Board of Missions joined forces to raise another million. It was then decided to include the Board of Ministerial Relief, the National Benevolent Association, and the Board of Church Extension. R. A. Long, wealthy Disciple layman, boosted the goal still higher with an offer to give a million dollars if the Brotherhood would raise an additional $5,300,000 and include higher education in the project. The audacity of this "package deal" goal awakened the stewardship consciousness of Disciples for the first time in their history. They began to think "big." Promotion of the Every Member Canvass (with weekly offering envelopes) was introduced as a feature of the movement so that givers from all economic levels could participate. Disciples were challenged to send 1,000 trained workers into full-time Christian service and raise $6,300,000 to support missions, benevolences, and education.[2]

In 1917, when the drive was well under way, Butler College and other institutions, because of the war economy, were

---

[2]For a fuller report of the Men and Millions Movement, *see,* Executive Committee, A. McLean, chairman, *The Men and Millions Movement, History and Report, 1913-1919* (Cincinnati: Men and Millions Movement, 1919); *World Call,* September, 1919, pp. 54-60.

316

piling up huge operating deficits. To relieve this situation it was decided to have a War Emergency Drive, beginning in 1918. This drive was a successful adjunct to the Men and Millions Movement; a sum of over two million dollars was pledged. Hoosier Disciples, like those in other states, adopted war slogans and nomenclature to bring the program to the people. The editors of the *Indiana Worker* wrote of "making the world safe for democracy" and of "keeping the home fires burning" as promotional gimmicks for sending the fund "over the top." Hoosiers were admonished, "Do you care? If not, the Kaiser has won his battle already in your heart."[3] The War Emergency Drive increased Men and Millions pledges to $7,105,342.63; Indiana raised $403,439.42 of this amount. The results of the life-commitment phase were even more astounding; 8,412 young people signed cards pledging themselves to go to college and consider volunteering for full-time Christian service when half-way through. Of these, 669 were Indiana young people. Butler College, the chief beneficiary of the program in Indiana, eventually received $300,000; $12,906.44 was given to the Indiana School of Religion, $7,857.27 to the Indiana Christian Missionary Association, and $50.00 to the Angola Bible Institute.[4] The phenomenal success of the Men and Millions Movement, the biggest financial drive ever undertaken by any religious group in America, was an incentive for similar campaigns by other religious bodies.

Cauble Becomes State Secretary

Just before the war broke out in Europe, Hoosier Disciples were thinking in terms of a "Diamond Jubilee" convention,

---

[3]*Indiana Worker,* February, 1918.
[4]*Indiana Worker,* January, 1915.

advertised as a seventy-fifth anniversary gathering (it was actually the 76th convention) to take place at Terre Haute in May, 1914. The first big assignment given to newly-elected State Secretary, C. W. Cauble[5] was to prepare for this convention. The year before, under special appointment, Cauble had added $10,000 to the receipts of the association ($5,000 added to matching funds given by Marshall T. Reeves of Columbus). This allowed the State Association to employ five full-time evangelists, assist five mission churches in the Calumet district, and help in the support of a student pastor at Purdue University. Delegates at the Terre Haute convention heard glowing reports from each of the five evangelists.[6] People were especially impressed with the brand new "Model T" roadsters these men were driving, another gift of Marshall T. Reeves. Reeves not only gave the automobiles, but he paid for their upkeep and driving expenses the first year. Not everyone could afford an automobile in those days; the Reeves' gift upgraded the state program. L. C. Howe, convention president, reported, "The inharmonious 'kickers' and the chronic growlers are becoming fewer and less influential in our state work, as the good years come."[7] Apparently the good years had come because $16,592.77 had been received for the state work (income tripled), and there were nine full-time staff employees in addition to the five missionary pastors.[8]

---

[5]Commodore Wesley Cauble (1874-1935) was a native Hoosier. He was a graduate of the College of the Bible and Indiana University and also studied at Harvard University. He served the Sixth Street Church at Indianapolis, and the churches at Greencastle and Martinsville. In 1908 he toured Egypt and Palestine. In 1914, Cauble became State Secretary. The state work advanced under his aggressive leadership. In his thirteen years as State Secretary he earned a national reputation as a church dedicator, a field which he entered exclusively in 1928. He was president of the Bethany Park Assembly for many years. Cauble is especially known for his book, *Disciples of Christ in Indiana,* written at the request of the convention and published in 1930.

[6]These evangelists were A. L. Martin (northern district), T. J. Legg (western district), G. I. Hoover (eastern district), Melnotte Miller (southwestern district), and Fred R. Davies (southeastern district).

[7]*Indiana Worker,* February, March, April, 1914; *Christian-Evangelist,* June 11, 1914.

[8]*Indiana Worker,* June, 1914. W. H. Book preached the convention sermon. Other speakers were B. A. Abbott, Carey E. Morgan, S. J. Corey, and C. C. Morrison.

Pioneer Program in Religious Education

Hoosier Disciples played a conspicuous part in the released time religious education program which originated at Gary in 1914. Children were excused from their regular public school classes for one period a week, on request of their parents, to receive religious instruction from denominational representatives. Myron C. Settle was induced by Robert M. Hopkins, secretary of the Bible School Department of the American Christian Missionary Society, to go to Gary in 1914 as one of the pioneer teachers on this project. Settle was experienced in the field of religious education, having been Disciple state director of Christian Endeavor in Kansas and state director of Religious Education for the Ohio Christian Missionary Society. The work at Gary was done in cooperation with the Indiana Christian Missionary Association and the American Christian Missionary Society.

The week-day teaching program was conducted in the Central, Glen Park, and Tolleston churches. Some 250 eighth grade children were originally enrolled at the three centers, each child receiving two hours of religious instruction weekly in addition to the church school period on Sunday. The week-day schools were conducted on a denominational basis in Gary for three years prior to the formation of a Board of Religious Education which had representatives from several denominations. By 1923 the week-day program of religious education was ministering to 4,000 children in that city, many of whom came from homes of the foreign-born. The movement spread to several communities in Indiana and to other states.[9]

---

[9]For reports of the Gary week-day program, *see, Indiana Worker,* December, 1914; March, May, November, 1915; September, 1920; *World Call,* April, 1921; Indianapolis *Star Magazine,* November 8, 1964.

The Indiana Mission Field, 1915-1919

The financial "pump priming" of Marshall T. Reeves paid off in the performance of the state evangelists in 1914 and thereafter. These men held 67 evangelistic meetings in 1914, organized five new churches, and added 1,054 persons to the membership of the churches. The following year, Reeves agreed to add one dollar to each two dollars received on personal pledge cards, to the extent of $4,000.[10] This gave support to the Every Member Canvass system, a stewardship program being promoted by Secretary Cauble.

Marion was a community of 25,000 inhabitants in 1915. Disciples there claimed to have the biggest Christian church and the finest preacher in the state. R. A. Bennett, pastor of the congregation, reciprocated by stating that he had the finest flock in Indiana. All this abundant good will provided a pleasant atmosphere for the State Convention in 1915. The five full-time evangelists carried a lot of prestige with their well-marked "tin lizzies" parked conspicuously in front of the church for all to envy and admire. Speakers from outside Indiana included R. H. Miller who represented the Men and Millions Movement; A. McLean and W. R. Warren brought the missionary messages. A. C. Smithers, who reported the convention for the *Christian-Evangelist,* wrote, "Nobody appeared to the cross-grained or crotchety."[11] The special emphasis on the amiable disposition of the delegates during the past few conventions seems to suggest that there had been conventions in the memory of some, at least, which were not all sweetness and light.

The State Association conducted a comprehensive survey of Indiana Christian churches in the spring of 1916, and a com-

---

[10]*Indiana Worker,* January, February, 1915.
[11]*Christian-Evangelist,* May 20, 1915.

plete report of the results was given at the Danville convention in May. The survey showed that there were Christian churches in every county of the state, some 848 congregations.[12]

Twelve cars a day left Indianapolis on the traction line that carried Hoosier Disciples to the Danville convention in 1916. Frederick D. Kershner, then editor of the *Christian-Evangelist,* a man later to play an important role in Indiana Disciple history, spoke on the subject, "Consecration, the Secret of Success." The convention called a sixth full-time person to serve as evangelist, and the budget was set at an all-time high of $20,000. Secretary Cauble claimed that it was now quite evident that Indiana was leading all the states of the union in effectiveness and organized activities.[13]

The Main Street Christian Church in Kokomo was headquarters for the annual convention of the State Association in 1917. General Pershing had just been recalled from an expedition into Mexico where he was searching for the elusive Pancho Villa, and the United States had declared war on Germany the month before. The brethren believed this was an appropriate time to urge Congress and the President to prohibit the manufacture and sale of alcoholic beverages as a war measure. They passed such a resolution. It suggested that since homes and churches were freely giving up their best young men, immediate and vigorous steps should be taken to safeguard properly their moral and spiritual life. A special committee which had recently visited the Indiana State House

---

[12]*Christian-Evangelist,* May 26, June 29, 1916. Of the 848 churches, 672 were listed as cooperative, 131 as non-cooperative, and eleven were mission churches. The membership of the cooperative churches was given as 132,441, and the Sunday school enrollment as 109,265. There were 191 churches with full-time preaching, three with three-fourths time preaching, 186 with half-time preaching, 241 with one-fourth time preaching, and 12 with occasional preaching. Fifty churches were listed as being active yet with no preaching. Ninety counties were organized for cooperative work. This survey was made on the field by state workers.

[13]*Indiana Worker,* April, October, 1916; *Christian-Evangelist,* May 25, 1916. F. E. Smith was president of this convention.

(J. C. Todd, T. C. Howe, and George L. Moffett) gave a specific report on what could be expected from Disciple ministers in support of the war effort. Governor James B. Goodrich was given assurance that the services of the ministers and the resources of the churches were available "in this crucial period of the nation's and the world's history." The hope was also expressed that the Governor would make it possible for the ministers to cooperate with the military authorities in preserving the moral and religious integrity of the soldiers by providing recreational programs and supplying chaplains for the armed forces. The ministers offered themselves, in the battle line if necessary, to the service of the state, "until under the providence of God, the prayer and passion of our hearts for peace can be satisfied by the establishment of justice and democracy in all the world."[14]

By special arrangement in the latter part of 1917, Secretary Cauble's salary was paid by the American Christian Missionary Society. He served this organization also while continuing as State Secretary. This plan lasted until January 1, 1921.[15]

The theme of the New Castle State Convention in 1918 was "The Church and the War." Advertisements appeared in the *Indiana Worker* to promote the sale of war-connected products. "Honor Rolls" with the names of those in military service inscribed thereon could be purchased for display in the churches. The Hackleman Music Company offered a new song for sale entitled, "Get-the-Kaiser." It was supposed to be especially adapted for humorous quartettes to give "red hot" thrusts at the Kaiser, defend democracy and condemn autocracy. Secretary Cauble's annual report gave the assurance that there was not an unbeliever in the trenches, and that the camps were "the most religious spots in the nation." On the

---

[14]*Indiana Worker*, April, June, 1917.
[15]*Indiana Worker*, June, 1924.

more realistic side, many pastors reported that they had given temporary service as camp chaplains.[16] The traditional convention reports indicated that the state work was on the move. In spite of the big drives that had been made for the Red Cross, Armenian Relief, Y. M. C. A., and other organizations, State Association receipts from all sources amounted to $20,484.46. Over 10,000 Indiana women were enrolled in the C. W. B. M. that year, an increase of 1,000 members. Muncie had the largest auxiliary with 315 members. Mrs. O. H. Greist was reelected president of the Indiana C. W. B. M.[17]

Marshall T. Reeves continued his liberal support of the state work until 1918. At that time he demanded, as a condition of further financial assistance, that the director and employees of the Association sign as statement of doctrinal belief which he had prepared. Cauble and his associates refused to sign on the basis that this document bore a suspicious resemblance to a written creed and as such it violated the fundamentals of the Disciples' movement. Reeves argued that it was not a creed but a way to his pocketbook. He made his final contribution of $450 to the Association on October 14, 1918.[18]

A half-million persons in the United States died in an influenza epidemic of massive proportions which swept the country in the fall of 1918. The State Board of Health placed a ban on public gatherings of every description. This made church services, revival meetings, convention and conference work impossible. The epidemic was especially severe at Butler College and in the military training camps.

The year of 1919 was a significant one for all Disciples. The armistice of November 11, 1918, brought cessation of

---

[16]*Indiana Worker*, April, May, 1918.

[17]*Indiana Worker*, May, 1918; *Christian-Evangelist*, May 23, 1918.

[18]*Indiana Worker*, June, 1924. Reeves made a similar proposition to the Board of Directors of Butler College the year before. Though none was required to sign the "loyalty" document, tacit approval was given in the form of a watered-down resolution. See Butler College *Minutes*, Book No. 7, October 10, 1917.

hostilities, and the churches started restructuring their programs for an era of peace. The war had increased the economic resources of most families, changed standards of living, and increased migration to large urban centers. Some of the old problems that troubled the churches were resolved, and many new ones had arisen. Secretary Cauble expressed this quite well in a leading article in the *Indiana Worker*. He wrote:[19]

An awakened public conscience will demand of the church a prophetic call to social righteousness; an adequate ministry of welfare service; a commensurate program of world evangelization; and a mighty influence in the preservation of the peace. The church with all other institutions will be subject to the stern judgment of a suffering world. The church's program must include both ministry and message.

The first number of the new magazine, *World Call*, was issued January 1, 1919. It continued *Missionary Tidings, The Missionary Intelligencer, Business in Christianity, The American Home Missionary,* and the *Christian Philanthropist*. With W. R. Warren and Mrs. Effie L. Cunningham as editors, the publication office was set up in the College of Missions building. The *World Call* envisioned a united front for Disciple missionary and benevolent work throughout the world. Other achievements of the period included the successful culmination of the Men and Millions Movement, institution of a Pension Plan for ministers, and the creation of the United Christian Missionary Society.[20]

The Third Christian Church, Indianapolis, Thomas W. Grafton, minister, entertained the State Convention in 1919.

---

[19]*Indiana Worker*, January, 1919.

[20]The United Society included the following agencies: American Christian Missionary Society, Foreign Christian Missionary Society, National Benevolent Association, Christian Woman's Board of Missions, Board of Church Extension, and the Board of Ministerial Relief. Headquarters was established at St. Louis.

Indianapolis Disciples furnished lodging and breakfast free to delegates. The meals provided by the Third Church ladies must have been excellent because it was reported that their fame in the culinary arts was known for many miles around Indianapolis.[21]

Upgrading the Religious Education Movement

Interest in the Sunday School had been high for several years prior to 1920, and the Sunday School program with its attendance contests, audience participation, and special entertainments (orchestras, bands, and other publicized features) received the lion's share of the church members' loyalty. Many churches had a large attendance in Sunday School; a pitifully small group stayed for the "preaching" service. To correct this, Garry L. Cook, as early as 1915 promoted a plan of unified and merged services. The churches at Oxford and Edinburg were often cited as good examples of the value of this technique. Wherever instituted, the plan helped to provide a larger congregation for the minister and eventually served to restore the church service to its place of primary importance. The Sunday School and Christian Endeavor departments of the State Association were combined in 1915, and Garry L. Cook supervised both organizations. By 1917 some of the larger churches began to take the task of religious education more seriously and started to call full-time persons to look after this work. In other churches the minister accepted the responsibility for religious education, and the pastor-superintendent idea became popular. A new regional division for religious education was created in 1918. Cook was placed in charge of the work in Indiana, Illinois, and Wisconsin as rep-

---

[21]*Indiana Worker*, April, 1919; *Christian-Evangelist*, June 5, 1919.

resentative of the Bible School department of the American Christian Missionary Society. The Sunday School department of the State Association then became associated with the larger organization. The new graded lesson curriculum with emphasis on departmental work was introduced about this time.[22]

Experimenting in Social Settlement Work

In 1914, students at the College of Missions were looking after three projects in social work. One of these was known as Bethany House; it was a social settlement house for a factory community at Haughville. Another was the teaching of foreigners in night schools in Indianapolis. The third project was the Flanner House social settlement for Negroes in Indianapolis. This undertaking was the most extensive and probably the most productive. The Flanner House had its beginning in 1898 when Frank W. Flanner, Indianapolis mortician, donated a property to the Charity Organizations Society for use as a Negro social service center. Flanner was a liberal supporter of the project until his death in 1912. The institution appealed for help to the Christian Woman's Board of Missions at this time and reorganized to permit C. W. B. M. representation on the board. In 1918 the C. W. B. M. purchased four buildings at the corner of West and St. Clair streets, remodeled and equipped them. The Flanner House endeavored to find employment for the people in the neighborhood, conducted cooking and sewing classes, sponsored clubs for young people, and operated a day nursery for working mothers. Later, a laundry school and a makeover shop were established. In 1919 a branch library was set up, a Sunday School program was started, and playgrounds for children put

---

[22]*Indiana Worker*, February, May, 1915; June, October, 1917; May, July-August, 1918.

in operation. The program was sponsored by the C. W. B. M. until 1923.[23]

Origin of the Christian Foundation

When Frederick D. Kershner was on the editorial staff of the *Christian Standard* he conceived the idea of establishing a foundation to bestow grants on worthy Christian projects, especially in the field of higher education and particularly for the training of ministers. He moved to Des Moines in the spring of 1920 and became professor of Christian doctrine at Drake University. Kershner knew a great number of wealthy Disciples who were potential donors and sought to interest them in the plan. William G. Irwin of Columbus, Indiana, seems to have been sympathetic with the project from the beginning, even to the extent of supplementing Kershner's income while he was laying the groundwork. Kershner taught but two courses at Drake; he was expected to divide his time among teaching, raising money for Drake University, and promoting the Christian Foundation.

The Foundation was organized in temporary form at Indianapolis, April 1, 1920, and the minutes of the organization date from this time. George W. Peake was elected president; Frederick D. Kershner, secretary; and William G. Irwin, treasurer. Headquarters were established at Indianapolis with a western office at Des Moines (Kershner's mailing address). In an explanation published in the *Christian-Evangelist*[24] im-

---

[23]For reports on the Flanner House *see Indiana Worker*, December, 1914; February, 1916; *World Call*, September, December, 1919. Supervisors of the Flanner House have been Miss Sarah Colton Smith (1898-1899), Mr. and Mrs. Robert Brokenburr (1912-1914), Charles O. Lee (1914-1925), and Henry L. Herod (1925-1935). Cleo Blackburn became superintendent in 1936. Blackburn, a graduate of Southern Christian Institute and Butler University, was research assistant at Tuskegee Institute when called to the Indianapolis work. He instituted a successful self-help program that gained national recognition. It was a pilot project for people in the neighborhood to help one another in the building of their own homes. With the help of the American Friends Service Committee new buildings were erected, and the whole area in that part of the city was upgraded. Blackburn's work in the self-help home building project is reported in the *Reader's Digest*, November, 1955.

[24]*Christian-Evangelist*, April 8, 1920.

mediately after the organization meeting, Kershner stated that the "foundation" idea was not new but had never before entered the field of religion. He suggested that if a foundation could be established to feed the poor it could also be established to proclaim the gospel; if the conquest of disease is a worthy goal, why not the conquest of sin? He further explained that the Christian Foundation was a trust fund created for a specific purpose and managed in a specific way. It was not a missionary society, benevolent or educational board. Kershner further stated that the Foundation was expected to help Disciples' educational work to the largest possible extent, a work now in a critical condition. The article listed a number of well-known Disciples as incorporators[25] and stated that the charter provided for a self-perpetuating board.

The Christian Foundation was incorporated in a permanent form by a special act of the Indiana State Legislature on March 10, 1921. Marshall T. Reeves became one of the first large donors to the Foundation. He made an annuity gift of $144,500 on October 12, 1921; by the end of 1923 his contributions reached the $260,000 mark, and his total contributions to the time of his death in 1925 amounted to $611,000. Many others also contributed to the Foundation at this early period. Minutes of the board meeting of February 21, 1922, show assets of $596,926.84. Kershner wrote later that donors to this time were Marshall T. Reeves, Henry McMillin, Mary E. Wood, Mrs. Florence W. Collins, Miss Kathryn Kohler,

---

[25]Original incorporators: James L. Clarke (Indiana jurist, Butler College trustee, member Danville church), William G. Irwin (Columbus banker and manufacturer), Marshall T. Reeves (Columbus manufacturer and banker), Hugh Th. Miller (Columbus businessman, former professor, two terms Lt. Governor of Indiana), Lucas C. Brite (Marfa, Texas, cattleman), Thomas W. Phillips, Jr., (Pennsylvania businessman, trustee of Bethany College and Phillips University), Ben D. Phillips (Pennsylvania businessman, trustee of Hiram College), George W. Hardin (Johnson City, Tenn., supporter of Milligan College), and George B. Peake (Des Moines, President of Central Life Assurance Company). Hilton U. Brown of Indianapolis was elected in 1923 in place of George W. Hardin, deceased. When Marshall T. Reeves died in 1925, Clarence L. Goodwin was elected to fill his unexpired term and Hilton U. Brown was made chairman of the trustees.

and William G. Irwin.[26]

The Kershner correspondence covering this period[27] indicates that the Foundation did not receive general approval. It was opposed by the Disciples' Board of Education. Z. T. Sweeney was uneasy about it because he believed that the program should have the endorsement of the International Convention before appealing to the brotherhood. Judge Clarke held the fear that Drake University and not Butler College would be the chief beneficiary. A business recession in the early 1920's slowed down the giving to the fund. A board session on May 27, 1923, shows the following distribution of grants: $100.00, Johnson Bible College; $1,532.81, Near East Relief; $4,123, mission work in Lake County, Indiana; $175.00, Purdue University Bible School; and Drake University, $2,666.56.[28]

Indiana Work Continued, 1920-1923

There were 308 delegates at the eighty-second annual convention of the State Association at Vincennes in 1920. J. Boyd Jones served as president. Dr. Royal J. Dye captivated the convention with missionary stories from Africa. At this convention it was proposed that the Emily E. Flinn Home for aged women, Marion, Indiana, be given to the National Benevolent Association. The convention passed a resolution urging the N. B. A. to accept the proposal and proceed as soon as convenient to organize the direction and management of the home as one of the institutions of the Brotherhood. Not long after this it was announced that the gift had been accepted, that the twelve non-Disciple residents already there would receive

[26]*Christian-Evangelist*, November 24, 1921; November 23, 1923, April 14, 1932.
[27]On file at Christian Theological Seminary archives.
[28]*Christian-Evangelist*, June 14, 1923.

care under the contract, and that Mr. and Mrs. E. C. Chaffee would be in charge.[29]

The state C. W. B. M. became a part of the United Christian Missionary Society in 1920, and the women changed the name of their organization to Indiana Woman's Christian Missionary Society. Local societies, formerly auxiliaries to the C. W. B. M., became auxiliaries of the United Society.[30]

The Board of Temperance and Social Welfare had its beginning in 1907 as a temperance board under the leadership of Dr. Homer J. Hall of Indiana. Luther E. Sellers, Christian Church minister in Indiana, eventually became its field secretary. Milo J. Smith, also of Indiana, became associate secretary through the financial help of the Men and Millions Movement. The American Christian Missionary Society had a standing committee on social service; Alva W. Taylor handled the work of this committee on a voluntary basis. Taylor, head of the sociology department of Christian College, Columbia, Missouri, finally accepted this work as a full-time responsibility, beginning June 1, 1921. The original temperance committee was expanded to include social service work under auspices of the U. C. M. S. Headquarters were maintained in the Occidental Building at Indianapolis, offices which also housed the Indiana Christian Missionary Association and regional headquarters for the United Christian Missionary Society.[31] *Social Trends,* a publication of the Board of Temperance and Social Welfare, was issued at Indianapolis with Alva W. Taylor as editor, beginning in 1928 and continuing to 1932.

The young people's camp and conference movement in Indiana had its beginning at the thirty-eighth session of the

[29]*Christian-Evangelist,* June 3, July 22, 1920; *Indiana Worker,* June, 1920.
[30]*Indiana Worker,* November, 1920.
[31]*Survey of Service, op cit.,* pp. 587-589; *Indiana Worker,* December, 1920.

Bethany Park Assembly in 1920. Over one hundred young people enrolled in this pioneer youth conference which "presented modern church work in all its phases." F. E. Davison was director, and L. Doyle Mullen was in charge of recreational facilities.[32]

The State Convention of 1921, held at the West Side Christian Church in Tipton, heard of the resignation of G. I. Hoover as evangelist of the Eastern District. He became associate secretary of the Disciples' Board of Education.

The State Convention of 1922 was held at the Jackson Street church in Muncie where S. G. Fisher was minister. Hoosier Disciples went to Frankfort, a community of 14,000 persons, for their annual convention in 1923.[33] A great interest was shown in the purchase of the Fairview campus in Indianapolis for Butler University.

Z. T. Sweeney of Columbus had the first volume of *New Testament Christianity* published in 1923. It was a unique compilation of excerpts from sermons and other writings of pioneer Disciples. The book sold for one dollar, but only to ministers over fifty years of age! Ministers under fifty received this book and the two subsequent volumes issued in 1923 and 1930 free on request.

The Ku Klux Klan Infiltrates Hoosier Disciple Ranks

The Ku Klux Klan was a post-war social phenomenon which caught on with native, white, Protestant Americans. At the peak of its popularity in 1924 some four million persons are said to have taken the Klan oath and donned the white robes and masks. Indiana had the largest concentration of klansmen in the nation; there were over 500,000 Hoosiers in the move-

---

[32]*Indiana Worker*, September, 1920.
[33]*Indiana Worker*, May, July, September, 1921; *Christian-Evangelist*, June 21, 1921; May 31, 1923; *World Call*, November, 1923.

ment. Because of the character of its constituency and the nature of its structure the Disciples' movement was especially susceptible to its appeal. Many Indiana pastors of the opportunist school used the K.K.K. to bolster their local programs. Others were pressured into support of the organization by zealous and ardent klansmen in their churches. Some ministers who kept silent or opposed the Klan openly had to endure persecution for their views. The organization seemed to mushroom all at once. Then, due to scandals and arrests in 1925, it subsided and went out of business. Nevertheless, the Klan left its scars of prejudice and bigotry on many Disciples' congregations in the Hoosier state.

Frank E. Davison's experience with Klan "pressure" is a vignette of what must have occurred in many places. From the vantage point of a quarter century of history he told his story in the book, *Thru the Rear-View Mirror*.[34] Davison called his Klan experience his first "baptism of fire." He wrote that 200 members were added to the church in a recent revival meeting and that his ministry was a very happy one until some of his elders came to him and said they would make him the greatest preacher in the state if he would support the current 100% Americanism movement. Such a move, they told him, would give him an opportunity to make many speeches and substantially increase his income. He refused the temptation. Soon, without his knowledge, Klan meetings were being scheduled in his church. Davison made a public protest to the congregation. He explained that if a majority of the members desired to have the building used in this way they had the right to grant permission, but he let them know that meetings already held had been without his knowledge and consent and over his protest. The matter made front page news for

---

[34]Frank Elon Davison, *Thru the Rear-View Mirror* (St. Louis: Bethany Press, 1955), pp. 75-79.

several days; Davison would not change his mind, and his resignation was forthcoming.

The Indiana Mission Field, 1924-1927

Over 1,000 Hoosier Disciples attended the annual convention at Rushville in 1924. Automobile rides to the historic Little Flat Rock church and visits to the graves of Knowles Shaw and John P. Thompson were conducted. President Aley of Butler University announced plans for the founding of a College of the Bible to be housed in the Butler University building. He told the convention that he hoped the Christian Churches in Indiana would raise the money for the Bible College building and that it would probably become the center of Disciple activity in the state.[35]

Ray H. Montgomery, Sr. presided over the sessions of the State Convention at Marion in 1925. Delegates were pleased with the newly-acquired Emily E. Flinn home, and many went to visit it. The Council of Indiana Ministers' Wives, an outgrowth of a small meeting at Bethany Park the year before, was organized at this convention. Mrs. L. C. Howe was elected president, and Mrs. L. E. Lee of Poseyville, secretary. Membership was extended to wives and widows of Indiana ministers.[36]

After serving the Tabernacle Christian Church in Columbus for twenty years, William H. Book[37] resigned this pastorate in 1925 to enter into general evangelistic work. He was successor to Z. T. Sweeney at the Columbus Church.

---

[35]*Indiana Worker*, April, June, 1924; *Christian-Evangelist*, May 22, 29, 1924.

[36]*Christian-Evangelist*, June 4, 11, 18, 1925; *Indiana Worker*, June, July, 1925.

[37]William H. Book (1863-1946) was a native of Virginia. He was ordained in 1882 and held the M. A. degree from Milligan College. After serving pastorates in Virginia he was called to the Columbus Tabernacle church in 1905. He served as trustee of Butler University and on the Board of the Indiana Christian Missionary Association. Book was author of *Real Life and Original Sayings of W. H. Book* (1900), *Columbus Tabernacle Sermons*, I and II, (1909, 1913), *Indiana Pulpit* (1912), and *Sermons for the People* (1918).

The Church Life Foundation, a movement for the spiritual enrichment and efficiency of the churches was launched at the Marion Convention. The Foundation was to be concerned with church attendance, enriching the church service with planned orders of worship, and providing adequate time for meditation and communion.[38] William S. Lockhart of Huntington was chosen to lead the movement, and an executive committee was appointed.[39] The Church Life Foundation, with headquarters in Indianapolis, had a program needed by Hoosier Disciples. Director Lockhart was soon in demand for local church conferences, state and district conventions, and on college campuses. Some thirty-three "orders of worship" were prepared for consideration in planning the worship program of the local church. The movement spread to other states, and ministers began thinking in terms of more dignified public worship and better architecture to support it. Though the Foundation ceased to exist after a few years, its program had a good effect on the brotherhood. The Director published an excellent book on the subject, one of the first of its kind among Disciples.[40]

Hoosier Disciples were responsible for the opening of the Indiana Christian Hospital at Indianapolis on April 1, 1925. A private venture seeking Disciple support, the Indiana Hospital Association, Garry L. Cook, executive secretary, rented the old Deaconess Hospital property in downtown Indianapolis. The hospital was in operation for a few years. An attempt was made in 1928 to purchase this property and remodel it. A resolution of moral support was all that could be

---

[38]*Christian-Evangelist*, March 12, 1925.

[39]Executive Committee: James H. Lowry, chairman; C. H. Winders, vice chairman; Reily C. Adams, treasurer; R. S. Sterling, F. H. Bowers, S. L. Hurlbut, F. P. Sterling, Sumner Clancy, and Miss F. M. Sterling.

[40]*Indiana Christian*, July, 1928; July, December, 1929. *See* William S. Lockhart, *The Ministry of Worship* (St. Louis: Christian Board of Publication, 1927).

obtained from the Christian Ministers' Association of Indianapolis. The State Convention also refused to aid the financial campaign in 1929 on the grounds of prior commitment to the $8,000,000 Pension Fund drive.[41]

The State Convention met at Bloomington in 1926. C. W. Cauble, who had served for thirteen years as state secretary, resigned earlier in the year but continued in office on a part-time basis until a replacement could be secured. He wished to devote his entire time to church dedicating (raising money for new buildings). Cauble reported that the state membership of the Disciples had reached 160,000 persons, an increase of 6,000 in the past year. Fifty-eight ministers' wives attended a tea at the Bloomington parsonage; Mrs. William B. Matthews was hostess. This was the second meeting of their newly formed Council.[42]

G. I. Hoover[43] became general secretary of the Indiana Christian Missionary Association in September, 1926. Having served for several years as evangelist of the Eastern District and later on the Disciples' Board of Education, he was well acquainted with the Indiana field and with promotional work.

The year 1927 marked the beginning of preparation by Disciples for the "nineteen-hundredth anniversary of Pentecost" in 1930. A comprehensive program on a brotherhood-wide basis was set up. These goals included gaining a half million members and establishing a World Convention in 1930. The Pentecost Committee was quite sure the 1930

---

[41]*Indiana Christian,* September, November, 1928; June, 1929; *Christian-Evangelist,* March 21, 1929.

[42]*Indiana Worker,* May, June, 1926; *Christian-Evangelist,* June 17, 24, 1926.

[43]Guy Israel Hoover (1873-1943) was born in Croton, Ohio. He was graduated from Hiram College in 1899 and ordained to the Christian ministry the same year. Later, he received the M.A. and B.D. degrees from the University of Chicago Divinity School. Hoover held pastorates at Zanesville and Minerva in Ohio, the First and West Pullman churches in Chicago, and the West Street Church in Tipton, Indiana. He was full-time evangelist for the Eastern District in Indiana, 1914-21; promotional secretary for the Board of Education, 1921-26; and general secretary of the Indiana Christian Missionary Association, 1926-1940. Hoover taught courses in the field of practical theology at the College of Religion, Butler University, 1925-32.

date was correct because Dean Frederick D. Kershner had solicited opinions of eminent biblical scholars from Yale Divinity School, Union Theological Seminary, and the University of Chicago; three out of five authorities favored the year 1930.[44]

By the time of the Lafayette State Convention in 1927 there had been a rapid upturn in economic conditions throughout the nation, a situation which helped the financial condition of churches and agencies. H. G. Connelly presided over the business sessions. There was much said about Hoosier participation in the Pentecost program. Though C. W. Cauble had retired from the state work the convention recommended that he proceed with writing a history of Indiana Disciples and regard it as one of the goals for Pentecost. He agreed that all records, books, and historical data gathered in his research would later be placed in the library of the College of Religion of Butler University. The convention also set goals of planting fifty new churches in the state by 1931 and increasing the state membership to 200,000 persons.[45]

Florence Carmichael, elementary superintendent for church schools, reported through the *Indiana Worker* that the Vacation Church School idea was getting a good foothold in the Hoosier State and many churches had sponsored schools during the summer.[46] The second high school youth conference was held at Bethany Park in August, 1927. Genefrede Harris served as dean, and Frank Hopper directed the recreation. There were fifteen faculty members and 167 students. The

---

[44]*Indiana Worker,* January, 1927; *World Call,* February, 1927. The original Pentecost Committee was organized with Charles Reign Scoville, chairman; Cleveland Kleihauer, vice chairman; Jesse M. Bader, executive secretary; and H. H. Peters, treasurer. The committee was enlarged later to 120 persons to conform with Acts II.

[45]*Indiana Worker,* June-July, 1927; *Christian-Evangelist,* June 9, 1927.

[46]*Indiana Worker,* June-July, 1927. Vacation church schools were held in Indianapolis at Central, Third, Linwood, Bethany, Fairfax, Beech Grove, Downey Avenue and North Park churches; Lafayette, New Castle, Noblesville, Oxford, Rockville, Garrett, Mitchell, Richmond, Bloomington, Terre Haute, Logansport, Warsaw, Winchester, Huntington, and Frankfort.

following week the young people's conference was held at the same place with nineteen faculty members and 158 students.[47]

Though Bethany Park was still being used it was becoming apparent by this time that the assembly program, as originally conceived, was now outdated. Many Hoosier Disciples would like to have seen Bethany Park restored, but this was not in the wave of the future. By 1927, leaders of the project were discouraged; the buildings were antiquated, the grounds neglected, and there was a loss of patronage and interest.[48]

The *Indiana Worker* appeared with a new format in September, 1927. The overall size was increased, and newspaper style was copied. Circulation was given at 4,100 copies per issue. G. I. Hoover was listed as managing editor, and there were several departmental editors.[49] When the October issue appeared it bore the name, *Indiana Christian*.

Bible Chairs in Indiana

The Angola Bible Chair at Tri-State College was instituted in 1911 through the cooperation of the college, the C. W. B. M., and the Angola Christian Church. Vernon Stauffer was one of the early workers. He was succeeded by O. F. Rakestraw. When the C. W. B. M. withdrew its support of the project the Standard Publishing Company took over the work. In 1916, the Bible Chair idea was dropped in favor of the Angola Christian Institute. J. O. Rose, former secretary of the Indiana Christian Missionary Association, became the instructor. It was claimed that over 200 young people entered full-time Christian service through the influence of the Angola

---

[47]*Indiana Worker,* September, 1927.
[48]*Indiana Worker,* September, 1927.
[49]Departmental editors: Florence Carmichael, Genefrede Harris, A. A. Coil, A. L. Martin, Cecil Franklin, Charles Shultz, John W. Marshall, Fred R. Davis, and V. P. Brock.

project. In 1929, there were three classes in Bible study enrolling fifty students, three classes in public speaking that enrolled ninety-six, and one class in the fundamentals of business ethics in which thirty-nine were enrolled. Under the influence of J. O. Rose, who was connected with the institute for sixteen years, forty-five student preachers were reported to have started their careers. Recitation rooms for the institute were furnished by the Angola church, and the Standard Publishing Company contributed $1,000 annually.[50]

The day after Christmas in 1914, the Bible Chair building at Indiana University was destroyed by fire. This was a serious setback to the project, but a room in the biology building nearby was offered as temporary headquarters.[51] The Bloomington Bible Chair became the Indiana School of Religion in 1917. Professor Harley Irwin Croyle was called as professor of Old Testament languages and literature at that time. Though a church workers' course was presented, students were advised that all who intended to prepare for the ministry would have better opportunities at Butler University. The School of Religion purchased property adjoining the campus in 1921. Dean Joseph C. Todd, writing in 1927, explained that Indiana University could not include religion in its curriculum but that the School of Religion at Bloomington provided biblical and religious instruction and chapel services, and that it stimulated religious life among the university students. It depended entirely on churches and individuals for support.[52]

Conventions to the Right and to the Left

A new kind of general convention was proposed in 1927. W. R. Walker, of Ohio, speaking to the Christian ministers

---

[50]*Indiana Worker*, September, 1927; *Indiana Christian*, July, 1929.
[51]*Indiana Worker*, February, 1915.
[52]*Indiana Worker*, September, October, 1917; *World Call*, January, 1927.

338

in Indianapolis, made it clear that the proposed new convention was not a meeting of protest against any organization or society but a meeting of good fellowship to emphasize the fundamental elements of the Disciples' plea and magnify their mission. It was called the North American Christian Convention, and the first meeting was held at Indianapolis in Cadle Tabernacle. The convention was promoted by individual Disciples and directed toward individuals. Attendance was between 2,500 and 3,000 persons, though the local attendance was said to be disappointing. A great number of doctrinal sermons and addresses were given, and conferences dealing with various facets of church work were held.[53]

The twenty-seventh annual session of the Disciples' Congress met in Indianapolis four months later in 1928. It was advertised as a free, impartial, open forum. The sponsors claimed of the Congress that "It represents no party, promotes no propaganda, serves no special interest." President Rothenburger's address, "Between Dogmatism and Progress," pointed the convention in the direction opposite to that of the North American group. Most of the speakers looked forward to new positions for the Disciples within a sociological-political-religious framework.[54] Both conventions were outside the structural pattern of the organized Brotherhood. One had a nostalgic backward look at old traditions and theological positions; the other looked to the future in quixotic, utopian expectation.

---

[53]*Indiana Worker,* August, September, 1927; *Indiana Christian,* November, 1927. Program personalities: Wallace Tharp, George P. Taubman, J. H. O. Smith, W. N. Briney, Ira M. Boswell, T. H. Johnson, S. W. Traum, F. J. Gielow, M. B. Miller, Virgil Wallace, Paul Henry Packard, Mark Collis, J. Quincy Biggs, J. F. Messenger, O. P. Spiegel, C. C. Taylor, J. H. Stambaugh, W. A. Sourgeon, Judge Gilbert O. Nations, C. R. Scoville, Bruce Kershner, Edwin S. Sweeney, Joseph L. Fisher, and Jesse R. Kellems.

[54]*Indiana Christian,* January, 1928. Speakers at this convention were William F. Rothenburger, Alva W. Taylor, Charles T. Paul, Ernest N. Evans, Robert E. Lewis, H. C. Armstrong, Mrs. F. E. Smith, Miner Lee Bates, Charles C. Morrison, Clarence E. Lemmon, and Albert W. Palmer.

Emphasis on Layman's Work

In the closing years of the 1920's business was good in America. Fortunes were being made on the stock market, and increasing prosperity seemed to indicate an expanding and secure economic future for all. The businessman was the high man on the totem pole of American life. In recognition of the possible role that businessmen could play in religion, a Business Men's Commission was set up at the Lafayette State Convention in 1927. It began with a special banquet at which seventy-five men were present. The second Business Men's banquet was held at the Claypool hotel in Indianapolis later that year. These were but the beginning of a series of similar dinner meetings held throughout the state to interest laymen in the work of the Indiana Christian Missionary Association.[55] Beginning in February, 1928, a "men's work" column was featured in the *Indiana Christian*. It was edited by M. R. Denison of the Studebaker Corporation at South Bend, chairman of the Business Men's Commission.

The United Society Moves to Indianapolis

When the United Christian Missionary Society was formed in 1919 the affiliated organizations set up headquarters at St. Louis. Later, after the College of Missions moved from Irvington to Hartford, Connecticut, the C. W. B. M. offered the abandoned College of Missions building to the United Society. The Society had been in St. Louis for eight years, and since its lease had expired anyway it was necessary to seek another location in St. Louis or elsewhere. An investigation revealed that the missions building was adaptable to the United Society

---

[55]*Indiana Christian*, January, February, 1928. Dinners were held at Marion, Fort Wayne, Elkhart, New Albany, Madison, Seymour, Rensselaer, La Porte, Logansport, Crawfordsville, Greencastle, Terre Haute, Noblesville, Kokomo, Anderson, New Castle, Rushville, Franklin, Bedford, Vincennes, and Evansville.

program and that Indiana laws were more favorable for the operation of an organization such as this than the laws of Missouri. The move to Indianapolis was inevitable, though U. C. M. S. employees were reluctant to break their ties with St. Louis. The St. Louis offices were closed on August 22, 1928, and headquarters were established at 222 South Downey Avenue, Indianapolis. The Christian Churches of Indianapolis held a formal reception for the U. C. M. S. employees at Central Christian Church. The new people were formally introduced at this time.[56] The move from St. Louis to Indianapolis meant an ever-increasing influx of national leaders into the Indianapolis churches and definitely made Indiana, particularly Indianapolis, the center of the power structure of the Disciples' movement.

Hoosier Disciples, 1928-1930

So many exciting things were happening in Disciple Hoosierland that all the sessions of the annual State Convention at Bedford in 1928 were crowded. Eating took on a new significance about this time because it was discovered that meals were a good way to bring groups together for special meetings. So the Bedford convention was replete with a missionary breakfast, ministers' dinner, businessmen's banquet, youth banquet, ministers' wives' luncheon, convention banquet, and numerous committee luncheons. Many convention addresses[57] were followed by conferences (workshops). Items that received special attention included the preservation of the Eighteenth Amendment, the Pension Plan, a new hospital in Indianapolis, and Pentecost goals. W. D. Bartle presided over

---

[56]*World Call,* April, June, October, 1928.
[57]Speakers included Cynthia Pearl Maus, Genefrede Harris, W. A. Shullenberger, W. P. Dearing, L. F. Sargeant, B. A. Abbott, T. C. Howe, Homer C. Boblitt, and Frederick D. Kershner.

341

the business sessions. Secretary Hoover reported that the State Association receipts for the fiscal year were $29,459.94 and that there had been 1,019 additions to the churches through the efforts of the state evangelists.[58]

The old Board of Ministerial Relief became the Pension Fund by act of the International Convention in 1928. Though it did not become operational until 1930 it meant that another agency destined to be of primary importance to the Disciples would have its headquarters in Indianapolis. Many Hoosiers served on the Board of Trustees.[59] Thomas C. Howe was president; F. E. Smith, who was called from a pastorate at Muncie, was secretary; and Samuel Ashby was treasurer. The great depression of the 'thirties arrived just as the Pension Fund drive for $8,000,000 for a prior service fund was launched. Though goals were not reached at this time the Fund started on a limited basis, eventually exceeded its objectives, and became firmly entrenched in brotherhood life.

Central Christian Church at Huntington, B. F. Cato, pastor, entertained the state convention in 1929. Charles E. Jefferson, popular New York City preacher, was a featured speaker. The Pentecost theme was emphasized.[60] Nearly a thousand delegates registered for the next convention at Central Christian Church in Indianapolis in 1930. Many looked forward to attending the International and First World Conventions later that year at Washington when the Pentecost program would reach its culmination. C. W. Cauble's book, *Disciples of Christ in Indiana,* was introduced at this convention.[61]

---

[58]For convention reports, see *Indiana Christian,* May, June, July, 1928; *Christian-Evangelist,* June 21, 1928.

[59]*World Call,* November, 1928. Pension Fund Trustees: Thomas C. Howe, Robert A. Long, Edward S. Jouett, William R. Warren, Oreon E. Scott, Samuel Ashby, William A. Shullenberger, Charles M. Rodcfer, Myrtle Slayton Moorhouse, Leila Avery Rothenburger, Isaac J. Cahill, Andrew D. Harmon, Frank Buttram, Buckner A. McKinney, and James R. McWane.

[60]*Indiana Christian,* June, 1929.

[61]*Indiana Christian,* April, 1930; *Christian-Evangelist,* June 5, 1930.

College of Missions, to 1928

The College of Missions, which had its beginning in 1911, had a favorable growth and rendered conspicuous service for many years. A standard degree program was not offered at first; missionaries in training received certificates of achievement. The catalog for the academic year 1916-17 announced an opportunity to gain M.A. and B.D. degrees in the future. The Ph.D. degree was offered, beginning in 1921. The requirements for this degree included three years of postgraduate study and the preparation of a thesis. There is no evidence that either the B.D. or Ph.D. degree was ever awarded. Several M.A. degrees were granted, however, the first of these being to Wallace Reed Bacon and Lois Anna Ely in 1919.

By 1922 it was apparent that there was dissatisfaction with the location of the College at Indianapolis. This site was originally selected because it was the headquarters of the Christian Woman's Board of Missions, since moved to St. Louis. College authorities believed that a location on the campus of a large university would be advantageous; a university center would give the missionaries a wider range of course selections, enlarged library facilities, and contact with life in a cosmopolitan center. They believed that the "academic tone and culture" of a university center would be beneficial to the students and that missionaries needed the prestige gained by a degree from a large university.[62] When the work of the C. W. B. M. was coordinated with the United Christian Missionary Society, control and management of the College of Missions passed to the United Society. A charter amendment in 1926 permitted reorganization of the school so that it had a self-perpetuating board of trustees with power to

---

[62]*World Call*, July, August, 1922.

select faculty and determine policies. The faculty[63] remained the same. This placed the College of Missions on a similar basis with other institutions of higher education. The new board was administratively independent of the United Society but acted for it.[64]

By this time (1927) it had become increasingly difficult to raise funds to support the school. Since there was a desire to move it to a university campus, investigations of possible other locations proceeded. Added motives for the change included a cut-back in the operating budget and lack of available funds to enter new missionary fields. Actually, the supply of trained missionaries exceeded the demand, if not the need. In view of this it was decided to suspend operation of the College of Missions for the academic year 1927-28.[65] In 1928 it was decided that the College would affiliate with the Kennedy School of Missions at Hartford, Connecticut. It was agreed that the College would reserve its full legal and institutional identity but that Disciple students could have access to all courses and residential accommodations on an equal basis with Kennedy students. The College of Missions library cooperated with the Hartford school as far as supplementing resources permitted. Professor Clarence H. Hamilton and some special lecturers represented the College of Missions at Hartford. The Kennedy School of Missions, an interdenominational institution, came into existence after the founding of the College of Missions but was in a better finanical position to maintain this unique type of work.[66]

---

[63]Faculty: Charles T. Paul, president; George William Brown, Oswald Joseph Grainger, Albert Raymond Miles, William Charles Morro, Mrs. Jessie Williams Paul, Everard Roy Moon, Toyozo W. Nakarai.

[64]*Christian-Evangelist*, June 24, 1926; *World Call*, August, 1926. New Board of Directors: W. F. Rothenburger, president; Mrs. Ellie K. Payne, secretary; C. H. Winders, T. C. Howe, Samuel B. Ashby, W. A. Shullenberger, Mrs. Effie Cunningham, Mrs. Ida W. Harrison, A. W. Fortune, O. L. Hull, Mrs. Alda Teachout, and J. H. MacNeill.

[65]*World Call*, July, 1927.

[66]*World Call*, August, 1928.

A United Christian Missionary Society survey completed in 1925 showed that the College of Missions offered graduate courses in all the mission fields occupied by the Disciples of Christ. It had especially strong departments on India and Latin America and one of the strongest working missionary libraries in America with a unique treatment on Tibet. Courses were offered in Tibetan, Lonkundo, Hindi, and Urdu languages. The report stated that since the school had opened some 410 students had enrolled and 309 had graduated. Of the total enrollment, 356 former students were working under the direction of the United Christian Missionary Society.[67]

Butler University, 1914-1930

Butler College made no radical changes between 1914 and 1917. Though there was an increase each year in the student body, there was a corresponding increase in the operational deficit. It was apparent that more classrooms and more professors were needed. The $300,000 received from the Disciples' Men and Millions Movement helped meet the emergency but did not solve the college problem permanently. When the United States entered the World War in 1917 the school faced far-reaching changes in curriculum, structure, and administrative procedures. Butler College was never the same after this experience.

A unit of the Students Army Training Corps was established in 1917. All regularly enrolled male students were given the opportunity of being inducted. After induction they became soldiers in the United States Army and were subject to military discipline. Until barracks were erected on the campus inductees were quartered in private homes and in the annex of the Downey Avenue Christian Church. Meals were served at the

---

[67]*Survey of Service, op. cit.*, pp. 523-524.

College of Missions building.[68] The athletic program was abandoned. Instructors from the War Department augmented the regular faculty. Young men desiring to be commissioned as officers, who perhaps otherwise would not have chosen to enter college, enrolled to take advantage of the S. A. T. C. program. This made an additional strain on college resources. The influenza epidemic of 1918 was especially severe on the campus. The school was closed to all except S. A. T. C. men, and they were compelled to wear medical masks at all times. The general order for demobilization of the S. A. T. C. unit came from the War Department on November 26, 1918. The mustering-out program began on December 4 and was completed by December 24th.[69]

Statistics on Butler College participation in the War were included in the minutes of the meeting of the Board of Directors on July 9, 1919. These show that 710 men of the Butler College "family" were active in the war effort. Of these, 266 students were enlisted in the S. A. T. C., and seventeen served in the Y. M. C. A. Thirteen men lost their lives; five were killed in action, and eight others died while in the service.[70] A special memorial service was held later in the chapel, and a bronze tablet containing the names of these men was presented to the school.[71]

By 1919, the Board of Directors, under pressure of increased post-war enrollment, realized that a program of long-range planning was needed. They faced the problem of deciding whether to spend vast sums in remodeling and new con-

---

[68]*Indiana Worker*, May, 1917; September, 1918.

[69]*Indiana Worker*, November, December, 1918.

[70]Those who lost their lives were as follows: Lt. Hilton U. Brown, Jr., Lt. Conwell B. Carson, Lt. Kenneth V. Elliot, Lt. Charles Good, Lt. Robert Edward Kennington, Sgt. Henry Reinhold Laukhardt, Private William Russell Mercer, Corp. Guy Griffeth Michaels, Corp. Mash Whitney Nottingham, Private Marvin Francis Race, Lt. Bruce Pettibone Robison, Lt. McCrae Stevenson, Apprentice Seaman Henry Clarence Toon.

[71]*Indiana Worker*, January, 1920. See Kathryn M. Graydon, *Butler College in the World War* (Greenfield: William Mitchell Printing Co., 1922).

struction on the Irvington campus or relocating on a new campus. The latter course was chosen. It was decided to employ an agent to conduct a financial drive for $1,000,000 and to search for a new site at once. The target date of September 23, 1923, was set as the day when the college would move into its new buildings.[72]

In view of a current $50,000 operating deficit the proposal to raise a million dollars and relocate on a new campus was a bold one. Apparently, the challenge got through to the alumni. A special "Alumni Committee of Twenty-Five" was formed at a meeting held in connection with the International Convention of the Disciples at Cincinnati in October, 1919. This committee took the initiative in the fund-raising program. The Alumni Committee recommended that John W. Atherton,[73] son-in-law of Hilton U. Brown, be appointed as financial secretary and campaign director; his appointment by the Directors was forthcoming. Atherton opened a campaign office in downtown Indianapolis at once and proceeded to engage in raising an emergency fund of $100,000. The drive for the larger amount was postponed to a later date.[74]

The Alumni Committee believed that one way to attract attention to the college was to have a strong athletic program. The example of formerly little known Notre Dame University's coming into national prominence through Knute Rockne's successful football teams may have been the incentive. Whatever the reason, one of the first achievements of the Alumni

---

[72]*Indiana Christian,* May, 1919.

[73]John Whistler Atherton (1878-1947) was a native Hoosier who had been graduated from Butler College in the class of 1900. After further study at the University of Chicago he taught in the high schools at Gary and Kokomo. At the time of his appointment as financial secretary of Butler College he was one of Charles Scribner's Sons' representatives. Atherton helped to organize the Butler Foundation as a holding company in 1921. He was influential with Butler alumni and Indianapolis men, "selling" them on the "new" Butler. In 1940 and 1944 he was elected state senator from Marion County. He served on the Board of Directors of Butler University and the Christian Board of Publication. After his death a student building was erected on the Butler campus which bears the name, "John Whistler Atherton Center."

[74]*Indiana Christian,* December, 1929.

Committee was to persuade the Board of Directors to pass on a staggering athletic program. An increase of $10,000 was authorized for expenditures in athletics. This was the beginning of emphasis on games and sports, a program which ended almost disastrously a few years later. Harlan O. "Pat" Page, assistant to Coach Stagg at the University of Chicago, was given a three-year contract as athletic director and made a member of the faculty.[75]

Thomas C. Howe retired as president in September, 1920; Dean J. W. Putnam was made acting president. Howe had been chief administrative officer for thirteen years and had been connected with the college for thirty-one years. During his administration the enrollment of the college increased from 300 to over 1,000 students. Robert J. Aley[76] became Howe's successor in 1921.

The School of Ministerial Education continued with programs leading to three-year B.D. and one-year M.A. postgraduate degrees until 1920. At this time the B.D. degree was again dropped; the M.A. degree program was continued with the "professional" courses eliminated from the curriculum. College authorities apparently wanted to take a new look at ministerial education before pursuing their current curriculum any longer. President Howe and a special committee from the Faculty and Directors had a conference with Frederick D. Kershner (Kershner was then with the *Christian*

---

[75]*Indiana Worker,* February, March, 1920.

[76]Robert Judson Aley (1863-1935) was born in Coal City, Indiana. He was graduated from Valparaiso University with the B.S. degree in 1882; attended Indiana University where he received the degrees of B.A. (1888), and M.A. (1897). Franklin College awarded him the honorary degree of LL.D. in 1909; the same degree was received from the University of Pennsylvania in 1917. Aley was a rural school teacher in Indiana, 1877-81; taught in the Coal City schools, 1881-82; was principal of the high school at Spencer, 1882-87; instructor in mathematics at Indiana University, 1887-88; professor of mathematics at Vincennes University, 1888-91; and on the faculty of Indiana University to 1909. In 1909-10 he was superintendent of public instruction for Indiana. Aley became president of the University of Maine in 1910. He was president of the National Educational Association, 1916-17, and belonged to many learned societies. Aley was inaugurated as president of Butler University on Founders Day, February 7, 1922. Another honorary LL.D. degree was conferred on him at that time. He, in turn, conferred the same degree on former president Thomas C. Howe.

348

Standard) in 1919 relative to establishing a new "College of Applied Christianity." The discussions resulted in a report to the Board of Directors to the effect that the establishing of such a college would be advisable. The committee also recommended that the college should have a separate board of directors which could include seven out of twelve from the Butler board. The committee suggested that if the college were instituted it should be in every sense an integral part of Butler College, but it would not be a substitute for the department of religious education (undergraduate department of religion) at Butler.[77]

The way was not clear for Butler College to engage in an extensive financial drive until the school was first prepared to receive grants from the large foundations. Senate Bill Number 274, providing for the organization of a holding company, became a law by act of the Indiana legislature in 1921. This circumvented the special conditions existing in the original corporation of Butler University, and safeguarded endowment funds from possible trouble that could arise from the old stock corporation disbanded in 1909.[78] The Butler Foundation (or holding company) elected its first officers on June 10, 1922. William G. Irwin[79] was selected as president.

The catalog for the academic year 1923-24 indicated a restoration of the name, "Butler University." This required no charter amendment. The school had been called Butler College since 1896; it was changed from university to college

---

[77]Butler University *Minutes,* Book No. 7, April 9, 29, 1919.

[78]*Butler Alumnal Quarterly,* April, 1921.

[79]William Glanton Irwin (1866-1943), churchman, philanthropist, banker, industrialist, was born at Columbus, Indiana, the son of Joseph I. Irwin. He received the B.A. degree from Butler University in 1889 and was awarded an honorary LL.D. degree from the same institution in 1938. He was president of several companies and director in many others. These include the Irwin Union Trust Company, Union Starch and Refining Company, Indianapolis Gas Company, and Columbus and Southern Traction Company. At the time of his death he had served as trustee of Butler University since 1908. He was associated in an official capacity with the Butler Foundation, The Christian Foundation, and the National City Church Corporation, contributing generously to all these causes.

at the beginning of the University of Indianapolis period. The catalog also indicated that the Metropolitan School of Music, the Indiana Law School and the College of Missions were affiliated with Butler by cooperation, and that the John Herron Art Institute offered courses which could be credited toward a baccalaureate degree in fine arts at Butler University. Frederick D. Kershner, who was to become dean of the College of Religion the next year, was listed as a member of the Butler University faculty in 1923-24.

The big financial drive got underway in 1923 with a conditional grant of $300,000 from the Rockefeller Foundation. William G. Irwin and his sister, Mrs. Z. T. Sweeney, made a joint contribution of $200,000; Arthur V. Brown gave $50,000, and Clarence L. Goodwin added $35,000. There were several gifts of $25,000. The first contribution mailed to the endowment campaign was from Roderick A. MacLeod (B.D., 1916) who was a Disciple missionary in Tibet. It was announced that by the end of 1923 that $900,000 was pledged to the Butler Foundation for endowment, and $600,000 for the building fund.[80]

Under assurance of the Endowment Campaign Committee[81] that financial goals would be reached, the Board of Directors closed the deal for the purchase of a new campus on the north side of Indianapolis. The new site, known as Fairview Park, contained 246 acres and had been used by the street railway company as an amusement park. It was thought at that time that the city planned to construct an artificial lake a half mile wide and three miles long and that the new Butler

---

[80]*Butler Alumnal Quarterly*, April, 1923; *World Call*, July, 1923; *Christian-Evangelist*, November 1, 1923; January 24, 1924.

[81]General Endowment Committee Personnel: William G. Irwin, chairman; Arthur V. Brown, vice chairman; J. W. Atherton, executive secretary; Hilton U. Brown, Robert J. Aley, Allan B. Philputt, Arthur R. Baxter, L. C. Huesmann, Emsley W. Johnson, A. M. Rosenthral, and Fred C. Dickson.

campus would eventually extend the whole length of the east shore of the lake.[82]

Large gifts continued to come to the Butler project in 1924, and the campaign to raise money for endowment and buildings went forward in a satisfactory manner. Architects Robert Frost Daggett and Thomas Hibben started to work on plans for the new buildings.[83] The dream of a "new" Butler was coming into focus. In the spring of 1925 William G. Irwin and his sister, Mrs. Z. T. Sweeney, offered another joint gift of $300,000 on condition that it would be matched by $700,-000 in new gifts.[84] This gave new incentive to the program, and more large gifts were soon received. Arthur Jordan,[85] who had already contributed $25,000, gave an additional $350,-000. In 1927 Jordan added another $625,000, bringing his total to $1,000,000.

In recognition of his philanthropy the new central building on the Butler campus was designated "Arthur Jordan Memorial Hall." Ground was broken for this building in the fall of 1926.[86] The new athletic plant was also under construction by this time. It cost over a million dollars but was built by a separate corporation. The university rented this facility until the stockholders generously surrendered their stock and title to the school.[87]

---

[82]*Christian-Evangelist*, May 3, 1923; *World Call*, July, 1923.

[83]*Butler Alumnal Quarterly*, January, 1925.

[84]*Christian-Evangelist*, March 5, 1925; *Butler Alumnal Quarterly*, April, 1925.

[85]Arthur Jordan (1855-1934) capitalist, was born at Madison, Indiana, and was a graduate of the high school in Indianapolis. He was in the poultry, eggs, and butter business for many years. An adroit business man, he soon ventured into other fields. Among these were the City Ice and Coal Company, the Keyless Lock Company, the Meridian Life Insurance Company, the Cloverdale Company (retail grocery chain), the International Machine and Tool Company, and the Printing Arts Company. He was a trustee of the Indianapolis Y.M.C.A., and served on the board of the Indianapolis Community Fund and Crown Hill Cemetery. In addition to the gift of $1,000,000 to Butler University he donated the Y.M.C.A. buildings at Rangoon, Burma, and Tisinan Fu, China. In 1928 he established the Arthur Jordan Conservatory of Music at Indianapolis, and the Arthur Jordan Foundation which he endowed with $2,000,000.

[86]*World Call*, January, 1927; *Christian-Evangelist*, September 22, 1927.

[87]Hilton U. Brown, *A Book of Memories* (Indianapolis: Butler University, 1951), p. 99.

The cornerstone for Arthur Jordan Memorial Hall was laid on November 10, 1927, with appropriate ceremonies. P. H. Welshimer, minister of First Christian Church at Canton, Ohio, delivered the principal address.[88] The new field house and stadium were dedicated on November 10, 1928, at the Butler—University of Illinois football game. It was announced in May, 1928, that contracts for two new dormitories to be erected on the south side of the quadrangle had been signed. The new Jordan building was almost completed by this time, and some of the fraternities had started their building.[89]

The move from Irvington to Fairview was made in the summer of 1928. Academic activities began on the Fairview campus with the fall semester of that year. The academic year 1928-29 was a happy one for students and faculty. The new campus met general approval. There were 3,047 students enrolled at the university during the year; ten years before this the enrollment was 946. Schools affiliated with the university at this time were the Arthur Jordan Conservatory of Music, the John Herron Art Institute, the Teachers College of Indianapolis, and the Claire Ann Shover Nursery School. Indiana Law School was listed in the catalog in an associate capacity.[90]

The university received a hard blow to its prestige when it was expelled from the North Central Association of Colleges

---

[88]*World Call*, January, 1928. Others on the program were Mayor L. Ert Slack of Indianapolis, President Robert J. Aley, Arthur V. Brown, Arthur Jordan, Frederick D. Kershner, and T. W. Grafton.

[89]*Indiana Christian*, May, 1928.

[90]Organization: Robert J. Aley, president; Elijah N. Johnson, treasurer; and Charles W. Wilson, secretary. Hilton U. Brown was president of the corporation and Directors; William G. Irwin was vice president of the Board of Directors, president of the Butler Foundation, and chairman of the General Endowment Committee; John W. Atherton was executive and financial secretary of Butler University and secretary of the Butler Foundation; and Emsley W. Johnson was chairman of the Alumni Endowment Committee. Directors: John W. Atherton, Crate Bowen, Arthur V. Brown, Hilton U. Brown, Lee Burns, Scot Butler, John E. Canaday, James L. Clark, Perry H. Clifford, Clarence L. Goodwin, Thomas W. Grafton, William G. Irwin, Emsley W. Johnson, Arthur Jordan, Henry Kahn, Robert A. Long, Hugh Th. Miller, P. C. Reilly, William C. Smith, Albert G. Snider, and Mrs. Z. T. Sweeney.

and Secondary Schools in March, 1930. It was understood
that the quality of its academic program was not involved;
Butler University had over-emphasized athletics. A new
athletic director had been employed in 1927. His salary of
$10,000 was considered excessive and out of proportion
to the general financial status of the institution. Rumors that
some of the football players were being paid for their services
were also being heard.[91]

College of Religion

The three-year postgraduate curriculum in ministerial education was dropped in 1920 in view of later establishing a
program on a better basis. A new College of Religion was announced in the 1924-25 catalog as a constituent college of
Butler University. It was to be administered by a dean and
a faculty of its own, acting under the immediate supervision
of the Church Committee of the university Board of Directors.
The new college was to have its own special endowment fund,
and eventually its own building on the Fairview campus. The
B.S.L., B.D., and M.A. degrees would be offered and diplomas
were to be given for shorter terms leading to positions of
church secretaries and ministers' assistants. Frederick D.
Kershner,[92] already a member of the university faculty, was

[91]*Butler Alumnal Quarterly,* October, 1927; July, 1930; *Christian-Evangelist,* July 17,
1930; *World Call,* July, 1930.

[92]Frederick Doyle Kershner (1875-1953) was a native of Maryland. He received
the Litt.B. degree from Kentucky University in 1899, and the M.A. degree from
Princeton University in 1900. Bethany College awarded him the honorary degree of
LL.D. in 1913; the same degree was received from Transylvania College in 1916. He
studied in Europe on various occasions between 1903 and 1911. Kershner was dean,
Kee Mar College, 1901-05; staff lecturer of the American Society for the Extension
of University Teaching, 1902-06; president of Milligan College, 1908-11; president of
Texas Christian University, 1911-15; professor of Christian doctrine at Drake University,
1920-24; and dean of Butler University College of Religion, 1924-54. Between 1915 and
1917 he was editor of the *Christian-Evangelist,* and he served on the editorial staff of
the *Christian Standard,* 1918-19. Kershner's published works include: The *Religion
of Christ* (1912), *Christian Baptism* (1913), *The Restoration Handbook* (1918), *Sermons on Special Days* (1921), *The Christian Union Overture* (1923), *The Spiritual
Message of Great Art* (1928), *Pioneers of Christian Thought* (1930), and *Those Gay
Middle Ages* (1929). He authored a page, "As I Think on These Things," for thirty
years in the *Christian-Evangelist.* He was a member of the American Society of
Church History and the American Theological Society.

designated dean of the new college.

The College of Religion opened for its first session in September, 1925. The curriculum was divided into five departments: Old Testament, New Testament, Church History, Christian Doctrine, and Practical Theology. In addition to Dean Kershner, five full-time persons constituted the faculty.[93]

Thirty-eight students were enrolled the first year. The enrollment increased to 74 in the 1926-27 academic year. The College of Religion graduated its first class on June 13, 1927.[94]

The College of Religion occupied rooms in the old Butler University building at Irvington for the sessions of 1925-26 and 1926-27. The next year classrooms in the College of Missions building were made available. The theological library was separated from the university library at this time and moved temporarily to the Missions building. Beginning with the academic year 1928-29 the College of Religion was given its own quarters in the Arthur Jordan Memorial Hall on the new Fairview campus. In the period between 1926 and 1930 several new members were added to the faculty.[95]

Beginning with the summer of 1927 the College of Religion held a summer session regularly. In addition to course work,

[93]Faculty: Frederick D. Kershner, A.M., LL.D., dean and professor of Christian doctrine; Bruce L. Kershner, A.M., professor of New Testament languages and literature; Guy I. Hoover, A.M., B.D., assistant professor of Old Testament languages and literature; H. Parr Armstrong, A.M., professor of practical theology; and Hugh W. Ghormley, A.M., B.D., associate professor of Old Testament.

[94]*Butler University Bulletin,* 1927-28: B.D. degrees were received by Alexander Aitken (Spokane University, 1925), William F. Bacon (McCormick Theological Seminary, 1912), Alva J. Lindsey (Butler University, 1925), and William Hauley Rowlands (Butler University, 1925). Thomas J. Bennett and Irvin James Kerrick received B.S.L. degrees. M.A. degrees with majors in religion were awarded to Alfred T. DeGroot, Yo Kawamura, and Harold L. Proppe.

[95]New faculty members were as follows: Morris M. Feuerlicht, B.H.L., A.B., professor of semitics; Tolbert F. Reavis, A.M., Ph.D., LL.D., professor of church history; William F. Bacon, B.D., instructor in Old Testament and semitics; Janet Malcolm Macdonald, Ph.D., associate professor of classical languages and archeology; Thomas W. Grafton, A.M., university chaplain and instructor in practical theology; Toyozo W. Nakarai, A.M., assistant professor of Old Testament; A. Campbell Garnett, A.M., Litt.D., professor of apologetics; Allena Grafton, A.M., instructor in practical theology; Dean Everest Walker, B.D., instructor in church history; and Alfred T. DeGroot, M.A., B.D., instructor in Old Testament.

a program of summer institutes was offered which proved to be popular through the years. The College of Religion catalog for 1930-31 lists 42 students registered for graduate work, and 117 enrolled as undergraduate students.

Learning the Hard Way

The emphasis on stewardship beginning in 1914 raised the level of giving to the State Association. The Association was then able to engage in a responsible program of evangelism and serve the five districts of Indiana with full-time resident representatives. World War I did not mean much to Hoosier Disciples until the United States became involved in 1917. The character of the movement was then altered by the population flow to urban centers, improved economic conditions, and frequent pastoral changes. New employment and social contacts made Disciples aware of the claims of other religious groups and forced them to challenge some of their own traditional views. Liberty Bond and various war-related relief appeals had a tendency to unify religious forces in a common cause as well as to educate church leaders in the techniques of large-scale financial drives.

The College of Missions was a pioneer project originating with the Disciples. If the financial support of missionary expansion could have kept pace with the vision of College of Missions leaders it might not have been necessary to close the school. However, when the United Society occupied the vacant building as headquarters it made Indiana, especially Indianapolis, the center of the Disciples' movement. The "new" Butler on the Fairview campus and the establishing of the College of Religion were especially significant for Hoosier Disciples; this made an extraordinary impact on the cultural, educational and religious life in Indiana.

Though Hoosier Disciples did not realize it then, "black" Thursday, October 24, 1929, the day of the stock market crash, was the beginning of a new and tragic era in American life. The economic depression settled in slowly but cast an ominous shadow over the next decade.

X

Under Clouds of Depression
1931-1941

THE WALL STREET CRASH OF 1929 which ushered in the Great Depression of the 1930's was not taken seriously by the churches at first. When lay-offs and wage cuts came a few months later church people began to realize the gravity of the situation. Hoosier Disciples, for the most part, were inclined to go along with the prevalent view that prosperity was "just around the corner," that in a few months conditions would right themselves and the national economy return to normalcy. In the meantime, people began to exhaust their financial resources; by 1931 they were really worried. James A. Crain, writing in *World Call*[1] at this time, was of the opinion that the depression had finally reached its greatest depth. Many experts felt that with business 23 per cent below normal and five million workers idle, conditions could not get much worse.

Since the government was not prepared to cope with the problem of giving immediate assistance to the great numbers of families in desperate need the churches were the first to come to the rescue. Some of the city churches found it necessary to open soup kitchens or provide relief in other ways for

---
[1]*World Call*, February, 1931.

people in their community. A reverse population shift took place when families returned to the farms and small towns they had left and doubled up with relatives who were willing to share the hardships of the times.

Period of Despair, 1931-1936

Congregations which had not incurred building and re-modeling debts in the prosperous late 1920's were more fortunate than the others. By reducing ministers' salaries and cutting back in other ways they managed to exist on a survival basis. Congregations carrying heavy mortgages, the missionary societies and other agencies of the churches faced virtually impossible obstacles by 1931 when incomes were shut off almost completely. The Indiana Christian Missionary Association closed its fiscal year in 1931 with a deficit of $6,956.60.[2] It was necessary to reduce the number of evangelists on the field. The State Convention at Logansport that year was not a happy one, though the program was thought to have had unusual strength. Hilton U. Brown, former editor of the *Indianapolis News* and first layman-president of the convention, addressed his brethren on "The Vandal Years." The speech was a challenge to the church to be strong to meet the changing times.

By 1932 Hoosier Disciples realized that the depression had not yet reached its depth but that they must unhappily look forward to years of continued hard times. It was a period of disillusionment. The *Indiana Christian*[3] carried an article by Roger W. Babson, the economist, which bears out this view. He stated that people had lost faith in "bankers, business leaders, and political leaders just as business men had

---

[2]*Indiana Christian*, May, June, 1931; *Christian-Evangelist*, June 11, 1931.
[3]*Indiana Christian*, July-August, 1932.

lost faith in each other." Babson advised churches not to curtail activities and compared doing so to hospitals running on half time because of an epidemic.

Whatever judgment is pronounced on the churches and their outreach agencies between the stock market crash of 1929 and the beginning of World War II in Europe must be made in the context of almost catastrophic economic conditions throughout the world.

The depression was noticeable at the Seymour State Convention of 1932.[4] There were only 400 delegates registered. J. N. Jessup, vice president of the State Board, reported "we have everything but money." Another deficit year was announced by the general secretary. There was talk of retrenchment and how far this could go without jeopardizing the cause. The usual number of luncheon and dinner meetings were held; the price ranged between 35 cents and one dollar per plate. M. R. Denison, of the Studebaker Corporation at South Bend, served as president of the convention. The general theme of the gathering was "Back to Christ! Forward with Christ."

The International Convention of the Disciples of Christ was held in Indianapolis in October, 1932. Delegates were treated to an impressive array of prominent speakers.[5] Many ministers at this convention, especially the program participants, were dressed in formal daytime attire; cutaway coats, striped trousers and winged collars were conspicuous on downtown Indianapolis streets during the week of the convention.

When President Franklin D. Roosevelt was inaugurated in

---

[4]*Indiana Christian*, June, 1932; *Christian-Evangelist*, June 2, 1932.

[5]*Indiana Christian*, October, 1932. Speakers: Hilton U. Brown, D. W. Morehouse, J. W. Black, R. H. Miller, Homer W. Carpenter, Ludwig von Gerdtell, Lin D. Cartwright, John A. Tate, Roger T. Nooe, M. E. Sadler, R. H. Crossfield, A. D. Harmon, Col. P. H. Callahan, J. Warren Hastings, W. H. Pinkerton, Willard Wickizer, George Walker Buckner, Jr., H. H. Peters, Mrs. Kent Hughes, C. R. Stauffer, C. M. Yocum, George A. Buttrick, J. G. Warren, Edwin R. Errett, Harold E. Fey, Marvin O. Sansbury, Alexander Paul, J. H. Goldner, Fred Corwin, Graham Frank.

1933 unemployment in the United States had reached an estimated 13 million people, and the country was in the throes of a banking panic. The first hundred days of the new administration saw the birth of numerous government agencies which came to be recognized later by their initials.[6] This was the New Deal in action, a force which was felt in every Hoosier community. With people in such desperate straits church thinking was ready to accept anything that promised relief, that is, anything except the repeal of the 18th Amendment which ended the Prohibition era in American life! Church people had their doubts about this. The New Deal experiment gave no immediate relief to missionary work. Contributions to state and national missionary societies continued to decline. When 52 missionaries were withdrawn from the foreign field, Stephen J. Corey, president of The United Christian Missionary Society, called it a "major catastrophe." Budgets had to be cut by more than 40 per cent, and missionary work on foreign and home fields was reduced to where it had been in 1912.[7] Many Christian churches in Indiana were threatened with the loss of their properties, and the State Association carried the additional burden of seeking financial help to save them.

One achievement on the state program for this period was the project of forming a Bethany Park beautification club. The State Association made a beginning in buying the stock in this organization so that the park could belong to the Christian churches. The club made plans to rehabilitate the buildings and grounds during the spring and summer. Volunteer labor was solicited for the Association-owned grounds, and private property owners were asked to paint

---

[6]Some of these "alphabet" agencies were the CCC, FERA, NRA, CWA, FDIC, HOLC, and TVA.

[7]*World Call*, March, 1933.

and otherwise improve their cottages. The program was successful, and extensive improvements were made.[8]

Rainy weather, floods, and a sagging economy kept the number of registered delegates down to 273 at the State Convention at Connersville in 1933. The Central Christian Church, under the leadership of its minister, George D. Wyatt, had redecorated its building and laid new carpets for the occasion. E. E. Moorman, who was convention president that year, introduced the theme, "Thy Will Be Done." The majority of the ministers in attendance had taken drastic salary cuts; some had not been paid at all. The total income of the State Association had been reduced to $16,713.26 in the fiscal year, and the deficit for operating expenses had increased.[9]

Depression clouds still hovered over Hoosierland when the next convention[10] of the State Association was held at Crawfordsville in 1934. Elmer Ward Cole, president of the convention, addressed the brethren on the subject, "The Paralysis of Defeatism." He traced the defeatism of the times to the disillusionment and mistaken hopes which had followed World War I. The delegates visited the study (then a Hoosier shrine) of General Lew Wallace, famous author of *Ben Hur,* who had attended the Sunday school of Central Christian Church in Indianapolis as a boy. The theme of the Crawfordsville convention was "The Church Meeting the Needs of the World Today." The churches were now making a realistic adjustment to depression conditions; the State Association, though not out of debt, had operated within its income the past year. It had sponsored fifteen area meetings for laymen, and 1,388 men had been reached in this manner.

---

[8]*Indiana Christian,* May, 1931; May, 1932; July-August, 1933.

[9]*Indiana Christian,* April, June, 1933; *Christian-Evangelist,* June 1, 1933.

[10]*Indiana Christian,* April, May, June, 1934; January, 1935; *Christian-Evangelist,* May 31, 1934.

The brethren finally decided they would not wait for the depression to go away but would try to do the best possible job with what was available to them. Looking forward to the 100th anniversary of the State Association in 1939, progressive centennial goals were set up at the Crawfordsville meeting. It was decided to make an effort to add 32,000 persons to the state membership and $10,000 to the permanent funds of the Association in the next five years.

A prophetic article[11] entitled, "The Church and the New Society," written for *World Call* by Charles O. Lee, indicated that after five years of depression the church was finally getting a new foothold and a new vision. Lee suggested that a new world was emerging from the midst of a far-reaching social cataclysm. He asked, "What form will it take? Will it swing to the left and plunge us into a more or less godless communistic control, or swing to the right and land us in a reign of almost equally godless fascism? . . . we are today saying that insecurity is the bane of our existence; that security must be vouchsafed for us all."

Frederick D. Kershner, dean of the College of Religion at Butler University, presided over the sessions of the annual convention[12] at Marion in 1935. Economic conditions were slightly better, and people had learned to adjust themselves to a depressed economy. The one thousand or so persons who attended the sessions heard variations on the theme, "Forward with Christ." Events in Europe drew attention away from domestic problems. Italy's invasion of Ethiopia, Hitler's rise to power in Germany, and the American embargo on the sale of munitions to belligerents reflected the isolationism of America (especially in Indiana) and provided a strong motivation for the peace movement in the churches.

[11]*World Call*, January, 1935.
[12]Convention reports: *Indiana Christian*, March, April, May, June, July, 1935; *Christian-Evangelist*, May 9, 1935.

Harold E. Fey of New York City (native Hoosier), secretary of the Fellowship of Reconciliation, was the special speaker for the ministers' banquet. A convention resolution expressed disapproval of the naval maneuvers currently being staged in the Pacific. Another resolution recommended that individuals and churches show by actions that there was no distinction of race and color in Christianity. One new church had been established during the year, but some church buildings were still in danger of being sold at sheriffs' sales.

The State Convention in 1936 was held at Bloomington. J. N. Jessup of Lafayette was president. Many ministers were unemployed at this time, and those who were employed were serving on very low salaries. They had, therefore, a great interest in either obtaining pastorates or changing to more lucrative ones. This led to unrest in the ministry and unethical conduct on the part of some ministers. Recognizing this, the convention passed a resolution concerning the un-dignified and un-Christian methods sometimes employed in securing pastorates, recommending that ministers and churches should cooperate with the state office to improve conditions and make the work more effective.[13]

Hoosier Disciples were rather proud of the fact that of the one hundred largest churches in the brotherhood, Indiana had twelve. These were:[14]

Richmond, First	1,298	Bedford, First	1,685
New Castle, First	1,379	Indianapolis, Central	1,715
Indianapolis, Olive		Columbus, Tabernacle	1,808
Branch	1,380	Lafayette, First	1,900
Kokomo, South Side	1,400	Indianapolis, Third	2,374
Anderson, Central	1,500	Indianapolis, Engle-	
Indianapolis, Hillside	1,584	wood	2,748

---

[13]*Indiana Christian*, April, June, 1936; *Christian-Evangelist*, May 28, 1936.
[14]*Indiana Christian*, March, 1936.

Religious Education, to 1937

Genefrede Harris, who had been regional director of religious education since 1923, left Indiana to work for the Christian Board of Publication in 1931. C. A. Burch, a former missionary, was appointed in her place. He served until 1934. H. L. Pickerill then became state director of religious education. Pickerill was succeeded by John W. Harms in 1935. In the meantime, the State Association, in cooperation with the National Department of Religious Education, agreed on a plan of joint administration through a Commission on Christian Education.[15] The work through the Commission began in March, 1935. Harms, though responsible to both state and national organizations, gave full-time service to religious education in Indiana.

By 1937 Indiana Disciples sponsored six summer conferences for high school youth and older young people. A series of week-end youth meets had their inception in 1937. The youth meets were sponsored jointly by the Indiana Woman's Christian Missionary Society and the Indiana Department of Religious Education. John W. Harms and Edith Clare Walden were co-directors of these projects.[16] Under the new co-operating administration a "Learning for Life" conference for adults, a laboratory training school for children's workers, and a special school for town and country workers originated in 1937.[17]

---

[15]State Commission Members: Robert T. Beck, chairman; J. Allan Watson, vice chairman; LeRoy F. Carter, secretary; Paul E. Million, Allen R. Huber, W. E. Moore, E. D. Day, E. D. Love, Lee Tinsley. Ex officio members: Roy G. Ross and G. I. Hoover. Cooperating Member: Mrs. O. H. Greist.

[16]*Indiana Christian,* February, 1937.

[17]*Indiana Christian,* May, 1937. John W. Harns served until 1938 when he entered a new position as executive secretary of the Council of Churches and Christian Education of Maryland and Delaware. Miss Anna M. Clarke then took his place in the Indiana work.

Purdue Christian Foundation

The Purdue Christian Foundation was organized officially in 1936. The next year Barton Hunter was called to Lafayette to become the Purdue representative of the Christian churches of Indiana.[18] The work among Disciple students at Purdue University was not a new one. It had been in existence for twenty years, beginning with a Sunday school class for Purdue students in the Christian church at Lafayette. J. N. Jessup, minister of the church, perceived a real need for a ministry of this kind, and Robert Knight was employed as pastor to the students. He began his work in December, 1916. Knight supervised several Sunday school classes, counseled with students, and provided social and recreational programs for twenty years. His ministry to students was a pioneer work and was very effective. The Indiana Christian Missionary Association and The United Christian Missionary Society helped the church in the support of this work.

Depression Clouds Begin to Lift

The North American Christian Convention held another meeting in Indianapolis, April 21-25, 1937. Sessions convened at Cadle Tabernacle. The convention was well attended, and a great number of prominent ministers gave addresses.[19] It was described in the *Indiana Christian* as a "rally of the forces of our brotherhood supporting independent missions."[20] T. K. Smith, pastor of the Tabernacle Church at Columbus, was chairman of the convention program.

---

[18]*Indiana Christian*, July, 1937.
[19]Speakers: George P. Taubman, Stephen J. England, Morris B. Book, Charles R. Scoville, LaVerne Taylor, W. R. Walker, Claude E. Hill, Paul Henry Packard, R. C. Snodgrass, Ralph Records, William E. Sweeney, Dean E. Walker, R. H. Miller, Bert Wilson, George Klingman, Basil Holt, Robert S. Tuck, and P. H. Welshimer.
[20]*Indiana Christian*, March, April, 1937.

The State Convention[21] of Hoosier Disciples was held at Fort Wayne in 1937. W. E. Carroll, minister of the Northwood Christian Church in Indianapolis, was president. Four Fort Wayne Christian churches assumed the responsibility of entertaining the convention. Edgar DeWitt Jones, Disciple president of the Federal Council of the Churches of Christ in America, and Hugh Thompson Kerr, former moderator of the Presbyterian Church of the U. S. A., were the principal speakers. The theme, "Memorializing Our Past and Understanding Our Future," was emphasized. Mrs. O. H. Greist[22] was honored guest at a dinner given by the state women's board in recognition of her 28 years of faithful service to women's missionary work in Indiana.

When the International Convention of the Disciples of Christ met at Columbus, Ohio, in 1937, Dean Frederick D. Kershner of the College of Religion was elected convention president for 1937-38. This was the fifth time that a Hoosier was elected to the highest office of the Disciples. Other presidents from Indiana had been A. B. Philputt (1903), Z. T. Sweeney (1904), T. W. Grafton (1923), and William F. Rothenberger (1934).[23]

The New Castle church, Robert T. Beck, minister, was celebrating a 75th anniversary when the State Convention[24] was held in 1938. The fascist nations in Europe were on the march, and World War II was about to occur; but the

---

[21]*Indiana Christian*, April, May, June, 1937.

[22]*Indiana Christian*, June, 1937. Mrs. Greist came to the state work as district secretary in 1907. She was vice president of the Indiana C.W.B.M. from 1909 to 1913; president, 1913 to 1919. Later, as general secretary she assisted in the organization of 232 local societies in the Christian churches. She contributed a column regularly to the *Indiana Christian*. Mrs. Greist was succeeded by Mrs. C. O. Nease.

[23]*Indiana Christian*, November, 1937. Philputt and Sweeney were presidents of the American Christian Missionary Society when this organization acted as the general convention. Hoosier presidents since have been W. A. Shullenberger (1942), and F. E. Davison, 1949.

[24]*Indiana Christian*, April, May, June, 1938; *Christian-Evangelist*, May 26, 1938.

brethren seemed to be interested primarily in upgrading their own local programs. It appeared to some that this convention which emphasized the theme, "Strengthen the Church to Advance the Kingdom of God," failed to deal realistically with the concrete situations of the day. Registrations reached the one thousand mark, and attendance was so large that many sessions had to be held in the high school gymnasium. Though the national economy had improved it was not reflected in the budgets of most churches nor in the agencies. The State Association had operated within its income during the fiscal year—even showed a balance of $10.24—but the income was only $12,035.13. The upgrading of the giving to Christian causes was a slow and sometimes painful procedure.

Since 1934 Hoosier Disciples had been anticipating the Centennial celebration of their state work in 1939, they were not disappointed with the progress report made at the Indianapolis centennial convention that year.[25] Considered against the background of a depressed economy the churches had done quite well. The state membership goal of 200,000 was not reached, but the churches made a net gain of 3,000 persons in the five-year period. Some new sanctuaries and educational buildings had been erected, others had been remodeled, and a few congregations had even purchased parsonages. Many church properties which had been threatened with loss had been restored. Operating deficits that were incurred in the first years of the depression were, for the most part, cleared; the churches were again working with balanced budgets. The theme for the centennial convention was appropriate, "Christ Glorified Our Past—He Commands Our Future."

---

[25]*Indiana Christian,* May, 1939; *Christian-Evangelist,* April 27, 1939.

Ephraim D. Lowe was president of the 100th anniversary convention. There were 1,875 registrations. Sessions were held at Cadle Tabernacle and Central Christian Church. Daniel Poling, guest preacher, gave three inspiring sermons. Mr. and Mrs. Owen Walker, Virgil P. Brock, William Moon, and Frank Huston led in the song services; Mrs. Arlene Dux Scoville sang several solos and played the piano. The older ministers were honored at a veterans' campfire luncheon. George Campbell of the *Christian-Evangelist,* Edwin R. Errett of the *Christian Standard,* George W. Buckner, Jr., of the *World Call,* and W. E. Garrison of the *Christian Century* were present to give addresses and report the convention to their journals. A pageant depicting the first State Meeting in 1839, written by Dean E. Walker and enacted by Butler University students, was given. The convention came to a climax with an address by Dean Frederick D. Kershner, "A Century of Witnessing to Christian Unity." The brethren did not dwell entirely on the past. Before the business sessions were closed they had approved resolutions against war, for peace, on Christan union, on foreign policy and against the liquor traffic.[26] Officers, directors, and staff of the Indiana Christian Missionary Association were present to be introduced and to make reports of their work.[27]

Working Through Commissions

A means by which the State Association was working effectively by this time was through its various commissions.

---

[26]*Indiana Christian,* June, 1939; *Christian-Evangelist,* June 1, 1939.

[27]Officiary of the Indiana Christian Missionary Association at the time of the centennial convention: G. I. Hoover, general secretary; Mrs. Emma E. Powell, office secretary; and Miss Anna M. Clarke, director of Christian Education. The state evangelists were W. C. Ashanhort, H. J. Buchanan, and E. L. Day. The general evangelists were T. J. Wilson, Charles E. Shultz, and Lawrence Elshoff. Directors: R. C. Dillman, H. L. Erlewine, Bruce Nice, L. S. Ashley, T. K. Smith, R. H. Kenady, R. H. Montgomery, H. H. Purkhiser, S. G. Fisher, E. D. Lowe, Joel Lee Jones, R. H. Hosier, Carl Barnett, Smith J. Gray, and E. C. Corts.

The Rural Church Commission was particularly effective during the depression. Originating in 1934, it was appointed to study rural life in Indiana, especially among the Disciples, and to cooperate with similar commissions in other states. The first commission meeting was held at Butler University, and the discussion centered on the training of rural ministers and the conducting of rural church institutes.[28] The next year an experimental rural church workers' school was held at Bethany Park to train adult leaders in rural church work.[29] A second school was held at Bethany Park the next year. Depression conditions are reflected in the fees for participants. The cost per person was $5.50, plus the following provisions: two quarts of canned beef, pork, or chicken; one pound of bacon or ham; one pound of butter, one dozen eggs, three quarts of canned fruits, five pounds of potatoes, five pounds of tomatoes, two pounds of cabbage, one glass of spread, one quart of pickles, and sandwiches for supper the first evening.[30] On June 6, 1937, the Commission joined with the Nineveh Christian Church and the children of John Chapman Miller to dedicate a farm to full-time Christian service. By 1938 the Commission had gained national recognition and was arranging with rural churches for gifts of food to maintain a cooperative house for Negro ministerial students at Butler University.[31] That year the Commission conducted 22 rural church institutes in Indiana in which more than 250 churches with a total membership of over 5,000 persons participated.[32]

---

[28]*Christian-Evangelist,* June 21, 1934. Commission members: Lee Tinsley, chairman; Professor E. C. Cameron, George F. Powers, Harry T. Bridwell, and F. C. McCormick.

[29]*Christian-Evangelist,* August 29, 1935. Faculty: George V. Moore, Ross J. Griffeth, Emory C. Cameron, George F. Powers, Mrs. Julia Elliot Harris, and Mrs. Edith Taylor.

[30]*Christian-Evangelist,* June 11, 1936.

[31]*Indiana Christian,* January, 1938. Many present-day Negro leaders among the Disciples were residents of this cooperative house.

[32]*Christian-Evangelist,* April 13, 1939.

The State Association met the needs of the times also through the efforts of a commission on men's work, a commission on the city church, and a commission on social welfare and social action. The last named commission considered such matters as securing direct relief for church members and citizens of the community, federal help for destitute children and aged persons, advising with fellow church members on the federal pension plan for employees, and cooperating with local welfare agencies.[33]

From Depression to War Economy

Germany's invasion of Poland and the Franco-British declaration of war in September, 1939, had repercussions in Hoosierland. Many of the leading ministers in the state took different views on what should be done about it. Some held for peace at any price, others advised intervention; some advocated neutrality, and others believed that the business of the church was reconciliation only. Events in Europe and Asia moved faster than views in America could crystalize. Russia annexed the Baltic republics; Hitler's military machine overran Norway, Denmark, the low countries, and France; Italy entered the war as an ally of Germany; British troops were forced to evacuate Dunkirk, and Britain's island fortress was bombed. Then Japan joined the axis powers and occupied Indochina. In America, the destroyers for bases deal was consummated with Great Britain; an embargo on iron and steel scrap was declared; and the Burke-Wadsworth Act created the Selective Service program. When the gross farm income between 1940 and 1945 rose from 11 to 25 billion dollars, and defense spending rose from one and one-half

---

[33]*Indiana Christian*, March, May, 1938.

billion to 81 billion dollars, it had a tremendous effect on American economy—and the churches.

A continuation committee appointed at the close of the North American Christian Convention at Indianapolis in 1937, chose October, 1940, for another convention in the same city. Because the International Convention was not being held that year and the Toronto World Convention had been cancelled, the committee believed this would be a good time to hold sessions. Using the slogan, "Preach the Word," speakers at this convention stressed the traditional plea for Christian unity, restoration of the church of the New Testament, and the evangelization of the world.[34]

The Selective Training and Service Act passed by Congress in 1940 provided for compulsory military service of all men between the ages of 21 and 35. Since the cause of pacifism was popular with the clergy at this time, and laymen in general were committed to neutrality, this Act posed problems for the church. Some of the persons in the eligible group were conscientious objectors. By action of the International Convention in 1939 a procedure was established for Christian churches to enroll their conscientious objectors so that draft boards could certify them to Civilian Service Camps for alternative service. They had to be supported by church funds. This caused tension in some congregations.[35]

The convention of the State Association, held at Portland in 1940, was a "resolution-happy" gathering.[36] The brethren approved of resolutions urging church members to promote social justice, renew efforts in Christian unity, raise more money for missions, and support the local option system; they condemned liquor advertising and the sale of obscene

[34]*Indiana Christian*, March, 1940.
[35]*World Call*, April, 1940; *Disciples of Christ Year Book* (Indianapolis: Year Book Publication Committee, 1941), p. 8.
[36]*Indiana Christian*, June, 1940; *Christian-Evangelist*, May 30, 1940.

371

literature. A resolution requesting President Roosevelt to recall Ambassador Myron C. Taylor from the Vatican was defeated. One reporter commented that there was an "almost complete absence of reference to the conditions confronting the churches in the present world situation at home and abroad."

There were 850 registrations at the Portland convention. A. N. Shockney was host pastor, and E. C. Corts, minister at Sullivan, presided over the sessions. Since the convention marked the beginning of the second century of history for Hoosier Disciples it was advertised as a "Century of Progress," and addresses were developed around the slogan "Forward with Christ." P. H. Welshimer of Canton, Ohio, was the guest preacher. In recognition of many years of service to the Association, G. I. Hoover, who was retiring from his position as general secretary that year, was awarded a watch and a purse by the state ministerial association. Joseph G. Wick, 18, pastor at Alfordsville, was also given recognition for being the youngest minister present.[37]

The depression made Hoosier Disciples conscious of the value of establishing permanent funds for the State Association. A pledge of $1,000, made by G. I. Hoover some years before as a memorial to his wife, became the nucleus of this fund. It was hoped that contributions would raise this amount to $300,000.

By 1940, when the clouds of depression had almost passed from sight, it was thought advisable to liquidate the operating deficit incurred by the State Association in the early 1930's. The Budget Commission of the International Convention gave approval for a $20,000 campaign for this purpose. W. C. Aschanhort and H. J. Buchanan were assigned to the

---

[37]*Indiana Christian,* June, July, 1940; *Christian-Evangelist,* May 30, 1940.

task. By 1942 the indebtedness was reduced to $8,000; the next year it was cut to $2,891.[38] With the coming of the war economy the last vestige of depression indebtedness was liquidated. The breaking of ground in the fall of 1940 for the new building of the Tabernacle Christian Church at Columbus was another expression of confidence in the future. When dedicated in 1942 it represented an expenditure of $750,000. The building was planned by Eliel Saarinen, famous Finnish-born architect, and it was destined to be one of the great church buildings among the Disciples.[39]

G. I. Hoover gave notice of his retirement as general secretary of the State Association several months in advance. He served in this office for fourteen years. After careful consideration Ephraim D. Lowe[40] was chosen to take his place. Lowe was in his nineteenth year as successful pastor of the Olive Branch Christian Church in Indianapolis and entered the state work on January 1, 1941, with the advantage of a considerable amount of experience.

The twelfth and final gathering of a series of nationwide convocations of the Disciples of Christ was held at Indianapolis Third Christian Church in March of 1941. A number of brotherhood leaders on the national level came to the city to lead discussions on such subjects as "What will the

---

[38]*Indiana Christian,* April, 1940; April, 1941; July-August, 1943.

[39]*Indiana Christian,* September, 1940. Four articles in *The Shane Quarterly,* October, 1943, pp. 244-257, describe this building.

[40]Ephraim D. Lowe (1893-   ) was born near Anderson, Indiana. He was graduated from Indiana Central College and later engaged in graduate studies at Butler University, Indiana University, and the University of Chicago. Butler University awarded him the honorary Doctor of Divinity degree in 1940. Lowe served twice as president of the Indiana Christian Ministers' Association; was president of the Indianapolis Christian Church Union, vice president of the Board of Church Extension, president of the Disciples state convention in 1939, and was president of the Board of Directors of the Indiana Christian Missionary Association for many years. Before becoming general secretary of the State Association he had been pastor of churches at Terre Haute, Anderson, and the Olive Branch Christian Church at Indianapolis. He retired from his office with the Indiana Christian Missionary Association in 1958 after serving seventeen years.

churches do in meeting religious needs in a time of the national defense program? What can be done about the evacuation of Americans in China? What of the effect of the new government social program relating to old people's homes and the Pension Plan?" Also, "What of the draft on our colleges and universities?"[41] By this time the war seemed to be getting closer to America, President Roosevelt had given his "Four Freedoms" speech, and the Lend-lease agreement had been approved.

Indiana Disciples convened at Bedford for their annual convention in 1941. W. E. Moore of Bloomington was president of the group; George Morris was host pastor. The theme of the convention, "Christ Is the Answer," expressed the general opinion toward world problems held by the 600 delegates who were present. Many of them being non-interventionists, they were dissatisfied with President Roosevelt's policy; it was thought that he had disregarded the alternative of a just peace through mediation before declaring an unlimited national emergency and resorting to the threat of unlimited force.[42]

By the end of the decade of the 'thirties the depression years had almost run their complete course, and the over-extended business economy had readjusted itself. Federal relief programs and "pump priming" had helped to restore public confidence and had stimulated recovery. The war in Europe, however, played no small part in the return of prosperity to America. Because merchant ships carrying supplies across the Atlantic were often torpedoed by German U-boats the United States supplied naval cover for the convoys and adopted a "shoot at sight" policy in September,

---

[41]*Indiana Christian*, March, 1941.
[42]*Christian-Evangelist*, June 19, 1941.

1941. By this time, ministers' salaries had been upgraded; mortgages on church properties (previously adjusted downward by mortgage holders) were being paid off, and a new church building and remodeling "boom" had its inception. The Japanese attack on Pearl Harbor came on December 7, 1941. Declaration of war on Japan, Germany, and Italy followed immediately. The cataclysmic events which ensued reached into every home and church in Hoosierland.

The Christian Foundation

The depression of the early 1930's slowed down the income growth of the Foundation. In 1931, the organization applied for admission to the International Convention of the Disciples as a reporting agency. The *Year Book* of the Disciples of Christ for that year showed some changes on the Board of Directors.[43] A financial report was published in the *Year Book* for 1932 which showed that the permanent fund had grown to $599,870, and that the endowment receipts the year before amounted to $31,830.82. William G. Irwin and his sister, Mrs. Linnie I. Sweeney, contributed an additional $1,800,000 to the Foundation in 1938. This increased the assets of the Foundation to $2,258,796.93.[44] According to the *Year Book* of 1942, assets had grown to $2,604,163.47 by June 30, 1941. Since a separate College of Religion building on the Butler University campus was being contemplated about this time the large gift of William G. Irwin and Mrs. Z. T. Sweeney was intended to support the capital funds and endowment needs of this project.

---

[43]Directors: Hilton U. Brown, president; James L. Clarke, vice president; William G. Irwin, treasurer; Frederick D. Kershner, secretary; Benjamin D. Phillips, Charles M. Setser, Clarence L. Goodwin, Edwin R. Errett, Hugh Th. Miller, and Girnie L. Reeves.

[44]*Christian-Evangelist,* May 26, 1938; *Indianapolis Star,* May 18, 1938.

Butler University, 1931-1941

The depression of the 'thirties cast its grim shadow over Butler University and cancelled the progressive plans for the "new" Butler for several years. The criticism of the North Central Association made at the time of the school's suspension from this body was accepted; the trustees and administration set about to fulfill the requirements imposed. By early 1931 it was possible to announce that the university was reinstated with the Association.[45] Robert Judson Aley, who had been president since 1921, resigned that year, and Walter S. Athearn[46] called to take his place. Athearn, former dean of the School of Religious Education and Social Service of Boston University, was believed to be ideally qualified for this position. He was inaugurated on Founders' Day in December, 1931.[47]

By 1932 the enrollment reached over 1,900 students. A seventy-fifth commencement and fiftieth anniversary of Butler's Teachers' College was observed at the same time. The Teachers' College was founded in 1882 by Eliza Blaker. It merged with the university in 1930, becoming a division of the College of Education, with W. L. Richardson as dean.[48]

---

[45]*World Call*, May, 1931.

[46]Walter Scott Athearn (1872-1934) was born in Iowa. He received the B.Ped. degree from Drake University in 1900. The University of Iowa conferred the B.A. degree on him in 1911, and the M.A. degree in 1914. He was granted the LL.D. degree from Fargo College in 1920. After teaching in the rural schools of Iowa he became an assistant professor at Drake University, 1900-1904. Athearn left Drake University in 1906 to become dean of Highland Park Normal College. He was professor of religious education at Drake University, 1909-1916. He then became professor of religious education at Boston University, 1916-1918; dean of the School of Religious Education and Social Service, 1918-1929. He was a voluminous writer, the author of twenty-six books and numerous monographs. Athearn was president of Butler University, 1931-1933. At the time of his death he was president of Oklahoma City University.

[47]*Christian-Evangelist*, January 7, 21, 1932; *World Call*, April, 1932. John H. Finley, associate editor of the *New York Times*, and Dean Charles W. Gilkey of the University of Chicago were speakers on this occasion. Six honorary degrees were conferred in connection with the inauguration: LL.D., Paul C. Stetson, superintendent of Indianapolis Public Schools; LL.D., Daniel W. Morehouse, president of Drake University; Sc.D., Henry L. Bruner, head of the zoology department of Butler University; Sc.D., George H. A. Clowes, director of research for the Eli Lilly Company; and Litt.D., John H. Finley, assistant editor of the *New York Times*.

[48]*World Call*, March, 1932.

It was moved to the Fairview campus in 1933. In the fall semester of 1932 a new division of evening and extension courses was added to the academic program. Professor Albert Edward Bailey, formerly of Boston University, was chosen as dean of this division. He succeeded Professor George F. Leonard who had been head of the department of evening courses the past two years. The new division was designed to promote the cause of adult education for the citizens of Indianapolis. Classroom work was offered at strategic points around the city. It was Athearn's declared aim to make Butler University the academic and cultural center of the city.[49] President Herbert Hoover visited the Butler campus in the last fall of 1932 and spoke to an audience of 20,000 people in the field house. Debaters from the University of Dublin (Ireland) met the debating team of Butler University that fall. The subject under debate was, "Resolved: that capitalism has broken down." This subject indicated the extreme political and economic views that had been motivated by the world-wide depression. The Dublin team spoke to the affirmative, and the Butler debaters took the negative position.[50]

By January of 1932 the depression was critically felt by Butler students. An employment bureau was set up to help find part-time work for those who needed financial help in order to stay in school. These students were willing to take jobs mowing lawns, washing dishes, clerking in stores or helping with housework. Many classes were grouped on a half-day schedule so that students could have gainful employment the other half day. Over 40 per cent of the student body was engaged in part-time work.[51] In 1933 the students

---

[49]*Christian-Evangelist*, August 18, 1932.
[50]*Christian-Evangelist*, December, 1932.
[51]*World Call*, January, 1932.

sponsored a charity drive through the *Butler Collegian* and gathered up 315 pairs of shoes, 50 overcoats, 35 suits, 150 dresses, 110 hats as well as other articles of apparel for the "needy" of Indianapolis. This drive was repeated in years that followed.[52]

Enrollment during the 1932-33 academic year reached 1,529 in the day session and 920 in the night courses. There were 146 teachers on the faculty. The President's remarks at the 1933 commencement indicated that he did not believe that the depression should be an impediment to progress in education but that the only safe policy for the institution in such a period was to adopt a "pay as you go" plan. He acknowledged the need for a new chapel, new library, new student union building with a cafeteria, new dormitories and other items of physical equipment, but he also stated that it was not reasonable to ask for these because the prolonged depression had exhausted the resources of the people.[53]

The President's plan to reduce operating expenses and improve academic standards, though approved in principle, was opposed by the business office and the faculty; the reorganization of the university was in line with sound academic standards. When fifty-seven professors were dismissed on the grounds of a "pay as you go" fiscal policy and many of the vacant positions filled by newcomers it appeared to be more of a "purge" than a reorganization plan. Faculty members would have preferred "across the board" salary cuts rather than to have their colleagues lose their positions. The dissension mounted and eventually led to a serious altercation between the President and the "downtown" business office. The President felt that the business

---

[52]*World Call*, February, 1933.

[53]*Indiana Christian*, September, 1933; *Butler Alumnal Quarterly*, July, 1933, pp. 105-108.

office was interfering in the academic policies of his administration; the business office felt that the President was exercising unwarrantable authority in financial matters. An open break in relationships was inevitable. The Board of Directors found it necessary to take action on the matter, and the President was relieved of his responsibilities.[54] Athearn's final act was the publication of a report of the work of his administration from July 7, 1931, to October 28, 1933. The report indicated what he believed to be the extent of his academic reorganization, the reasons for the changes he had made, and what he thought remained yet to be done. It was published in a twenty-seven page booklet under the title, *Dual Control of an Urban University.*[55]

James W. Putnam,[56] vice president of the university, was made acting head of the school in October, 1933. This was the third time he had acted in this capacity. Dr. Putnam was a wise and genial person, conciliatory by nature, and the right man for the position at that time. He "toned down" his predecessor's reforms and did much to heal the wounds of a trying period. Putnam was officially inaugurated as President of Butler University, February 7, 1935.

With approximately one-tenth of the population of Indiana receiving some form of public relief and many others living on a bare subsistence income, families could not provide much assistance to young people in college. The state organi-

---

[54]*Indianapolis Star*, October 31, 1933; *Christian-Evangelist*, November 9, 1933.

[55]Walter Scott Athearn, *Dual Control of an Urban University* (Indianapolis: Butler University President's Report, 1933).

[56]James William Putnam (1865-1940) was born in Illinois. Illinois College awarded him the A.B. degree in 1894 and the A.M. degree in 1898. Later, he received the A.M. degree from Cornell University and the Ph.D. from the University of Wisconsin. He also held the honorary degree of LL.D. from Illinois College and Hanover College. He taught at Illinois College, University of Wisconsin, Northwestern University, and the University of Missouri. His faculty career at Butler University started in 1909 as professor of economics. Before his appointment as president he served as department head, director of evening classes, dean of the liberal arts college, vice president, and acting president. Dr. Putnam was also a member of the Board of Temperance and Social Welfare, and of the Board of Education of the Disciples of Christ.

379

zation of the Civil Works Administration (CWA), William Book, Jr., director, offered special work opportunities for students beginning the second semester of 1934; three-fifths of the student's tuition was met by the government in this way and two-fifths by the university. In 1936, local units of the National Youth Administration (NYA) gave assistance to 147 undergraduates through work projects. The students were allowed to earn a maximum of $65.50 toward their tuition each semester.[57]

President Putnam and the Board of Directors established a College of Business Administration and a Junior College in the fall of 1937. The College of Business Administration absorbed the old department of business administration, and the next year M. O. Ross was announced as dean of the new school. The Junior College was instituted to meet the needs of students who could not afford to pursue a four-year curriculum but wanted to specialize in some field. Associate in Arts (or science) certificates were awarded to Junior College graduates.[58]

Dr. Putnam resigned as president of the university on April 12, 1939, and Daniel Sommer Robinson,[59] head of the philosophy department at Indiana University, was named as his successor. Dr. Robinson, a graduate of Butler College in

---

[57]*Butler Alumnal Quarterly*, April, 1934; April, 1936.

[58]*Butler Alumnus*, October, 1937.

[59]Daniel Sommer Robinson (1888-19   ), a native of Indiana, was born near North Salem. He entered Butler College to study for the ministry and was graduated with the A.B. degree in 1910. He continued his education at Yale University, receiving the M.A. degree in 1911 and the B.D. in 1912. After study at the University of Breslau in Germany he entered Harvard University where he received the Ph.D. degree in 1917. Marietta College awarded him the Litt.D. degree in 1937. His career in the ministry included pastorates at Billings, Montana, and Newport, New Hampshire. His teaching career started at the University of Wisconsin where he was instructor in philosophy, 1919-1920; assistant professor, 1920-1922. He was professor of philosophy at Miami University, 1922-1929; head of the department of philosophy at Indiana University, 1929-1939; and president of Butler University, 1939-1942. He became director of the School of Philosophy, University of Southern California, 1946-1954. Robinson was visiting professor at Bethany College, 1954-1955, and professor at Macalester College and Hamline University, 1951-1957. He served in the Chaplains Corps, U. S. Navy, 1918-1919; commander in U. S. Naval Reserve, 1942-1944. Robinson is the author of numerous books in the field of philosophy.

the class of 1910, assumed office in June, 1939, and was inaugurated at the field house on February 7, 1940. On the inaugural occasion, honorary degrees were conferred on Eli Lilly, president of the Eli Lilly Company; Harry Lester Smith, dean of Indiana University School of Education; and T. K. Smith, minister of Tabernacle Christian Church, Columbus, Indiana.

At the time Robinson began his service with Butler University the war in Europe seemed to be going favorably for the axis powers; America was greatly concerned with the outcome. By June, 1941, the United States was committed to the extent of almost anything but a "shooting" war. President Robinson cooperated with the government in its recruitment program for the armed forces. Courses in military science were given through the department of physical education of the university, and special courses were offered for employees in Indianapolis industries engaged in filling defense contracts.[60]

College of Religion, 1931-1941

The College of Religion enrolled 145 students during the 1930-31 academic year. Of these, forty-seven were graduate students. The next year the enrollment increased to 191. The catalog dated June, 1932, lists an impressive faculty.[61] The work of the College of Religion was organized into two divisions in the spring of 1932. There was a graduate division

---

[60]*Christian-Evangelist*, December 18, 1941.
[61]Faculty in catalog of 1932. Dean Frederick D. Kershner, M.A., LL.D.; Bruce L. Kershner, M. A.; G. I. Hoover, B.D., A.M., D.D.; Everhard Roy Moon, A.M., B.D., D.D., F.R.G.S.; Morris M. Feuerlicht, B.H.L., A.B.; Janet Malcolm Macdonald, A.M., Ph.D.; Arthur C. Garnett, M.A., Litt.D.; Toyozo W. Nakarai, A.M., Ph.D.; Allena Grafton, A.M.; D. E. Walker, A.M., B.D.; A. T. DeGroot, M.A., B.D.; Morris H. Pullin, M.A.; Walter E. Bachman, M.R.E., D.R.E., D.D.; Albert E. Bailey, A.M. Between 1932 and 1934 the following were added to the faculty: Joseph C. Todd, A.M., B.D., D.D., LL.D.; Elmer J. Homrighausen, B.D., S.T.M., A.M., Th.D., D.D.; W. A. Shullenberger, D.D.; Max T. Krone, M.S.; D. C. Gilley, M.M.; Ross J. Griffeth, A.M., B.D.; E. C. Cameron, B.D., A.M.; and Arthur Holmes, M.A., Ph.D., Th.M., Th.D., LL.D.

with curricula leading to the degrees of B.D. and M.A., and an undergraduate division which offered the degrees of B.S.L. and B.S. (in religion). By including undergraduates in the College of Religion, Dean Kershner attracted a large number of students. A directive[62] from President Athearn in the spring of 1933, given in the interest of raising academic standards and reducing operating costs, discontinued the undergraduate division in the College of Religion and placed it under the direction of the College of Liberal Arts and Sciences. The directive also suspended the department of missions, combined some other departments, and relieved four professors from their duties. This left the College of Religion with four full-time professors, the promise of part-time instruction from professors of other departments of Butler University, and a student body reduced by one-half. The College of Religion was designated as a professional school only, offering graduate-level courses leading to the degrees of B.D. and M.A. The undergraduate department of religion at Butler University then offered the B.S.L. and B.S. (in religion) degrees. To Kershner, it looked as if his work to build up a large school for the training of ministers had been completely undermined; it was a severe blow. Though the move was sound academically, connected as it was with the dismissal of faculty members and the loss of students, it was unpopular with the faculty and church constituency and was a primary factor in antagonizing public opinion against President Athearn. The releasing of Disciples professors and replacing them with part-time non-Disciple personnel was looked upon with disfavor. The next year under a new administration at Butler University a new compromise program was adopted. The program provided

---

[62]Directive from W. S. Athearn to F. D. Kershner, dated March 21, 1933. Kershner claimed that neither he nor his faculty had prior consultation on this matter.

that the College of Religion would have charge of all under-graduate work in religion in the upper division of the College of Liberal Arts and Sciences, students being allowed to enroll in the College of Religion when they had reached the third year in undergraduate college. The College of Religion was again permitted to grant the degrees of B.S.L. and B.S. (in religion) as well as the B.D. and M.A. degrees.

In the fall of 1938 it was announced that the College of Religion had been elected to membership in the American Association of Theological Schools. The immediate effect of affiliation with the A.A.T.S. was that the College of Religion found it necessary to become a purely graduate school. The undergraduate division was again turned over to the College of Arts and Sciences of Butler University where it became the undergraduate department of religion. There were 78 graduate students and eleven undergraduates in the College of Religion, so the move toward standardization did not hurt as much as it had in 1933; the claim could still be made that among standardized graduate schools of the Brotherhood the College of Religion had the largest enrollment.[63]

Because most of the students in this period served churches on week-ends there was never much time for extra curricular activities. They did have a basketball team for a number of years. Regularly scheduled games were played with Johnson Bible College, Milligan College, Cincinnati Bible Seminary and some local fraternities, but the College of Religion team was rarely victorious. The most popular feature of these contests was the dinner given to both teams by the University Park Christian Church. Eventually, the athletic program was abandoned. One organization which has had a continued

---

[63]*Indiana Christian,* January, 1939; *Christian-Evangelist,* January 12, 1939.

existence since 1933 is the Zelotai. It was organized in the home of Mrs. Frederick D. Kershner in the fall of that year. This club, composed of the wives of students and faculty members, has become increasingly meaningful and helpful. The Beta Chapter of the International Society of Theta Phi, established at the College of Religion in 1938, also became a permanent organization. This is an honor society for students, ministers, and religious workers. Membership is based upon scholarship, promise, and achievement in religious and related fields.[64]

The necessity of improving library resources became apparent with the coming of standardization. Dean Joseph C. Todd of the Indiana School of Religion had collected over 2,000 books and periodicals relating to the Disciples of Christ, and this collection was acquired for the College of Religion in 1938.[65] Later that year, Enos E. Dowling was employed as the first full-time librarian of the school. The file of the *American Christian Review* was purchased about this time from the Daniel Sommer family. The *Review* was primarily an Indiana item founded in 1856 by Benjamin Franklin, pioneer Disciple editor. In 1887 the name was changed to *Octographic Review*. Some 600 volumes from the old Cotner College library were added at this time. The Christian Foundation made it possible for the school to purchase the Nathaniel Schmidt collection of over 7,200 items (4,200 books) in 1940. Dr. Schmidt was a Swedish scholar who had been professor of oriental history and Semitic languages at Cornell University. There were hundreds of rare and valuable books in this collection, including some

---

[64]Charter members were Dr. Arthur Holmes, Dean Frederick D. Kershner, Dr. Ludwig von Gerdtell, and Dr. Toyozo W. Nakarai. Dr. von Gerdtell, a native of Germany, had been added to the faculty the year before. Other members added in 1938 were Bruce L. Kershner, D. E. Walker, H. Wilson, Edwin Hayden, and W. Barney.

[65]*World Call*, February, 1939.

of the oldest polyglott Bibles.[66] In 1941, the College of Religion acquired 2,500 volumes from the private library of President Alva Ross Brown of Johnson Bible College.[67]

The Disciple collections acquired in this period were added to the collection of Disciples literature started in 1900 by Dean Jabez Hall. It then became the most extensive collection of literature of the Disciples in existence. The Nathaniel Schmidt collection of theological books added depth to the expanding resources of the College of Religion library.

The faculty of the College of Religion saw the need for a special publication of its own to interpret world conditions in the light of spiritual convictions, present College of Religion lectureships in printed form, and portray the Disciples' movement in some of its historical aspects. To meet this need, *The Shane Quarterly,* with Dean Frederick D. Kershner as editor, made its first appearance in February, 1940.[68] This was the beginning of the school's publication program.

When Butler University moved to the Fairview campus in 1928 the College of Religion occupied quarters in the Arthur Jordan Memorial Hall. It was fully intended that it should have a building of its own in the very near future. The depression of the 'thirties postponed this project for nearly ten years. In the meantime the Christian churches of Indiana made financial contributions to the project, these contributions accelerating as the depression lifted and economic conditions improved. The fund grew to $150,000 by 1940,

[66]*Indiana Christian,* October, November, 1940; *Christian-Evangelist,* June 22, 1940. For a description of the Schmidt collection *see,* Toyozo W. Nakarai, "The Nathaniel Schmidt Library," *Shane Quarterly,* January, 1941.

[67]*World Call,* November, 1941.

[68]*The Shane Quarterly* continued until 1956 when it was succeeded by Volume 17 of *Encounter,* an ecumenical theological quarterly. For a complete description and history of *Shane Quarterly, see* editorial by Ronald E. Osborn in *Encounter,* Vol. XVII, No. 1 (Winter, 1956).

and it was decided that it was possible to start the building program.[69] The project was delayed a few months while the committee[70] determined where the structure should be located and the style of architecture to be used. It was finally announced in the late fall of 1940 that construction would begin. The new building was to be of Georgian colonial architecture because this characterized the early buildings along the Atlantic seaboard. It was thought that the difference in architectural style between the proposed building and Arthur Jordan Memorial Hall would set the College of Religion building apart as a separate unit. It was announced that William G. Irwin would give $100,000 through the Christian Foundation to the building project. The Foundation also proposed to provide a grant of another $400,000 for the maintenance of the College of Religion over a period of ten years.[71]

College of Religion alumni were pleased that the "new building" dreams were finally coming true. Some of these former students got together at the state convention in Bedford in 1941 and organized the College of Religion Alumni Association. The alumni project was sponsored by David S. McNelly, E. R. Andry, and E. E. Russell for the purpose of promoting closer relationships among alumni and stimulating interest in the College of Religion.[72]

About the time that construction of the new building was an assured fact a rumor was circulated surreptitiously to the effect that the Dean and his faculty members, in order to

---

[60]*Christian-Evangelist,* June 22, 1940.

[70]Building Committee: William J. Irwin, J. W. Atherton, Hilton U. Brown, Edwin R. Errett, Hugh Th. Miller, and Emsley W. Johnson, Sr.

[71]*Indiana Christian,* July, October, December, 1940; *World Call,* September, 1940; *Christian-Evangelist,* January 2, 1941.

[72]*Indiana Christian,* June, 1941. E. R. Andry was elected president; R. Melvin Thompson, vice president; and E. E. Russell, secretary-treasurer. Eugene Timbrook and Howard Anderson, added to these, comprised the first executive committee.

have their salaries guaranteed, had been compelled to sign a creedal statement which bound them to teach the religious views held by those who controlled the Foundation resources. The rumor was picked up by brotherhood and interdenominational journals, and the College of Religion was condemned almost immediately without investigation of facts. Charges of "creedalism" and the stifling of academic freedom headed the list. On interrogation of faculty members it was discovered that they were completely unaware of the existence of such an alleged creedal instrument.

The contract made between Butler University, Butler Foundation, and the Christian Foundation, dated June 12, 1940, was written evidence of a business agreement made between these parties concerning prior contributions to the Butler Foundation by William G. Irwin, Mrs. Z. T. Sweeney, and Clarence L. Goodwin, and the contribution made to Butler University by Marshall T. Reeves. Since the intent of the donors had been that the income derived from the use of this endowment should support the training of ministers for the Disciples of Christ, it was agreed that this income should be used in the maintenance of the College of Religion. The Christian Foundation agreed to pay all the remaining expenses of equipping and maintaining the College of Religion (including salaries and maintenance) as well as the College of Religion's proportionate share of the administrative and general expenses of the University.[73] Under the contract, the University would use the $150,000 on hand (which had been subscribed by the churches) to build a College of Religion building, and the remaining cost of the building ($100,000) would be paid by the Christian Founda-

---

[73]According to the *Year Book* of the Disciples of Christ, the Christian Foundation had $2,261,206.93 in its permanent funds at this time and receipts from investments the past year had yielded $22,692.77.

tion. All parties in the contract were bound to carry out the terms of the agreement for a period of ten years; if agreeable to all parties of the contract the terms could be renewed annually. The title to all real estate was to remain with Butler University unless the University should be taken over by some other corporation or body. In such an event the College of Religion and the campus immediately contingent would be deeded over to the Christian Foundation.

There was nothing in the contract of June 12, 1940, specifying what doctrines should be taught at the College of Religion or how any should be taught. The University, however, agreed that the work and teachings conducted in the College of Religion should be under a five-member committee of the Board of Directors of the University, three members of whom had been recommended by the Christian Foundation.

The contract was a guarantee to the Christian Foundation that the Disciples of Christ would not lose control of the College of Religion in the event that Butler University became structured outside of the Disciples' fellowship. Officials of the Christian Foundation made no effort to impose a creed on the College of Religion. Actually, they wanted the College of Religion to be free to operate inside the framework of the Disciples' movement and in accord with the purposes of the founders of Butler University. Since the Disciples were not structured as an authoritarian body there was no other course they could follow.

At the time that charges of creedalism were made the Christian Foundation was affiliated with the International Convention of the Disciples and made regular reports to this body. Hilton U. Brown, president of the Christian Foundation, was president of the Board of Directors of Butler

University and a director in the Christian Board of Publication. W. A. Shullenberger, president of the International Convention of the Disciples, had been teaching for two years at the College of Religion and would continue to teach for many more years. Among others on the faculty were Ephraim D. Lowe, general secretary of the Indiana Christian Missionary Association, and Rabbi Morris Feuerlicht. The contract of June 12, 1940, did not restrict their academic freedom or the teaching freedom of any other faculty member.

The entering of its own building by the College of Religion marked a new era in the history of ministerial education at Butler University. The catalog for the academic year 1941-1942 indicated that courses would be offered leading to the degrees of B.D., Th.M., and M.S. (in religion) and promised that in the near future a Th.D. program would be inaugurated. Prior to 1941 there had been some unofficial references to the institution as the School of Religion of Butler University; the catalog published in 1941 made this name a reality.[74]

The Years of the Locust

The history of Hoosier Disciples in the period 1931-1941 can be understood only in the context of the great depression. If the prosperity of the late 'twenties had continued through the next decade the story would have been different. Unemployment, insecurity, unrest, and fear of the future brought out some of the best—and some of the worst—characteristics

---

[74]College of Religion committee on the Board of Directors of Butler University in 1941; William G. Irwin, chairman; Crate D. Bowen, Hilton U. Brown, Edwin Errett, and Hugh Th. Miller. Faculty and lecturers: Frederick D. Kershner, dean; Bruce L. Kershner, Toyozo W. Nakarai, D. E. Walker, Arthur Holmes, Ludwig von Gerdtell, William J. Moore, Peyton H. Canary, M. M. Feuerlicht, W. A. Shullenberger, T. K. Smith, Wayne Berry, Ephraim D. Lowe, Abram E. Cory, Lucille Calvert, and Harold F. Hanlin. Enos E. Dowling was librarian.

of the movement. By the end of the depression decade, as calamitous as it was to the churches and its agencies and institutions, the movement was again on the march. Unfortunately, war was soon to come. With it came new problems, new choices to be made, new testing of the faith, and new opportunities. The year 1941 marked the end of another era for Hoosier Disciples.

XI

Facing War and Prosperity

1942-1953

THE ATTACK ON PEARL HARBOR on December 7, 1941, involved the United States in war. During the first five months of 1942 the Japanese captured Manila, Singapore, and the Netherlands East Indies. Bataan and Corregidor soon fell to the enemy. It was reported at the Indiana State Convention in 1942, however, that the ranks of Hoosier Disciples were not shattered by war hysteria. The convention was held at Logansport. Mark Anthony of New Albany was president. Mrs. Charles K. Green, representing the British Churches of Christ, was the speaker featured at the banquet for ministers and their wives. For many it was the first opportunity of hearing a direct report of the experiences of their British colleagues in the Battle for Britain. The Indiana brethren were confronted at this time with the necessity of making a fresh appraisal of their responsibilities and obligations as members of the church and as citizens of the nation. The convention passed but one resolution; it was a request to churches in defense and new-construction areas to expand their programs to meet the urgencies of the times. The resolution also called upon all Christian churches and upon state and national groups to give financial aid to support the churches engaged in such programs and urged all Indiana congregations to keep in touch with men in the service and members who had moved to defense centers.[1]

The Churches and World War II

The implementation of the Logansport resolution was highlighted in central Indiana when the government began construction of an army camp to accommodate 36,000 trainees (Camp Atterbury). Richard E. Lentz, pastor of the Tabernacle Christian Church at Franklin, reported that the camp would be four miles from the city of Franklin when completed. He stated that the civilian population increased from 15,000 to 20,000 persons by June, 1942, due to employment of construction workers. The four downtown Franklin churches, in cooperation with ministers, chaplains, and U.S.O. (United Service Organizations) directors, established a central church office. This office issued weekly bulletins to the men in the barracks, distributed religious literature, volunteered their ministers for counseling, scheduled union services, and developed recreational programs.[2]

The Disciples' brotherhood was in its fourth year of a Five Year Program of Advance in 1941. When this nation-wide stewardship project was launched no one knew of the cataclysm that would soon be let loose on earth. It was necessary in the fall of 1941 to plunge into an Emergency Million drive as the fifth year emphasis of the Program of Advance. The object of the drive was to raise an extra million dollars to carry the ministry of the church to the service personnel. The campaign was successful and cared

---

[1]*Christian-Evangelist*, June 18, 1942; *Indiana Christian*, May, June, 1942. Among the speakers at the convention: R. Powell Mead of Anderson, Fred R. Davies of Charlestown, Richard E. Lentz of Franklin, Willard Wickizer of Indianapolis, Raymond F. McLain of Transylvania College, and Raphael H. Miller, Sr., of St. Louis.

[2]*Indiana Christian*, July-August, 1942.

for the emergency demands for a two-year period. An additional $250,000 was requested in 1943 under the name of the War Time Service Fund. Hoosier Disciples were responsible for contributing their share to these funds.[3]

The structure and program of the State Association in 1942 centered in the offices in the Occidental Building in Indianapolis. The Board of Trustees with Ephraim D. Lowe, general secretary, held quarterly meetings at this place. Work was carried on through the state secretary, three district evangelists, and a director of religious education. These persons were responsible for field work, counseling with churches, and holding evangelistic meetings. The Association operated within a budget of $22,000 the year before, and $52,000 had accumulated in the permanent funds.[4]

In 1943 the United States forces were successful in the Pacific area and defeated the axis powers in North Africa. American air power was smashing at European targets, and it appeared that the tide had finally turned in favor of Great Britain and her allies. In this country, because of the shortage of man-power in industry, nearly all able-bodied persons found some kind of employment. Some men worked two shifts; many worked extra time on weekends. Wives and mothers worked in war plants, stores, gasoline filling stations and on many other jobs formerly held by men. Young people, still in school, found part-time employment to aid the war effort. The shortage of consumer goods and the imposition of food and gasoline rationing, plus rent controls, provided many families with an income larger than could be spent. This was partly offset by the purchase of war bonds and by an inflated economy which spiraled upward at an

---

[3]*World Call,* October, 1941; September, 1943; *Indiana Christian,* November, 1941; April, 1942; June, 1944; *Christian-Evangelist,* August 11, 1943.
[4]*Indiana Christian,* October, 1942.

accelerated rate. The increase in family income was not reflected in ministers' salaries; many ministers had to take part-time extra jobs in industry in order to meet their living expenses. Family mobility was high in the war years. Some congregations lost as many as one-third of their members annually. Fortunately, new members, people who had moved from other communities, made up for the loss. There was a rapid increase in marriages, and the birth rate increased. Church work had to be carried on by persons in the middle or older age brackets and by young people not old enough to enter the armed services. The demands of the times posed serious problems for the churches. Almost every family was harassed by special tensions brought on by abnormal living conditions.

Under the inspiration of the slogan, "Faith—Works—Victory," the State Convention for 1943 met at Kokomo. There were only 656 registrations, but the Main Street Christian Church was often filled to overflowing. Gasoline rationing and flood conditions over central Indiana made this convention quite local in representation. S. Grundy Fisher, minister at University Park Christian Church in Indianapolis, was president. Mrs. Kenneth B. Bowen of Covington, Kentucky, who addressed the meeting of the ministers' wives, was the only speaker from outside the state. Forums were conducted on pertinent subjects. Because of food rationing there was but one group meal. It was called the "convention" dinner.[5]

The spacious, newly decorated sanctuary of the Central Christian Church at Anderson was the locale of the State

---

[5]*Indiana Christian*, January, May, June, 1943; *Christian-Evangelist*, June 2, 1943. D. Irvin Sheets spoke to the Ministers' Association on the subject of returning service men; George Harris gave an address on the rural church; W. F. Rothenburger and R. H. Montgomery presented the convention sermons; C. M. Yocum and Alexander Paul lifted up the cause of missions; Richard E. Lentz spoke on character education in the home; Norman E. Berry told of the needs of the benevolent homes; and Dougal K. McColl gave an address on evangelism.

Convention of Hoosier Disciples in 1944. The brethren seemed to have a will to match the problems of the war and subsequent post-war world with renewed devotion to Christ and the church. The youth of the state accepted their share of the national program of winning 250,000 young people to Christ in the year ahead and recruiting 500 young people for missionary education and the mission fields. Indiana Disciples assumed their portion of the $300,000 goal for the training of 150 new missionaries to work in the post-war world. G. F. Powers of Nineveh presided over the convention sessions. A spirit of optimism characterized the gathering as the speakers centered their remarks on the general theme, "Strengthen the Church for the Present Crisis." Several resolutions were considered by this convention. One of these respectfully requested the National Selective Service Board to reconsider deferment of pre-ministerial students; another favored asking the United Nations to make a statement of Christian peace aims to the rest of the world immediately with the thought of ending the conflict at the earliest possible moment on the basis of such terms; the third resolution concerned a financial campaign of $18,000 on behalf of the Bethany Park Assembly to be raised among the churches during the current year. All three resolutions were approved.[6]

The State Association in 1944, in recognition of its 100th anniversary in 1949, planned a five year program of advance. Appropriate goals were set up. Among these were 10,000 additions to the churches each year, five full-time evangelists in the field, 25 young men led into the ministry, ten new Indiana fields entered, 20 closed churches opened, 50 new pastoral unities, 2,500 subscriptions to the *Indiana Christian,* and 2,000 registered delegates at the centennial convention.[7]

---

[6]*Indiana Christian,* May, June, 1944; *Christian-Evangelist,* June 21, 1944.
[7]*Indiana Christian,* September, 1944.

By the end of 1944 the war against the axis powers was going quite well. The invasion of the Marshall Islands had taken place, Bougainville and the Gilbert Islands had been captured, the Marianas were invaded, allied landings in Normandy and southern France took place, Paris was liberated, the United States forces recaptured Guam, the reconquest of the Philippines began, and B-29 raids on Japan from Saipan had their inception. In December, 1944, the Germans projected their last great thrust in the Battle of the Bulge. May 8, 1945 was V-E day, marking the breaking down of German resistance. Following the dropping of atomic bombs on Japan in August, that nation soon surrendered. The United Nations was organized in San Francisco in 1945 before the end of the war. President Roosevelt, serving his fourth term in office, died in 1945 and was succeeded by Harry S. Truman. The termination of hostilities brought an end to wartime rationing and the gradual elimination of many wartime civilian restrictions. These momentous events, plus the return of the military personnel to their homes and the changeover to a peace-time economy posed many problems for the churches by the end of 1945. It meant the beginning of a tremendous period of reconversion and reconstruction for the nation.

"With Christ We Build Anew"

The State Convention for 1945, the ministers' mid-winter institute, and many other gatherings of Hoosier Disciples had to be canceled in 1945 because of government restrictions. By the spring of 1946 state-wide activities were resumed. The 107th State Convention was held at Central Christian Church in Terre Haute in 1946. Thomas J. Bennett was host pastor. R. Powell Mead, president, gave the key-note address on the theme, "With Christ We Build Anew." J. Warren Hastings of the National City Christian Church was the convention preacher. The brethren, still disturbed by the war, especially by the implications of the use of the atomic bomb, nevertheless, were happy to meet again in fellowship. Resolutions concerning family life, race relations, world peace, the liquor traffic, famine and student work were passed.[8]

A "Crusade for a Christian World," the national brother-hood promotional program for 1946-1950, originated from the suggestion of a self-appointed committee of church leaders to the Commission on Budgets and Promotional Relationships of the International Convention of the Disciples of Christ. Convention approval for the crusade was secured in August, 1946. It was designed to motivate a resurgence of the Christian life through evangelism, education, stewardship, Christian unity, world fellowship, world mission, reconstruction, and Christian world order; it was to culminate in a "package deal" drive for $14,000,000 to be shared by national agencies, colleges, and state missionary societies which had participated.[9] The Crusade came to the attention of Hoosier Disciples through a series of assemblies and a voluminous amount of literature distributed in the churches. Indiana goals were announced as 33,811 new members, 10,-312 newly trained leaders, 15 new pastoral unities, 92,000 baptisms, every Disciple home reached with Christian teaching, 20 new churches, 100 new lifework recruits, 51,972 tithers, and 50 new churches. R. Powell Mead, then minister of the East Lynn Christian Church at Anderson, was elected

---

[8]*Indiana Christian*, March, June, September, 1946; *Christian-Evangelist*, July 3, 1946.
[9]*Crusade Information, Questions and Answers* (Indianapolis: A Crusade for a Christian World, 1946), pp. 1-5, 15-17.

chairman of the Indiana campaign, and F. W. Wiegmann of the Downey Avenue Christian Church in Indianapolis was made vice chairman.[10]

On February 28, 1951 the promotional activity for the Crusade was closed on the national level, though churches were expected to continue to remit offerings. The total receipts reported in the *Year Book* of the Disciples for 1951 show that $8,307,893 had been received. Some 348 Christian churches in Indiana participated in raising $684,779 toward the total goal. The giving in Indiana was exceeded only by that of Texas.

R. Melvyn Thompson was president of the 108th State Convention held at Winona Lake in 1947. There were 2,000 registrations. Those in attendance heard variations of the theme, "Creative Christians for the Atomic Era." The youth sessions were attended by 400 young people. Resolutions approved by the convention called for the appointment of a committee to encourage closer relationships with the Baptists, opposition to patterns of segregation, restoration of civil rights to conscientious objectors convicted of violating the Selective Service Act of 1940, opposition to peacetime compulsory military training, strengthening the United Nations, approval of keeping atomic energy control in the hands of a civilian commission, endorsement of the Crusade for a Christian World, and objection to the Roman Catholic hierarchy receiving public money for parochial schools.[11]

The State Convention was held at First Christian Church in Marion in 1948. L. Doyle Mullen of Lafayette was presi-

---

[10]*Indiana Christian*, January, March, April, 1947; *World Call*, January, 1947.

[11]*Indiana Christian*, April, May, June, 1947; *Christian-Evangelist*, August 6, 1947. Program participants: R. Melvyn Thompson, Fred West, Elton Trueblood, Harry B. McCormick, Gaines M. Cook, Jessie M. Trout, Wayne Guthrie, John McCaw, Cleo Blackburn, Edwin T. Dahlberg, Gerald G. Sias, A. Reid Liverett, Ernest L. Harrold, and Rosa Page Welch.

dent of the gathering, and C. L. Johnson was host pastor. The laying of the cornerstone for the new addition to the Emily E. Flinn Home was a highlight of the meeting. More than 1,000 persons gathered on the spacious lawn of the institution to witness the ceremonies and hear an address by J. Eric Carlson of the National Benevolent Association. Before adjourning, the convention passed strong resolutions on the support of the Crusade for a Christian World, Christian Unity, and the first meeting of the World Council of Churches at Amsterdam, Holland, to be held later that summer.[12]

The 110th convention of Hoosier Disciples, held at Central Christian Church in Indianapolis in 1949, had been designated five years before as a "centennial" convention. It marked the passing of 100 years since the organizing of the Indiana Christian Home Missionary Society, forerunner of the Indiana Christian Missionary Association. The original society, brainchild of Elijah Goodwin, was organized at Central Christian Church in Indianapolis, October 6, 1849; it was the first of the state society organizations among the Disciples of Christ. W. A. Shullenberger was host pastor of the convention in 1949, as was Love H. Jameson in 1849. Not all the goals set up for the centennial year were reached. Instead of 10,000 additions each year there had been 7,000. The goal of five full-time evangelists in the field was achieved. Many more than 25 young men had entered the ministry, and more than ten new fields were entered. The opening of twenty closed churches was not realized, however, nor was the one of establishing 50 new pastoral unities. The desire to have a subscription list of 2,500 for the *Indiana Christian* exceeded expectations; it increased from 1,100 to 3,517. Instead of 2,000 registered

---

[12]*Indiana Christian*, May, June, 1949; *Christian-Evangelist*, July 21, 1948.

delegates to the 1949 convention (goal set in 1944), there were 2,503.[13]

The dedication of the new addition to the Emily E. Flinn home at Marion on August 28, 1949 was also an achievement of the year. Miss Glenn Harter was superintendent of the home at the time. The $260,000 addition made it possible to care for several more aged men and women.[14]

Lebanon, the county seat of Boone County, a community of 7,000 persons, entertained the 111th State Convention. Fred W. Wolff was pastor of the host church; Paul E. Million of Crawfordsville served as president of the convention. The 1950 meeting followed the usual pattern. Anna M. Clarke planned the youth sessions. Rosa Page Welch was convention song leader. The Lebanon convention marked the last session of the Indiana Woman's Christian Missionary Society. Mrs. B. H. Bruner, general secretary, announced that the Indiana Christian Women's Fellowship would now take its place. The Constitution of the old organization had been revised where necessary and ratified at the State Board meeting at Anderson on March 22, 1950, to go into effect the following July 1.[15]

Postwar Expansion and the Korean Conflict

Though vital material for construction of such non-defense buildings as churches, parsonages, and educational units was not available until the conclusion of World War II, many churches purchased parsonages and made minor property

---

[13]*Indiana Christian*, May, June, 1949; *Christian-Evangelist*, May 18, 1949. Officers of the convention: Raymond H. Montgomery, Sr., president; Robert T. Beck, vice president; H. O. Pritchard, treasurer; and Kenneth Brady, recorder. Speakers: Roy A. Burkhart, Raymond F. McLain, Kirby Page, Ben Hagelbarger, Dennis Savage, John A. Tate, and Mrs. Laurence Lew. Ephraim D. Lowe, general secretary, and H. R. Hosier of Gary, president of the State Board, brought progress reports to the convention.

[14]*Christian-Evangelist*, March, April, 1950.

[15]*Indiana Christian*, March, April, 1950.

improvements, during this period. Prosperity raised the giving level of the average church family, and much of this extra income received by the churches was used to pay off debts which had accumulated during the depression; mortgage-burning ceremonies were popular at this time. Looking to the future when building construction would again be permitted, many downtown city churches purchased real estate in the suburbs where there would be ample room for the parking of cars and an expanded program of activities. A church building-boom started in earnest at the close of World War II. The shortage of essential materials and the steady acceleration of building costs served to curtail the construction phase until about 1948. Since this was a lush period for raising money there were many drives for capital funds. Professional fund-raising concerns, engaged by the churches to conduct financial drives, multiplied rapidly. When churches realized that building costs were not going to decline, because of the inflationary economic spiral, they plunged into the construction phase of their programs. By the middle of 1950 the possibility of involvement in the Korean War stepped up the program; some churches broke ground ahead of schedule to get their building programs underway before possible government restrictions were issued. There was a lull in new construction between 1951 and 1953, but after the truce in Korea the building and remodeling boom started again. Not counting advancement in appraisal values of their existing real estate holdings, the Disciple churches in Indiana increased their capital investments by millions of dollars. New and remodeled sanctuaries, for the most part, conformed to approved architectural design and served to influence the religious thinking and worship patterns of the Disciple constituency.

In June, 1950, soldiers of the communist-dominated North

Korean government commenced streaming over the 38th parallel (arbitrary dividing line between North and South Korea after the end of World War II) into South Korea. The United Nations Security Council backed the Republic of South Korea in trying to stay the advance of the communists. The North Korean military maneuvers looked like a repetition of the aggressive acts of Hitler and Mussolini. Therefore, when the communist armies of North Korea plunged southward across the 38th parallel it was looked upon as an attack on the free world. The United Nations military forces, made up largely of United States military contingents, succeeded in pushing the enemy back to his own lines, but force was needed to hold this position. General MacArthur, impatient for a complete victory, engineered a strategic military maneuver in November, 1950, in landing a strong force behind the North Korean lines. The Chinese, as they had threatened to do if so provoked, entered the war actively and drove the United Nations forces back across the 38th parallel and out of North Korea. Hostilities finally ended in a stalemate. An armistice was signed at Panmunjom on July 27, 1953. Eventually most of the American troops were finally withdrawn from South Korea and were returned home.

The churches, for the most part, looked upon the Korean conflict as a righteous action. After the humiliating defeat at the hands of the Chinese the war was taken more seriously, and demands for an amicable settlement were voiced frequently. Though the expected government restrictions on building programs did not come, the difficulty in getting heavy material for construction, especially steel, slowed down the completion of many projects. The Korean conflict did not reach into every home as had World War II; there were some casualties and no little tension concerning the eventual outcome.

The State Association Expands Its Resources

The Kokomo Main Street Christian Church, which had recently celebrated its centennial with a remodeling program, entertained the State Convention in 1951. Jo M. Riley was host pastor; Benton B. Miller of Indianapolis was convention president. After considerable discussion, the convention voted to approve a campaign for an extra $200,000 during the next three missionary years. The fund to be raised was designated to purchase camp sites in northern and southern Indiana, rejuvenate Bethany Park, aid the Indiana Campus Christians' Foundation and the Purdue Christian Foundation. Convention resolutions included support of the forthcoming Disciples' World Convention at Melbourne, Australia, Unified Promotion, the Campbell Home restoration project, the Emily E. Flinn Home, the Indiana Council of Churches, and the School of Religion at Butler University. It was also agreed at this convention that the charters of all Indiana Disciples-related agencies should be changed so that board members could be elected at the convention of the State Association each year.[16]

The first new camp site purchased under the authority of the State Convention was one four miles southeast of Bedford. Dedication ceremonies for Bedford Christian Camp took place on May 27, 1951. Later that year, the State Association in cooperation with Disciples in the northern counties of the state, purchased a fifty-acre tract of ground bordering the east end of the Barbee chain of seven lakes in Kosciusko

---

[16]*Indiana Christian*, May, June, 1951. William H. Book, then vice president of the Indianapolis Chamber of Commerce, addressed the convention on the subject, "Some Suggestions from the Pew to the Pulpit;" *see Christian-Evangelist,* July 11, 1951. Other speakers: Jonas M. Berkey, Archie Mackey, Ronald E. Osborn, Walter W. Sikes, Dwight E. Stevenson, Theo O. Fisher, Lonnie H. Hass, Harlie L. Smith, Leslie R. Smith, George H. McLain, Harry M. Davis, Mrs. Kenneth M. Bowen, Mrs. Clarence H. Hamilton, Robert T. Beck, Floyd Hines, and Gaines M. Cook. There was a panel discussion on the state work. Participants: Mrs. B. H. Bruner, Miss Anna M. Clarke, Ephraim D. Lowe, Miss Bessie Myers, Lonnie H. Hass, and Laurence Elshoff.

County, ten miles north of Warsaw. Barbee Christian Camp was dedicated during the sessions of the State Convention at Winona Lake in 1952. John H. Booth, campaign director, reported in 1953 that progress was being made on the $200,-000 drive. Half of the amount had already been received in cash. In 1954, the thirty-three-acre site, known as Indian Lake Christian Retreat, was ready for use. It was located fifteen miles from the heart of Indianapolis. This became a central camp and conference grounds for year around use.[17]

The State Convention for 1952 was held in June so that Hoosier Disciples could better enjoy beautiful Winona Lake. The theme, "That His Way May Be Known," was used for this convention and related to the long-range program of the Disciples. Glen L. Tudor, minister of the Central Christian Church at Elkhart, served as convention president. William Robinson, British Disciple and a member of the faculty of the School of Religion at Butler University, brought the devotional studies each morning. Rosa Page Welch of Chicago was in charge of the music. Special addresses were given by J. Warren Hastings, Bernard C. Clausen, A. Dale Fiers, and John Updegraff.[18]

The Oxford Court Case

Occasionally in Indiana, as in other states, local congregations have divided over controversial issues and turned to the courts to establish rightful ownership of real estate and other church property. Such a case occurred with the Christian Church at Oxford, Indiana. Beginning in 1936 there was a difference in opinion among members as to whether the congregation should be known as the Christian Church (Dis-

---

[17]*Indiana Christian*, May, June, September, 1951; May, 1952; July, 1954; *Christian-Evangelist*, July, 1954.
[18]*Indiana Christian*, April, 1952.

ciples of Christ) or as the Church of Christ. The underlying issue was whether or not the congregation should continue in the cooperative fellowship within the framework of the Disciples or become an independent congregation. The final break came in 1950 when the cooperative group withdrew to hold services at another location. The Church of Christ division retained possession of the building. The Christian Church division then filed civil suit for aid against the minister and trustees of the Church of Christ division in repossessing the church property. The Christian Church won the case after eighteen months of litigation, the decision being based on the finding of the court that the plaintiffs had adhered to the original doctrines and practices held at the time the property involved (church building and parsonage) was acquired.[19] The schism at Oxford was unfortunate, but the decision rendered by the court should have set a precedent favorable to the Christian Churches (Disciples of Christ) in Indiana.

John A. Farr of Jeffersonville presided over the 114th convention of the Christian churches in 1953. It was held at the Central Christian Church of Huntington where J. Maurice Thompson was host pastor. Addresses and workshops stressed the theme, "Through Christian Fellowship We Advance." There were 2,670 registrations.[20]

The Vicissitudes of Bethany Assembly

Many successful summers were scored at Bethany Park with the assembly programs. By 1928, however, interest in the

---

[19]*See* Cause No. 1686, Complaint to declare a trust in real estate and an injunction, Benton County Circuit Court, September Term, 1950; Albert Greenwood, *et al. vs.* Marvin C. Schramm, Special Finding of Facts, Benton County Circuit Court, April Term, 1952.

[20]*Indiana Christian*, February, April, June, 1953. Jesse M. Bader, executive secretary of the National Council of Churches gave four addresses. Orval D. Peterson of Yakima, Washington was guest preacher. Toyozo W. Nakarai of Butler's School of Religion presented a series of Bible studies.

"Chautaqua" type of presentations began to wane, and it was difficult for youth conferences to adapt to existing facilities. When the depression came in the 'thirties Bethany Park began to experience financial problems. By the end of 1940 Bethany Assembly owed $7,500 to the Permanent Funds of the State Association. Herbert J. Buchanan, many years field evangelist for the Association, became manager of the park in 1946. There was a revival of interest in the project when it was under his guidance. He was successful in getting many property owners to improve and modernize their holdings. However, many of the public buildings had become obsolete and needed to be totally removed and replaced. A serious fire in 1952 destroyed the hotel and restaurant buildings; three forthcoming youth conferences had to be cancelled. The $13,000 recovered from the insurance on these buildings paid off the standing indebtedness and left a small amount of money which was applied to the Bedford and Barbee camp projects. Mrs. Effie L. Cunningham had willed her Bethany Park home to the Assembly, and this sold for $5,000. These proceeds were applied to the Indian Lake Retreat. All the public buildings except one were sold by 1954. This action closed out Bethany Park as a camp grounds for Hoosier Disciples. Though the park had a glorious history and had met the needs of Disciples for many years, it had become a liability by this time. One of the first youth conferences in America was held there in 1920. Exciting and inspirational events had transpired on the old camp grounds, but the program of Christian work had so changed by the end of 1950 that it was thought not feasible to invest additional thousands of dollars to maintain a project that belonged to days long since past. The wave of the future was moving in another direction.[21]

---

[21]*Indiana Christian*, June, 1946; January, March, November, 1952; October, 1954.

Leadership Changes Among Hoosier Disciples

Mrs. C. O. Nease, secretary of the Indiana Woman's Christian Missionary Society, closed her work with the Society in September, 1946. She had been an effective laborer in the missionary cause for many years. In her last official report for the missionary year, 1945-1946, she indicated that there were then 362 local societies, 14,115 members, and that $70,-913 had been raised during the current year for world outreach.[22] Mrs. B. H. Bruner became her successor. Hoosier Disciples were honored in 1948 when William H. Book, executive vice president of the Indianapolis Chamber of Commerce and elder in Third Christian Church in that city, was chosen to be president of the Pension Fund of the Disciples of Christ. He had been a trustee since 1942.[23] Edward L. Day retired as secretary-evangelist of the Marion County Christian churches in 1949. A dinner was given in his honor at the Olive Branch Church in Indianapolis, recognizing an active Christian service record of 51 years.[24] Orville W. Williams, new secretary-evangelist of the Marion County Church Union, began his work the next year.[25] Miss Bessie M. Myers came to Indiana from California to be state director of children's work in 1950. She worked in association with Miss Anna M. Clarke and Mrs. B. H. Bruner.[26] In 1950, Lonnie H. Hass also began service with the Association as director of the Town and Country Church program.[27] Laurence Elshoff, a district evangelist of the State Association for fifteen years, returned to a former pastorate in 1953.[28] In September of that

---

[22]*Indiana Christian*, September, 1946.

[23]*World Call*, March, 1948.

[24]*Indiana Christian*, October, 1949.

[25]*Indiana Christian*, December, 1950.

[26]*Indiana Christian*, January, February, 1950.

[27]*Indiana Christian*, June, 1950.

[28]*Indiana Christian*, June, 1953.

same year Maxwell T. Smith became director of the Christian Men's Fellowship for Indiana.[29] A month later, E. Lyle Harvey, pastor of the Milroy church, was made director of the Indiana Department of Religious Education.[30] He succeeded Miss Anna M. Clarke.

Headquarters for the State Association had been maintained in the Bankers Trust Building in Indianapolis since 1945. Offices were moved to a large home on Kessler Boulevard in 1954. The first story of the new quarters served as the residence for Ephraim D. Lowe, and the five rooms on the upper story were used for the state offices.[31]

Significant Persons Lost by Death

Several Hoosier Disciples, prominent in the work of the Christian Churches in Indiana, died during this period. Frank Huston, author of some 400 gospel songs, often song leader for evangelistic meetings, died in 1942.[32] The next year, G. I. Hoover, state secretary, 1926-1940, passed away.[33] He was working on the depression debt liquidation project of the State Association at the time of his death.

William G. Irwin died December 14, 1943.[34] Christian layman and philanthropist, he had been a member of the Board of Directors of Butler University for many years and was one of the large contributors to the fund for the "new" Butler on Fairview campus. His sister, Linnie (Mrs. Z. T. Sweeney), also one of the generous benefactors of Butler, died February 3, 1944 at the age of 84. She taught a Sunday school class at the Columbus Tabernacle church for many

---

[29]*Christian-Evangelist*, November 11, 1953.
[30]*Indiana Christian*, October, 1953.
[31]*Indiana Christian*, January, 1954.
[32]*Indiana Christian*, January, 1943.
[33]*Indiana Christian*, February, 1943.
[34]*Christian-Evangelist*, December 29, 1943.

years. One of her last acts was to participate in the corner-stone laying ceremonies of the new Saarinin-designed church building at Columbus.[35]

Mrs. Effie L. Cunningham died on June 18, 1945 at her Bethany Park home. She had been treasurer, recording secretary and president of the Christian Woman's Board of Missions in Indiana. Mrs. Cunningham was also editor of *Missionary Tidings* in 1909; later, she was associate editor of *World Call.*[36] William H. Book died at Orlando, Florida in 1946. He had been pastor of the Tabernacle church in Columbus for many years and was well known as a lecturer and minister.[37] Hugh Th. Miller died on May 26, 1947. As a young man he served ten years on the Butler University faculty and was later a member of the Board of Directors. At the time of his death he was treasurer of the Butler Foundation.[38] John W. Atherton died June 2, 1947. Atherton was a Christian layman and served in an important capacity in the raising of funds and in the construction of the new Fairview campus at Butler.[39] Miss Anna M. Clarke, who was director of the Indiana Department of Religious Education from 1939 to 1953, died June 10, 1953. Miss Clarke pioneered with Junior High groups in summer camps. A new family camp plan was launched in Indiana under her leadership. During her service with the State Association the number of camps and conferences increased with five to fifteen. She was responsible for developing a broad program of religious education in the Hoosier state.[40]

---

[35]*Indiana Christian,* February, 1944.
[36]*World Call,* September, 1945.
[37]*Indiana Christian,* July, 1946.
[38]*Christian-Evangelist,* June 18, 1947; *Indiana Christian,* December, 1947.
[39]*Christian-Evangelist,* June 18, 1947.
[40]*Indiana Christian,* June, 1953.

409

Foundations at University Centers

PURDUE UNIVERSITY

The work with Disciple students at Purdue University was started in First Christian Church at Lafayette. Robert Knight became a full-time student worker in 1916 and carried on the task for twenty years. The project was recognized at this time as a responsiblity of all the Christian churches in Indiana. A house was purchased in 1945, and it was formally opened to students on January 26, 1946. A new location at the center of the campus was established in 1953. Some of the leaders who followed Robert Knight in the work of the Purdue Christian Foundation between 1920 and 1954 were Barton Hunter, Forrest L. Brock, Hubert Reynolds, Doyle Mullen, Mrs. Everett Wright, Joseph G. Wick, and C. A. Underwood.

INDIANA UNIVERSITY

The Bible Chair established at Indiana University eventually became the Indiana School of Religion, and the work was carried on primarily through the efforts of Joseph C. Todd. The School of Religion celebrated forty years of history in 1940. There were three faculty members at this time: Joseph C. Todd, Robert S. Eccles, and Harold E. Hill.[41] It did not claim to be a school to train ministers, but courses in the Bible and religion were made available to university students.

INDIANA CAMPUS CHRISTIAN'S FOUNDATION

The work of this foundation, established by First Christian Church of Bloomington, began when a director was called

---

[41]*Indiana Christian*, February, 1951. Directors in 1951: Raymond H. Montgomery, Sr., Mrs. E. C. Rumpler, Merrill R. Wilson, Bin T. Smith, E. C. Shirman, Jean S. Milner, Roy O. Pike, Mrs. Betty B. Andrews, Jess E. Martin, Vern W. Ruble, F. S. Cannon, Rodney D. Smith, C. E. Cook, Frank R. Greer, Mrs. F. O. Branch.

in 1945. Meetings were held in the Campbell House, next to the church buildings. A student Bible class was started in the Sunday School, and special worship services for university students were held at the church. Robert T. Huber was called in 1954 to supervise the activities of campus Christians. He was made assistant minister at the Bloomington church so that he could integrate the students into the work of the local church.[42]

Butler University, 1942-1953

The university community was shaken by the advent of World War II. It meant personal involvement to a majority of the male students. On December 8, 1941, most of the students gathered around portable radios in fraternity and sorority houses, in the campus club, and in offices to hear President Roosevelt ask Congress for a declaration of war against Japan. Ten days later, Butler's President Robinson spoke to the students and faculty on the subject of a second world war. Robinson emphasized the current national emergency and declared that the existence of a free people was at stake. He stated that he believed that all of the students then registered under the Selective Service Act would be called into service before the opening of the next semester. War emergency councils for both faculty and students were created. In separate and joint sessions the matter of how Butler University could best serve the nation, the Red Cross, and other service organizations was discussed.[43]

The university had 226 men in military service by February, 1942. Five were members of the faculty. In April, 53 more names were added to the service list. Construction work began on June 1, 1942 to convert the fieldhouse and gym-

---

[42]*Indiana Christian,* February, October, 1951; January, 1955.
[43]*Butler Alumnus,* January, 1942.

nasium to war use as a training station for 800 navy signal-men. The west end of the gymnasium was used for lodging quarters; the basketball playing area was covered with asphalt. There was a hospital and isolation ward along the south side of the building, and a food, clothing and storage room was set up on the northwest end. The fieldhouse was officially turned over to the navy on June 17, 1942, with impressive cere-monies. Henry F. Schricker, governor of Indiana, and Mayor Reginald Sullivan of Indianapolis were speakers on this oc-casion.[44]

Daniel Sommer Robinson had resigned as president of the university by this time, after being in office less than three years. Later, he received a commission as Lieutenant Com-mander of the Chaplains' Corps of the Naval Reserve. M. O. Ross,[45] dean of the College of Business Administration, was made acting president on February 23, 1942; he was named president later that year.

Ross J. Griffeth, professor of Biblical history and liter-ature at Butler University since 1933, was called to the presi-dency of Northwest Christian College at Eugene, Oregon, in 1944. He had been secretary of the Rural Life Commission of the Indiana Christian Missionary Association since 1937. Griffeth was succeeded at the university by E. Robert Andry, minister of the Downey Avenue Christian Church in Indian-apolis. Frederick D. Kershner retired as dean of Butler's

[44]*Butler Alumnus,* February, April, June, 1942; *Christian-Evangelist,* May 7, 1942.

[45]Maurice O'Rear Ross (1897-   ), a native of Kentucky, received the A.B. degree from Kentucky Wesleyan College in 1918; M.A. University of Chicago, 1824; Ph.D. *ibid.,* 1936. He also held honorary LL.D. degrees from Kentucky Wesleyan College, Wabash College, and Indiana Central College. After serving the Sturgis, Kentucky, schools in an administrative capacity he became assistant professor of economics at Earlham College in 1924. He was dean of Earlham College, 1932-1937. He became dean of the College of Business Administration at Butler University in 1938, and president in 1942. Ross retired from the presidency of Butler University in 1962 and accepted a position to teach in the field of business administration at Chapman College, Orange, California. He is the author of several books and treatises in the field of economics. The current phase of the Butler University expansion program had its beginning in the last years of the Ross administration. The men's residence hall at the university is named Ross Hall in his honor.

School of Religion in 1944, becoming dean emeritus and head of the department of Christian doctrine at this institution.[46]

Normal campus life at Butler University was suspended for the duration of the war. Women outnumbered the men in the regular enrollment, and great numbers of men were in uniform. Butler University became an important military training center. In addition to the Signal Corps training school in the fieldhouse, an Army Aviation Cadet Center was established on the campus. Five fraternities evacuated their houses and turned them over to the incoming aviation cadets. Faculty members assisted the Air Corps instructors. The university had to adjust itself to new schedules and new courses. Students and faculty members were restricted by government rationing programs. Many campus rallies were held to assist the war effort, especially in the sale of war bonds and stamps. At one such rally on December 6, 1945, more than $51,200 worth of stamps and bonds were sold.[47]

The Indianapolis College of Pharmacy was acquired by the university in 1945. It became known as the Butler University College of Pharmacy. A drive to raise $400,000 was projected immediately to provide for a modern pharmacy building on the campus.[48]

Campus life returned to normal at the beginning of the 1945-46 academic year. Nearly 3,900 students sought admission to college courses as the post-war educational program got underway. Two years before this there were 1,200 regular students enrolled, and 85 per cent of these were women. When the veterans came back the student body doubled. Because many entered for "late" semester work, administrative and academic problems were increased. Coach Paul D.

---

[46]*Indiana Christian,* March, 1944; *Butler Alumnus,* April, 1944; *Christian-Evangelist,* May 3, 1944.

[47]*World Call,* February, 1945.

[48]*Butler Alumnus,* December, 1945; *World Call,* December, 1945.

"Tony" Hinkle was especially welcomed back to the campus. He had gained much recognition as coach of basketball and football teams at the U. S. Naval Training Station, Great Lakes, Illinois.[49]

As a climax of a three-year study of educational facilities at Butler University this school was placed on the approved list of the Association of American Universities in 1946.[50]

It was estimated that 2,094 Butler University men and women were in some branch of government service during the war. Fifty-two of these were chaplains. In recognition of the service personnel, and especially of the 92 Butler men who lost their lives in World War II, a special memorial service was held in Sweeney Chapel on the Butler campus on May 1, 1947.[51]

The Campus Club was almost totally destroyed by fire in 1947. It had been used by the students as a lounge and recreation center. The Campus Club was replaced by the student union building, dedicated at the opening of the school year in 1949. The new building was named the John Whistler Atherton Center and was considered as a memorial to this man who had served the institution for 27 years. The new center contained a cafeteria, sandwich grill, bookstore, and recreation and conference rooms.[52]

Enrollment reached an all-time high in the 1947-48 academic year; 6,977 students were registered for the various sessions. In 1948, degrees were received by 674 students.[53] The J. I. Holcomb annual Faculty or Staff Award was established that year. It was to be presented at commencement to

---

[49]*Butler Alumnus,* October, 1946; *World Call,* January, February, 1946; *Indiana Christian,* September, 1946. Butler fieldhouse was named "Hinkle Fieldhouse" in his honor in 1965.
[50]*Butler Alumnus,* December, 1946; *World Call,* January, 1947.
[51]*Butler Alumnus,* July, 1947.
[52]*Christian-Evangelist,* October 10, 1947; *Indiana Christian,* December, 1949; *World Call,* June, 1949.
[53]*Christian-Evangelist,* February 2, 1949.

the person selected as having made the most significant contribution to the welfare and progress of the university during the preceding year.[54] The university began its 97th year in the fall of 1951. By this time the new pharmacy building was completed, and a merger had been arranged with the Jordan Conservatory of Music, an accredited four-year college that had operated in downtown Indianapolis for 21 years.[55] Governor George N. Craig of Indiana gave the commencement address in 1953. The LL.D. degree was conferred on him on this occasion.[56] The year 1953 closed with plans under way for a new $250,000 observatory and planetarium on the campus. J. I. Holcomb, member of the Board of Directors, was the donor of the building. It contained a 38-inch telescope, the largest in Indiana at the time.[57]

School of Religion, 1942-1953

The School of Religion (formerly College of Religion) of Butler University observed "open house" on January 28, 1942. Those who were interested had an opportunity to inspect the new building, the latest on the Butler campus. Two days of special programs followed the "open house" ceremonies. Special addresses were given by Edwin R. Errett, Daniel S. Robinson, Frederick D. Kershner, and Hilton U. Brown. The building was dedicated on June 5, 1942. Raphael H. Miller,

---

[54]*World Call*, February, 1948.

[55]*Butler Alumnus*, Fall, 1951; *World Call*, May, 1950.

[56]Butler University Directors, 1953: Hilton U. Brown, president; J. I. Holcomb, vice president; Crate D. Bowen, Keller T. Brock, Glenn R. Hillis, Richard T. James, Emsley W. Johnson, Jr., Mrs. Hugh Th. Miller, J. Irwin Miller, Raphael H. Miller, John F. Mitchell, Jr., G. Barret Moxley, Kurt Pantzer, John R. Rees, M. O. Ross, Mrs. Ralph M. Spann, Mrs. Robert S. Tangeman, Evan B. Walker, Kenneth W. Wolling, Mrs. William A. Zumpfe. Administration: M. O. Ross, president; Ray C. Friesner, dean of the College of Liberal Arts and Sciences; Orman L. Shelton, dean of the School of Religion; J. Hartt Walsh, dean of the College of Education; H. C. Graebner, dean of the College of Business Administration; Edward H. Niles, dean of the College of Pharmacy; Harry C. Crull, director of University College; R. H. Van Cleave, director of the Evening Division; Clide E. Aldrich, director of the Division of Graduate Instruction; John T. Barnett, director of Public Relations; C. R. Maxam, registrar; Elizabeth Ward Durflinger, dean of women; L. Gray Burdin, dean of men.

[57]*World Call*, December, 1953.

editor of the *Christian-Evangelist,* was the featured speaker. Dean Kershner paid tribute to three men who made the building possible: William G. Irwin, John W. Atherton, and Hilton U. Brown. Hugh Th. Miller led in the dedication service; T. K. Smith gave the dedication prayer, A. E. Cory read the scripture, and President M. O. Ross gave a brief address.[58]

There were 115 students enrolled at the School of Religion when the new building was dedicated. They came from 37 colleges and seminaries. Among them, they served 151 churches in Indiana as student pastors.[59] A strong faculty[60] awaited the students who enrolled for the fall semester in 1942. The curriculum provided for students to pursue studies leading to the degrees of A.M., B.D., Th.M., and Th.D.

World War II cut deeply into the ranks of Butler University School of Religion student body. Beginning about the time the school moved into its new quarters, several ministerial students (most of whom were ordained clergymen) became chaplains. Many former students of the School of Religion also accepted commissions in the Chaplains' Corps. A large number of men in both categories served in this capacity through the duration of the war. Among them were:

Kenneth Webster Ball	Jason M. Cowan
William V. Barney	George A. Curtis
Luke Bolin	Douglas A. Dickey
Ormonde Stanley Brown	Harold G. Elsam
Hubert H. Callahan	Theodore O. Fisher
George W. Cartwright	Fredric J. Forney
Walter H. Coburn	Clarence W. Franz

---

[58]*Indiana Christian,* February, May, 1942; *Christian-Evangelist,* June 11, 1942; *World Call,* September, 1942.

[59]*Indiana Christian,* June, 1942.

[60]Faculty, 1942: Frederick D. Kershner, T. W. Nakarai, Bruce L. Kershner, D. E. Walker, Arthur Holmes, Ludwig von Gerdtell, W. J. Moore, Harold F. Hanlin, and Lucille Calvert. Lecturers: A. E. Cory, M. M. Feuerlicht, W. A. Shullenberger, Ephraim D. Lowe, and E. Wayne Berry.

Luther C. Goebel
Albert F. Grothe
(Lutheran)
Victor R. Griffin
Harold F. Hanlin
Robert E. Hanson
Stewart W. Hartfelter
(Presbyterian)
Kenneth E. Hartman
(Lutheran)
Vernon F. Kullowatz
Carl S. Ledbetter
Julian B. Linkous
Arthur J. Lively
R. LeRoy Logan
A. B. McDiarmid
(New Zealand Army)
Johnnie V. McHenry
Charles H. Marler
J. Fenton Messenger, Jr.
Raphael H. Miller, Jr.
Raymond R. Miller

Richard W. Moore
H. Daniel Morgan
Albert R. Moss
Charles E. Mull
William O. Norris
John W. Osberg
Russell E. Palmer
David C. Pellett
Hartwell M. Ramsey
Frederick C. Sears
Charles L. Smith
(Baptist)
William Martin Smith
Herbert W. Sprowls
Gerald E. Timbrook
Henry Toogood
John A. Tyrell-Baxter
William N. Weaver
Hayes H. Webster
Thomas Clyde Wolfe
Orville L. Wright

The standard liberal arts colleges of the Disciples, prior to the early 1920's took pride in a large enrollment of ministerial students. This was usually a strong group of every campus. Students preparing for the ministry could take a four-year ministerial course with a terminal "ministerial" A.B. degree. This was considered adequate preparation for the Disciples' ministry. The ministerial curriculum, filled with what would currently be called professional courses, crowded out many basic undergraduate courses in English, history, science, and the humanities. The "ministerial" A.B. curriculum was loaded with Bible courses considered necessary in the ministerial profession. When the liberal arts colleges, to uphold their academic standing and meet the requirements of accrediting agencies, increased the number of basic liberal arts courses it meant that professional courses had to be eliminated. A limited number of credit-hours in Bible study were allowed within the framework of the A.B. curriculum, but such courses were not sufficient or adequate to qualify a graduate to be a candidate for ordination. The liberal arts colleges began to encourage pre-seminary training on the undergraduate level, designed to provide a sound, basic background for future graduate studies. This meant that Disciple students could no longer complete their ministerial education in the four-year period represented by the A.B. degree. A temporary vacuum was created in the Disciples' program for ministerial education when ministerial candidates, desiring to complete their education in the traditional four years, found it was no longer possible in the standard colleges.

To meet the shortage of trained ministers in the brotherhood, many well-meaning persons became interested in the so-called Bible college idea. A number of Bible colleges were established in the 'twenties and 'thirties for the primary purpose of training ministers within a four-year period. These Bible colleges and Bible institutes became popular with students desiring to enter the ministry, and there was a rapid development of schools of this nature. Many students took the position that if they could get a degree (usually Bachelor of Sacred Literature) in four years it was not necessary to enter upon a seven-year program of college and seminary training. Since the Bible colleges were not recognized by the standard accrediting agencies many students from these colleges found they were seriously handicapped later when they had a desire to upgrade their education.

Dean Kershner believed that the School of Religion was in a position to help these "Bible college" trained men to improve their academic standing by taking graduate work at the School of Religion while making up their undergraduate

418

deficiencies at the College of Liberal Arts and Sciences of Butler University. He envisioned the School of Religion as a "central" graduate school embodying the highest academic standards of the ministerial profession; it was to be sort of a "finishing" school for the Bible colleges. Kershner's program was effective in recruiting great numbers of students and improving the academic qualifications of Bible college graduates. It had, however, two major faults; many students thus gained were predisposed unfavorably against the cooperative mainstream of the Disciples' brotherhood (the Bible colleges took an independent position), and the acceptance of great numbers of students from unaccredited institutions jeopardized the standing of the School of Religion as a graduate seminary. Thus, an unfavorable image for the School of Religion was created in the eyes of mainstream Disciples.

Dean Kershner was hospitalized in January, 1943. For a number of years he had been handicapped with poor vision. After his hospital experience he had a relapse for several months and was confined to his home. An unsuccessful cataract operation was performed in the latter part of 1943, and it was apparent that his health would not permit rigorous administrative duties. After his resignation as dean, the Butler University Board of Directors, on April 12, 1944, appointed Orman L. Shelton[61] as his successor. Shelton began his work as dean on September 1, 1944. Kershner then became dean

---

[61]Orman Leroy Shelton (1895-1959) was born in Kansas. He received the A.B. degree from Phillips University in 1929 and the D.D. degree from the same school in 1935. Shelton was ordained as a Christian Church minister in 1923. He served pastorates at Marlow, Oklahoma, 1923-25; Denison, Texas, 1928-32; Ponca City, Oklahoma, 1932-38; and Kansas City, Missouri, 1941-44; dean, School of Religion, 1944-1958; president, 1958-1959. In the period 1923-25 he was public relations director at Phillips University. He was president of the state conventions in both Oklahoma and Texas; was chairman of the Home and State Missions Planning Council of the Disciples, 1938-41; member of the Board of Managers of the United Christian Missionary Society, 1938-41; member of the Board of Trustees of the United Society, 1941-44. His affiliations included the National Association of Bible Instructors, the American Academy of Political and Social Science, and the American Association of University Professors. Shelton was author of a widely read book on church administration. It was entitled, *The Church Functioning Effectively*. At the time of his death in 1959 he was the first president of Christian Theological Seminary.

emeritus and head of the department of Christian doctrine. Shelton was formally installed on October 25, 1945. Raphael H. Miller, chairman of the School of Religion committee of the Butler Board of Directors, gave the installation charge. The speaker for the occasion was Albert W. Palmer, president of Chicago Theological Seminary.[62]

The alumni of the School of Religion instigated a program in 1944 to have the portrait of Frederick D. Kershner painted. E. Robert Andry was appointed to select the artist and complete the raising of the necessary funds. The portrait was completed in July, 1945, and hangs in the library of Christian Theological Seminary.[63]

The twenty-first year of the School of Religion opened in the fall of 1946. There were 188 students enrolled in the various sessions that year, the largest student body of any Disciple seminary.[64] There were a number of veterans in this group and former chaplains interested in refresher courses.[65]

PERSONNEL CHANGES ON THE FACULTY AND STAFF

Two new professors were added to the faculty in 1945. They were S. Marion Smith and L. Gray Burdin. Professor Smith, who had been teaching at Phillips University, was called to teach in the New Testament field, replacing Professor Harold F. Hanlin who had entered the chaplaincy. Professor Burdin took charge of the speech department in the place of Lucille Calvert who was on leave of absence. In 1946, David C. Pellett became an instructor in Semitic languages and the literature of the New Testament. The next year Frank J. Albert was added as instructor in Christian doctrine and

[62]*Indiana Christian,* November, 1944.
[63]*Indiana Christian,* September, 1944; June, July, 1945.
[64]School of Religion *Catalog,* September, 1946.
[65]*Indiana Christian,* October, 1945.

church history. A. C. Watters came to the faculty in 1958 as assistant professor of missions. Watters had been in educational work in Great Britain for twenty years; prior to that he was a missionary in India for thirteen years. W. Robert Lewis became placement secretary at the School of Religion in 1949. He came to this position from the pastorate of the Seventh Christian Church in Indianapolis. Bruce L. Kershner, head of the New Testament department, 1925-43, died in 1949. He was a brother of Dean Kershner and a former missionary to the Philippines.

Dean E. Walker, head of the church history department, was called to the presidency of Milligan College in 1949. Ronald E. Osborn succeeded him, beginning September 1, 1950. Osborn had been on the faculty of Northwest Christian College at Eugene, Oregon; before that, he was editor of *Front Rank,* Disciple youth magazine. Franklin E. Rector began service on the faculty at the same time as head of the department of town and country church. The third new faculty member to begin service in September, 1950, was Beauford A. Norris. His teaching assignment was in the field of city church and pastoral work. Professors Osborn, Rector, and Norris were officially installed at a special service in Sweeney Chapel on November 7, 1950. Henry P. Van Dusen, president of Union Theological Seminary, was the speaker for the occasion. On the death of Ernest W. Lundeen, cataloger, Thelma F. Hodges became cataloger in 1950.

James Blair Miller, for six years pastor of the Christian Church at Bethany, West Virginia, and teacher at Bethany College, joined the School of Religion faculty on February 1, 1951, to become head of the department of religious education. Later that year, William Robinson, British theologian and educator, came to the School of Religion to teach Chris-

421

tian doctrine and theology. Miller and Robinson were installed on February 5, 1952, at a special service. Wilhelm Pauck of the Federated Theological Faculty was the speaker of the occasion. Alfred R. Edyvean was appointed head of the department of speech and radio in 1951, replacing Grover B. Gordon who entered the chaplaincy. Enos E. Dowling, librarian, joined the faculty of Lincoln Bible Institute in 1951. His successor, Myrddyn W. Jones, was appointed in 1953. Walter W. Sikes of the department of social welfare of The United Christian Missionary Society became head of the department of philosophy and Christian ethics in 1952, succeeding Arthur Holmes who had retired. On November 4, 1953, an official installation service was held for Edyvean, Jones, and Sikes. Dean Liston Pope of Yale Divinity School spoke at this time on the subject, "The Role of the Christian Minister Today."

By 1953, the personnel and character of the faculty of the School of Religion was completely changed from what it had been ten years before.[66] Many of the younger men who were added had already finished most of their work on the Ph.D. degree, and they were given generous consideration in programs of upgrading their academic standing through completing their doctoral programs.

Though occasional lectureships had been presented from time to time a regular system of spring and fall lectureships was established in 1945. The spring lectureships were usually held in connection with the Indiana Christian Ministers' Retreat. By these means, students and settled ministers in Indiana became acquainted with distinguished scholars and were

---

[66]Catalog listing of faculty for 1953: Orman L. Shelton, D.D., Toyozo W. Nakarai, M.A., Ph.D., S. Marion Smith, M.A., B.D., David C. Pellett, M.A., B.D., William Robinson, M.A., D.D., S.T.D., Walter W. Sikes, M.A., B.D., M.S.T., Th.D., Frank J. Albert, B.D., Ronald E. Osborn, M.A., B.D., A. C. Watters, M.A., Ph.D., Beauford A. Norris, M.A., B.D., Ph.D., Franklin E. Rector, M.S., James Blair Miller, B.D., Alfred R. Edyvean, M.A., B.D., Ph.D., Grover B. Gordon, M.A., Arthur Holmes, M.A., Ph.D., Th.M., Th.D., LL.D.

brought up to date with current religious thought.[67] Additional special lectures were presented occasionally on particular subjects.

During the calendar year of 1950 there were 596 students enrolled in the School of Religion and in the undergraduate department of religion at Butler University. Of these, 344 had declared for full-time Christian service careers.[68] There were 332 students from thirty-five states and three foreign countries enrolled in the various sessions of the School of Religion in 1953; eighty-nine universities and colleges, and eleven seminaries were represented in the student body. At commencement in 1954, four students received B.D. degrees, nine received either the M.A. or M.S. degrees, one received an M.R.E. degree, and one the Th.M. degree.[69]

DEANS KERSHNER AND SHELTON, A COMPARISON

Though in poor health and finally blind in his later years, Dean Kershner continued to meet his classes for several years after he gave up administrative responsibilities. When his final illness and death on August 24, 1953 came, it marked the end of an era for the School of Religion. He was a leading educator among the Disciples of Christ and made a significant contribution to theological education in his times. Dean Shelton was also a man dedicated to theological education. In the first few years of his administration at the School of Religion he worked in the shadow of Dean Kershner. Through loyalty to their beloved Dean Kershner, some faculty members found it difficult to adjust to the new administration. Eventually,

---

[67]Among the lecturers who appeared from 1945 to 1953 were Dr. Reinhold Niebuhr, Dr. W. E. Hocking, Dr. R. H. Pfeiffer, Dr. William Robinson, Dr. Amos N. Wilder, Dr. George La Piana, Dr. Georges Florovsky, Dr. Halford E. Luccock, Dr. M. Searle Bates, Dr. Lewis J. Sherill, Dr. W. F. Albright, Dr. Perry E. Gresham, Dr. Douglas Horton, Dr. Emile Clavier, and Dr. Hampton Adams.

[68]*Christian-Evangelist,* August 30, 1950.

[69]School of Religion *Catalog,* September, 1954.

Dean Shelton, through patience and forbearance, won the respect of his faculty and constituency.

Both men loved their students; there was a cordial and personal relationship between the deans and each member of the student body. Kershner's background was that of a life-long scholar, author, and editor. He had very little experience in the pastoral ministry. In contrast, Shelton's background was almost completely in the pastoral ministry. He came to the School of Religion from several successful pastorates among outstanding congregations. In his editorial work on both the *Christian-Evangelist* and *Christian Standard,* Kershner served before the issues which caused dissension between the cooperative and independent groups had crystallized and apparently conceived his role as that of being a mediator between the two, a mediator whose views were weighted on the conservative side. Shelton, on the other hand, because of a lifetime on the front lines with the cooperative movement and years of working with agencies of the brotherhood was much more sensitive to actual brotherhood needs and more aware of the trends of his times toward an ecumenical fellowship. In a patient, inoffensive, and quiet manner he introduced a new philosophy of seminary education to the institution he served. Though he respected faculty members and students who were inclined toward anti-agency and anti-International Convention views, he consistently and in a Christian way began integrating the School of Religion into the mainstream of the Disciples of Christ.

New professors called in the Shelton administration were encouraged to serve the organized life of the brotherhood whenever and however possible. Kershner was inclined to leave such activity to the initiative of the men themselves. Shelton, perceptive in the choice of faculty members, seemed to have the ability to see a prospective professor's potential as a scholar and as a religious leader even before he gained such recognition through achievement. He insisted that budget provision be made for professors to attend meetings of the learned societies and share in the experience of other scholars. A special achievement on the part of one faculty member was a matter of rejoicing for the whole faculty. Shelton was also very generous in giving blocks of time to professors who were completing their doctoral programs. He was truly ecumenical in his views and cooperated wholeheartedly with local and state church federations and the national and world councils of churches. He brought outstanding scholars to the school for lectureships so that students could appreciate contributions made outside the ranks of the Disciples of Christ. Through summer institutes he provided a means of "refresher" courses for ministers of the brotherhood. Dean Shelton was never satisfied with the school as it was; his program was to upgrade the faculty, upgrade the curriculum, upgrade the academic and spiritual life of the students, and upgrade the church on all levels.

Both Kershner and Shelton had one thing in common. They wanted to provide good ministers—and many of them—for the church. Both were ambitious to make the School of Religion the largest seminary in the brotherhood. With a two-day curriculum which allowed their students to put a primary emphasis on their pastoral duties, and with the admission of great numbers of students from unaccredited schools, seminary life became an adjunct to the student's experience rather than the center of it. Dean Shelton was aware of this and knew that such a program jeopardized the standing of the school, but his obsession to reach as many students as possible made him act very slowly to correct this situation.

Reflections, 1942-1953

If the history of Hoosier Disciples, 1931-1941, can be understood only in the context of the great depression, it can be understood only in the context of two wars and unparalleled prosperity in the period, 1942-1953. No one could have imagined in the 'thirties the nature of the problems of the 'forties. The two periods were entirely different. Yet it would seem that the Christian churches of Indiana met their new challenges quite realistically, and for the most part, effectively. They were more bewildered by the depression than they were by the two wars. Both the depression and the wars had a leavening effect on the churches; the depression turned their views inwardly, and the wars turned them outwardly. Perhaps the tensions of both decades served to equip them better for the most bewildering period of all, the space age.

XII

Confrontation with Responsibility
1954-1965

HOOSIER DISCIPLES HAD TO ADJUST to a new and different world in the years following the great depression and World War II. The possibility of annihilation through atomic warfare, the dangers of "fallout" from atomic testing, the population explosion, the breaking up of colonial empires, the realignment of nations into capitalistic and communistic groupings, the freedom movement of American Negroes, automation in industry, the conquest of space, and the trend toward union of great religious bodies caused no little concern for the churches. The new world was a reality. Scientists, statesmen, theologians, and educators were confronted with baffling responsibilities.

An awareness of the need of the church to come to grips with the state of the world was disclosed at the State Convention in Evansville. Held in 1954, it marked the first time such a gathering had convened in southwest Indiana in 115 years. F. W. Wiegmann of Indianapolis was the presiding officer. Rallying under the slogan, "Christ's Call to Mission," the missionary aspects of the Christian movement were stressed. C. M. Yocum, retiring executive secretary of the foreign division of The United Christian Missionary Society,

427

labeled the Christian Church of Indiana as the "mother of the foreign missions movement." He stated at Evansville that three of the first five Disciple missionaries to India and two of the first missionaries to Japan were Hoosiers. Mae Yoho Ward, secretary of Latin American missions, made a plea for the church to hear the call of the world for food, shelter, clothing, and spiritual sustenance. She pointed out that this could be accomplished only when Christians practice what they preach and live as they pray. A resolution destined to have far-reaching consequences was passed by the convention. It called for a study commission to make a three-year survey of Christian work in Indiana with a view toward presenting proposals for greater coordination and efficiency in the future. The convention also approved of a resolution calling for church support of the School of Religion by underwriting the School's annual operating budget to the extent of $30,000 each year.[1]

Unification Procedures, 1955-1958

The State Convention met at Richmond in 1955; George L. Florence of Seymour served as president. The First Christian Church of this city, founded by Elijah Goodwin in 1859, was the host congregation. Special group meetings, workshops, reports of the state work, and meetings for young people were featured at this gathering. The initial report of the study commission was accepted at the convention, and the commission was advised to proceed with a plan of merger which would embrace the Indiana Christian Missionary Association, the Indiana Department of Religious Education, the Indiana Christian Women's Fellowship, and other such agencies so

---

[1]*Christian-Evangelist*, June 23, 1954.

that a plan could be presented for consideration at the next annual convention.[2]

Frank G. Helme, minister of the Main Street Christian Church of Rushville, was president of the State Convention at Elkhart in 1956. There were 4,072 delegates, a record number. In his opening address, President Helme stressed the need of man's responsibility to know God, build on the heritage of the past, understand himself as a reborn person, and sacrifice as much as necessary to demonstrate his love.[3]

The program of the 118th State Convention, held at Indianapolis in 1957, centered on the theme, "Thy Mission High Fulfilling." Neither the fact that it rained constantly nor that sessions were scattered between the Northwood, Third, and Downey Avenue churches, the Murat Temple, and the School of Religion dampened the enthusiasm of over 5,000 Hoosier Disciples who registered for this meeting. Theo O. Fisher, minister of the Northwood Christian Church in Indianapolis, presided over the sessions. In the Sunday pulpit exchange some fifty ministers of the convention were guest speakers in Indianapolis churches. Mrs. George F. Gill, president of the Indiana Christian Women's Fellowship, challenged Indiana women to accept a goal of $175,000 for the total work of the Disciples during the next fiscal year. The study commission, appointed to work on a unification plan, proposed the Constitution and By Laws necessary for operation under this plan, and this instrument was accepted by the convention. Action

---

[2]Convention speakers: William Robinson, Jesse M. Bader, Franklin E. Rector, Miss Mareta Smoot, Mrs. Dorothy M. Dolbey, Roy A. Burkhart, and C. O. Hawley. F. E. Davison previewed his book, *Thru the Rear View Mirror,* at the ministers' luncheon. Mrs. Barton A. Johnson of Covington, Kentucky, spoke at the ministers' wives' luncheon. Dean O. L. Shelton was devotional leader for the convention, and William Robinson presented the Bible studies.

[3]*Indiana Christian,* June, 1956; *Christian-Evangelist,* August 22, 1956. Program personalities: William Robinson, F. E. Davison, Ira G. Langston, Harlie L. Smith, Beauford A. Norris, C. O. Hawley, and Mrs. Emory Ross.

was also taken on the ordination of ministers. It was decided that ordination services could take place at the State Convention upon request of the candidate's sponsoring congregation if such request had the support of three local congregations. The convention, however, encouraged only such applicants for ordination as had completed or nearly completed work on either the B.D., M.R.E., or M.S.M. degrees. Harmon O. Pritchard, actuary of the Pension Fund, was elected to his fourteenth term as treasurer of the convention.[4]

The program of the State Convention at Fort Wayne in 1958 sounded the theme, "Today's Church Faces Tomorrow's World." Raphael H. Miller, Jr., pastor of the East Side Christian Church at Evansville, was president. George W. Wascovich, Robert T. Beck, and E. Clayton Gooden were the host pastors. With Constitution and By Laws for unification of the state work already adopted it was necessary for the convention to take action on enabling acts so that the new organization could be effective by July 1, 1959. A finance committee was appointed to work with the existing boards in preparing a tentative budget for the fiscal year 1959-60 to be presented to the Commission on Brotherhood Finance in 1959. The study commission was empowered to request the nominating committees of the three existing boards to serve with the State Convention nominating committee for 1959 to aid in the selection of personnel for offices in the unified structure. A campus life commission had been created the year before, but without financial resources. This commission recommended that a consultation on campus life be called by the convention through the commission in the fall of 1958 to study the re-

---

[4] *Indiana Christian*, June, 1957; *Christian-Evangeilst*, May 6, July 22, 29, 1957. Among convention speakers: John Paul Pack, Mae Yoho Ward, Halford E. Luccock, and Robert G. Nelson. James R. Carley of the School of Religion was in charge of the music.

sponsibiilty and opportunity of the campus life program in Indiana.[5]

Institutional Expansion

In response to a genuine need in Indiana for an outlet specializing in books and supplies for Christian churches, the Bethany Book Store was established. Located in the Missions Building, it was dedicated November 15, 1955.[6]

The Charles T. Paul Library in the Missions Building was organized by Mrs. Ada Mosher who served as its voluntary librarian for eleven years following her retirement from the Cleveland, Ohio, public library system. After her death in 1956, her brother, H. B. McCormick, former president of the United Society, established the Ada M. Mosher memorial section. This missionary library of 30,000 volumes is a valuable adjunct to the work of The United Christian Missionary Society. Miss Doris Autrey is the present librarian.[7]

The United Society was motivated in 1955 to reactivate the College of Missions through an annual summer session at Crystal Lake, Michigan. This session supplements the preparation of Disciples' missionaries by providing orientation to policy and program of the United Society. Ralph T. Palmer is dean.[8]

The cornerstone for the new headquarters of the Board of Church Extension was laid on June 17, 1958. Located at 110 Downey Avenue in Indianapolis, the building was an architectural innovation. A circular structure, known as an

[5]*Indiana Christian*, April, May, 1958; *Christian-Evangelist*, June 23, 1958. Speakers: Mrs. W. K. Evans, president of the International Christian Women's Fellowship; William G. West, Chattanooga, Tennessee; and True D. Morse, U. S. undersecretary of agriculture. Daily Bible lectures were given by S. Marion Smith of the School of Religion.

[6]*Christian-Evangelist*, November 9, 1955.

[7]*World Call*, July-August, 1954; February, 1957; *Christian-Evangelist*, December 5, 1956.

[8]*World Call*, February, 1957.

"office in the round," it was dedicated December 9, 1958.[9]

Ground was broken on March 19, 1958 for a four-story office wing and adjoining auditorium for the Missions Building in Indianapolis. Dedication ceremonies were held on March 4, 1959. The new addition provided space for several new offices; the new auditorium was built to accommodate 300 persons. The International Convention moved its offices from downtown Indianapolis to the new building. Several other agencies were also thus provided with more adequate quarters.[10]

Early in 1965 the Association of Christian Churches in Indiana became one of six bodies cooperating in building an Interchurch Center on land provided by Christian Theological Seminary on the west end of its new campus. The new building, in addition to housing the Association will provide headquarters for the Indiana Synod of the Presbyterian Church, the Indiana Area of the Methodist Church, the Indiana-Kentucky Conference of the United Church of Christ, the Indiana Council of Churches, and the Church Federation of Greater Indianapolis. The new Interchurch Center is expected to be a dramatic architectural symbol of ecumenical reality and may be ready for occupancy in late 1966.

Personnel Changes in the State Work

Dean W. Brigham of San Angelo, Texas, became associate secretary in the department of men's work of the State Association on April 1, 1958. He had been civilian personnel director at Goodfellow Air Force Base in Texas. James H. Behler, who had been associated with the United Society in the department of home missions, was appointed executive

[9]*Christian-Evangelist*, May 19, July 14, 1958. *Christian Evangelist-Front Rank*, January 4, 1959; *World Call*, July-August, September, 1958; February, 1959.

[10]*Christian-Evangelist*, April 7, 1958; *Christian Evangelist-Front Rank*, March 15, 1959; *World Call*, May, 1959.

director of the Indianapolis Christian Church Union, beginning April 1, 1958. He succeeded Orville W. Williams who has resigned. Behler was succeeded in this position by Ronald L. Secrist on July 1, 1961. Ephraim D. Lowe, executive secretary of the State Association since 1941, retired on March 1, 1959. F. E. Davison was named interim executive secretary to serve until the unified board had an opportunity to choose a new general secretary for the state work. Davison served in this capacity for four months. The board was not yet ready to name the new secretary at the time Davison resigned, so Lonne H. Hass, director of town and country work for the State Association since 1950, was asked to take this interim position. Hass continued with the state organization until September 1, 1960, when he accepted a position as national director in the department of church development of the United Society. John W. Harms,[11] executive vice president of the Church Federation of Greater Chicago, became general secretary of the Association of Christian Churches in Indiana on January 1, 1960. Harms, an experienced administrator in the field of organized religious work, was already acquainted with the Christian churches in Indiana, having been state director of religious education, 1934-1938.

Unification in Practice

Hoosier Disciples gathered in the historic old city of Vincennes for their annual State Convention in 1959. Frank

---

[11]John W. Harms (1902-   ) was born at Blue Springs, Nebraska. He received the A.B. degree from Phillips University in 1931, and the M.A. degree from the University of Chicago in 1952. The honorary degree of LL.D. was awarded to him by Phillips University in 1952; Christian Theological Seminary granted him the honorary D.D. degree in 1960. He was business manager of the Central Christian Church at Enid, Oklahoma, 1926-1929; director of religious education (Eastern Area) of The United Christian Missionary Society, 1931-1934; state director of religious education for Indiana, 1934-1938; executive secretary of the Council of Churches of Maryland and Delaware, 1938-1942; vice president of the Church Federation of Greater Chicago, 1943-1959; and general secretary of the Association of Christian Churches in Indiana, 1960-. He was ordained in the Disciples of Christ ministry in 1931. Harms was a member of the Disciples' delegation to the first assembly of the World Council of Churches at Amsterdam, Holland, in 1948. A contributor to many periodicals, he is also author of the book, *Prayer in the Market Place,* 1958.

E. Davison served in a dual capacity on this occasion; he was interim general secretary of the Association and president of the convention. The convention theme, "The Church—A Creative Fellowship," was emphasized by the speakers and program participants.[12] A colorful academic procession by the faculty of Christian Theological Seminary and a recognition service for retired General Secretary Ephraim D. Lowe; highlighted the events, but the thoughts of the delegates centered primarily on the new program of unification of the state organization.

The study commission on unification, appointed by F. W. Wiegmann at the convention in 1954, met regularly for three years to draft a plan for the unification of all departments of the state work. This was a large and representative group; sessions, many of which were held at either the School of Religion or the Downey Avenue Church, were well attended. Few precedents were found for the new undertaking. Dean O. L. Shelton, a specialist in the field of church administration among the Disciples, was often called upon for assistance. He gave valuable advice concerning a basic philosophy for the unification program. By the time of the 120th State Convention in 1959 the proposals of the study commission had been acted upon by the convention, the Constitution and By Laws received approval, and enabling acts had been passed; unification was to be a reality by July 1, 1959. The boards of the State Association, the Christian Women's Fellowship, and the department of Christian Education were to become one. All agencies and commissions of existing boards were to work under the direction of one new board to be elected at the Vincennes convention. The plan anticipated a unified office

[12]Convention speakers: F. E. Davison, Ronald E. Osborn, Beauford A. Norris, William Martin Smith, Roger T. Nooe, and Margaret Lawrence. Rosa Page Welch directed the convention music.

434

for those on the staffs of the three former organizations.[13] With unification, the name Indiana Christian Missionary Association ceased to exist. As of July 1, 1959, all the functions, programs, holdings, and legal obligations were taken over by the new organization which identified itself as the Association of Christian Churches in Indiana.[14]

With a unified board once established, it was necessary to have a planning conference to consider immediate and future steps to be taken by the new organization. Such a conference was held at the Meadlawn Christian Church in Indianapolis, January 18-20, 1960. The first day of the conference served to orient those in attendance to the nature of the task before them. Areas for specific consideration were lifted up at this time. The national long range program of the Disciples, called a "Decade of Decision," was to get under way in 1960. This program sought to encourage growth in evangelism, stewardship, Christian education, and world outreach. The Meadlawn conference took into account state-level planning for the first year of the Decade of Decision and those to follow. John W. Harms, new general secretary for the Association, had his initiation into the state work on this occasion.[15]

The next step after the unification of the various boards of the state, was unification of the staffs of these organizations. On October 31, 1960, the new board unanimously adopted the plan of the personnel committee as submitted by its chairman, Raphael H. Miller, Jr. This plan proposed the staff to be made up as follows: John W. Harms, general secretary; E. Lyle Harvey and Donald O. Legg, associate general secretaries; Mrs. Ward I. Nicholas, associate secretary for the Chris-

---

[13]*Indiana Christian*, July, 1955; February, April, June, November, 1958; May, 1959; *Christian-Evangelist*, July 29, 1957; June 23, 1958.

[14]*Indiana Christian*, September, 1959.

[15]*Indiana Christian*, February, 1960.

tian Women's Fellowship; Dean Brigham, associate secretary for the Christian Men's Fellowship; Harold R. Johnson, associate secretary for church life development, Christian education, and other functional services; Mrs. Doris Demaree, director of leadership development; Ronald L. Secrist, associate secretary for Greater Indianapolis; and Vinton D. Bradshaw, director of student-church relations (in cooperation with Christian Theological Seminary).[16]

While Hoosier Disciples were experiencing unification of their organizations on a state level the program and services of the National Christian Missionary Convention (Negro Assembly organized at Nashville, Tennessee in 1917) merged with the program and services of The United Christian Missionary Society, effective July 1, 1960. Some members of the National Convention staff and board were placed on the staff and policy-making agency boards of the United Society.[17] The Market Street Christian Church in Carthage and the Second Christian Church in Indianapolis were the only two churches in Indiana affiliated with the National Christian Missionary Convention; both had long since been integrated into the Indiana Christian Missionary Association.

The State Convention at South Bend in 1960 was not looked upon as several simultaneous gatherings of state-level organizations holding annual meetings, but as the church in official session in Indiana. Unification had made the convention the corporate voice of the Indiana brotherhood. The convention theme, "We Now Unite—Our Christ Revealing," was an expression of this new image. Monroe G. Schuster of Anderson was president of the convention; the host ministers

---

[16]*Indiana Christian,* November, 1960.

[17]*Christian Evangelist-Front Rank,* October 18, November 1, 1959. When the 45th Assembly of the N.M.C. was held at Roanoke, Virginia, in 1961, William K. Fox, president, and Emmett J. Dickson, executive secretary, claimed that the merger of staffs strengthened the churches affiliated with the National Missionary Convention.

were Hartford C. Inlow, Donald B. Taylor, and Raymond D. Harris. A vast number of resolutions were passed. They were concerned with the controlling or eliminating of nuclear weapons testing, fostering temperance education in the churches, developing a program of information on Disciple polity for new members, approving the expansion and development plans for Christian Theological Seminary, and encouraging emphasis on family life programs. Churches were encouraged to make no discrimination among races in their memberships, the Decade of Decision was endorsed, and it was recommended that special stress be given to the traditional heritage of the state convention and definite goals be set for the 125th state convention in 1964.[18] These resolutions were offered and adopted so quickly it called attention to the need of preconvention procedure for such proposals and greater use of commissions and committees, especially in the area of social action. The convention approved a proposal by F. W. Wiegmann, chairman of the State Board, that three properties on Downey Avenue in Indianapolis be purchased for use as headquarters for the new state office, the churches to raise $50,000 for this purpose before June 30, 1960.[19]

No Longer a Provincial People

It was apparent by the middle of the twentieth century that Hoosier Disciples could no longer be considered a provincial people. Over 200 Indiana Christian Church members from 45 Indiana communities attended the World Convention of the Christian Churches at Edinburgh, Scotland, in 1960. This probably testifies as much for their economic stability as for interest in the world-wide aspects of their faith.

---

[18]*Indiana Christian*, April, May, June, 1960. Convention speakers: Harold E. Fey, Spencer P. Austin, Doyle Zaring, Kathryn Turney Garten, Irvin E. Lunger, Mae Yoho Ward, James L. Stoner, Samuel A. Carruth, and John W. Harms.

[19]*Indiana Christian*, June, 1960.

Nevertheless, the public image of the Christian Church, for whatever it is worth, was greatly improved in Indiana by this time. Missionary headquarters, a university, and a seminary at Indianapolis gave evidence of a large concentration of religious leadership in the state. Lay members of Christian churches were prominent in the cultural, economic, and political life of Indiana. Matthew E. Welsh, trustee and elder in First Christian Church of Vincennes, was elected Governor of Indiana in 1960. J. Irwin Miller, Columbus industrialist, was elected for a three-year term as President of the National Council of the Churches of Christ in the U. S. A. that same year. His election marked a new place for the laity in the life of American Protestantism. Miller, a member of North Christian Church in Columbus, also served on the Board of Directors of Butler University and as chairman of the trustees of Christian Theological Seminary. On July 1, 1962, Elvis J. Stahr, Jr., former secretary of the army, member of the Christian Church, became President of Indiana University. Since then, he has become an elder in the First Christian Church, Bloomington.

Conventions at Anderson and Lafayette

J. Maurice Thompson of Huntington was president of the 122nd State Convention held at Anderson in 1961. His keynote address was on the convention theme, "Fervent in Spirit, Serving the Lord." The usual number of dinners, luncheons, committee meetings, and workshops were held. The big decision of the convention, however, was the response made to an unusual proposal by the Commission on Budgets and Promotional Relationships. It was a request for an emergency drive to raise $2,738,426 in a three-year period as Indiana's initial responsibility to the Decade of Decision capital funds goal of $7,745,454 for participating agencies on the state and national level. No such comprehensive program had ever been attempted before by any Disciple state organization; nevertheless, after thorough discussion the following resolution carried:

Resolved: That the State Convention approve the Indiana Commission's plan to pool all capital needs of the national and state agencies for the years 1960-64, the total amounting to approximately $2,738,426, and to conduct a special three-year "crash campaign" to secure the total objective from individuals as well as church budgets . . .

In June, 1961, the Association made the decisions necessary to implement this program. In the fall of that year the Capital Funds project was brought to the attention of the churches through rallies in the various districts throughout the state.[20]

The annual report of the officers and staff to the State Convention at Anderson in 1962 indicated that the staff had been brought up to full strength during the year. Edwin R. Allender had become associate secretary for Christian education and executive chairman of the division of functional church services; Robert R. Smythe had been appointed director of youth services and family life education, and Leon K. Weatherman had taken the place made vacant by Dean Brigham as associate secretary for men's work. The Indiana Christian Women's Fellowship, Mrs. H. I. Rudduck, president, reported that 750 Indiana women attended the International CWF Quadrennial Assembly on the Purdue University campus in July, 1961. The Fellowship then had 280 organized units in local churches with a total membership of 50,060 women. The offerings raised through the Indiana Christian Women's Fellowship in

---

[20]*Indiana Christian*, April, May, 1961. Among speakers at the convention: Alfred Dudley Ward, P. Hunter Beckelhymer, Howard Anderson, Monroe G. Schuster, J. Maurice Thompson, Mrs. J. Warren Hastings, F. W. Wiegmann, Richard E. Lentz, Russell J. Humbert, and A. Dale Fiers. George A. Harris directed the communion service.

the past year amounted to $170,312. The Christian Men's Fellowship sponsored three retreats during the year, reaching 476 men. Ernest Fawcett of Kokomo was president of this group. The report on the college and university campus ministry showed that Clayton F. Daugherty had been minister and director of the Purdue Christian Foundation; James F. Martin, through the Campbell House of First Christian Church at Bloomington, had directed the Indiana University campus ministry; Mr. and Mrs. James Quisenberry directed the Campbell fellowship at Central Christian Church in Terre Haute, serving Indiana State Teachers' College students, and Robert H. Anderson guided the ministry to students at Ball State College through the program of the Disciples' Student Fellowship of the Hazelwood Christian Church in Munice. A Campus Christian Life Foundation had been established in Indianapolis, the work being done through Vernon H. Scott of the University Park Christian Church.[21]

Howard Anderson of Bloomington was president of the 123rd State Convention at Lafayette in 1962. It was described in the *Indiana Christian* as a "lively" convention, the business sessions being well attended. This convention held much interest because by then the state work was unified under a new board, there was a unified staff to administer the program, and an audacious United Capital Funds Appeal campaign was about to be launched. The convention was at last moving toward responsible action on current issues. This did not mean that past history was downgraded; in fact, it was lifted up. On request of the convention the state board appointed a history committee (this became a commission later) to develop an authoritative and definitive history of the Christian Churches, and to provide the historical emphasis for the coming 125th

---

[21]*Indiana Christian*, April, 1962.

aniversary convention in 1964. Ronald E. Osborn, dean and professor of church history at Christian Theological Seminary accepted the chairmanship of this committee. The theme of the convention, "Provided with Power," was well chosen.[22]

The United Capital Funds Appeal

A state-wide rally attended by 1,200 Hoosier Disciples to launch the drive for the United Capital Funds Appeal was held at the Indiana State Fairgrounds in Indianapolis on October 24, 1962. It was the first of its kind in Hoosierland. The $2,738,426 goal was based on the needs of the agencies as follows: the State Association, $1,054,515; Christian Theological Seminary, $1,155,000; National Benevolent Association, $105,192; United Christian Missionary Society, $322,-464; Disciples of Christ Historical Society, $5,355, and the Board of Church Extension, $95,900.[23]

At a campaign luncheon meeting held in Indianapolis on November 30, 1962, Doyle Zaring, general lay chairman of the drive, read a letter which served as an exciting incentive for the successful completion of the program. It was from Miss Elsie I. Sweeney, president of the Irwin-Sweeney-Miller Foundation of Columbus, Indiana. The letter stated that the Foundation had made a commitment of $300,000 toward the

---

[22]*Indiana Christian,* March, April, May, 1962. Among convention speakers: Leslie R. Smith, president of the International Convention; Howard Anderson, pastor of First Christian Church at Bloomington; Beauford A. Norris, president of Christian Theological Seminary; Henry A. McCanna, director of the town and country department of the National Council of Churches; Fred Hoskins of Chicago Theological Seminary; and Mae Yoho Ward, vice president of The United Christian Missionary Society.

[23]*Indiana Christian,* September, 1962. Leadership personnel of the campaign: Doyle Zaring of Indianapolis, general lay chairman; Mrs. Frank Thomas of Anderson and Floyd A. Hines of Connersville, associate general chairmen; Theo O. Fisher, pastor of Northwood Christian Church, Indianapolis, R. H. Miller, Jr., pastor of East Side Christian Church, Evansville, and George E. Wascovich, pastor of First Christian Church, Fort Wayne, general minister co-chairmen. Four general women co-chairmen who led in organizing the work among the districts were Mrs. H. I. Rudduck of Mishawaka, Mrs. Forrest Brock of Richmond, Mrs. J. T. Moore of Seymour, and Mrs. C. A. Underwood of Gosport. Donald O. Legg of the Association staff served as publicity and information chairman, and Clyde R. Yater as treasurer.

total goal of $2,738,426. In addition, the Foundation promised another grant of $200,000 when the total goal was reached. Miss Sweeney wrote, "I believe you know that this represents the interest in the Appeal of myself, Mr. and Mrs. Robert S. Tangeman, and Mr. and Mrs. Irwin Miller." Statewide solicitation began on January 6, 1963. The Capital Funds Appeal was properly interpreted in terms of church development, buildings, equipment, and physical improvements, and was well received by Disciples in Indiana.[24]

The United Capital Funds Appeal exceeded its goal by $523 by the time of deadline date of November 30, 1963. This earned Indiana Disciples the additional challenge gift of $200,-000 from the Irwin-Sweeney-Miller Foundation for a total campaign achievement of $2,938,949. It was, according to John W. Harms, the boldest venture in faith Indiana churches had taken in the 125 years of their cooperative life.[25]

Preparing for an Expanded Program

Under unification of state organizations, responsibility for the continuing program of the Association became the primary concern of the State Board. The Board is made up of three persons elected from each of the fourteen districts, consisting of 42 persons in all. The chairmen of the program units and district presidents also meet with the Board in an *ex-officio* capacity. This Board met six times during the 1962-63 fiscal year. In this period the Board took action on several important matters; most of these were policy items related to the receiving and purchasing of property for new churches, grants-in-aid to needy congregations, and safeguarding property for use by the Christian Churches in Indiana. Among

---

[24]*Indiana Christian*, December, 1962.
[25]*The Christian*, December 29, 1963; *Indiana Christian*, January, 1964; *World Call*, March, 1964.

other actions, the State Board also reaffirmed its intention to purchase the old Third Christian Church building in Indianapolis and use it for the experimental "Broadway Inner City Project" in cooperation with The United Christian Missionary Society. Altogether, the State Board considered nearly fifty separate actions involving policy decisions and future long-range program planning.[26]

The Central Christian Church of Terre Haute, R. Powell Mead, minister, entertained the 124th State Convention of Hoosier Disciples in 1963. G. Lavon Fisher of Marion presided over the sessions. Disciples were in the midst of their United Capital Funds Appeal at the time. Though this program received proper emphasis the convention also looked forward to its 125th anniversary in 1964 by sounding an historical note. The history commission sponsored a special luncheon which was well attended, especially by local church historians. They were encouraged to write and publish historical material on their congregations. Vignettes, covering interesting features in Hoosier Disciple history, were sandwiched in between the regular addresses. It was announced that Henry K. Shaw, librarian at Christian Theological Seminary, had been commissioned to write a new history of the Christian Churches in Indiana to be published in 1966. It was to be considered as a means of continuing the historical emphasis of the 125th anniversary of the State Convention and as a contribution to Indiana's sesquicentennial celebration that year. The recommendations committee, under the leadership of Mrs. Ronald E. (Naomi) Osborn, chairman, set a high standard for responsible action at this convention. Instead of meeting during the convention only, this committee had an all-day session in January, several sessions during the plan-

---

[26]*Indiana Christian*, April, 1963.

ning conference in March, an all-day meeting in April, and finally another all-day session the day before the convention opened. Adequate preparation was thus made for the business sessions, and it was possible to transact convention business more efficiently.[27]

The 125th Anniversary Convention

The program committee (convention officers and executive committee) made a strong effort to guarantee that the State Convention in 1964 would be the most outstanding one in Hoosier Disciple history. One hundred twenty-five years had passed since the first State Meeting had been held in the old Kentucky Avenue meetinghouse (Central Christian Church) in Indianapolis. The theme, "Our Rich Heritage—A Challenging Future," was emphasized by the program participants. From the opening session on Thursday, April 2, to the climactic special session on Sunday afternoon, the heritage of the churches was lifted up. Five dramatic presentations, "Procession of the Churches Across 125 Years," were given. These dramatic sketches, written by Mrs. Jay R. (Audrey) Calhoun, opened with a portrayal of present times and worked back to the period, 1800-1839. Sessions were held in the spacious new Clowes Hall on the Butler University campus. Other features of this convention included: Christian unity sermons on Sunday in Indianapolis churches by guest ministers from across the state, dedication of a bronze plaque marking the first State Meeting at Central Christian Church, dedication of the main entrance way of the new campus of Christian Theological Seminary, presentation of the drama, "The Cup

---

[27]*Indiana Christian,* February, March, April, May, September, 1963; *The Christian,* June 2, 1963. Featured speakers: Mr. and Mrs. Juan Marcos Rivera, Indiana missionary partners; Harley E. Patterson, pastor of Central Christian Church, Indianapolis; Mrs. Helen Pearson, vice president of International CWF; Howard E. Short, editor, *The Christian;* and Floyd A. Hines, churchman of Connersville. Howard E. Anderson, First Christian Church, Bloomington, was the morning devotional leader.

of Trembling," by the CTS players under the direction of Alfred R. Edyvean, youth sessions at Northwood Christian Church, and a history luncheon at the State Fairgrounds. On the last named occasion there was a recognition of the history commission members, local church historians, and descendants of pioneer Disciples. Willis R. Jones, president of the Disciples of Christ Historical Society, gave the featured address, "Meet Elder John O'Kane."

Doyle Zaring, layman of the University Park Christian Church in Indianapolis, was president of this convention. There was 3,200 registrations, and Clowes Hall was filled for every session.[28]

Commission on the Ministry

One of the functions of the State Association staff across the years was to counsel with churches and ministers about ministerial relations. When the commission on the ministry was appointed this function came under its sponsorship. One of the first tasks of the new commission was to try to develop a recommended process for the recruitment, licensing, ordination, and calling of ministers. Attention was given to compensation, length of tenure, and how to achieve the highest level of churchmanship by ministers and congregations. Myron C. Cole of Indianapolis was first chairman of this group. He was followed by Frank G. Helme, pastor of the Main Street Christian Church, Rushville. On the retirement of Frank G. Helme, Herbert C. Barnard, minister of the Eastgate Christian

---

[28]*Indiana Christian*, January, March, April, May, 1964; *The Christian*, April 26, 1964. History commission: Ronald E. Osborn, chairman; L. H. Carpenter, vice chairman; Miss Elsie I. Sweeney, secretary; J. Edward Moseley, Paul Million, Jr., Miss Doris Autrey, Mrs. William Park, William H. Book, Mrs. John Boyd, Henry K. Shaw, Wayne Guthrie, Louis A. Warren, Mrs. T. W. Nakarai, John W. Harms, and Mrs. John Borland. Convention speakers: Doyle Zaring, Ronald E. Osborn, W. A. Welsh, Miss Helen Spaulding, Mrs. James D. Wyker, John Oliver Nelson, Perry E. Gresham, Charles E. Wells, Willis R. Jones, and Henry K. Shaw. L. Eugene Brown led the Bible devotions.

445

Church in Indianapolis, became chairman. The commission, working on a philosophy for a responsible ordination process, proceeded on the basis that those who entered the full-time ministry as a life service should be ordained, and that the ordination of ministers was a concern of the whole church even though it was primarily a local church function. The interdependence of congregations was also recognized in the procedure of ordination. It was recommended, therefore, that two or more congregations with state-wide representatives of the churches through the Association, join in establishing an ordination council which recommends or disapproves a candidate for ordination. If the local church and the commission grants approval the act of ordination is carried out by the local church with representatives of all the churches (through the commission) participating. The new policy did not state that candidates should have the B.D. or other professional degree in religion, but it presumed that in most instances such degrees should be considered as minimum preparation for the ministry and that ordination with the approval of the commission should not take place otherwise. In establishing this policy the commission took into consideration the suggestions of the central committee on ministerial services of the Home and State Missions Planning Council, the national office of ministerial services of The United Christian Missionary Society, and other state commissions on the ministry which had worked on the upgrading of ministerial leadership.[29]

Descendents of the Pioneers

As part of the continuing emphasis on history and by recommendation of the history commission, Indiana descen-

---

[29]*Indiana Christian*, April, 1961. A complete statement on the policy and procedure for licensing and ordaining ministers which went into effect on July 1, 1963, as recommended by the commission on the ministry, appeared in the *Indiana Christian*, February, 1964.

dants of pioneer Disciples were honored at district conventions in the fall of 1964. A pioneer Disciple was defined as one who was a member of the Christian Church in 1839 or earlier, in Indiana or some other state; a descendant is one who traced his/her ancestry to such a person. Attractive certificates were awarded to "descendants," and their names were published in the October, 1964, issue of *Indiana Christian,* and in succeeding numbers.

Guide Lines to Restructure

When unification was adopted in 1959 a Study Commission was created by the State Convention to complete the process. The work of this commission came to fruition under the leadership of F. W. Wiegmann who had first proposed reorganization several years before this. Recommendations of the commission were adopted by the State Conventions in 1964 and 1965. These recommendations greatly strengthened the Association by giving its two main structures, the State Convention and the State Board, clearly defined functions. The Study Commission is under commitment for continuing study of structure and function in order that the Association may have the necessary guide lines to meet the needs of changing times.

Leadership Development Institutes were held in 1962 and 1963. They were designed for district and state leaders in Indiana as an expression of the new national concept of leadership training which proposed to probe deeply into basic considerations of the life of the church. A "position paper" entitled, "Concept of the Church in Indiana," grew out of the 1963 institute. As a result of the work of these institutes there was a staff recommendation to the State Convention concerning a broad state-wide emphasis upon a study of the nature of the church with the "position paper" being used as the basis of this study. In 1964-65 a series of sub-district conferences of six-hour

447

duration were held, involving leaders from many Christian churches in Indiana. This project took the place of restructure participation meetings sponsored by the International Convention of the Christian Churches.[30]

State Convention, 1965

The Convention[31] was held at Marion in 1965; Mrs. George E. Gill of Indianapolis was president. Mrs. Gill, an elder in the Downey Avenue Christian Church at Indianapolis, was the first woman ever to be elected to this position. With the success of the 125th anniversary convention of 1964 still in focus, delegates went to Marion in 1965 anticipating that this gathering would surely be an anticlimax; they were agreeably surprised. They returned home feeling that this was one of the great conventions. They were inspired by the addresses, amused by the vignettes, and moved by the drama, "The Wounded," presented by CTS Players. Delegates were also impressed with the "Message on the State of the Church in Indiana," a special committee report prepared by a group of twenty-five state leaders for presentation at the opening session. The committee was made up of people with specialized vocational experience and recognized leadership in the church. Raphael H. Miller, minister of the East Side Christian Church,

---

[30]*Indiana Christian*, April, 1964. *See* "Concept of the Church in Indiana" (fourth draft of position paper originally prepared by Lester G. McAllister). Indianapolis: Study Commission of the State Convention, F. W. Wiegmann, chairman, March, 1964.

[31]*Indiana Christian*, March, April, 1965. Featured speakers at the convention: James Jeffrey, director of the Fellowship of Christian Athletes; Clinton W. Marsh, director of evangelism, North Central Area, United Presbyterian Church, U.S.A.; Walter F. MacGowan, minister of the Union Avenue Christian Church in St. Louis; Virgil A. Sly, president of the United Christian Missionary Society; A. Dale Fiers, executive secretary of the International Convention of Christian Churches; Robert G. Nelson, executive secretary of the department of Africa and Jamaica, U.C.M.S.; James P. Lamberson, minister of music at Northwood Christian Church, Indianapolis; Miss Ruth May Harner, U.C.M.S. missionary to India; Lester G. McAllister, professor at Christian Theological Seminary; B. MacDonald Layne, executive director of youth work, world outreach education department, U.C.M.S.; Miss Fannie M. Bennett, division of church life and work, U.C.M.S.; and Mrs. George E. Gill, president. Mrs. Calvin L. Porter presided over the meeting of the Indiana Ministers' Wives' Association, and Harold E. Cline presided over the meeting of the Indiana Christian Ministers' Association.

Evansville, was chairman. The "message" was a realistic appraisal which pointed out strengths and weaknesses in the total life of the church and suggested direction for the future. It was the basis for discussion in the fourteen district assembly meetings during the convention. Its strong challenge for the Christian Churches (Disciples of Christ) to become relevant to life in the modern world drew some adverse criticism, but on the whole it was well received.[32]

Amendments to the Constitution and By Laws of the Association, presented in the March, 1965, number of the *Indiana Christian* and repeated in the April number, were the results of further thought and planning by the Study Commission. They were acted upon at the Marion convention.

At the beginning of the Decade of Decision and in response to general brotherhood-wide planning, some long range objectives had been developed. These included the establishing of forty to sixty new churches, building an office building for the Association, strengthening services to local churches, additional attention to college and university campuses, and improvement of camp and conference facilities at Barbee, Bedford, and Indian Lake. As a feature of the 125th anniversary of the State Convention these long range objectives were reconsidered, and revised objectives and goals for the Decade of Decision were adopted. They contained twenty-eight major objectives and fifty-seven secondary goals.[33]

Hoosier Disciples were beginning to learn who they were, where they had been, and the direction they wanted to go in the future. It was announced at this gathering that the State Conven-

[32]*Indiana Christian*, March, 1965. *See* "Message of the State of the Church in Indiana" and Discussion Guide. (Indianapolis: Message Committee, R. H. Miller, chairman, 1965).

[33]*Indiana Christian*, April, 1964. *See* "Revised Objectives and Goals for Christian Churches (Disciples of Christ) in Indiana, 1964-1970." (Indianapolis: Association of Christian Churches in Indiana, First edition, March, 1964).

tion for 1966 would be held at Vincennes with Ray H. Montgomery, Jr., as president.

Homes for Aging Disciples

In 1949, when Miss Glenn Harter was superintendent of the Emily E. Flinn Home at Marion, the structure was enlarged to provide care for more residents. By 1952 when Mrs. Fred Wolff was superintendent, a campaign was started to liquidate the capital indebtedness, complete work on the third story, and provide a hospital unit on the fourth story. Construction was started on a new wing of the building in 1962. James M. Hull was administrator of the Home by this time. The new wing was dedicated on April 19, 1964. It provided accommodations for 61 additional residents, a separate heating plant, and a lounge and recreational center. This was the third major building project since the Home was founded in 1904.[34]

Through the gift of the Martinsville Mineral Springs Hotel to the National Benevolent Association by the W. A. and Charles S. Kennedy Foundation in 1957 it was possible to establish a national pay-type home for retired persons at Martinsville. Called the Kennedy Memorial Christian Home, it was remodeled and modernized so that it could accommodate guests by November 1, 1957. The Home was dedicated on September 20, 1958. W. Dean Mason, northeast area representative of the National Benevolent Association, became administrator of the Home.[35]

Some members of First Christian Church at Greencastle established the Greencastle Christian Home in 1963. It is controlled by an autonomous corporation and serves as a non-

[34]*Indiana Christian,* July, 1953; April, 1954; June, 1960; November, 1962; April, 1964; *World Call,* December, 1962.

[35]*Indiana Christian,* June, October, 1957; September, 1958; *Christian-Evangelist,* August 18, October 13, 1958; *World Call,* January, 1958.

denominational home for men and women 62 years of age or older. There are sixty apartment units in this building and special facilities for group activities. The Greencastle Christian Home is recognized and approved by the National Benevolent Association and the committee on the aging and aged of the State Association.[36]

Butler University, 1954-1965

The period, 1954-1965, was one of enormous expansion in buildings and equipment at Butler University. The men's residence hall (later designated Ross Hall) had its beginning with a ground-breaking ceremony on February 6, 1953. By the first semester in 1954 it was being occupied by 160 students. A new addition to this building, doubling its size and capacity, was open for students in the fall of 1963. J. I. Holcomb, Indianapolis industrialist, made it possible to construct an observatory and planetarium on the Butler campus which was dedicated on November 5, 1954. Prior to this he had established the J. I. Holcomb Botanical Gardens on a twelve acre tract on the north side of the campus. Later, as a memorial to his wife, he provided funds for building a carillon bell tower on a hilltop overlooking the gardens. The bell tower was dedicated on October 4, 1959.

The centennial of the university was celebrated in 1955. Special observances were held throughout the year. The Indianapolis City Park Amphitheatre (later called the Hilton U. Brown Theatre) was started in 1954 and dedicated on June 26, 1955. It became an attractive and useful place for summer musicals and other events. Butler University summer Commencement was first held there in 1955 and in subsequent years. As a feature of the centennial observance, many

---

[36]*Indiana Christian,* July, 1963; April, 1964.

honorary degrees were awarded from time to time during the year.[37]

Hilton U. Brown, who had been a member of the Board of Directors since 1885 and president of the Board since 1903, resigned in the centennial year at the age of ninety-six. James I. Holcomb succeeded him as president of this Board.

President M. O. Ross of Butler University and Dean O. L. Shelton of the School of Religion made a simultaneous announcement in the early summer of 1958 that the Christian Foundation and the Irwin-Sweeney-Miller Foundation had given one million dollars to Butler University and two million dollars to the School of Religion (soon to incorporate as Christian Theological Seminary). The grants were designated for capital improvements. This represented the largest single gift at the time to a private college or university in Indiana. Prior to this, negotiations had been under way between the School of Religion and Butler University to provide that Christian Theological Seminary (successor to the School of Religion) could operate under its own board of trustees and acquire a new campus adjoining that of the university. The two million dollar gift was allocated for that purpose. The university had long been in need of a library building, and the one million dollars given by the two Foundations was added to the library building fund. Because of this generous grant it was possible to begin construction on a beautiful new library building which was formally dedicated as the Irwin Library

---

[37] Recipients of honorary degrees: Jessie M. Trout, vice president of the United Christian Missionary Society; Kenneth B. Seeley, minister of Central Christian Church, Kalamazoo, Michigan; Honorable R. S. Garfield Todd, Prime Minister of Southern Rhodesia; U. S. Senator Homer E. Capehart; Arthur Clay Pope, scientist and Butler graduate of 1929; Donald A. McGavran, missionary-educator; Fabian Sevitzky, conductor of the Indianapolis Symphony Orchestra; Ovid Butler, distinguished forester; Edward G. McGavran, Butler graduate of 1924 and dean of the School of Public Health, University of North Carolina; I. Lynd Esch, president of Indiana Central College; Dwight Billings, Duke University; Charles B. Brownson of Indiana; Winfred E. Garrison, former president of Butler University and professor at the University of Houston; and Oreon E. Scott, Disciple layman and chairman of the Christian Board of Publication.

on May 1, 1965. It was so named to honor members of the Irwin family who had been responsibly connected with Butler University since it was founded in 1855.

A women's residence hall was opened for students in the fall of 1956. It needed to be expanded to accommodate more students; a west wing was completed in the fall of 1963 and an east wing finished a few months later. This building became known as the Louis Schwitzer Memorial Hall in honor of the Indianapolis industrialist and civic leader. Jordan College of Music merged with Butler University in 1951 and became the Jordan College of Music at Butler University. In 1959, Lilly Endowment, Incorporated, offered a conditional grant of one million dollars to erect a new fine arts building on the Butler campus. The Arthur Jordan Foundation provided an additional grant of $500,000, making it possible to erect the building. Known as Lilly Hall, it was dedicated on December 9, 1962.

Through the generosity of Mrs. George H. A. Clowes and her two sons, Allen Clowes of Indianapolis and Dr. George H. A. Clowes, Jr., of Cleveland, it was possible to erect Clowes Memorial Hall on the campus. This hall is a huge auditorium for the performing arts; it immediately became a cultural center for Indianapolis, offering highest quality drama, ballet, and opera. Regular concerts are played here by the Indianapolis Symphony Orchestra. Clowes Hall also serves the university as its auditorium for special events.

In recent years some sororities and fraternities have erected new buildings or made additions to their existing structures. With the adding of all these new facilities Butler University came into its own as a great educational institution.

J. I. Holcomb proposed a Science Research Institute in 1958. His will provided an endowment of $12,500,000 for the projected institute which was to have its main stress on the biological sciences. The development of this project is in the wave of the future for Butler University.

M. O. Ross retired from the presidency of the university in 1962. He had served the school since 1928, first as dean of the College of Business Administration, and for twenty years as president. Alexander E. Jones,[38] dean of the College of Liberal Arts and Sciences, was made acting president on September 1, 1962, and was elected president the next year. He was inaugurated in Clowes Hall on February 7, 1964, as the fifteenth president of Butler University. J. I. Holcomb, president of the Board of Directors of Butler University, died in April, 1962. Harry T. Ice, Butler graduate of the class of 1926, and an Indianapolis attorney, was elected to this position.[39]

The School of Religion Becomes
Christian Theological Seminary

By 1954 the School of Religion was rapidly becoming identified with the ecumenical aspects of the program of the church. Ronald E. Osborn, head of the department of church history, was given a leave of absence in 1954-55 to serve on the Faculty of the Graduate School of Ecumenical Studies at Celigny, Switzerland. Robert Tobias, since 1953 in ecumenical fellowship service in Europe, accepted an appointment on the Faculty of the School of Religion, beginning in September, 1954. At the same time he also became director of

---

[38]Alexander Elvin Jones (1920-   ) was born at Independence, Missouri. He received the B.A. degree from DePauw University in 1942; M.A., University of Minnesota, 1949; Ph.D., *ibid.*, 1950; and LL.D., DePauw University, 1964. He was a member of the faculty of the University of Minnesota, 1949-50; University of Arkansas, 1950-1956; MacMurray College, 1956-59; dean of the College of Liberal Arts and Sciences, Butler University, 1959-63; president, 1963. Jones served with the United States Naval Reserve, 1942-45. He is a member of the National Educational Association and the Modern Language Association. He authored the book, *Creative Exposition,* 1957, and is co-author of *Writing Good Prose,* 1961.

[39]Mr. Ice also is secretary of the Board of Trustees of Christian Theological Seminary.

the department of ecumenical service of the Disciples' Association for the Promotion of Christian Unity. S. Marion Smith, head of the New Testament department, spent the summer of 1954 studying in Palestine. That same summer, Walter W. Sikes, head of the department of philosophy and Christian ethics, conducted a second annual European traveling seminar. The School of Religion was well represented at the Second Assembly of the World Council of Churches held at Evanston in 1954. Robert Tobias was a delegate, William Robinson and J. Irwin Miller (trustee) were consultants. Dean Shelton was an accredited visitor, and Ronald E. Osborn was a member of the news staff.

The School of Religion was by this time definitely on the move. It was selected by the Russell Sage Foundation in 1955 as one of five theological seminaries where pilot studies on the place of the social sciences in ministerial education would be carried on. The purpose of this program was to study the roles the modern parish minister performs in an effort to find out how the social sciences could contribute effectively to provide him with the knowledge and skills he needed. The study was conducted by Samuel W. Blizzard who was on leave of absence from Pennsylvania State University. An advisory committee of Dean Shelton, B. A. Norris, Walter W. Sikes, James Blair Miller, F. E. Rector, and S. Marion Smith worked with Dr. Blizzard.[40]

Both William Robinson and A. C. Watters requested retirement from the Faculty in 1956. Dr. Robinson wished to return to England, his homeland, and Dr. Watters accepted the pastorate of the church at Bulawayo, Southern Rhodesia, where he was employed by The United Christian Missionary

---

[40]*World Call,* February, 1955; *Christian-Evangelist,* January 12, 1955. *See* Samuel W. Blizzard, *Training for the Ministry Project* (New York: privately published, n.d., mimeo).

Society. Over 200 people attended a special "farewell" dinner given in their honor in June, 1956. Joseph M. Smith, former missionary of The United Christian Missionary Society, succeeded Dr. Watters as head of the department of religions and missions, beginning September, 1956. James G. Clague, principal of the College of the Churches of Christ in Toronto, Canada, succeeded Dr. Robinson on the Faculty in the department of systematic theology and doctrine.

Two faculty members received distinct honors in 1956. Robert Tobias was awarded the Cross of Commanders of the Royal Order of Phoenix by King Paul of Greece for having contributed in a special way to the welfare of the Greek nation. Toyozo W. Nakarai received a citation from Histradut Ivrit of America on the occasion of the fortieth anniversary of this organization in 1956. Histradut Ivrit of America recognized through this citation that Butler University had been presenting courses in Hebrew almost continuously for seventy years, and that for the past thirty years the School of Religion had been outstanding among seminaries in Hebrew languages and culture. Prior to this, in 1953, Dr. Nakarai was given the B'rith Abraham Award for the advancement of Hebrew learning.[41]

The School of Religion first began publishing *Shane Quarterly* in 1940. Though the scope of this journal was not limited to Discipliana it was primarily concerned with this feature. A need was felt for a more adequate outlet in the publication of scholarly papers and serious essays. In a meeting with other seminaries and agencies of the Disciples of Christ general agreement was expressed on the desirability of such a journal. Because the resources were not forthcoming nothing more was done toward publication. In the spring of

---

[41]*Indiana Christian,* March, 1956; *Christian-Evangelist,* March 28, 1956.

1956 the faculty and administration of the School of Religion decided to enlarge the service formerly rendered by *Shane Quarterly* in a journal with a new format and a new name. The first issue of *Encounter* (Vol. 17, No. 1) appeared in the winter of 1956. The name, *Encounter,* was chosen in the hope that its readers would find themselves increasingly engaged in genuine and challenging dialogue with authors of many traditions. Ronald E. Osborn was made editor of the journal. Calvin L. Porter became co-editor with him in 1965. O. L. Shelton was managing editor until his death in 1959. Henry K. Shaw was then appointed to this position. Don R. Wismar became book review editor in 1965. *Encounter* soon came to be recognized as one of the leading theological journals in America. It has the distinction of being indexed regularly in the *Index to Religious Periodical Literature* of the American Theological Library Association, and abstracted in *Religious and Theological Abstracts.* It also became one of twenty-seven English language periodicals on the Check List of Basic Periodicals in *Aids to a Theological School Library.*

Four professors were officially installed on November 14, 1956. They were James R. Carley, Robert Tobias, James G. Clague, and Joseph M. Smith. Representatives from forty colleges, universities, seminaries, and agencies were present for the occasion. Walter N. Roberts, president of the United Theological Seminary in Dayton, Ohio, and secretary of the American Association of Theological Schools, gave the address, "The Idea of a Theological Seminary."[42]

Expanding Facilities—Upgrading Curriculum

By this time it was apparent that neither the existing building of the School of Religion nor its financial resources

---

[42]*World Call,* January, 1957.

could be considered adequate for its expanding program. Considering the future when a new building could be erected and the institution adequately endowed and incorporated as a seminary with its own board of trustees, a new development program was announced in 1956.[43] In the meantime, Dean Shelton appointed a special faculty committee to study theological education for the purpose of upgrading the program and curriculum of the School. B. A. Norris was chosen as chairman of the committee; he was assisted by Ronald E. Osborn and S. Marion Smith. This special committee worked for two years on the project, bringing provisional reports to the Faculty for free discussion. With faculty emendations, the monthly reports developed into a basic document useful as a future guide for administration, faculty, alumni, and students. It was adopted by the Faculty on January 16, 1959, approved by the Board of Trustees on May 11, 1959, and published under the title, *Special Study of Theological Education, Faculty Report*. The new program and curriculum had its inception in the fall semester, 1960.[44]

George C. Stuart, pastor of First Christian Church, Bloomington, Illinois, was called to be head of the department of preaching, beginning with the fall semester of 1957. Henry K. Shaw, pastor of the Washington Avenue Church of Christ at Elyria, Ohio, was named librarian, beginning at the same time. They were officially installed as members of the Faculty on November 13, 1957. George A. Buttrick of Harvard University gave the special address for the occasion. Lowell G. Colston, formerly on the staff of the counseling center at the University of Chicago, was appointed head of

---

[43]*Indiana Christian*, April, 1956.
[44]*See*, Christian Theological Seminary, *Special Study of Theological Education, Faculty Report* (Indianapolis: C.T.S. Press, 1959).

the department of psychology of religion and pastoral care, beginning September 1, 1958.

The project of establishing a new campus of its own and separating administratively from Butler University (though preserving many academic relationships) envisioned a ten million dollar expansion program for Christian Theological Seminary. It was estimated that five million dollars would be needed for new buildings and five million dollars for permanent endowment. D. Wright Lunsford, pastor of Central Christian Church, Wichita, Kansas, began his work as director of financial resources on July 1, 1957. Jack E. Sanders and Ervin L. Thompson became associate directors. Thompson was former pastor of the Christian Church at Eldorado, Arkansas, and Sanders served the church at Alva, Oklahoma. The announcement in 1958 of a pledge of two million dollars from the Christian Foundation and the Irwin-Sweeney-Miller Foundation demonstrated confidence in the project and became an exciting incentive to complete the program.

As a result of two years of study prior to 1958 by a committee representing the interests of Butler University and the School of Religion, a separation agreement was reached which was satisfactory to both groups. The university needed the use of the School of Religion building and the surrounding real estate for its own expansion program; the School of Religion needed several acres of land adjoining the west end of the Butler campus for its building site. Steps were taken for the School of Religion to incorporate as a separate institution definitely related to the Christian Churches (Disciples of Christ), but functioning with the university as an academic unit. On September 17, 1958, the former School of Religion became legally incorporated in the State of Indiana as Christian Theological Seminary. This made it possible for the Seminary to own its own property, accumulate endowments, receive bequests, and conserve its assets. The undergraduate department of religion at the university, under this arrangement, continued to serve the Christian Churches of Indiana as an undergraduate department of religion, and the seminary was looked upon as the theological seminary of the university. Orman L. Shelton was then named president of Christian Theological Seminary; Beauford A. Norris, assistant dean of the School of Religion, became academic dean of the Seminary.[45]

An alumni council was formed in 1958 by former students of the School of Religion. The council proposed to sponsor a program of closer relationships and active cooperation with the Seminary and support the new development and expansion project.[46]

President Shelton, though he rarely spoke of it, was the victim of heart attacks in 1953 and 1954. He was so engrossed in reaching certain goals for the upgrading of the institution that he undervalued his own physical capacity. The long illness of his wife and subsequent death in 1956, due to a spinal injury sustained in an automobile accident, was an added burden he had to carry. The heavy responsibility connected with the separation agreement with Butler University, negotiating with property owners for the site of the new Seminary campus, and the projection of the expan-

---

[45]*Christian-Evangelist*, May 12, October 20, 1958; *World Call*, July-August, 1958; *Indiana Christian*, October, 1958. C.T.S. incorporators: Hilton U. Brown of Indianapolis; Raphael H. Miller, Sr., former editor of the *Christian-Evangelist;* J. Irwin Miller, Columbus industrialist; J. R. Rees, agriculturalist and state senator; Earl Pulse, president of the Union Starch and Refining Company; Theo O. Fisher, pastor of the Northwood Christian Church, Indianapolis; and O. L. Shelton. Dr. Shelton was named temporary chairman of this group of incorporators; it was considered as the core of the Board of Trustees to be developed. William F. Welch, Indianapolis attorney, was elected temporary secretary-treasurer.

[46]*Christian Evangelist-Front Rank*, January 4, 1959; *World Call*, March, 1959. Ronald L. Secrist was elected president of the council; Howard F. Miller was made vice president; and Lonnie H. Hass became secretary-treasurer. Other members were Thomas Henry, Herschel M. Reed, and William Martin Smith. E. L. Thompson served as alumni secretary.

sion program took its toll on his health. He was hospitalized in the middle of December, 1958, never to return to the Seminary again. He died at the home of his daughter, Mrs. E. L. Thompson, on March 3, 1959.[47]

Beauford A. Norris, President

Beauford A. Norris,[48] then dean of the Seminary, was asked by the trustees to become acting president. He was elected to the presidency on April 15, 1959. The inauguration of Dr. Norris as second president of Christian Theological Seminary took place on October 28, 1959, at University Park Christian Church. J. Irwin Miller, chairman of the Board of Trustees, presided on this occasion; Dean Liston Pope of Yale Divinity School gave the special address. More than 150 persons, representing colleges, universities, seminaries, ecclesiastical organizations, and learned societies, participated in the academic procession.[49]

President Shelton had the difficult task of bringing Christian Theological Seminary into existence; President Norris built a responsible academic and administrative structure on this foundation. David C. Pellett served as acting dean until

[47]For a full account of the life and work of Orman L. Shelton, *see,* "Portrait of a Churchman," by Ronald E. Osborn, *Encounter,* Spring, 1959 (Volume 20, No. 2), pp. 132-167. The Faculty commissioned an artist to do a painting of President Shelton in 1961. It hangs in the library of Christian Theological Seminary.

[48]Beauford A. Norris (1909-   ) is a native of Kansas. He received the A.B. and A.M. degrees from Phillips University in 1932; the B.D. degree, *ibid.,* 1933. In 1950 he was granted the Ph.D. degree from the University of Edinburgh (Scotland). Ordained to the Christian ministry in 1932, he served the Christian churches at Milford, Kansas, 1933-35; Washington, Pennsylvania, 1935-39; and Pampa, Texas, 1939-48. During World War II he was chaplain, U.S.A.A.F., serving in the Asiatic-Pacific theatre of operations, and attaining the rank of major. Dr. Norris joined the Faculty of Butler University School of Religion in 1950; became assistant dean in 1954; dean and president of Christian Theological Seminary, 1959. He was fraternal delegate to the British Churches of Christ, 1949; vice president of the Home and State Missions Planning Council (Disciples). 1957-58; vice chairman and trustee of the Accredited Theological Seminaries of Ohio and Indiana, 1959-1965. He has contributed a number of articles to religious journals.

[49]*See, Addresses Given at the Inauguration of Beauford A. Norris, President, Christian Theological Seminary, October 28, 1959* (Indianapolis: CTS Press, 1959).

the appointment of Ronald E. Osborn[50] as dean in 1959. Dr. Pellett was then named director of graduate studies and summer session. At this time, Henry K. Shaw, librarian, became also the director of publications, and Cassius M. Fenton was appointed business manager and treasurer. D. Wright Lunsford resigned as director of financial resources in 1959 to accept the pastorate of First Christian Church, Omaha, Nebraska; E. L. Thompson, his associate, resigned to become state secretary for the Christian Churches in Pennsylvania. Bill L. Barnes, pastor of the Affton Christian Church at St. Louis, Missouri, and alumnus of the School of Religion, was called in 1960 to become director of development. He is responsible for all gift incomes, communications, church relations, and recruitment; Howard B. Goodrich, Jr., pastor of the Dearborn, Michigan, Christian Church, also an alumnus, became associate director of development in 1963.

Vinton D. Bradshaw joined the staff as director of student-church relations in 1958. J. Daniel Joyce was called to the Faculty as associate professor of New Testament in 1959 and was intalled on May 2, 1961. That same year, Lester G. McAllister was called from the Faculty at Bethany College to become professor modern church history, and Keith Watkins joined the Faculty to teach in the field of worship and parish ministry. The four new professors—Lowell G. Col-

---

[50]Ronald Edwin Osborn (1917-   ) was born in Chicago. Phillips University awarded him the degrees, A.B., 1938; M.A., 1939; and B.D., 1942. He received the Ph.D. degree from the University of Oregon in 1955. He was pastor of the Christian Church at Jonesboro, Arkansas, 1942-43. Dr. Osborn was editor of youth publications for the Christian Board of Publication, 1943-45; on the faculty of Northwest Christian College, 1946-50; faculty, School of Religion at Butler University, 1953-59; dean, Christian Theological Seminary, 1959-   ; lecturer, Graduate School of Ecumenical Studies, near Geneva, Switzerland, 1954-55; visiting professor, Union Theological Seminary, Manila, Philippines, 1965. He was a delegate to the World Conference on Faith and Order, Lund, Sweden, 1952, and president of the Disciples of Christ Historical Society, 1950-53. He has been editor of *Encounter* since 1952. Dr. Osborn has contributed numerous articles to religious journals, and is the author of *Ely Vaughn Zollars, a Biography*, 1947; *The Spirit of American Christianity*, 1957, German translation, 1960; *The Reformation of Tradition* (editor), 1963; and *A Church for These Times*, 1965.

ston, Lester G. McAllister, Vinton D. Bradshaw, and Keith Watkins were installed on December 7, 1961. Seward A. Hiltner of Princeton Theological Seminary gave the address on this occasion.

J. Daniel Joyce became dean of the Graduate Seminary of Phillips University in 1962, and Calvin L. Porter was called to his position in the New Testament field that same year and installed February 12, 1963. Jack E. Sanders resigned his position in the development department on November 1, 1962. Walter W. Sikes retired as professor of Christian ethics and philosophical theology in 1963 and was given the emeritus rank. Don R. Wismar became assistant professor of preaching in 1963, taking the place of George C. Stuart who had resigned. In 1964, Franklin E. Rector resigned from the Faculty to become associate secretary for research and planning of the Illinois Council of Churches, and Joseph M. Smith resigned to accept the position of executive secretary of the department of East Asia of the United Christian Missionary Society. Harold E. Fey, former editor of the *Christian Century,* became visiting professor of Christian social ethics in 1964.

Vinton D. Bradshaw was given a leave of absence in 1964-65 to work on a doctoral program, and Frank G. Helme of the State Association staff took his place. Frank C. Rustemeyer, also of the State Association, became Helme's successor beginning with the fall semester in 1965. Edwin L. Becker of the Divinity School of Drake University was called to the faculty of Christian Theological Seminary in 1965 as professor of the sociology of religion. Toyozo W. Nakarai, faculty member since 1927, retired in the summer of 1965 and was given emeritus rank. A recognition dinner was given in his honor on April 22, 1965. Moses Bailey, retired from the faculty of Hartford Seminary Foundation, became visiting professor of Old Testament in the fall of 1965.[51]

The first commencement as Christian Theological Seminary was held on June 8, 1959, at University Park Christian Church. J. Irwin Miller, chairman of the Board of Trustees, was the speaker for this event. Including those graduated in August, 1959, ninety-six students received B.D. degrees; four more received the Master of Religious Education degree and two the Master of Theology degree. The honorary degree of Doctor of Divinity was conferred on Paul Hunter Beckelhymer, minister of the Christian Church at Hiram, Ohio; John E. Ross, Butler University alumnus and medical missionary to the Belgian Congo; and William Martin Smith, School of Religion alumnus and general representative of the Pension Fund of the Disciples of Christ.[52]

MOVING TOWARD FINANCIAL STABILITY

Lilly Endowment, Incorporated, made a grant of $194,570 to the Seminary in the spring of 1960. It provided for the purchase of special equipment, establishing of research and training facilities; scholarships for pastoral counseling interns, research assistants in urban church planning, and assistants in communications, as well as for a comprehensive survey of

---

[51]For a complete listing of faculty, trustees, staff, and administration in 1965, see Appendix, pp. 471-472.

[52]Honorary doctoral degrees were awarded in 1960 to John W. Harms, general secretary of the Association of Christian Churches in Indiana, and to Professor LeRoy Waterman of the University of Michigan. Professor Allen B. Stanger of Lynchburg College and J. Maurice Thompson, pastor of First Christian Church at Huntington, Indiana, and School of Religion alumnus, were given honorary degrees in 1961. In 1962, Eldon Campbell, general manager and vice president of television station WFBM, and Robert G. Sulanke, pastor of Hazelwood Christian Church, Muncie, Indiana, were recipients of honorary degrees. Honorary degrees in 1963 were granted to William G. Baker, Butler University alumnus in Edinburgh, Scotland, and Professor Royal F. Humbert of Eureka College. Raphael H. Miller, Jr., pastor of East Side Christian Church at Evansville, Indiana, received an honorary degree in 1964.

the library facilities and program.[53] An additional grant of $138,275 was made by Lilly Endowment, Incorporated, in 1963, to continue these programs for another three years.[54] A grant of $100,000 for the purpose of increasing faculty salaries, to be totally spent within a ten-year period, was made by the Christian Foundation in 1961.[55] The Earl Burton Pulse Memorial Scholarship was made possible in 1962 by a gift of $24,000 from the Irwin-Sweeney-Miller Foundation, Cummins Eugine Foundation, and the Union Starch Company. Mr. Pulse, who died in 1959, was president of this company and a trustee of Christian Theological Seminary.[56] In 1963, the Christian Foundation gave the Seminary a grant of $1,995,000 for operating expenses during the next seven years.[57] At a special convocation on November 19, 1963, Mrs. Robert Tangeman, president of the Board of the Christian Foundation, announced that ownership of about $5,600,-000 in securities had been transferred by the Foundation to the Seminary. This transfer was an unrestricted gift and assured the Seminary of a permanent income which then amounted to 43 per cent of the operating budget. In accepting this gift, President Norris stated that he believed it was the largest gift ever made to an American Seminary from a single source, if not the largest contribution made to any seminary. Mrs. Tangeman stated that it was the conviction of the Foundation that Christian Theological Seminary was making an increasingly significant contribution to theological education and that it had the ability to achieve the high goals it had set for itself.[58]

---

[53]*The Christian*, April 17, 1960; *Indiana Christian*, April, 1960; *World Call*, May, 1960.
[54]*World Call*, March, 1963.
[55]Christian Theological Seminary *Bulletin*, October, 1961.
[56]Christian Theological Seminary *Bulletin*, April, 1962.
[57]*Indiana Christian*, September, 1963.
[58]*The Christian*, December 15, 1963; *World Call*, January, 1964; *Indiana Christian*, February, 1964.

THE FACULTY UPGRADES ITSELF

Many professors, at the time they were called to the Faculty, had not yet completed their work on doctoral programs. The Seminary was generous in allowing them time for this purpose. Because of this, ten members of the Faculty were enabled to complete studies for doctor's degrees, 1954-1965.

Faculty members have also been successful in the field of publication. James R. Carley's book, *Hymns for Today,* was published in 1960. *The Context of Pastoral Counseling,* co-authored by Lowell G. Colston and Seward Hiltner, was published in 1961. James Blair Miller authored *Our Church's Story,* a Bethany graded youth book, published in 1961. *Shin Tosa Nikki* was written by Toyozo W. Nakarai and Donald E. Bower. Published in 1962, it is the account of the mission to Japan by the Indiana Lincoln Foundation. Ronald E. Osborn's *Spirit of American Christianity* was published in 1957 (German translation, 1960). Dr. Osborn was a contributing author of a book by Cynthia Pearl Maus, *The Church and the Fine Arts,* published in 1960. *The Reformation of Tradition,* volume one of the series of papers by the Panel of Scholars, was edited by Dr. Osborn and published in 1963. In 1965, his book, *A Church for These Times,* was released. David C. Pellett contributed twenty-three articles for the four-volume *Interpreter's Dictionary of the Bible,* published in 1962. Walter W. Sikes authored *The Stranger in My House* (1957), and *Christian Faith and Experience* (1962), curriculum books for older youth and young adults. Joseph M. Smith wrote *The World Christians Live In,* a Christian Discipleship series book published in 1964. A book by Robert Tobias, *Communist-Christian Encounter in East Europe,* was published in 1956. The book, *Preaching on Christian Unity,* issued in 1958, was edited by him. In 1954-1965, faculty members contributed numerous articles to the scholarly journals.

The Lectureship program continued at Christian Theological Seminary during this period. For many years these lectures were in the categories of departmental lectureships, lectures on preaching, lectures on church mergers, and lectures on the ecumenical movement. In 1962, the Hugh Th. Miller lectureship in the fall was established to explore in breadth the involvement of the church in the contemporary world; the Oreon E. Scott lectureship in the winter was established to explore in depth some area or issue of theological thought.[59]

A NEW CAMPUS

Edward Larrabee Barnes of New York was selected in 1960 as the architect to design the new campus for Christian Theological Seminary. He proceeded at once to make plans for a building complex to be located on a bluff overlooking White River southwest of the Butler University campus. Groundbreaking ceremonies were held on March 10, 1964, for a pre-Gothic building to house twelve seminar rooms, five lecture halls, faculty offices, administrative offices, a board room, lounge and recreation center, dining area, a communications workshop, and an auditorium. Plans also called for a twenty-unit dormitory, a chapel, and a library to be erected later. The new seminary building was occupied in the spring of 1966.[60]

---

[59]Among the lecturers from 1954 to 1965 were: Harold A. Bosley, Quirinus Breen, E. Martin Browne, Ernest Cadman Colwell, George R. Davis, F. E. Davison, P. D. Devanandan, W. E. Garrison, Cyrus H. Gordon, Warren Grafton, Hans Harms, William J. Jarman, John Knox, Richard Kroner, Clarence Lemmon, Ralph W. Lloyd, John Alexander Mackay, Rajah Manikam, Martin E. Marty, Otis Maxfield, J. Irwin Miller, Martin Niemoeller, G. Edwin Osborn, Wilhelm Pauck, Waymon Parsons, Jaroslav Jan Pelikan, Charles W. Ranson, Elfan Rees, Walter W. Sikes, Virgil Sly, Roy Snodgrass, Granville T. Walker, Hans Hermann Walz, Daniel Day Williams, Jesse H. Ziegler.

[60]Building Committee: Harry T. Ice, Richard B. Stoner, B. A. Norris, David C. Pellett, James Blair Miller, Ronald E. Osborn, and Robert Tobias.

467

Beginning with the fall semester of 1965 the Master of Sacred Theology degree (S.T.M.) was offered by Christian Theological Seminary as a service to ministers who wished to continue their theological education after graduation and after having served in the parish ministry. The School of Religion conferred 481 degrees between 1927 and 1958; Christian Theological Seminary conferred 437 degrees between 1959 and 1965. This is a total of 919 degrees. Of these, 851 were Bachelor of Divinity degrees; 31 were Masters of Religious Education; 31 were Masters of Theology, and six were Masters of Sacred Music. Butler University also conferred a great number of M.A. and M.S. degrees in this period, the course work having been provided by the School of Religion or Christian Theological Seminary.

Dimensions of Progress

The Christian Church (Disciples of Christ) in its frontier phase was really a freedom movement. Those who embraced its doctrines considered themselves liberated from authoritarian creeds, hierarchical control, stewardship commitment, and even a professional clergy. They soon found out that their very existence as a body of Christian people was seriously threatened by this extremist position. Their concern for evangelism and expansion was jeopardized for lack of means to accomplish their purpose. Through bitter experience they learned that their cherished freedom often led to fragmentation and separation; their liberty led to license, and their independence led to anarchy.

The organizing of a State Meeting in 1839 was the first step taken by Hoosier Disciples to guarantee and protect their liberation by responsible ecclesiastical structure. The establishing of North Western Christian University (Butler University) in 1855 by the State Meeting was the first fruit of cooperative effort. The primary struggle by Hoosier Disciples for a century and a quarter was a search for guide lines of effective cooperation. During the last decade the issue was met squarely by the State Association and other agencies, and unification was the result. Unification has meant the protection of freedom for the churches, efficiency in administration, and the upgrading of the ministry. It has provided a groundwork for responsible expansion into many areas of Christian concern.

Hoosier Disciples, for a century and a quarter, have been searching for ways and means of being a responsible unit of the church universal. The search has not ended, nor should it ever end. Proposals are even now under consideration by the Commission on Brotherhood Restructure of the International Convention of Christian Churches (Disciples of Christ) which will have far-reaching influence upon the life and work of each state and area organization. The general commitment, not yet finally adopted, to become the Christian Church (Disciples of Christ) and not merely a movement of local churches, is already shaping the thinking of Hoosier Disciples. Their history to this time indicates that they will not only be influenced by these currents of renewal in the church, but that they will take a significant place in the reshaping of the entire Disciples' brotherhood. A survey of the Christian Churches in Indiana in 1966 points out that Hoosier Disciples have come a long way from Blue River, Silver Creek, Little Flat Rock and the Edinburg conference; much has been accomplished on the state level, but however important the past, it is but a precursor of greater things to come in the future.

APPENDIX

Christian Theological Seminary
1965-1966

FACULTY

Beauford A. Norris, B.A., M.A., B.D., Ph.D. *President*

Ronald E. Osborn, B.A., M.A., B.D., Ph.D. *Dean*

David C. Pellett, B.A., M.A., B.D., Ph.D. *Director of Postgraduate Studies*

*Frank J. Albert, B.A., B.D., Ph.D.

Moses Bailey, B.A., M.A., B.D., S.T.M., Ph.D., LL.D.

Edwin L. Becker, M.A., B.D., M.A., Ph.D.

Vinton D. Bradshaw, B.A., B.D.

James R. Carley, B.A., M.M., D.S.M.

James G. Clague, B.A., B.D.

Lowell G. Colston, B.A., B.D., Ph.D.

Alfred R. Edyvean, B.A., B.D., M.A., Ph.D.

Harold E. Fey, B.A., B.D., D.D., Litt.D., HH.D.

S. Marion Smith, B.A., M.A., B.D., L.H.D.

Lester G. McAllister, B.A., B.D., Th.D.

James B. Miller, B.A., B.D., Ed.D.

Calvin L. Porter, B.A., B.D., Ph.D.

Henry K. Shaw, B.A., M.A.Ed., D.D.

Keith Watkins, B.Th., B.D., Th.D.

Don Roy Wismar, B.A., M.A., B.D., Th.D.

---

*Deceased, 1965.

471

472

APPENDIX

The Association of the Christian Churches in Indiana

1965-1966

STATE CONVENTION OFFICERS

*Ray H. Montgomery, Jr., *President*

Mrs. George E. Gill, *Past President*

Mrs. Vera Kingsbury, *Vice President*

Floyd A. Hines, *President-elect*

*Donald B. Taylor, *Vice President*

ADMINISTRATIVE STAFF

*John W. Harms, *General Secretary*

*Donald O. Legg, *Associate General Secretary, Stewardship Services and Financial Promotion*

*Russell Hensley, *Associate Secretary, General Services*

Mrs. Ward I. Nicholas, *Associate Secretary, Christian Women's Fellowship*

*Leon K. Weatherman, *Associate Secretary, Christian Men's Fellowship*

*Edwin R. Allender, *Associate Secretary, Division of Program Services and Director of Campus Christian Life*

*L. Richard Hudson, *Associate Secretary, Research and Development*

Mrs. Herald Demaree, *Director, Leadership Development and Children's Work*

---

*Ministers.

473

APPENDIX

*Richard L. Lauer, *Director, Youth Work and Family Life Education*

*Ronald L. Secrist, *Associate Secretary for District No. 11, Christian Church Union*

*Frank C. Rustemeyer, *Director, Student-church Relations*

STATE BOARD MEMBERS, 1965-1966

Mrs. Harold S. Johnson, *Chairman*

*James L. Stoner, *Vice Chairman*
Mrs. Lee Moffett, *Recording Secretary*

Clyde R. Yater, *Treasurer*
Ray Thorn, *Assistant Treasurer*

	District		District
Merritt O. Alcorn	14	Mrs. Graham Marsh	4
*Howard E. Anderson	12	Robert Mitchell	10
Berne E. Boruff	12	Mrs. Lee Moffett	3
*L. Eugene Brown	10	Mrs. Mabel Monteith	1
John N. Bunnell	2	Mrs. Forrest Moore	10
Mrs. Jack Carpenter	6	*Wm. H. Neeriemer	4
Leewell L. Carpenter	5	Richard Pauley	12
John Chapman	2	Andrew W. Ramsey	11
Richard Curts	4	*Ralph H. Richardson	14
Mrs. Clarence Foreman	14	Dr. C. J. Scherrens	11
Jay B. Gardner	1	Arthur Schlamp	13
Stanley Hall	3	*Earl B. Seitz	7
Raymond D. Harris	2	*Fred Sharp	6
*C. T. Herod	7	Mrs. Carlin Smith	11
Mrs. Russell Horner	3	*James L. Stoner	9
*Robert L. Howell	6	*Ralph Thomas	13
A. Russell Hutchinson	5	Mrs. Marion Warpenberg	13
Mrs. Harold S. Johnson	5	Dr. Mary Ruth Winebrenner	6
*Paul E. Kerr	1	Clyde R. Yater	9
Mrs. Walter Kimball	7		
Mrs. Emerson Laughner	8		

*Ministers.

474

The Association of the Christian Churches in Indiana

MEMBERS AT LARGE

*Forrest L. Brock   *George L. Florence   Donald R. Smith
*Russell A. Deitch   Mrs. Peter Macko

MEMBERS EX OFFICIO

Miss Dorothy Ault, *Chairman, Division of Program Services to Local Churches*

*Herbert C. Barnard, *Chairman, Commission on the Ministry*

Wayne F. Burke, *Chairman, State Camp Committee*

*Harold E. Cline, *President, Indiana Christian Ministers' Association*

*Howard R. Dungan, *Chairman, Department of Survey and Strategy*

*Allen S. Estill, *Chairman, Commission on Christian Social Concerns*

Joseph G. Lehman, *Chairman, Communication and Public Relations*

*Lester G. McAllister, *Chairman, History Commission*

Mrs. William H. Park, *President, Christian Women's Fellowship*

Frank E. Parker, *Chairman, Commission on Church Development, Town and Country*

Mrs. Calvin Porter, *President, Indiana Christian Ministers' Wives Association.*

David E. Reese, *Chairman, Commission on Campus Christian Life*

Mrs. H. I. Rudduck, *Chairman, Committee on Housing for the Aging*

*Monroe G. Schuster, *Chairman, State Office Building Committee*

*Earl P. Seitz, *Chairman, Finance Committee*

*George W. Smith, *Chairman, Commission on Ecumenical Relations*

Charles Tracy, *President, Christian Men's Fellowship*

*George G. Wascovich, *Chairman, Committee on Budgets and Promotional Relationships*

---

*Ministers.

475

CHRISTIAN MEN'S FELLOWSHIP

Charles Tracy, *President*

Paul T. Morris, *Vice President*   Edgar L. Casey, *Secretary*
Kenneth Clark, *Vice President*   Marion D. Smith, *Treasurer*

DISTRICT PRESIDENTS

Tillman Abbott	4	*Jerome E. McCoy	7
*Charles Allan	13	Richard Panley	12
Max Breeding	9	*J. Kenneth Powell	11
Edgar L. Casey	5	*David E. Reese	3
Arnold C. Eadler	6	Thomas Stratton	8
Charles R. Jones	10	Mrs. Edna Vaught	1
*Daniel C. Kechel	2	Randall Walker	14

CHRISTIAN WOMEN'S FELLOWSHIP

Mrs. William H. Park, *President*

Mrs. Teal O. Younce, *Vice President*

Mrs. Frank Thomas, *State Study Director*

Mrs. Joseph A. Meurer, *Recorder*

Mrs. Edward H. Sparks, *State Service Director*

Mrs. Harold S. Johnson, *Financial Secretary*

Mrs. George A. Harris, *Chairman, Business Women's Committee*

Mrs. Wm. L. Helvie, *State Worship Director*

GENERAL SECRETARIES, 1860-1966§

1860	Elijah Goodwin	1889	J. P. Ewing
1861	H. Z. Leonard	1890	J. L. Parsons
1863-1865	R. L. Howe	1891-1893	L. L. Carpenter
1866	W. R. Jewell	1893-1896	E. B. Scofield

---

*Ministers.

§Until recent years the holder of this office was known as the Corresponding Secretary. In the early years many men served this office in the sense of sharing an undesirable duty with no fixed remuneration. R. L. Howe was the first man to give the office full-time status. Later, others served in a part-time capacity; some years there was no secretary at all. The modern conception of the function of a state secretary began with C. W. Cauble's administration. John W. Harms is the first administrative secretary to be responsible for the entire state program.

1866	J. H. Bauserman	1897-1900	T. J. Legg
1867	N. A. Walker	1904-1909	J. O. Rose
1870-1871	J. H. McCollough	1910	E. M. Barney
1871-1874	L. L. Carpenter	1911-1913	L. E. Murray
1875	W. R. Couch	1913-1925	C. W. Cauble
1875-1878	L. L. Carpenter	1926-1940	G. I. Hoover
1879-1880	L. Berry Smith	1941-1958	Ephraim D. Lowe
1881	W. H. Drapier	1959	Frank E. Davison
1885	T. M. Wiles	1959	Lonnie E. Hass
1887-1888	J. H. O. Smith	1960-	John W. Harms

APPENDIX

*Presiding Officers of State Conventions**

John M. Alexander	1915	Roy E. Deadman	1922
Howard E. Anderson	1962	M. R. Denison	1932
		John A. Farr	1953
Mark Anthony	1942	Joseph Fassett	1847
W. D. Bartle	1928	G. Lavon Fisher	1963
A. R. Benton	1881, 1888	Theo O. Fisher	1957
W. C. Bramwell	1850-1856	S. Grundy Fisher	1943
Hilton U. Brown	1931		
L. E. Brown	1911	George L. Florence	1955
Ryland T. Brown	1871-1874		
		Elijah Goodwin	1857-1870
W. E. Caroll	1937	Mrs. George E. Gill	1965
Elmer Ward Cole	1934		
		Frank G. Helme	1956
John Cole	1845	Harry G. Hill	1912
H. G. Connelly	1927	L. C. Howe	1914
E. C. Corts	1940	Austin Hunter	1907-1909
E. L. Day	1910	J. N. Jessup	1936
E. F. Daugherty	1930	J. Boyd Jones	1920
Frank E. Davison	1959	O. E. Kelly	1929
		F. D. Kershner	1935

*In the earlier years of the convention the presiding officer was a chairman who was selected after the meeting was convened. Very little status was attached to the office. Since his name was not often included in the convention report sent to the periodicals (no minute books extant), there are gaps in this list prior to 1895.

478

E. T. Lane	1894	Benjamin F. Reeve	1848, 1849
Ephraim D. Lowe	1939	J. A. Roberts	1878-1880
G. M. McCord	1913	Monroe G. Schuster	1960
J. H. McNeill	1835	E. B. Scofield	1897-1899
R. Powell Mead	1946	F. E. Smith	1916
Benton B. Miller	1951	David H. Shields	1921
Raphael H. Miller, Jr.	1958	W. W. Sniff	1924
Paul E. Million	1950	J. Maurice Thompson	1961
W. E. Moore	1941	R. Melvyn Thompson	1947
E. E. Moorman	1933	O. E. Tomes	1923
L. Doyle Mullen	1948	Clay Trusty	1928
Ray H. Montgomery, Jr.	1966	Glen L. Tudor	1952
Ray H. Montgomery, Sr.	1925, 1949	D. R. Van Buskirk	1885
John B. New	1844, 1846	J. M. Vawter	1926
John O'Kane	1839	A. L. Ward	1917
J. L. Parsons	1875	F. W. Wiegmann	1954
A. B. Philputt	1903-1906	J. H. Wilson	1938
G. F. Powers	1944	Doyle Zaring	1964

APPENDIX

Year and Place of State Conventions

1839 Indianapolis	1863 Indianapolis	1889 Bethany Park
1840 Crawfords-	1864 Indianapolis	1890 Bethany Park
ville	1865 Indianapolis	1891 Bethany Park
1841 Indianapolis	1866 Indianapolis	1892 Bethany Park
1842 Connersville	1867 Indianapolis	1893 Bethany Park
1843 Noblesville	1868 Indianapolis	1894 Bethany Park
1844 Indianapolis	1869 Indianapolis	1895 Bethany Park
1845 Bloomington	1870 Indianapolis	1896 Greenfield
1846 Columbus	1871 Kokomo	1897 Bethany Park
1847 Greensburg	1872 Rushville	1898 South Bend
1848 Little Flat	1873 Wabash	1899 Irvington
Rock	1874 Bedford	1900 Valparaiso
1849 Indianapolis	1875 Indianapolis	1901 Anderson
1850 Indianapolis	1876 Fort Wayne	1902 Terre Haute
1851 Indianapolis	1877 Indianapolis	1903 Greenfield
1852 Indianapolis	1878 Noblesville	1904 Lebanon
1853 Indianapolis	1879 Greensburg	1905 Bedford
1854 Indianapolis	1880 Rushville	1906 Lafayette
1855 Indianapolis	1881 Union City	1907 Bethany Park
1856 Indianapolis	1882 Island Park	1908 Bethany Park
1857 Lafayette	1883 Island Park	1909 Bethany Park
1858 Bedford	1884 Bethany Park	1910 Anderson
1859 Indianapolis	1885 Bethany Park	1911 Columbus
1860 Greencastle	1886 Bethany Park	1912 Hammond
1861 Indianapolis	1887 Bethany Park	1913 Indianapolis
1862 Indianapolis	1888 Bethany Park	1914 Terre Haute

1915 Marion	1933 Connersville	1951 Kokomo
1916 Danville	1934 Crawfordsville	1952 Winona Lake
1917 Kokomo	1935 Marion	1953 Huntington
1918 New Castle	1936 Bloomington	1954 Evansville
1919 Indianapolis	1937 Fort Wayne	1955 Richmond
1920 Vincennes	1938 New Castle	1956 Elkhart
1921 Tipton	1939 Indianapolis	1957 Indianapolis
1922 Muncie	1940 Portland	1958 Fort Wayne
1923 Frankfort	1941 Bedford	1959 Vincennes
1924 Rushville	1942 Logansport	1960 South Bend
1925 Marion	1943 Kokomo	1961 Anderson
1926 Bloomington	1944 Anderson	1962 Lafayette
1927 Lafayette	1945 Not held "War"	1963 Terre Haute
1928 Bedford	1946 Terre Haute	1964 Indianapolis
1929 Huntington	1947 Winona Lake	1965 Marion
1930 Indianapolis	1948 Marion	1966 Vincennes
1931 Logansport	1949 Indianapolis	
1932 Seymour	1950 Lebanon	

BIBLIOGRAPHY

BOOKS

Andrews, Edward Deming, *The People Called Shakers, a Search for the Perfect Society.* New York: Oxford University Press, 1953.

Bestor, Arthur Eugene, Jr., *Backwoods Utopias, the Sectarian and Owenite Phases of Communitarian Socialism in America: 1663-1929.* Philadelphia: University of Pennsylvania Press, 1950.

Brown, Hilton U., *A Book of Memories.* Indianapolis: Butler University, 1951.

Brown, John T., *Churches of Christ.* Louisville: John P. Morton and Company, 1904.

Buley, R. Carlyle, *The Old Northwest, Pioneer Period, 1815-1840.* Vols. I, II. Indianapolis: Indiana Historical Society, 1950.

Cady, John F., *The Origin and Development of the Missionary Baptist Church in Indiana.* Berne, Indiana: The Berne Witness Company, 1942.

Carlton, Robert, Esq. (Pseud. for Baynard Rush Hall), *The New Purchase,* or *Seven and a Half Years in the Far West.* Indiana Centennial Edition, James Albert Woodburn, editor. Princeton: Princeton University Press, 1916.

Cartwright, Peter, *Autobiography of Peter Cartwright, the Backwoods Preacher.* W. P. Strickland, editor. New York: Methodist Book Concern, 1856.

Cauble, Commodore Wesley, *Disciples of Christ in Indiana, Achievements of a Century.* Indianapolis: Meigs Publishing Company, 1930.

Christian Churches (Disciples of Christ), Crusade Committee, *Crusade Information, Questions and Answers.* Indianapolis: A Crusade for a Christian World, 1946.

Christian Theological Seminary, *Addresses Given at the Inauguration of Beauford A. Norris, President Christian Theological Seminary,* October 28, 1959. Indianapolis: C. T. S. Press, 1959.

Central Christian Church History Committee, *125 Significant Years, The Story of Central Christian Church, Indianapolis.* Indianapolis: McDaniel Press, 1958.

Davidson, Robert, *History of the Presbyterian Church in the State of Kentucky.* New York: Robert Carter, 1847.

Davison, Frank Elon, *Thru the Rear-View Mirror.* St. Louis: Bethany Press, 1955.

Dunlavy, John, *The Manifesto, or a Declaration of the Doctrine and Practice of the Church of Christ.* Pleasant Hill, Kentucky: P. Bertrand, Printer, 1818.

Edson, Hanford A., *Contributions to the Early History of the Presbyterian Church in Indiana.* Cincinnati: Winona Publishing Company, 1898.

Edwards, J. H. (editor), *Orthodoxy in the Civil Courts.* Cincinnati: Standard Publishing Company, 1884.

Evans, Madison, *Biographical Sketches of the Pioneer Preachers of Indiana.* Philadelphia: J. Challen and Sons, 1862.

Finley, James B., *Sketches of Western Methodism: Biographical, Historical and Miscellaneous.* W. P. Strickland, editor. Cincinnati: Methodist Book Concern, 1854.

Forbes, John Douglas, *Victorian Architect: the Life and Works of William Tinsley.* Bloomington: Indiana University Press, 1953.

Garrison, J. H. (editor), *The Reformation of the Nineteenth Century.* St. Louis: Christian Publishing Company, 1901.

Gipson, Lawrence Henry, *The Moravian Indian Mission on White River, Diaries and Letters, May 5, 1799 to November 12, 1806.* Indianapolis: Indiana Historical Bureau, 1938.

Graydon, Kathryn M., *Butler College in the World War*. Greenfield, Indiana: William Mitchell Printing Company, 1922.

Green, F. M., *Christian Missions and Historical Sketches of Missionary Societies Among the Disciples of Christ*. St. Louis: John Burns Publishing Company, 1884.

Harms, John W. (editor), *Disciples of Christ Silver Anniversary of Religious Education*. Indiana edition. St. Louis: Department of Religious Education, U. C. M. S., 1935.

Harrison, Ida Withers, *Forty Years of Service, a History of the Christian Woman's Board of Missions,* 1874-1914. Indianapolis: C. W. B. M., n.d.

Hinsdale, B. A., *Ecclesiastical Tradition: Its Origin and Early Growth; Its Place in the Churches, and Its Value*. Cincinnati: Standard Publishing Company, 1879.

Holliday, F. C., *Indiana Methodism: Being an Account of the Introduction, Progress, and Present Position of Methodism in the State; and also a History of the Literary Institutions Under the Care of the Church, with Sketches of the Principal Methodist Educators in the State, Down to 1872*. Cincinnati: Hitchcock and Walden, 1873.

Kilgore, Charles Franklin, *The James O'Kelly Schism in the Methodist Episcopal Church*. Mexico City: Casa Unida De Publicaciones, 1963.

Knollenberg, Bernhard, *Pioneer Sketches of the Upper Whitewater Valley, Quaker Stronghold of the West*. Indianapolis: Indiana Historical Society, 1945.

Lindley, Harlow (editor), *Indiana As Seen By Early Travelers*. Indianapolis: Indiana Historical Commission, 1916.

Lindsay, Nicholas Vachel, *General William Booth Enters Into Heaven*. New York: The Macmillan Company, 1917.

Lockhart, William S., *The Ministry of Worship*. St. Louis: Christian Board of Publication, 1927.

Lockwood, George B., *The New Harmony Movement*. New York: D. Appleton and Company, 1905.

Lyttle, Charles H., *Freedom Moves West, A History of the Western Unitarian Conferences, 1852-1952*. Boston: The Beacon Press, 1952.

484

McLean, A. (chairman, executive committee), *The Men and Millions Movement, History and Report*. Cincinnati: Men and Millions Movement, 1919.

Mathes, James Madison, *Life of Elijah Goodwin, the Pioneer Preacher*. St. Louis: John Burns, Publisher, 1880.

Melcher, Marguerite Fellows, *The Shaker Adventure*. Princeton: Princeton University Press, 1941.

Miller, Hugh Th., *Tabernacle Church of Christ, Columbus, Indiana*. Columbus, Indiana: Privately printed, 1940.

Morrill, Milo True, *A History of the Christian Denomination in America*. Dayton, Ohio: The Christian Publishing Association, 1912.

Peters, H. H., *Charles Reign Scoville, the Man and His Message*. St. Louis: Bethany Press, 1925.

Richardson, Robert, *Memoirs of Alexander Campbell*. Philadelphia: J. B. Lippincott and Company, Vol. I, 1869, Vol. II, 1870.

Rogers, F. M. (editor), *Fifty Years' March of Mercy*. St. Louis: National Benevolent Association, 1937.

Scoville, Charles Reign, *Evangelistic Sermons*. Des Moines: Christian Union Publishing Company, 1902.

Shaw, Henry K., *Buckeye Disciples, A History of the Disciples of Christ in Ohio*. St. Louis: Christian Board of Publication, 1952.

Shumaker, Arthur W., *A History of Indiana Literature*. Bloomington: Indiana Historical Society, 1962.

Smith, William C., *Indiana Miscellany: Consisting of Sketches of Indian Life, the Early Settlement, Customs, and Hardships of the People, and the Introduction of the Gospel and of Schools, Together with Biographical Notices of the Pioneer Methodist Preachers of the State*. Cincinnati: Poe and Hitchcock, 1867.

Smith, William Henry, *The History of the State of Indiana*. Indianapolis: Western Publishing Company, Vol. I, 1903.

Smith, William Martin, *For the Support of the Ministry*. Indianapolis: Pension Fund of the Disciples of Christ, 1956.

485

Society of Friends, *Faith and Practice of Indiana Yearly Meeting of the Religious Society of Friends* (Book of Discipline). Richmond: Yearly Meeting Session, 1950.

Stone, Barton W., *The Biography of Eld. Barton Warren Stone, Written by Himself;* with Additions and Reflections by Elder John Rogers. Cincinnati: J. A. and U. P. James, 1847.

Stott, William T., *Indiana Baptist History, 1798-1908*. Franklin, Indiana: Privately printed, 1908.

Sulgrove, B. R., *History of Indianapolis and Marion County, Indiana*. Philadelphia: L. H. Evarts and Company, 1884.

Sweet, William Warren, *Circuit-Rider Days in Indiana*. Indianapolis: W. K. Stewart Company, 1916.

Sweet, William Warren, *Religion on the American Frontier, 1783-1840, The Presbyterians*. Chicago: University of Chicago Press, Vol. II, 1936.

Tiers, M. C. *The Christian Portrait Gallery*. Cincinnati: M. C. Tiers, Publisher, 1864.

Trollope, Francis, *Domestic Manners of the Americans*. Donald Smalley, editor. New York: Alfred A. Knopf, 1949.

Ware, Charles Crossfield, *Barton Warren Stone, Pathfinder of Christian Union*. St. Louis: The Bethany Press, 1932.

Warren, W. R. (general editor), *Survey of Service*. St. Louis: Christian Board of Publication, 1928.

West, William Garrett, *Barton Warren Stone, Early Advocate of Christian Unity*. Nashville: Disciples of Christ Historical Society, 1954.

White, Anna and Leila Taylor, *Shakerism, Its Meaning and Message*. Columbus, Ohio: Fred J. Heer Press, 1904.

Wilmore, Augustus Cleland, *History of the White River Conference of the Church of the United Brethren in Christ*. Dayton, Ohio: United Brethren Publishing House, 1925.

Winger, Otho, *History and Doctrine of the Church of the Brethren*. Elgin, Illinois: Brethren Publishing House, 1919.

Winger, Otho, *History of the Church of the Brethren in Indiana*. Elgin, Illinois: Brethren Publishing House, 1917.

American Christian Review. Religious journal which began as a monthly in 1856 and became a weekly in 1858. Started by Editor Benjamin Franklin as a middle-of-the-road conservative paper it became extremely conservative in later years. Appeared as *Octographic Review* in 1887, and as *Apostolic Review* in 1939. It developed into a journal to express the views of the anti-instrumental, anti-missionary society, anti-church college division of the Disciples' movement.

Butler Alumnal Quarterly. See *Butler Alumnus.*

Butler Alumnus. Quarterly journal of Butler University Alumni Association. Originated as the *Butler Alumnal Quarterly* in 1911, and became the *Butler Alumnus* in 1937.

Butler College Bulletin. Information bulletin of Butler College.

Central Christian. See *Indiana Christian.*

Christian, The. Weekly journal of the Christian Churches (Disciples of Christ) now published at St. Louis. Successor to the *Gospel Echo, Gospel Echo and Christian, Christian, Christian-Evangelist,* and *Christian Evangelist-Front Rank; The Christian* since 1960. Comprehensive index published jointly by the Disciples of Christ Historical Society and Christian Board of Publication in 1962.

Christian-Evangelist. See *The Christian.*

Christian Evangelist-Front Rank. See *The Christian.*

Christian Messenger. Monthly religious journal associated primarily with Barton W. Stone and the Christian (New Light) Church movement. Published at Georgetown, Kentucky, and Jacksonville, Illinois, 1826-1845; suspended 1837-1839.

Christian Monitor. A family magazine with religious emphasis. Edited primarily by Mrs. M. M. B. Goodwin it was directed toward women readers. Published 1863-1884 at Cincinnati, Indianapolis, and Kansas City, Missouri. It also appeared as *Christian Companion,* and *Ladies Christian Monitor.*

Christian Preacher. Monthly magazine of sermons and miscellaneous material published at Cincinnati, Ohio, and Georgetown, Kentucky, 1836-1840 by editors David S. Burnet and John T. Johnson.

Christian Record. A monthly religious journal published at Bloomington, Indianapolis, and Bedford, Indiana. Midwest news coverage for Christian Churches, but primary attention to Indiana news of the churches. Quasi-official journal for the Indiana State Meeting of Christian Churches; precursor of the *Indiana Christian.* Published at times by James M. Mathes. James M. Mathes and Elijah Goodwin, Elijah Goodwin, and James M. Mathes. Published as *Christian Record,* 1843-1866, and then sold to *Christian Standard.* Re-published in 1870 as *Christian Record; Christian Record and Living Laborer,* 1871-1872; *Christian Record and Sunday School Worker,* 1873-1875. Absorbed by *Evangelist* 1875. Re-published as *Christian Record,* 1882-1884.

Christian Record and Living Laborer. See *Christian Record.*

Christian Record and Sunday School Worker. See *Christian Record.*

Christian Standard. Published at Cincinnati, Ohio. Since 1866 a weekly religious journal for the Disciples of Christ. For many years the leading magazine in the mainstream of Disciples' thought. Beginning in the 1920's, critical of Disciples' structure and represents views of "independents."

Evangelist, The. Monthly religious journal edited by Walter Scott, 1832-1844. Appeared in 1836 as *Gospel Restored.* Superseded by *Protestant Unionist.* Published at Cincinnati, Carthage, and Pittsburgh.

Encounter. Quarterly journal of theological scholarship published at Indianapolis by Christian Theological Seminary. Superseded *Shane Quarterly,* 1940-1955, as volume XVII.

Gospel Luminary. Monthly religious journal of the eastern states "old" Christian Churches. Began publication at West Bloomfield, New York, in 1825, David Millard, editor.

Heretic Detector. Monthly religious journal edited by Arthur Crihfield of Middleburg, Ohio, 1837-1841. Directed toward detecting heresies in religious denominations other than the Christian Churches.

Indiana Christian. Monthly journal for Christian Churches (Disciples of Christ) in Indiana. It was published as a bi-monthly at Indianapolis as *Indiana Central Christian,* 1887-1889. It then became the Indiana Department of the *Christian Standard.* It was issued separately as a supplement to the *Christian Standard* in 1891. From 1892 to 1902 it was issued again in Indianapolis as a monthly paper. The *Indiana Christian* was suspended, 1903-1913, though several attempts were made to revive it. It was published as the *Indiana Worker,* 1914-1927, and as the *Indiana Christian* since 1928 it continues to be the official monthly journal of the Association of Christian Churches in Indiana.

Indiana Worker. See *Indiana Christian.*

Indianapolis Daily Journal. Indianapolis newspaper.

Indianapolis Star. Indianapolis newspaper.

Indianapolis Star Magazine. Sunday supplement to *Indianapolis Star.*

Millennial Harbinger. Monthly religious journal, 1830-1870. Edited by Alexander Campbell at Bethany, West Virginia during his lifetime, and later by W. K. Pendleton.

Missionary Tidings. Publication of the Christian Woman's Board of Missions, Indianapolis, 1883-1918. Superseded by *World Call* in 1919.

North-Western Christian Magazine. Monthly Christian Church journal edited by John Boggs. Published at Cincinnati, 1854-1858. Designed as an anti-slavery periodical.

N.B.A. Family Talk. Publication of the National Benevolent Association.

Octographic Review. See *American Christian Review.*

Reader's Digest. Monthly magazine article digest published at Pleasantville, N. Y.

Shane Quarterly. See *Encounter.*

Western Reformer. Monthly religious journal published at New Paris, Ohio, Centerville, and Milton, Indiana, 1843-1849.

World Call. Monthly Magazine of Disciples of Christ, reporting for the United Christian Missionary Society and other agencies. Published at St. Louis, Missouri; Indianapolis, Indiana, since 1919.

Bibliography

REPORTS

Athearn, Walter Scott (President's Report), *Dual Control of an Urban University*. Indianapolis: Butler University, 1933.

Blizzard, Samuel W., *Training for the Ministry*. New York: Privately printed, n.d.

Bureau of Census, *Special Reports, Religious Bodies;* 1906. Washington: Government Printing Office, 1910.

Christian Theological Seminary, *Special Study on Theological Education, Faculty Report*. Indianapolis: C.T.S. Press, 1959.

Miller, Raphael H., Jr. (Chairman Message Committee), *Message on the State of the Church in Indiana*. Indianapolis: Association of Christian Churches in Indiana, 1955.

Report of the Proceedings of the General Convention of the Christian Churches of the United States of America. Held in Cincinnati, Wednesday, October 23, 1849, together with the Third Annual Report of the American Christian Bible Society and the Second Annual Report of the Cincinnati Christian Tract Society, with Appendices. Cincinnati: American Christian Depository, 1849.

Year Book, Disciples of Christ. (July 1, 1940—June 30, 1941), International Convention of Disciples of Christ and cooperating agencies and organizations. Indianapolis: Year Book Publication Committee, 1942.

RECORDS

Catalogs: Butler University, Butler University School of Religion, Christian Theological Seminary, North Western Christian University.

Charter and By-Laws of North Western Christian University and an Ordinance for the Government of the Institution. Indianapolis: N.W.C.U., 1847.

Minutes of the Board of Directors of North Western Christian University (and Butler College); Book I, 1852-1863; Book II, 1864-1874; Book III, 1875-1885; Book IV, 1886-1892; Book V, 1892-1904; Book VI, 1904-1915; Book VII, 1915-1921.

490

Minutes of the Silver Creek Baptist Association, 1812-1835.

Special Finding of Facts: Cause No. 1686, Complaint to declare a trust in real estate and an injunction, Benton County Circuit Court, September Term, 1950; Albert Greenwood, *et. al. vs.* Marvin C. Schram.

UNPUBLISHED MATERIAL

Mathes, James Madison, *Life of Elder James Madison Mathes, Written by Himself for the Use of His Children When He is No More.* Bedford, Indiana: manuscript, circa 1870.

Wiley, Francis M., *The History of Central Christian Church.* Indianapolis: manuscript, 1933.

Index

Asterisk indicates reference is in footnotes

A

Abberly, R. W., 311*
Abbot, —, 179*
Abbot, B. A., 318*
Abbott, Tilman, 476
Abingdon College, 300
academies, early: Cambridge Seminary, 109; Centerville, 95; Fairview Academy, 110, 114,* 131, 149; Farmington Academy, 109, 109,* 110, 114; Haw Creek Academy, 109; Ladoga Academy, 105,* 109; Wayne County Seminary, 109, 169*
Adams County, 195
Adams, Hampton, 423*
Adams, Morton D., 241
Adams, Mrs. Morton D., 241
Adams, Reily C., 334*
Adams, Thomas M., 123*
Ade, George, 12
Agassiz, Louis, 228
Aiken, Alexander, 354*
Ainslie, Peter, 295
Akron, 288*
Albert, Frank J., 420-421, 426,* 471
Albion, 279*
Albright, W. F., 423*
Alcorn, Merritt P., 474
Alcott, A. C., 172*
Aldrich, Clide E., 415*

Alexander, John M., 478
Aley, Robert Judson, 333, 348, *biography* 348,* 350,* 352,* 376
Alfordsville, 372
Alkire, John, 35*
Allen, B. L., 284, 287
Allen, Charles, 476
Allen, Nancy, 169*
Allen County, 151, 195
Allender, Edwin R., 439, 473
Altisont Letters, 169*
American Academy of Political Arts and Sciences, 419*
American Association of Theological Schools, 383, 457
American Association of University Professors, 419*
American Christian Missionary Society, 127, 155, 156, 157, 158, 158,* 159, 162, 182, 183, 194, 216,* 289,* 298, 295, 295,* 299, 316, 319, 322, 324,* 326, 330, 366*
American Christian Review, 162, 170, 384
American Friends Service Committee, 327*
American Home Missionary, The, 324
American Housewife, 236
American Red Cross, 411
American Society for the Extension of University Teaching, 353*

493

497

Index

Callahan, Hubert H., 416
Calvert, Lucille, 389,* 420, 416*
Cambridge City, 128, 169,* 188, 288*
Cambridge Seminary, 109
Cameron, E. C., 369,* 381*
Camp and Conference movement, Youth: Barbee Christian Camp, 403-404, 406; Bedford Christian Camp, 403, 406; Bethany Park, 330-331, 336-337; Indian Lake Retreat, 404, 406; Junior High and family camps, 409
Camp Atterbury, 392
Camp Creek Baptist Church, 53*
camp meetings, 28, 34, 43, 64
Camp River Baptist Church, 55*
Campbell, Alexander, 32,* 38, 46, 48, 50, 52, 54, 59, 62, 63, 65, 68, 75, 78, 85,* 86, 88, 89, 90, 99, 112, 128-132, 133, 139, 140, 141,* 142, 143-144, 146, 147-148, 156, 163, 164, 165, 166,* 167, 168, 169,* 183-188, 191, 210, 220, 237, 246, 269, 286, 299,* 302
Campbell, Mrs. Alexander, 183
Campbell, D. W., 279*
Campbell, Eldon, 464*
Campbell, George, 109, biography 109,* 114,* 117, 118,* 120,* 123,* 126,* 127, 131, 135,* 149,* 151,* 182,* 188
Campbell, George (editor), 368
Campbell, G. (Ohio), 116*
Campbell, Jno. A., 184
Campbell, Thomas, 62, 273
Campbell House (Bloomington), 411
Campbellsburg church, 204
Campus Life Commission, 430
Campus ministries: Campbell Fellowship, Terre Haute, 440; Campus Life Foundation, Indianapolis, 440; Disciples; Student Fellowship, Muncie, 440; Indiana Campus Christians' Foundation, Bloomington, 403, 410-411, 440;

Campus ministries—cont'd
Purdue Christian Foundation, Lafayette, 318, 329, 365, 400, 403, 410, 440
Canaday, John E., 352*
Canary, Peyton H., 389*
Cane Ridge (Kentucky) Revival, 22, 29, 41
Cane Ridge Presbyterian meeting-house, 29
Canfield, John M., 255,* 279*
Canneltown, 279*
Cannon, F. S., 410*
Canton, Ohio, 372
Capehart, Homer E., 452
Carelton, Simeon P., 237*
Carley, James R., 430,* 457, 466, 471
Carlson, J. Eric, 399
Carmichael, Miss Florence, 336, 337*
Carnegie, Andrew, 304, 305
Carnegie Foundation, 306
Carns, Conrad, 35*
Carpenter, Mrs. Jack, 474
Carpenter, L. H., 445*
Carpenter, Leewell L., 196, 198, 199, 203, 204, biography 204,* 205, 206, 207, 208, 239, 240, 243, 245, 245,* 246, 248, 249, 250, 251, 252, 255,* 258, 279,* 474, 476, 477
Carr, Bruce, 234
Carroll, W. E., 366, 478
Carroll County, 195
Carruth, Samuel A., 437*
Carson, Conwell B., 346*
Carson, J. D., 279*
Carter, LeRoy F., 364*
Carter, William, 182*
Carthage church, 436
Cartwright, George W., 416
Cartwright, Peter, 23, 42*
Case, Mrs. J. D., 214*
Casey, Edgar S., 476
Cass County, 195
Catholics, see Roman Catholics
Cato, B. F., 342

503

Index

507

Index

Forrest, J. D., 298,* 299*
Fort Miamie, 13
Fort Ouiatenon, 13
Fort Sumter, fall of, 160
Fort Vincennes, 13
Fort Wayne, 18, 101, 104, 116,* 199, 340,* 366, 441,* 481
Fort Wayne Christian churches, 366
Fort Wayne State Society mission, 196
Fortune, Alonzo W., 82,* 344*
Foster, B. F., 106,* 179*
Fountain City, 37, 288*
Fountain County, 195
Fountain Park Assembly, 248-249
Four Mile church (Wayne and Union Counties), 21
Fourteen Mile Baptist Church, 53*
Fox, William K., 436*
Frank, J. A., 256,* 279,* 299*
Frankfort, 105, 116,* 304, 331, 481
Frankfort church, 105, 336*
Franklin, 106,* 187, 340*
Franklin, Benjamin, 97, 101, *biography* 101,* 104, 107, 112, 115, 116,* 118, 118,* 126,* 162, 179,* 182,* 235, 286, 384
Franklin, Cecil, 337*
Franklin, Daniel, 116*
Franklin, Joseph, 72, 179,* 184, 235
Franklin, W. M., 224
Franklin College, 133, 300, 348*
Franklin County, 118,* 195, 226*
Franklin-Hume Debate, 189
Franklin Tabernacle church, 392
Franz, Clarence W., 416
Frazee, Ephraim S., 14,* 135,* 136, 149,* 188, 233,* 235
Frazee, Fannie, 253
Frazees (the), 182*
Frazier, —, 79*
Frazier, E. L., 82,* 208, 279*
Frazier, Mrs. F. E., 253*
Frazier, Simeon, 201, 227,* 231,* 233*
Fredericksburg, 293*
Free Soil Democrat, 156*

French settlers, 13
Friesner, Ray C., 415*
Friendship Baptist Church, 55*
Front Rank, 421
Fugitive Slave Act, 1850, 145-146
Fulton County, 195
Fulton, Ohio, 116*

G

Gandy, L. B., 237*
Gantz, E. J., 245*
Gardner, Jay B., 474
Garfield, James Abram, 162,* 209, 224, 286
Garfield University, 259*
Garnett, Arthur C., 354,* 381*
Garrett, 336*
Garrison, J. H., 269, 286,* 289, 296, 303*
Garrison, Winfred E., 298,* 299,* 300-301, 303-304, *biography* 303,*368, 452,* 467*
Garst, C. E., 241
Garst, Mrs. C. E., 241
Garten, Kathryn Turney, 437*
Gary, 181,* 182,* 293,* 319, 347,* 400*
Gary churches: Central, 319; Glen Park, 319; Tolleston, 319
Gary, D. H., 208
Garvin, Hugh C., 257, 261, 262, 265-270, 272, 298
Gearhart, Herbert G., 472
General Christian Sunday School Association, 203, 240
General Convention of the Christian Churches, *see also* International Convention of Christian Churches (Disciples of Christ), 126-128, 194, 202, 209, 211, 212, 219, 255
Genius of Universal Emancipation, 37
Georgetown, Kentucky, 33, 112, 299*
Georgetown (Kentucky) church, 299*

508

Index

Index

Judah, John M., 229*
Junior High camps, 409

K

Kahn, Henry, 352*
Kansas City, Mo., 280, 419*
Kantz, R. F., 265*
Karslake, W. J., 298*
Kawamura, Yo, 354*
Kechel, Daniel C., 476
Kee Mar College, 353*
Kellems, Jesse R., 339*
Kelly, O. E., 478
Kelsey, W. A., 297*
Kemper, James, 25
Kenady, R. H., 368*
Kendalville, 291*
Kendallville church, 279*
Kendrick, H. C., 283*
Kennedy Memorial Christian Home, 450
Kennedy School of Missions, 344
Kennington, Robert Edward, 346*
Kentucky revival and the Shakers, 40
Kentucky University, 218,* 259,* 290,* 301, 302, 353*
Kentucky Wesleyan College, 412*
Kern, W. H., 235, 258
Kerr, Hugh Thompson, 366
Kerr, Paul E., 474
Kerrick, Irvin James, 354*
Kershner, Bruce L., 339,* 354,* 381,* 384, 416,* 421
Kershner, Frederick Doyle, 321, 327, 328, 336, 341,* 348-349, 350, 352,* 353-354, *biography* 353,* 354,* 362, 366, 368, 375,* 381,* 382, 384,* 385, 389,* 412-413, 415, 416, 416,* 418-420, 421, 423-425, 478
Kershner, Mrs. Frederick D., 384
Kewanna, 237*
Kidd, Walter L., 235
Kies, Marietta, 298*
Kimball, Mrs. Walter, 474
Kimmons, J., 166*

Kingsbury, Mrs. Vera, 473
Kinkade, William, 67
Klage, John, 39
Kleihauer, Cleveland, 336*
Klingman, George, 365*
Klum, Miss Ada, 223*
Knight, Robert, 365, 410
Knob Creek Baptist Church, 53*
Knox church, 279*
Knox County, 59, 195
Knox, John, 467*
Kohler, Kathryn, 328
Kokomo, 246, 261, 340,* 347,* 394, 440, 480, 481
Kokomo Main Street church, 204,* 279,* 321, 394, 403
Kosciusko County, 195, 403-404
Krone, Max T., 381*
Kroner, Richard, 467*
Krout, R. K., 137
Krutsinger, W. H., 234, 236
Ku Klux Klan, 1924, and the churches, 331-333
Kuhn, T. H., 251, 365,* 279*
Kullowatz, Vernon F., 417

L

Ladies' Christian Monitor, 190
Ladoga, 109, 184
Ladoga Academy, 105,* 109
Ladoga Methodist Church, 184
Lafayette, 18, 103, 183, 184, 249, 281, 291, 292, 336, 340, 398, 440, 480, 481
Lafayette church, 103, 175, 336,* 410
LaGrange, 279*
LaGrange County, 151, 195
Laird, A. M., 258
Lake County, 195, 329
Lake James Assembly project, 291*
Lamberson, James P., 448*
Lancaster, 237*
Land, ____, 237*
Land, J. M., 208
Lane, E. T., 251, 479
Lane, Henry S., 160, 184, 185

521

Index